More Praise for *Me Against My Brother*

"This is an important book about a subject that could hardly be more important. Anyone interested in how the world works should read it; though it will bring comfort to none."

—*The Sunday Telegraph*

"We owe a debt of gratitude to people like photojournalist Scott Peterson, who not only risked his life to witness the horrors and take pictures but who possesses the eloquence to describe what he has seen, which he does in a powerful, disturbing book."

—*Houston Chronicle*

"Scott Peterson's savage and penetrating new book makes clear, Africa is rarely as simple as it seems. *Me Against My Brother* is extensively researched and thoroughly documented. This is history at its most penetrating."

—*Atlanta Journal-Constitution*

"A spirited examination . . . Peterson melds his eyewitness accounts with considerable research. His reporting is fresh with colorful observation . . . it makes for powerful reading."

—Mark Bowden, *Policy Review*

"A sad, compelling, and depressingly accurate picture . . . this is first rate reportage from the front lines."

—Keith B. Richburg, author of *Out of America*

"A gripping piece of reportage by a courageous American journalist. Peterson takes his readers on a frightening journey to the very edge of human tragedy."

—Karl Maier, author of *This House Has Fallen: Midnight in Nigeria*

Scott Peterson is the Moscow bureau chief for *The Christian Science Monitor*. His photographs have appeared in *Time*, *Newsweek*, *Life*, *The New York Times Magazine*, and *Harper's*.

ME AGAINST MY BROTHER

AT WAR IN SOMALIA, SUDAN, AND RWANDA

A JOURNALIST REPORTS FROM
THE BATTLEFIELDS OF AFRICA

SCOTT PETERSON

Routledge
New York London

Published in 2002 by
Routledge
29 West 35th Street
New York, NY 10001

Published in Great Britain by
Routledge
11 New Fetter Lane
London EC4P 4EE

First Routledge hardback edition, 2000
First Routledge paperback edition, 2001
Copyright © 2000 by Routledge

All photographs by Scott Peterson, Liaison Agency, 11 East 26th Street, New York, NY 10010, tel: 212-779-6300, www.liaisonphoto.com.

Lyrics for "Down in the Bunker" by The Steve Gibbons Band used by permission of Steve Gibbons, Havic Records.

Printed in the United States of America on acid-free paper.

10 9 8 7 6 5 4 3

Library of Congress Cataloging-in-Publication Data

Peterson, Scott.
    Me against my brother: at war in Somalia, Sudan, and Rwanda: a journalist reports from the battlefields of Africa / Scott Peterson.
        p. cm.
    Includes bibliographical references.
    ISBN 0-415-92198-8 (hb) / 0-415-93063-4 (pb)
        1. Somalia—Politics and government—1991–   2. Insurgency—Somalia—History—20th century. 3. Sudan—History—Civil War, 1983–   4.Sudan—History—Civil War, 1983—Atrocities. 5. Rwanda—History—Civil War, 1994. 6. Rwanda—History—Civil War, 1994—Atrocities. 7. Genocide—Rwanda—History—20th century. 8. Civil war—Africa, Eastern—History—20th century. 9. Atrocities—Africa, Eastern—History—20th century. I. Title.

DT407.4.P48 2000
960.3'29—dc21   99-056411

For those Africans at war, that their courage and spirit may one day be put to better use building peace;

and for Willard S. Crow, my friend, grandfather, and traveling companion in China and the Arctic, whose adventures set the precedent

CONTENTS

ACKNOWLEDGMENTS

Encouragement comes in many forms, and this book owes much to many people. It would be impossible to name all those who inspired, taught, traveled with, and cared for me—wittingly or not—along the way.

Primary thanks must go to Africans of Somalia, Sudan, Rwanda, and far beyond, who opened their hearts often, despite the inherent rush and inescapable voyeurism of the deadline-pushed journalist. Some are named in the text, though many others are not. I am grateful for their hospitality, patience, boundless humor, and readiness to share. They make Africa so rich a place to be.

I especially thank the few Somalis—one in particular; he shall remain unnamed—who, unbidden except by their own humanity, saved my life on 12 July 1993 in Mogadishu. I don't know how I could begin to repay them.

Relief workers, diplomats, and journalists took me in in myriad places and shared their knowledge and companionship.

My editors at *The Daily Telegraph* in London made most of the journeys described in this book happen. Nigel Wade and Frank Taylor gave me the run of the continent, and early on Pat Prentice was strongly supportive. Paul Hill and Patsy Dryden on the foreign desk were constantly good friends—and Paul, a needed accomplice. Stretching further back, Meg Bakken at *The Seattle Times* has been a strong backer since long before we both wrote for that paper, and wrote for *The Highline Times*.

The Christian Science Monitor has kindly accommodated my need to revisit old stomping grounds and revise the manuscript. Editors Clay Collins and Faye Bowers have been good friends and especially encouraging on many fronts. The *Monitor* librarians—particularly Leigh Montgomery and Suman Bandrapalli—deserve special praise.

At the Gamma Liaison photo agency in New York, Jennifer Coley was an early believer in my work, followed in her support by Oliver Morris. Donnamarie Barnes, Evan Agostini, and Sandy Ciric have lived Africa, the Balkans, and the Middle East with me by generously editing tens of thousands of my photographs. At Gamma Presse Images in Paris, Didier Contant and Elizabeth Bernard have also been very supportive. Photo editors at *Time* magazine—especially Robert Stevens—and *Newsweek* have backed me with assignments for years.

I am grateful to my parents, Ken and Merry Ann, who never imposed limits upon their children, yet still provided such an important sense of "home." They also had the grace to accept my extended journeys abroad—with, at first, little apparent result.

Deep thanks to friends and colleagues who were kind enough to read portions of the manuscript: David Chen, Steve Hubbell, Jean-Philippe Ceppi, and Adam and Cathra Kelliher all made excellent critical suggestions and comments. For those that I did not incorporate—and any other errors of judgment or fact—I alone am responsible.

Steve Hubbell's friendship and guidance early on was crucial to getting this project off the ground. I am grateful to Gideon Weil and Kim Witherspoon at Witherspoon literary agency for embracing my writing and this daunting work. I thank Amy Shipper and Eric Nelson, my editors at Routledge, whose unflagging enthusiasm has helped sustain my efforts. Jennifer Hirshlag, also of Routledge, meticulously ensured quality production. Thanks to Michael Miller as well, whose fine cartography graces this book.

My young children, Olivia and Guy, have withstood long absences of their father—both when I travel as a correspondent and for this book. I hope that one day they will understand the importance of these pages to me, and, bubbling with expectant joy and waking bright-eyed to every new day, as they now do, that they will forgive me my capitulation to this book's selfish requirements.

My greatest appreciation is reserved for my wife, Alex, whose precious companionship, wonderful spirit, and sheer fearlessness have been a constant source of strength and love. She restored me after tough scrapes in Africa and relishes the continent as much as I. She also graciously and judiciously applied her editor's eye to this book in its most raw and every subsequent form. Only she knows how much she has contributed to its final flow.

INTRODUCTION

Which are we: beasts because we make war,
or angels because we so often seek to make it
into something holy?

—Barbara Ehrenreich, *Blood Rites*

There is a time and a place for everything "under the heavens," the Scriptures promise. And so for every foreign correspondent there is a first time for war. This was my first time, more than a decade ago in Africa, and I was nervous. Even by African standards, there were few more remote places than the Keren Front, lodged in the heart of Eritrea in northeast Africa, a moonscape laced with trenches that harkened back to the brutalities of World War I.

In the days before I had arrived, the Eritrean guerrillas—who had already been fighting for independence for a *generation*—had repulsed a major Ethiopian army offensive. There were said to be many enemy dead. Now I was on my way, though I had never seen a dead body in my life.

My journal records how I "grew more and more apprehensive as we neared the front." I was afraid, and my last sleepless night was spent reading Ernest Hemingway's *The Old Man and the Sea*. I marveled again at its exquisite writing—"two pages long, ten light years deep," we used to joke in school—although there was little solace in the words: "'But man is not made for defeat,' he said. 'A man can be destroyed, but not defeated.'"[1]

We started marching to the front line at 4:30 am, before first light, but the time didn't matter to me. In my state of anxiety, I hadn't slept at all, nor did I feel the need. We had left at 1:30 am and had driven an impossible stony path with headlights shaded—the Eritreans made all their movements at night, to avoid bombing by Ethiopian planes. We arrived at the rear base, a cluster of underground bunkers that, inside, smelled of hard living.

Through my bleary eyes as dawn broke, the trail to the front took on a surreal quality. For one and one-half hours, we followed a valley littered with shell casings and trees torn to splinters by heavy tank bombardment. Then we began climbing, and the trail became dotted with gauze and other bloodstained dressings. "The serum of life was splattered on the rocks," I wrote. "The rebels did not win without casualties."

The trench system was the top of the ridge, and the first bodies I saw were on the nearside—Ethiopian troops cut down by Eritrean gunfire as they charged the rebel trench. "Those are the ones who wanted the medals," smirked my translator, a lady warrior called Chu-Chu. She had spent a year fighting on the front herself, and so had seen all this before. These bodies had not yet begun to swell with their own gases. But the strong wind couldn't wipe away the sickly sweet smell of death. *Human* death. It was unique, a smell that I would become too familiar with over time but would never accept casually.

It was the everyday details that drew me in, as they still do. I knew the broad outlines of the conflict—I didn't need to serve as witness to understand that—but what told me most were the human elements. Peering over the edge of the trench, with the Ethiopian positions on the next ridge, watching me, I could see hands sticking up out of the dirt, and boots still worn and bayonets and tufts of hair. These were people that no one would ever bother to identify.

Some Ethiopian troops had made it to the trench, then died and were buried by rebels who dug away more dirt from the sides of the trench to cover the bodies. It was among them—the bodies under the dirt that we were actually standing and crawling on—that there was a rare moment of identity. I picked up a piece of folded paper jutting out of the "bottom" of the trench, and opened it.

It was like a schoolchild's notebook paper, ruled with perfect thin blue lines that imposed order on the unruly handwritten Amharic script. It was an unmailed letter from a soldier to his mother, and seemed to have been in a breast pocket. But it was spoiled with bloodstains and the telltale hole of a round from an AK-47 assault rifle—that through paper leaves a perfect 5.56mm ring of metallic gray residue. Opened up, the letter showed eight holes. Its writer could not have had a chance. In the proper revolutionary style demanded by the Marxist regime of dictator Mengistu Haile Mariam, it was signed "Forward Ethiopia."

And there was the poverty of this front line that struck me, a quality common to every war zone on the continent. Boots of the dead were held together with knotted yarn, and bullet sacks were made from cut-off trouser leggings. I had forgotten my fear, in the process of trying to absorb all this. "Eritrean fighters manned the lookouts draped with strings of bullets and carrying Kalashnikovs and shoulder-held anti-tank weapons," I wrote in a letter to *my* mother. "They were happy to see a visitor who is growing up fast—maybe faster than he would like."

I had made it to the front. I was feeling in control, but then I lifted my camera to record the carnage. After a few frames it jammed, bringing me right back to reality. We rushed into a wider trench section, bringing clouds of dust with us, and the rebels offered me tea while I fumbled with my camera. Here on the edge of the planet, on a ridge at war, I was being offered the quintessential hospitality of a cup of tea. Foul-tasting as it was—who knows where the water came from?—the guerrillas had prepared it using a little camp stove. Sugar came from a battered tin, and it was presented to me with a smile. The hospitality had a price: the diarrhea didn't stop for two days.

The camera was a mess, too, and as I fiddled with it I popped the back open, with the film still in it, so that the four frames I had taken were exposed to the light and ruined. I finally got the camera working, but it was an inauspicious start.

The missive home from Eritrea was somber: "I saw my slowly budding career flash before my eyes," I wrote, "in a nightmare of amateurism."

Africa has always known violence and war, its soil regularly stained with the blood of its people. But the conflicts of the last ten years of the millennium have been the most vicious, have created the most suffering, and so are most worthy of examination.

At the turn of the decade in 1990, with the close of the Cold War, a new sense of optimism for peace and democracy had swept across Africa. Nelson Mandela, the African liberation leader incarnate and a source of pride throughout the continent, was released from prison on Robben Island to lead South Africa from apartheid to multiethnic rule. Ethiopia's new president—a former rebel himself—granted Eritrea its independence, ending that war.

But with promises of inclusion in the New World Order still ringing in African ears, things fell apart elsewhere. Chaos and then famine emerged in Somalia. Peace broke down in Angola and Algeria. Civil war in Sudan, Liberia, and Burundi continued to burn. And in Rwanda, a genocide was unleashed in 1994 that, in time, would force realignments across central Africa. Many of these conflicts turned so severe that for combatants and civilians alike, Hobbesian self-survival often became the only goal.

This story was more promising elsewhere. The former Soviet satellite states in eastern Europe bid to join NATO, and Russia swallowed its pride and held out its begging bowl to the one remaining superpower, the United States. But in Africa fragile political systems continued their collapse, and human anguish intensified. Still, the "Dark Continent" never seemed to grab the world's attention until the vital signs—as in Somalia and Rwanda—became too severe to reverse.

Of course, Africa's conflicts vary from war zone to war zone, but certain characteristics—military, human, and spiritual—mark them all. This is where my interest lies, in the dust and the sweat, and the laughter mixed with misery that permeates the flavor of war in Africa.

This is not a pretty book. It doesn't describe Africa's stunning sunsets and wild animals, nor its exceptional beauty. And it does not really have a happy ending. But this book does aim to illuminate human tragedy in a way that shows how such tragedies may be easier to avoid in Africa and beyond in the future.

Instead of telling of tented safaris, this book is an uncompromising look at the pain that so many Africans suffer under those gorgeous sunsets, the death that they meet in countries that also happen to be populated with the elephants, lions, and mountain gorillas that captivate the West. Because for every sun-drenched day, there is one of rain. For every majestic lion, there are many more sickly hyenas and vultures ready to devour the horrible things that result from violence.

I prefer to think that in Africa there is a Jungian balance between remarkable good and intense evil. But it may be more of a Manichean battle between the forces of light and dark, because as worthy of spiritual celebration as the good may be, the degree of evil is also extraordinary. So let me make clear from the start: this book is about the extremes, as they can and do exist in Africa. In that sense it is biased, because not every African nation is at war. Not every country is starving and ruled by warlords. And not every tribesman in Africa dreams of inflicting genocide upon his rival.

There are, of course, also wonderful examples of Africans prevailing. I don't mean to downplay this good and have myself experienced much hope, love, and healing in Africa—enough to easily fill the pages of another tome.

But many nations are in conflict and suffer agonies largely unrecorded. These, I believe, require exploring for what they tell us about the human capacity to conduct evil, and also to survive it. So this book is about the Dark Side, and the hope, love, and healing that sometimes emerge despite it.

This book is not a memoir. It doesn't tell cowboy tales of the front line, and then how I retired to the bar every night to better my colleagues at the telling of war *stories*—something that, for me, rarely took place. Instead, in its essence, this book is about war *crimes*, and how people come to commit them. There are many crimes here, and do not think that the culprits are limited to Africans. American and other foreign forces in Somalia committed startling acts of savagery, hiding behind the banner of the United Nations; French authorities and some church officials in Rwanda were complicit in genocide—not to mention the shameful indifference, then hobbling of a ready-to-act UN Security Council by a gun-shy United States.

Questions of justice—even in a continent where the idea of a war crimes tribunal and accountability is so very new—should be paramount. Failure to address this issue will mean that more Africans themselves must answer this question, as it was put by the president of Burundi in August 1994, after the slaughter of 2,000 people in a town:

"How long is blood going to have to flow in this country?" he asked, attempting to deflate tensions.

"What do you gain when you start killing and shedding blood? Can you drink it? Can you make bricks from it? Who has ever benefited from blood running in the streets?"[2]

Spiritual journeys do not always start out as such, and mine in Africa certainly did not. Since I marched anxiously toward the front line in Eritrea in 1989—writing letters home about profound changes in my thinking—I have covered many other conflicts in Africa, the Balkans, and the Middle East.

In those days as a writer, I was driven by the ambitious precedent laid down by William Faulkner in his 1950 Nobel Prize acceptance speech. An especially perceptive English teacher gave me a copy before I could fully appreciate its importance. I kept it folded in my shoulder bag on early journeys. Faulkner advised the "young writer" to leave

> no room in his workshop for anything but the old verities and truths of the heart, the old universal truths lacking which any story is ephemeral and doomed—love and honor and pity and pride and compassion and sacrifice. Until he does so, he labors under a curse. He writes not of love but of lust, of defeats in which nobody loses anything of value, of victories without hope and worst of all without pity or compassion. His griefs grieve on no universal bones, leaving no scars. He writes not of the heart but of the glands.[3]

Armed with such teachings, I set off at the end of 1988 for Africa. I made two trips that took the greater part of two years: the first traveling overland north to south from Cairo to Cape Town; the second in the opposite direction, from Johannesburg to Algiers. I sent freelance stories along the way to the *Atlanta Journal-Constitution* and the British newspapers—whoever would have them. But my first war experiences in Eritrea and Sudan, then Mozambique and Angola, made clear how much there was to learn about the human spirit in Africa.

My original aim in Africa was to simply be an observant tourist—to have an adventure that might yield an interesting travelogue, or *something*. I had just graduated from Yale University with a double major in English and East Asian Studies. I had studied Chinese and traveled to China twice—the first time with my grandfather, who as my companion became the subject of the first story I ever wrote. Over time, I considered being a foreign correspondent. Since I expected to spend much of my career in Asia, I thought a two-month journey to Africa might be a change of scene.

But that innocent start slowly turned into a different journey altogether. I was becoming hooked on war, on the emotions it inspired and forced me to confront.

So when I flicked on my radio at a border post on the Niger-Algeria frontier, during a motorcycle trek across the Sahara Desert on 2 August 1990, and heard that Iraqi strongman Saddam Hussein had invaded Kuwait, it soon became clear that a new war would be taking place in the Middle East. *The Sunday Telegraph* in London agreed to base me in Cyprus, and I worked as a stringer from there in Lebanon, Syria, Turkey, and especially northern Iraq. I was relegated to Damascus during most of the Gulf War in early 1991, envious of my colleagues in Saudi Arabia and Iraq who were seeing the "real" war.

But I had my break in the spring, when Iraqi Kurds staged a rebellion. As the Gulf War drew to a close, President George Bush had indicated that toppling Saddam was up to the Iraqis, though any attempt from inside would have American help. The administration later denied making any such promise, but the Iraqis took the advice to heart.

A colleague, Peter Bakogeorge, and I resolved to get in. At a remote border village we paid Kurdish guides $800 to find safe passage into Iraq. I carried only the essentials: a thin Kevlar flak jacket; a gas mask (there were fears that Saddam would use gas to put down the insurrection, and in fact Iraqi forces *did* use mustard gas then against Shiite Muslim rebels in the south); loads of film; and a kilo and a half of oily black olives.

We left at night on a smugglers' route and got past Turkish troops that were on heightened alert because of the annual spring offensive of the PKK, Turkey's own separatist Kurdish rebels. We came across the concrete post marking the border—and saw the mines glinting in the moonlight. Even then I knew we were taking far too many risks. Unbeknownst to us, a BBC television crew had been killed the day before by their guide, apparently following this same route. We spent a dangerous and fearful night in a smugglers' cave and the next morning were delivered into the hands of the Iraqi Kurds, the *peshmerga* guerrillas.

Within days we had caught up with the front line. To be close to a satellite phone, Peter hooked up with a Kurdish leader. But after all these months of buildup and now with Baghdad already capitulated to US forces, I was determined to see whatever action remained. I hitchhiked alone beyond the town of Arbil, across a broad, grassy plain, and I found the war. Iraqi tank shells were falling like rain, as Kurdish rebels stood in small groups and argued about what to do. Baghdad had turned the tide and was pushing back the rebellion. The rebels began to retreat, and I too was crammed into a four-wheel drive vehicle. We drove wildly fast, and leaning out the window I saw why: two Iraqi helicopters were overhead, firing their rockets. I was struck with a queasy dread. We screeched to a halt, and the *peshmerga* jumped out and uselessly emptied their magazines at the helicopters.

I ran around, frantically trying to capture the moment on film and looking for cover. There was none, but what I saw in the midst of this firefight has enlightened my reporting ever since: even as we were being rocketed, even as Baghdad was crushing the rebellion, American jet fighters flew high overhead, watching everything and doing nothing to intervene. I had heard Bush's promise to help the Kurds and Shiites and had taken it as one. But that promise was being ignored. It was my first experience of American foreign policy gone tragically wrong, in a place very far from Washington. It prepared me for serious US mistakes later in Somalia and Rwanda.

I had to flee northern Iraq, along with 1.5 million Kurds. As we trekked overland back into Turkey, the question on my lips was the same asked me repeatedly by the Kurds, who had put so much store in a promise from America: "Where's Bush?"

After the Gulf War, I moved back to Africa and was taken on by *The Daily Telegraph* in London. Not staff, but well enough cared for and "retained," like all the Africa correspondents for British papers based in Nairobi, Kenya. It felt good to be back on my old stomping ground, and I expected to be covering an anticipated blossoming of democracy across the continent. That was not to be—I never once, in fact, wrote a story about democracy there. Instead, over the next four years I witnessed the violent upheavals that I attempt to portray in the following pages.

There was still so much to learn, and little did I expect that the laboratory of war in Africa would virtually renew our understanding of the Four Horsemen of the Apocalypse: War, Famine, Pestilence, and Death.

Back then I was still a believer in the goodwill of institutions and governments and was convinced that if they knew that bad things were happening in Africa, they would try to intervene. The world was getting to be a smaller place, and so ignorance was no longer a valid argument for inaction, when presented with evidence of crimes. It had been that way for some time. More than a century ago, after all, the head of the Red Cross, Gustave Moynier, rejoiced that knowledge would be the best weapon against wrongdoing. Writing in 1885, he said, "These days we know what is going on in every corner of the globe. News of the slightest skirmish spreads like wildfire, all but putting the dying on the battlefield in front of the reader."[4]

Of course, news today is live and instantaneous. With satellite technology, there is nowhere we can't be, and no place where television can't report. But as the examples of China's Tiananmen Square, Somalia, Bosnia, Rwanda, Chechnya, Kosovo, and East Timor show, such immediate news does more to appall than to spur timely intervention. The case of Rwanda's genocide in 1994 may have been the most outrageous: that bloodletting went on for 100 days and went almost unremarked by American and other Western leaders, who were more worried about its impact on their midterm elections and about avoiding legal obligations to intervene if they even *used* the dreaded, loaded "G"-word: genocide. Rwanda was the proof, one relief agency noted, that "we could have been watching Auschwitz live."[5]

What does it take to provoke action? If Rwanda is any measure, then I would agree with this analysis: that action may require "the collapse of continents rather than single states; oceans of dead rather than mere rivers—with repercussions that significantly affect rich countries as well as poor."[6]

This book shows how Africa's recent catastrophes have not been inevitable. Preventive action—coupled with a better understanding of Africa itself—could have averted much suffering. These conflicts do not arise out of some uniquely "African" weakness. Instead, they have often been made worse by wrongheaded foreign intervention. Learning the lessons will be critical to understanding modern conflicts in Africa and how the United States, the United Nations, and Africans themselves failed—and continue to fail—to bring peace. The difficulties posed by foreign intervention are valuable far beyond Africa's borders.

I have detailed Somalia's descent into clan conflict and the war against American troops, the spiritual and power-hungry excesses that spur Sudan's endless holy war, and a case of horrific transgression against the human spirit: the genocide in Rwanda.

There may seem little more connecting these three conflicts than a shared continent. This is true. They show very different facets of war, types of outside influence and intervention, and yield different lessons. Yet taken together, they give a good picture of the modern African experience of conflict.

Still, there are threads. War crimes are the most obvious. And the disastrous US policy in Somalia, for example—the most formative post–Cold War foreign debacle for America so far—led directly to another disastrous, shameful US policy of genocide denial in Rwanda.

In Somalia, famine and the fighting were first ignored, then neglected.

Eventually media images of the suffering were so powerful that the UN—and eventually the US—overreacted. This was going to be the test case of the New World Order. Iraq had just been driven out of Kuwait in 1991, in a stunning and bloodless (for the US-led allies) victory, which overnight swept away the memory of 58,000 dead American GIs in the mud and jungle of Vietnam. Iraq was a *modern* war, in which high tech came into its own. Military censors— even self-censorship by some news editors—meant that few images of the thousands of Iraqi deaths were shown in America. So the precedent had been set: here was a huge set-piece battle of armor on armor, the type of which may never be seen again.

And almost nobody died.

So expectations were high for an aid mission to Somalia—an infinitely lesser problem than the oil-important Gulf—and it should have been easy. Instead, on the American watch, the Mogadishu Line was drawn and crossed: the humanitarian mission—"God's work," as President Bush liked to say— chose sides in a local battle and became Somalia's chief warlord.

In Sudan, a civil war that has boiled along for most of the second half of the century has intensified in the past decade with a fresh injection of religious fervor. Cursed by the fact that there has been no defining moment to force closure to the crisis, Sudanese on both sides of the front line have fallen into a chronic rhythm of conflict virtually impenetrable from the outside. The fragmentation of the southern, African rebel group has caused yet more destruction and insecurity. The UN for years has carried out an interminable relief effort, and though it may have succeeded in saving lives, it also has prolonged the war by feeding the combatants.

In Rwanda, the lessons are different yet again. Here the signs of preparation for genocide were clear enough to anybody who cared to look. Thanks largely to American pressure to avoid "another Somalia," the killing was allowed to rage unchecked, then to burn itself out. Washington made sure that the UN force already there—which demonstrably could have saved tens of thousands of lives—was cut back to a skeleton force, sending a clear message to Rwanda's murderers that they could act with impunity.

So Rwanda was abandoned as the UN retreated. Then in the aftermath, the West added shame upon shame: as more than 1 million Hutus crossed *en masse* to Zaire, goaded by the organizers of genocide, who hid among them, the reaction to feed and care and relieve these people was immediate. Overnight, history was altered. These people—many of them intimately involved in the slaughter—became the "victims" of the genocide and were worthy of our help.

The result in the Rwandan camps, as it has been in Somalia and Sudan, was that professional do-gooders were routinely compromised by their own humane intentions. And Africa's warlords have taken full advantage. Civilians are the target of atrocities, and armed groups steal relief supplies, manipulate aid to further their war aims, and kill relief workers when they don't get their way. Hobbes would have been fascinated by the brutal universe in which so many Africans now struggle to get by, in which every man must fight for himself. For deep in Africa's darknesses, armed "fighters" abuse without reason, accountable to no one.

I don't consider myself to be a war junkie, flitting from front line to front line like a shit-eating bluebottle fly to feast on the gore of war, only hunting for the "worst" image or the most gruesome photograph to send to an uncomprehending audience that is already overexposed to violence. When I left Africa in mid-1995, I moved to the Balkans, where the final throes of a long-running war that brought us the phrase "ethnic cleansing" were winding down. Serbs had just sacked the UN "safe haven" of Srebrenica in Bosnia, ridding it of Muslims. The Croatian army kicked the Serbs out of the Krajina region. And the first and only action I saw was from Mount Igman above Sarajevo in August, when NATO planes bombed Bosnian Serb positions to break the three-year siege of the city. Then it was coverage of the Dayton peace deal and the unearthing of evidence for the War Crimes Tribunal on the Former Yugoslavia.

Revealing those crimes reminded me of the injustices I had seen committed in Africa, and how so little had been done—as if a decision had been made, somewhere, that Africa and Africans were not worth justice. In South Africa, the homemade Truth and Reconciliation Commission had helped heal deep trauma by digging for the truth. Ethiopia also conducted its own war crimes tribunal. But for the biggest crime of all, The International Criminal Tribunal for Rwanda, based in Arusha, Tanzania, got off to a shaky and underfinanced start.

After a year in the Balkans, during which I switched allegiances from the *Telegraph* to *The Christian Science Monitor,* I moved to Jordan to be the Middle East correspondent. Fascinating as these entrenched conflicts are, they are so ingrained that they are largely stale. To get at Mideast hatreds, you have to dig deeper and plumb histories that are as myth-ridden and prejudiced as those in the Balkans. Real hand-to-hand combat today is gone, and even flash points like Hebron are localized, where Israelis with guns and Palestinians with stones carry out set-piece running battles. Watching on television, you might think that the entire West Bank was aflame. But except in the rarest cases, you yourself can engage in these battles as a journalist, requiring a bulletproof vest, or take ten paces back and return to calm normality.

The minutiae of the Arab-Israeli peace process—detailed *ad nauseam* in the world's press—is often meaningless. But staid as this may be, relative to Africa, it is progress. Wouldn't a Somali, or Sudanese, or Rwandan prefer being bored reading about a fitful peace process than be consumed by full-blooded war?

One thing that should be understood is that the glamorous mythology that surrounds the life of the foreign correspondent is exactly that, a myth. For self-declared war correspondents, or even reluctant, de facto ones, certainly there are exceptional moments. I understand the words of the young Winston Churchill, when he wrote that "nothing in life is so exhilarating as to be shot at without result."

But a look at the figures makes clear that there is much else besides, especially in Africa. Endless hours are spent getting from place to place: waiting in airports or driving for days—as I did to get to the Keren Front—on back-breaking roads. Most of the rest of your time is spent churning out your report, and then—at least before the advent of the personal satellite phones—wasted trying to "get a line" to London or New York or wherever. The remaining fraction is divided further: of course there are interesting people to speak to and miracles to see—but add in feeling awful for lack of nourishment, from sleep to food, and all the while with your senses under constant assault. It can be, and in Africa it often is, painful.

And then, if you are in the right place at the right time, it may be that Churchill's "exhilaration" could happen to you—provided, of course, that you don't actually get shot.

There are other drawbacks. "We journalists are like garbage cans," Leon Uris notes. "Everybody sends us their filth. Through us comes all that is rotten in man."[7] So there are many coping mechanisms. But it is impossible not to be affected. Worn down by atrocities in Somalia, where he was a British official, Gerald Hanley knew how destructive the daily dose could be: "It was obvious that you could not live in violence and threat for overlong periods and not be diverted into those side lanes of fear and doubt. It was all too personal, too close, too tiring to one's reverence for charity, and pity."[8]

So I'm afraid that, if Me Against My Brother were to be shown on television, it would require a disclaimer often used for much weaker material: We must warn you that what you are about to see includes graphic images that some may find offensive.

But I make no apologies for the reality I found and for describing it as I saw it. It should tear at your heart and make you angry, very angry, as it does me, that such crimes are committed in Africa by Africans against each other and by outsiders at Africans' expense.

Along the way, I lost several friends and colleagues. Some are mentioned in the following pages, attacked and murdered by mobs or killed by stray and not-so-stray bullets. It is something that happens when one crosses the invisible line—unwittingly or not—that separates an observer from a combatant. A few of those lost friends were searching in Africa, like me, for something universal, something that was not just about the mystery of being African and at war, but that illuminated mysteries about *us*.

Writing this book has been a lot like traveling in Africa. It has been difficult. No part of it came easily. But there have been moments for me of epiphany and triumph, as well as those of great despair. There have been tears, too, that came unbidden in solitude.

When I hear the thumping of helicopter rotor blades today, a clench of *something* wells up in my throat, and I am transported back to Mogadishu, to the US airborne forces that crisscrossed that city day and night for months. Even while writing parts of this book at an isolated ranch at the base of Mt. Kenya soon after the events, when barn swallows made high-velocity swoops past my head, I heard the whistle-pop of a bullet just missing. Fireworks displays from a distance, to me, are volleys of mortar fire.

The act of writing has partly expunged those memories, shedding light on them, cleansing them, boiling them down to moments of essential emotion and value. Mysteries remain, of course. For despite the scale of this odyssey, I have only two eyes. And as much as these eyes may have seen, there is so, so much more in Africa and beyond that they have not.

Africa is the cradle of mankind, the place where life began. And it is also a place where human emotion can be as strong as God's Word. For me, Africa is all these things, and in this way I admit to a love affair that will last. Africans are imbued with a defiant spirit, as we all are, but like few others, they face an uncertain future. The history of the Dark Side, some of which I record here, is powerful. And to prevail in the future will not be easy. But the cost of more stumbling is great and is evident in the warm, loving embrace of every mother. Must this legacy of suffering be passed on, like a bludgeoning, inescapable inheritance?

I can't get away from the sensibility of William Wordsworth, and the high price of failure:

> A simple child,
> That lightly draws its breath . . .
> What should it know of death?"[9]

MAPS

SOMALIA

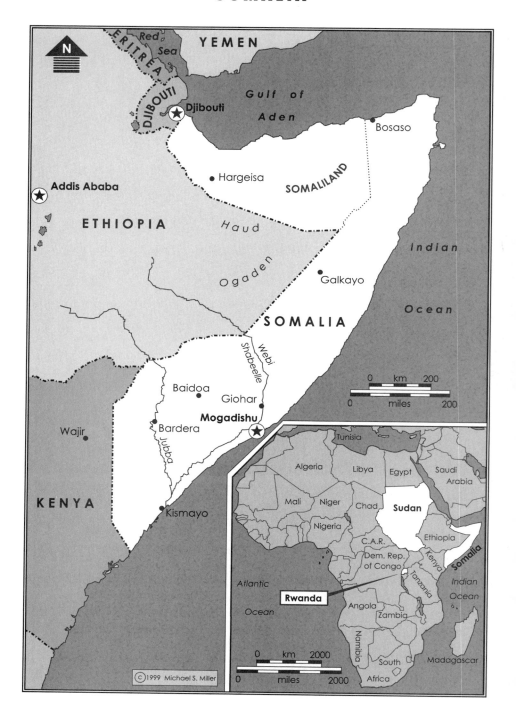

SUDAN

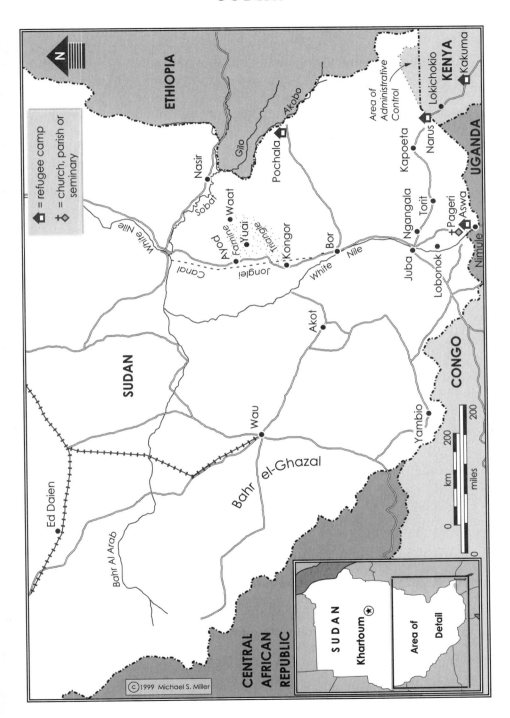

RWANDA

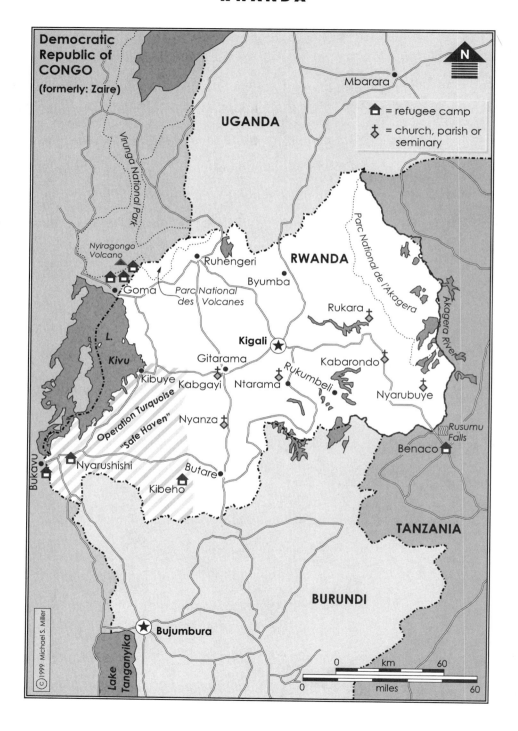

PART I

SOMALIA

WARLORDS TRIUMPHANT

Me and my clan against the world;
Me and my family against my clan;
Me and my brother against my family;
Me against my brother.

> —The hierarchy of priorities,
>   as ordered by a Somali proverb

ONE

LAWS OF WAR

But of all the races of Africa there cannot be one better to live among than the most difficult, the proudest, the bravest, the vainest, the most merciless, the friendliest; the Somalis.

—Gerald Hanley, *Warriors*

The morning turned hot, but kept still; too early for anyone's bile to rise, too early to show anger. Nevertheless, Abdi Kadir sat resentful in a derelict tea stall, his worn assault rifle by his side. Already he was enraged today. The journalists he had escorted to this southern Somali town had been too demanding, too dismissive of his youth, and too ready to command him and to complain. It had been as though he was not a gunman, not worthy of respect despite the violence that his childish fingers could inflict. The sweet dark tea trickled down his throat, soothing his empty stomach.

They had wanted to move from Bardera that morning in September 1992, but they were delayed because he had forgotten to fill the vehicle with fuel. They shouted abuse, swearing, offending his fragile pride. The money for compliance was good: a total of $300 each day, split between Abdi, two other gunmen, and the owner of the land cruiser. Most of the journey had been fun, rich with pleasure and deep laughter. But how quickly that had changed.

Abdi looked out the stall door, his narrow features struck head-on by the sun. Dust coated everything. A sour sweat spread between his skin and the metal of the uncomfortable chair. He controlled his emotion, a latent antagonism checked so far but simmering, ready to boil up with the heat of the day. Abdi was with the other gunmen, far from the car. So what if these journalists were late again and missed their plane out of Somalia? May they never see Heaven, he cursed. God willing, *Inshallah.*

Then around the corner ran the bald one, the British journalist—was his name Sam?—whose rage reddened his shaven head. Sam was howling. They were late, the plane was already at the airstrip a few kilometers away. Unconcerned, Abdi had seen it land, churning a hurricane of dust, as he quietly sipped his tea. For the two journalists, it was to be their escape; now they were going to miss it.

"Let's go! Let's go! LET'S GO!" screamed Sam, the one twisted vein in his forehead swollen. Without waiting for a reply, he turned and ran back to the car.

So Abdi and his men reluctantly left the dregs of their tea, took up their weapons, and strode along behind. At the land cruiser, I was locked out too and provided more abuse. Abdi spat.

Sam Kiley of *The Times* (London) and I had come to Bardera to speak to a warlord and to get a feel for an expanding relief operation. The 1992 famine was in full flower, and for looting gunslingers life had never been so rewarding. I had been coming to Somalia for more than a year, and we were both well versed in the rigors of this conflict.

But this was a special and expensive trip. We had driven south from the capital, Mogadishu, navigating minefields and coming across food convoys being looted at gunpoint. At the start, we were so happy to be "on the road" outside Mogadishu that we lit up cigars—cheap King Edwards, thanks to my freelance budget—and enjoyed the passing desert. In Bardera we'd already seen enough, and we were more than ready to get out. So Abdi's deliberate messing about made us angry.

Racing to the airstrip, Sam announced that if we missed the plane, no one would be paid. Abdi's vehemence deepened, his thin fingers quivering at such ingratitude, his protests lost in the rush of contempt. The vehicle wheeled onto the airstrip, but it was too late. Rotors whining, the UN relief plane had taxied to the far end and turned. Our rage blotting out our reason, we ordered the car to speed into the flight path in a desperate bid to signal the pilots. Our protests were drowned finally by the roar of the plane overhead and then dust as the plane's wheels lifted. Sam sunk his fist into Abdi's side, grunting more threats and finally crossing an imaginary line in Abdi's mind that separated insult from crime. Abdi was ready to kill, would have been happy to kill.

Then there was silence, as we slowed; the dust settled around us like fine snow, muffling noise.

"That's it. No money," Sam said contemptuously.

Abdi's face leered through the cloud. Something snapped, as it had done for so many Somalis so many times during the civil war, as their country collapsed. In such times here, as elsewhere in Africa and beyond, an armed man's rage percolated close to the surface, ready to move forcefully to ensure survival. Brazen hostility demanded a hostile reaction. And who were these foreign bastards who find me, Abdi the Prideful, so useless? I must prove that I am a *gun man*, unassailable, able to unleash quick revenge. I will draw the strength from my bloodline, a strength that—in this desert wilderness of my birth—demands vengeance, to defend honor.

Calm. The threat of fiscal punishment hung heavily as Abdi's private vow to secure justice poisoned his thoughts. Then another plane landed unexpectedly, causing both sides to bristle for the dispute. I loaded my bag onto the German Hercules and returned for Sam's duffel. But a scuffle erupted, immediately turning dangerous. Abdi was poised beside the car, menacing us with his weapon.

"Pay us the money—I need all of it!" he shouted, like a knife-wielding street kid afraid that he would not be taken seriously. Abdi's face crumpled beyond its years into deep lines, his pursed lips hiding for a moment the crazed wide grin that had adorned it for the past three days, laughing and scowling at once through polished white teeth. Every day he chewed the narcotic leaf qat, like a cow emasculating its cud. The succulent stems of *Catha edulis* are a stimulant like Benzedrine, and habit forming to chew. Over time his teeth would be darkly stained, but now in his youth they were innocent. The lips split again, teeth flashing brightly in anticipation of conflict.

"No way," Sam told him. "You have wasted our time. We're lucky to get out of here at all." The Germans unloaded ten tons of relief food, meant to help save the lives of Somalis made miserable by the reign of warlords and militia, by tempestuous gunmen like Abdi. These were the predators that made Somalis suffer, the militiamen who foraged to survive, abusing and looting at whim.

With the ability at his fingertips to end this argument *now,* Abdi turned bold. I reached for Sam's bag and Abdi also grabbed hold, his free right hand expertly double-clicking his Kalashnikov from safety to semi- to full automatic. Abdi felt confident, strong and blinded by rage at these impudent, cheap, weaponless foreigners. He swung the gun to my temple and laid his finger on the trigger. He then nodded at comrade Daher, a wild character who was skinny and older with dirty hair and teeth well stained with weed. Daher made his point by hoisting a heavy .30-caliber Browning machine gun to his hips. His scrawny body sagged under the weight of a bandolier of 300 rounds draped over his shoulders too, every sinew required just to hold this weapon aloft, never mind fire it. Daher's scarred face dripped with effort; he vowed to kill Sam.

Shouting intensified. The German flight crew were ready to depart, and they wound up their engines. But I didn't let go, and Sam didn't move. We were so angry at this blackmail that something irrational snapped inside me, as it had Abdi, causing a foolish reaction. But what else was there? Abdi and his men wouldn't hesitate to fire. They could hardly wait.

"Shoot me! Shoot me! Just SHOOT ME, you fuckers!" I bellowed, my voice increasing in pitch and in strength. My arms shook, my eyes jumping from one weapon to the other. "Let's go, Sam," I said, less sure. Abdi was amused at this pathetic defiance.

"Pay, or we *will* kill you!" Abdi shouted, an edge to every word. But a hint of hesitation was there. We wouldn't die.

We needed to be on that plane—it was our last chance out—but the Germans waved goodbye. This was not their problem. Sam and I reached for our wallets. To add insult, we paid in smaller bills. Abdi wanted new hundred-dollar notes. Frustrated at this further extortion, we talked hard but gave in, outgunned. Our patience had run out, and the Germans were sealing the aircraft door. Abdi demanded more cash, though this was never part of the deal. I wrestled with the bag gripped by Abdi's knotted fist. The Somali finally let me have it.

"No, no, no, NO! You've had enough, you thieving bastards!" I growled, as an unthinking final shot. Abdi's anger rose further, but this time he stopped. These ones would be back in Mogadishu before long, he thought, and I will get more then. This calculation made, he declared his friendship, which we did not reciprocate. The gunman and his cohorts—their "security" job done—drove away through the sand blizzard of the propellers, Abdi Kadir feeling the fresh wad of dollars in his pocket, happy at last.

Sam was not happy, and neither was I, as we climbed aboard the plane. Here was yet one more lesson of outsiders being abused by arrogant and ungrateful Somalis, a lesson that every foreign do-gooder who would come to Somalia should learn, but often perilously neglected.

"I just can't fucking *believe* these people," he said, cradling his bald head in his hands as the nose of the Hercules lifted off. "Do they think we *enjoy* coming to Somalia, that anyone *wants* to put up with that *shit* every day just to help them?"

I couldn't have agreed more. We were not exactly on a mission of mercy. But this violent episode was typical of many that I would come across during dozens of journeys to Somalia. Of course Abdi was an extreme example: so many Somalis I met were gracious and welcoming and friendly. I wanted to understand "these people"—these ancient nomadic warriors and peacemakers—who were thrown by default into a new era in which the measured calculus of killing with a spear had been displaced by weapons of much greater efficiency. Intelligent in so many ways, Somalis were unprepared for the scale of chaos afflicting them. This dangerous cocktail was curiously both ancient and modern, and it mixed medieval demands for vengeance with today's disturbing ability to thoughtlessly kill vast numbers of people.

This disease had not been limited to Somalia. Several African states, the Balkans, Caucasus—even Indonesia—have been similarly driven to battle for ethnic or tribal differences. In Africa it has always been so, but has proved all the more potent when destructive firepower is easier to find than food and when government disappears or is complicit.

Somalia's collapse may always serve as grist for the attentions of those who explore the Dark Side of the human mind, who strive to measure "abnormal" behavior by locating pockets of inhumanity hidden in certain folds of the cerebellum of Somali marauders like Abdi, though they are common to all. Nevertheless, Somalia's recent history is also a tale of grave miscalculations made by foreigners in a very foreign land. Knowing nomads happily demonstrated their supremacy and disdain for the outsiders; the so-called "fruits" of civilization were not seen as such by them.

But it was the efficient modern methods of taking life—in such hard-worn and pitiless hands—that complicated the equation. Because Somalis are, like gunman Abdi, as hard as their country.

The reputation of Somalis as fearless defenders of their own independence, their reliant faith in Allah, their clans, and the regenerative glory of camels has evolved since Somalia provided fragrance to the ancient Egyptian pharoahs. The earliest references to the people of this parched wilderness are inevitably as 14th-century warriors, fighting bravely for Islam against the Christian "infidels" of Abyssinia. Taking part in the *jihad,* or holy war, they were "constantly praised for their bravery and daring and for their devotion to the cause of Islam."[1]

But when not at the battlefront, Somalis were recorded as being "dangerous, savage brigands" accountable to no one but God, with a firm conviction that power came only from supremacy of force. The modern parallels are obvious, writes the historian Ioan Lewis. "Even under the Imam's banner, [Somali recruits] were often troublesome and difficult to manage. Frequently quarrels and struggles between Somali lineages took a similar course to that which they follow today."

To understand the roots of violence in Somalia requires knowing the uncompromising nature of the environment. The harsh life of nomads revolved solely around survival. Camels and water were important tools, but so were good relations with other people and their clans. Kinship ties were paramount and were expected to be upheld in war and peace.

Every Somali child knows by heart his or her genealogy more than 20 generations, back to the revered common ancestral eponym of all Somalis, *Somaale*, from the words "go and milk." Beyond this hero the line is traced presumptuously up to the Prophet Mohamed or to noble Arabian families.[2] From *Somaale*, the lineages divide into six clan families. Political allegiances are determined by the male line, so Somalis don't ask each other *where* they are from but *whom* they are from.[3] Everyone knows that their place on this intricate map determines their status, strength, and also the severity of revenge that would be carried out on their behalf.

Clan has always been the last refuge, the last security during crisis, the only proven guarantor of safety when the world falls apart. "The rains can fail, wells can dry up, pastures can turn to dust," explains John Drysdale, a Briton who has fought alongside and lived among Somalis for decades. "It needs binding faith and clan loyalty to keep everyone alive."[4]

The brutal climate also helped ensure that Somalis developed a code of conduct that—ideally—meant to protect the weak from the predations of the strong. So as idolized as powerful warriors might be, in poetry and folk tales, there were deterrents designed to limit the scope and destruction of hostilities.

Surprising as it sounds, in light of what has afflicted Somalia for the past decade, Somalis for centuries had developed peace making as an art form almost on par with war making. Some argue that these traditional restrictions could be considered a Somali version of the Geneva Conventions.

"Somali society traditionally offered men a choice of two ideally contrasting, and mutually necessary roles: that of warrior (*waranle*, literally 'spear-bearer') or man of God (*wadaad*)," writes Lewis. "It was the task of the latter not only to mediate between man and God, but also between men in the cause of peace and harmony."[5]

But across this stark and beautiful land, there always have been too few resources, and therefore too many reasons to fight. From ownership of camels and women to pride and cultural praise for a man engaged in killing, desert rivals rarely saw eye to eye. Camels were—and still are—especially beloved, according to Somali oral history. The camel was described this way, by poet Omar Istreliya:

> It is a living boulder placed by God in the wilderness;
> Demel and her young ones are as vital to life as the tendons
>   of one's back;
> Had it not grown out of solid rock it should have not been
>   so highly appreciated.[6]

But it was the camel's ability to sustain life—just as relief aid would be during the civil war of the early 1990s—that made it worth fighting for. Exactly 100 camels was the blood money to be paid to atone for the killing of a Somali man—no other currency would do. In terms of camels, women were worth 50.

"Camels and horses constituted the only property whose looting in the time of war was sanctioned by Somali custom due to the high value attached to these animals by society," say the oral historians. "Anyone who met his death while trying to loot camels . . . was considered to have died honorably in the course of a worthy undertaking."

Still, this oral history speaks to the virtues of peace over war, and of harmony over discord. "War results in the death of a son, but not the birth of one," explains one proverb. And another: "Men's ideal bedding is peace."

The result of these sometimes conflicting views was that "although war was a constant feature . . . acts of excessive brutality were seldom committed." The reasons were strictly a function of what it took to survive, as the Somali historians explain: "Since no group liked to be on the receiving end of such excessive violence, they took great care not to be the first to perpetrate it. They had every reason to believe that the example they set in victory would be the one followed by their opponents in the event of their own defeat." This result "was dictated more than anything else by the pragmatic consideration of ensuring protection for one's own vulnerabilities in the swinging fortunes of war."

Such careful calculations may have worked when raiding parties faced their enemies with spears. And making peace even then was a delicate undertaking that required mediators, long talk, and mutual respect. But this careful balance toward peace—achieved in the past despite even the most atrocious transgressions—has broken down during the modern age of the gun, as the old divisions between who was weak and who was strong disappeared.

After all, killing with a spear requires far more commitment to the act than simply pulling a trigger.

Hand in hand with this warring history, of course, was pride in total personal, and later national, independence. "Few writers have failed to notice the formidable pride of the Somali nomad, his extraordinary sense of superiority as an individual, and his firm conviction that he is the sole master of his actions and subject to no authority except that of God," Lewis notes.[7] This legacy bedeviled every would-be colonizer. Somalis fought rule by the Italians in the late 19th century, then against British forces that tried to impose law, order, and administration.

The crucial lesson for those considering intervention in Somalia was embodied in the case of Sheikh Mohamed Abdullah Hassan, dubbed the

"Mad Mullah" by the British.[8] Warriors united under the sheikh for more than 20 years at the turn of the century, defeating every force sent against them. The Mad Mullah issued white turbans and strings of Muslim prayer beads to the "Dervishes," as his 5,000 mustered loyalists were called. In the course of his military crusade he declared a "holy war" against the Christian infidels, and his nationalist example—along with a particular mastery of evocative poetry and song that inspired his fighters to extraordinary bravery—is often invoked today.

What isn't remembered so well but parallels the modern era of clan warfare is that battles between the Dervishes, their Somali rivals, and the British caused mass starvation. Somalis were reduced to eating rats, and by the end of 1912, officials believed that a third of the entire population had perished in what came to be called the "Time of Eating Filth."

After suffering heavy casualties in numerous ground campaigns—which included use of a mounted camel constabulary—the British finally put down the Mad Mullah in 1920 with Royal Air Force bombers, in a carefully planned land and sea assault. Even then victory over the rebellious Somalis was slight. The British only lightly imposed themselves thereafter by keeping fewer than 200 officials in the protectorate. "It is wonderful," remarked one British officer, "how little we have yet managed to impress the Somalis with our superior firepower."[9]

Their subsequent respect for Somali intransigence was made clear in a report on tribes in British Somaliland published by the military government in 1945. The "savage and despotic" Mad Mullah was praised for "exacting unquestioning obedience founded on fear" during his reign, though he forced British officers to pull back to just two coastal towns. The risks of less-than-iron rule were made plain: "With the withdrawal of British control of the interior, indescribable disorder and inter-tribal warfare broke out, and in the holocaust which followed it is estimated perhaps one-third of the male population of British Somaliland were speared to death."[10]

Unappealing as it sounded, Somalia had attracted me for a long time. When rebels were pushing at the gates of Mogadishu in December 1990, on the eve of the Gulf War, I was based in Cyprus for *The Sunday Telegraph* (London). I sent messages to check the interest but, predictably, there was none. When I moved to Africa the next summer, Somalia was at the top of my list.

Before my first trip in September 1991, foreigners who had spent any time in Somalia issued dire warnings. Civil war between these mysterious clans and its attendant anarchy were well under way, and I should beware. Every Somali was a born killer, I was told, and this instinct would be unleashed at the slightest insult. Except for paying gunmen "guards" with cash—which was dangerous enough—I should know that all Somalis were larcenous and that fiscal disputes could be as bloody as those about injured pride.

I was never told of Somalis' unflinching generosity toward friends and sometimes toward enemies. How many times would I be invited into someone's house for a feast beyond their means? But these warnings were also based on bad experience. Somalia's neighbors have always referred with disdain to this barren land as the home of the *shifta,* or bandit. Somalis have done little to dispel the stereotype, and refer to their own bandits as *moryan,* with a mixture of fear and respect.

Somalis constituted the most extensive and united "nation" in Africa before the arrival of European adventurers. Speaking the same language and adherents of the same Sunna Muslim faith, they should have been among the last to dissolve into internecine conflict. Among themselves they are divided only by clan, by relationships between extended families that stretch back over generations. The Somalis were deprived of their natural ethnic homogeneity before the turn of the century, however, when their "nation" was one of many victims of the whimsical carve-up of Africa by colonial powers at the Berlin Conference of 1884–85.

With these divisions imposed from abroad, the dismemberment of Greater Somalia would serve the ambitions of future leaders by providing a ready-made reason to war against neighbors. Differences among clans would in turn serve as reason to war against each other.

Spread already across the Horn of Africa, ethnic Somalis were split five ways. The border with Ethiopia lopped off much of the Ogaden and Haud deserts to the west; tiny Djibouti was excluded in the northwest and given to France; and the border with Kenya divided southern "Somalia." Aspirations of one day unifying Greater Somalia, of "liberating" those Somalis forced to live under foreign banners, were evident in the national flag unfurled at independence in 1960: five points of a white star, set on a blue background.

The dream of Greater Somalia was resurrected by Mohamed Siad Barre, the dictator who came to power in a military coup in 1969. He hid the mystery of his iron-fisted rule behind dark glasses. Protruding features bunched together below Barre's hairless nostrils. A tiny square Hitlerian mustache adorned lips that gaped like those of a foraging bottom fish. This look prompted a derisive nickname among irreverent Somalis: Big Mouth. Ruthless in every way, Barre maintained his stranglehold by tight control of the army and security services and—though attacking the cancer of tribalism in public—by quietly playing clans off one another. Possibly nothing less could have kept Somalis at relative peace under a central authority. The dictator himself anticipated the coming chaos. "Tribalism and nationalism cannot go hand in hand," he declared. "It is unfortunate that our nation is rather too clannish; if all Somalis are to go to Hell, tribalism will be their vehicle to reach there."[11]

In the 1970s and early 1980s, Barre's ideology of "Scientific Socialism" officially aimed to destroy the ancient clan system. Launching a national campaign, Barre held formal ceremonies to symbolically "bury" the grip of clans, often burning effigies representing tribalism and misrule.[12] Kinship greetings were completely outlawed, including terms referring to "former" clan status that were used to get around that rule. But no matter the whims of their leaders: ties of blood kinship were too embedded in the Somali psyche to be exorcised.

This abiding faith in clan, coupled with the modern weapons amassed by Barre during the Cold War, would lead to disaster. Unimportant as Somalia's natural resources are to the outside world—limitless sand and a few drops of low-grade oil—the country sits at a strategic gateway to the Middle East and Red Sea route to the Mediterranean Sea and Europe. Banking on this strategic fact, Barre was all too happy to ensure that Somalia figured in the Cold War calculations of the superpowers, first of the Soviets and later of the Americans. In 1974 Somalia was the first sub-Saharan African country to sign a friendship treaty with the Soviet Union, and the 6,000 Soviet soldiers and civilians there ran the place as though they were operating out of a "mini-Kremlin," according to one account. "They controlled the ministries of defense and information, the secret police and an important military facility at Berbera. They turned the ragtag Somali army into a 25,000-man fighting force, armed with heavy artillery and AK-47 assault rifles. They supplied the air force with MiG fighters, and the schools with teachers who taught more political theory than mathematics."[13]

The superpower rivalry was waged there at fever pitch. The US in the early 1970s was allied to Ethiopia—that historical scourge of Somalia, because of the "persecuted" ethnic Somalis in the Ogaden and Haud. American Peace Corps volunteers were stoned in the streets of Mogadishu, and by 1971 they were forced to withdraw. US diplomats were spat upon, and by 1977 the embassy staff was pared down to three. Mogadishu was plastered with posters that showed Somali peasants stomping on Uncle Sam. The value of Soviet weaponry alone infused into Somalia totaled $270 million.[14]

But in 1977, buoyed by this military hardware—and, no doubt, notions of natural superiority—the Somali army itself marched into the Ogaden. Ethiopian units fell back, and within two months 90 percent of the Ogaden was in Somali hands: the dream of Greater Somalia was partly realized.

The Soviets, however, had already begun to support the young Ethiopian revolutionaries who had deposed Emperor Haile Salassie. Their efforts to persuade Barre to form a Marxist alliance with Ethiopia failed, and the Somali leader forced the Soviets to make a choice. Tired of Barre's irascibility, the Soviets switched allegiances, prompting a remarkable Cold War flip-flop in the Horn of Africa. Overnight Soviet advisers moved from Mogadishu to Addis Ababa, and within months 15,000 Cuban troops, columns of Soviet tanks, and hardware—worth $1 billion—were deployed to "protect" Ethiopia's borders. In Somalia, the hitherto sacred trinity of Marx, Lenin, and Barre was never mentioned again.

As they had thrilled at fighting for centuries, Somalis were obsessed with the war. Health clinics were converted to make uniforms, and the demand for news of the front was so great that neither radios nor batteries could be found in the markets.[15] The Soviet realignment belatedly caused an American turn-around, as Barre played the Cold War card to find a new source for weapons. He begged Western and Arab countries for help to turn back Soviet-Cuban "imperialism" in Africa's Horn. President Jimmy Carter promised military aid but Congress insisted that Somalia first withdraw its troops from the Ogaden. The imperious leader, Big Mouth, had miscalculated.

Backed by overwhelming Soviet and Cuban firepower, Ethiopia began to recapture the Ogaden, despite Barre's personal direction of the final stages of the war. National pride was dealt a severe blow—a bad result for any Somali warrior, for whom victory alone assures power and credibility. Barre purged the top ranks of the military. But defeat was so total that Barre feared Ethiopian units would cross into Somalia. Arms were anxiously distributed to civilians and refugees in the north. Those weapons in angry public hands would haunt Barre until his fall.

For a decade from 1978, even as Barre hardened repressive measures, the US spilled $800 million into the country, one-quarter for military "aid," in exchange for its own military access to ports and airports. Somalia's former colonial master, Italy, contributed $1 billion from 1981 to 1990, more than half of which went for weapons.[16] The value of foreign aid to Somalia soared to $80 per person, the highest rate in Africa and equivalent to half the gross domestic product.[17]

The now limitless supply of mortars, 106mm anti-tank cannons, and how-itzers, along with the aging Soviet hardware, would serve to lubricate the nation's destruction. Since the Mad Mullah, there had hardly been a time when Somalia was not at war with itself or its neighbors. But with internal opposition growing, armed insurgency was inevitable.

As his unpopularity grew, and despite his lip service to ending clanism, President Barre systematically replaced top officials with his own clansmen. By 1987, half the senior officer corps in the army were Marehan or related clans.[18] Armed opposition groups emerged based on clan affiliation, and insurrection erupted in the north.

In 1988 the entire northern city of Hargeisa was leveled in a fruitless effort to rid the regime of an Isaaq clan-based rebel group. Somali Air Force jet fighters took off from the Hargeisa airport and then turned around to make repeated bombing runs on the city. One conservative estimate put the number of civilians dead at 5,000, and another—which includes the bombing raids—at more than 50,000.[19] Though this act of destruction finally brought US military support to an end, at the peak of the battle a controversial American shipment of 1,200 M-16 assault rifles and 2.8 million rounds of ammunition was delivered *by air* to the Somali army.[20]

Far from feeling any remorse, President Barre was beside himself with joy at his "triumph." According to one former Somali official who paid a visit: "I have never seen Barre so relaxed and happy throughout my long association with him. He did not look like a president who had just destroyed his second capital, causing so much suffering and anguish. He simply saw himself as a Darod [clan] chief who had totally annihilated an enemy clan."[21]

Conditions were so bad that Somalis who managed to escape and testify to human rights groups dispensed with the usual confidentiality and permitted their names to be used, despite risks to relatives still inside: "What more could they do to us?" they asked.[22]

Barre's methods altered the traditional laws—and limits—of war. He encouraged soldiers to loot and sell freely what they could steal,[23] setting in motion a strategy of banditry—until then little known in Somali conflicts, except during the reign of the Mad Mullah—that was later replicated by roaming militias. Forced conscription of all men between the ages of 18 and 40 made for an unhappy army of soldiers who deserted often with their military experience and weapons intact, ready for uprising.

Every Somali, like my young gunman Abdi, learned how to use an assault rifle. And though years later they laughed when I even mentioned the name Big Mouth—the dictator seemed like no more than a passing dark cloud by then—the result of Barre's militarism was part and parcel of Somalia's modern experience, and they knew it.

As the guerrilla groups began infiltrating the capital, more weapons became available on the black market. The anarchy reached a peak in the first days of 1991. The final edition of the government newspaper ran this telling banner headline: PRESIDENT SIAD EXTENDS AMNESTY TO REBELS, PEACE TALKS ANYTIME, ANYWHERE.[24] Even the 5,000-strong "Red Beret" presidential guard—all drawn from Barre's Marehan clansmen—abandoned their failed warrior king, taking with them the collected loot from dozens of embassies. They departed the capital in a convoy that stretched for more than 10 miles, flanked by tanks and armored vehicles. The president, who had vowed many times that "when I leave Somalia, I will leave behind buildings but no people," stayed on to finish the job.[25]

He did not have long to wait. In one of the last security reports to reach the president, found later by Somali journalist Mohamoud Afrah, the chief of intelligence had warned: "I have noted a certain uneasiness in the army and in our own clan, a crisis of confidence," the report read. "The army is tired and hungry and are as if under the influence of drugs. Many of them have sold their weapons and defected to the rebels."[26]

An amphibious unit of US Marines from the USS Guam, diverted from final preparations for Operation Desert Storm in Saudi Arabia and the Persian Gulf, evacuated 272 American Embassy staff from Mogadishu in early January.[27] By 26 January 1991, the rebels had fought their way to Barre's hill-top residence at Villa Somalia, forcing him to flee so abruptly in a tank that sacks of money were left behind near the parking bay.

The victors ransacked Villa Somalia and found miles of magnetic tape recordings from tapped phone lines and countless reels of film of "secret" meetings taken with hidden cameras. Just months later, I sifted through the debris, an odd act that seems to be the preserve of the foreign correspondent. The aim was never to find trophies, but to find clues. I thumbed through the cassettes and videotapes. There was a copy of the original declaration, printed on the day of Barre's coup in 1969, which praised the "Bloodless Revolution." My gunmen excitedly brought me shell casings and pointed out the bodies of fallen guards that had not been taken away. One room was stuffed with thousands of unopened plaintive letters sent during Amnesty International campaigns to free political prisoners.

But the most chilling evidence of all that I found were thick files marked "NEVER LET OUT," listing enemies of the regime condemned to die in their dungeons. Barre was the Ceausescu of Africa. After such suffering for so many years, the aftershock of newfound freedom struck like a collective post-traumatic stress disorder. But instead of peace—as one might have expected—the result was more bloodshed.

Gone overnight were the instruments of repression, the security service with its spies and torture, the increasingly lawless army—the fearsome glue that had held Somalia together and kept clan emotions in check for two decades. The power vacuum was readily filled by the ferocious ghosts of Somali warriors past. Fortified with the endless firepower of Barre's Cold War arsenal, a new and altogether modern version of the invincible Somali gunman began to transform his country, sucking the once noble, often brutal attributes of Somali nomadic life into a vortex of irreversible violence. Traditional restraints were giving way.

The result was predictable to any clear-eyed student of the Somali mind. "The first thing to understand about the Somalis is that they are not as other men," writes Lewis.[28] "Today this nomadic society, with its goats, sheep and camels, has hit the age of the Kalashnikov. Every family has a high-powered weapon, and uses it; no tally of bloodshed can be kept and responsibility for violence is not clear; so the old system of reconciliation has been undermined."

President Barre's mark on Somalia's star-crossed future was indelible. His army abandoned 40,000 weapons and hundreds of millions of live rounds to the guerrillas. Vast arms and weapons dumps were parceled out among clan leaders, putting into their hands the ability to rule Somalia by force, as warlords. The toys divided, these new warlords could begin reaching for power for the sake of their clan—just as Barre, the exemplar, had done with his. And they could perpetrate their own terror.

Most Somalis, proud and sure in their arrogance that they could govern themselves after toppling Barre, were helpless to prevent clan leaders from carving out their fiefdoms in Mogadishu and the countryside. The structures of civic rule crumbled, and over time I saw the new warlordism exert itself. Somalis deplored the reimposition of tribal divisions, but in Somalia's brave new world, citizens had no choice other than to seek protection from their clans. Little else could save them.

Remarkably, Barre's decline seemed to have been deliberately ignored or misunderstood by the US government. In 1989, the State Department charged Barre's army with a "widespread, systematic and extremely violent assault" on unarmed civilians."[29] But as late as 1990, Gen. Norman Schwarzkopf— who within months would command the US-led military alliance that reversed Iraq's occupation of Kuwait—told Congress that military aid to the Barre regime was critical "to help Somalia retain its political and territorial integrity."[30]

This was not the last misreading of Somalia by American policy-makers. Missing the signs of Barre's imminent fall, the US had built a $35 million embassy, its largest and most expensive in sub-Saharan Africa, replete with a nine-hole golf course that was more sand trap than putting green. It opened to great fanfare on 4 July 1989. Officials later conceded that the scale of the project may have given the "wrong impression," especially considering Somalia's diminishing importance at the close of the Cold War. The final lick of paint had barely dried in January 1991 when the regime collapsed and the shining new embassy had to be abandoned to eager hordes of looters.

In restrospect, the sacking of the embassy would prove to be the first line of an involved parable about American policy mistakes in Somalia. But little did I realize that Somalia would be the place in the New World Order where the United States would first lose its innocence.

Armed guerrillas and civilians scaled the high walls with ladders; *à la* Saigon, the ambassador was forced to flee by helicopter. It was impossible to know that four years later I would be on hand for a similar American and UN retreat—from the same compound, in fact—though the consequences would be much greater.

Not far away, at Mogadishu's main cathedral, another ceremony told even more about the sacrilege that would soon follow: a group of escaped prison convicts had burst open the tall wooden doors to loot the riches of the church. Beneath the ornate sculpted Stations of the Cross, they laid down their guns long enough to dig up the grave of the Italian bishop of Mogadishu, the first foreigner murdered in 1989 as President Barre's security services began to lose control.[31]

When they were finished they tossed aside the bare pale skull of the bishop, still stuck with freshly disturbed dirt, its teeth pried out for their gold fillings.

TWO

"CITY OF THE INSANE"

Death has become too commonplace to matter. The two greatest products in Mogadishu these days are shooting and rumors: from morning to night they manufacture rumors, from night to morning they manufacture shootings.

> —Mohamoud Afrah,
> *Mogadishu: A Hell on Earth*

In biblical times, the three wise men came from the land of Punt with their gifts of gold, frankincense, and myrrh. Such luxuries still grace Somalia's markets, but since the fall of Siad Barre weapons had been in much greater demand than perfume. Gold, such as that plucked from the bishop's teeth, was of value only for the protection it could buy.

Mogadishu's arms markets had grown unchecked since the eve of the dictator's collapse, when merchants quietly took clients aside to inspect their clandestine weapons stocks. Now the market teemed with criminals and self-appointed defenders and excited boys, the whole scene smelling of gun oil and testimony to an all-pervasive gun culture fed for decades by Italian, Soviet, and American "friends." Here in microcosm was the true wealth of the Barre regime.

This part of Mogadishu had been virtually off-limits to foreigners for well over a year, so I was apprehensive on my first visit in September 1991. My handful of gunmen—freelancers hired by people I trusted—said they could protect me. Strings of bullets of every caliber dangled from the thin frames of shop stalls like chunks of fresh camel meat or vegetables. They shared space with detergent and medicinal roots. I ducked from one display to the next in the narrow alley.

"Salesmen" gathered around me, locked into a possible sale, sure that here was a customer with money. They all wanted some of it, and the circle tightened, almost menacingly. Men with wheelbarrows loaded with ammunition stopped to partake of the palaver.

"You want gun? What you want?" demanded one man, his face well-used to a bitter wad of qat. That morning, he was happy to be facing a monied man. I fondled grenades in a box and sifted through an assortment of bullets that could be purchased singly—for simple jobs—or in lots. But his Hungarian Parabellum pistols were full of grit, so I moved on.

The tin roofs grew hot with the day, so weapons merchants fortified their dripping faces with bundles of fresh qat, chewing thoughtfully, making them more ready to absorb the daily horrors.

The gun merchants got twitchy when it seemed that I was looking only, not buying. Behind the stalls were stacked artillery rounds and mortars of all sizes like a selection of candy. There were oily boxes of screw-in detonators, banks of rocket-propelled grenades and launchers—some still packed in their factory grease—and long, slender missiles for big spenders. There was enough firepower to repel an invasion, and, in fact, that is exactly what it *would* be used for soon enough in 1993, to force American "peacekeeping" troops to go home.

But Somalia was in enough trouble already, without the Americans or anybody else. The capital was divided between the strongest clans, the Habr Gedir and the Abgal, which had fought together to oust Siad Barre. But then they squabbled over the spoils: who would be president? Like Beirut and Nicosia, Mogadishu was split between north and south by an unruly no-man's-land called the Green Line. It was there that the sparkling merchandise of the gun market was used, and it was at the gun market that the gunmen congregated to discuss the afflictions of the day. There was no law, there was no government. These men were it.

Arms were—and still are—Somalia's most useful currency. Along with food, they can ensure living until tomorrow. Without a weapon, your food will be stolen; but well armed, you can always steal food. An AK-47 assault rifle then cost just $70; two full clips of bullets cost less than a plate of goat meat.

One man broke away, brandishing his wares as the others fell back. A wild flash of the eyes lit up his face as he squeezed off a dozen rounds into the air. The spent cartridges ejected into the laughing crowd. A stem of qat quivered from where it was held between his teeth.

"Good gun, and cheap price for you!" he shouted, as the others began blasting into the air themselves, in competition. The rounds fell somewhere in the city, adding to the daily casualty rate of those maimed by stray bullets. The rain of bullets never seemed to stop. But all the shooting made my guards uneasy, and they motioned to go. If there were ever a single rule for getting by in a war zone, it must be this: when your gunmen get nervous, get nervous with them. So we left. That day at least, God's will could not be to die ignobly, not there.

Somali reverence for the weapon was obvious even at Mogadishu airport, when I landed that fall for the first of what would be dozens of journeys to Somalia. The relief plane I hitched a ride with had descended slowly along Somalia's rough coast, north toward the Mogadishu airport, over shallow gem-blue waters that hid the sharks that patrolled this shore, with their layers of razor-sharp teeth. The city emerged, at the edge only a sprawl of scrappy slum huts that turned into white buildings and then patches of green along main avenues. It all gradually gained in resolution as we dropped down through the mask of whipping dust and heat. The particular suffocating odor of the capital—a fermentation as total as if it had occurred in a sealed plastic bag—was a mix of hot sea and salted, rotting ocean waste and the decomposing refuse of sweating human beings. I can't forget it.

My lungs had barely adjusted to the heat and smell, and I began to sweat. I was presented with a visa form from the swindlers who had stolen the immigration stamps. In English and Italian, as nonchalantly as a request to note my age, I was asked to list the type, serial number, brand, and caliber of all the weapons I was bringing into Somalia, to catalog my own humble addition to the destructive potpourri. All those warnings prior to my departure quickly gained credibility.

Barren Somalia, already in the grip of militiamen with guns, was disintegrating further. The defilement of the bishop's cadaver was just the beginning, the petty prologue of violations that from 1991 would devastate the capital with the bloodiest clan war in Somalia's history. The rival warlords' quest for power—and the destruction wrought by Barre's own defeated clansmen—would lead to famine.

Gangs of bandits looted and foraged, exacting a fierce toll. By late 1991 there were nearly 40 distinct bandit groups in the capital alone. Their hands were always soiled with dirt, for they dug up every length of copper and phone wire under Mogadishu's streets. Militiamen were recruited with promises of loot. Large gray electrical transformers were cut down from their poles to get at the half pint of poor-quality oil inside. Factories were dismantled and sold complete to Arab countries by emerging "godfathers."

For those trapped in Mogadishu, a long agony was only beginning. I stayed that first time in a dingy hotel called the Nasa Hablood, where I was the only customer. The steak was good, and Somali papayas the size of watermelons—one half for dessert, with lemon slices—were a feast. My gunmen and I drove around, but our mobility was limited by the areas of fighting. The list of meetings was typical: relief agencies, hospital, local leaders. The scenes along the way were not.

On the streets were corpses of civilians who hadn't given up their vehicles quickly enough. I saw the body of one man dumped at a bus stop, his intransigence manifest by a bullet through the nose that, on exit, tore away the back bowl of his skull. No Somali waiting there gave a second glance, but instead, deliberately, did *not* look.

"Chaos" would be the wrong word to describe the plundering. For at the top of the informal clan power structure were the former guerrilla leaders and opponents of Siad Barre who had swept him away. Their claims to power—and willingness to impose those claims by force—turned their titles to "warlord."

"One of Siad Barre's worst legacies is power addiction," explains the Somali writer Mariam Arif Gassem. "The dark culture of his dictatorial regime injected into the minds of every single Somali the appetite for power, either for the individual or for the tribe. Power in Somalia is synonymous with wealth, freedom and personal security."[1]

The epitome of that power and its use was General Mohamed Farah Aidid (pronounced *I-deed*), warlord *par excellence* by the Somali definition. He was a strong man with a military sense of purpose and decisiveness: this much I could tell within minutes of our first meeting in September 1991. His features were chiseled and unforgiving, with the bearing of a hawk in constant pursuit of prey. And they held that way when he barked orders into a radio standing in a nondescript shipping container that doubled as a command center. This was the most important man in Somalia, judging from the fearsome, lean look of the armed convoy outside. Those gunmen had killed plenty.

Aidid took over from Siad Barre as chief of police in 1958, and during local elections had the hands of voters stamped to prevent their voting twice.[2] The rank of general was a holdover from his time in Barre's army. He encouraged its use to enhance his image as a ruthless warrior, a flamboyant man of arms. His twisted smile was decidedly wicked. But he was quick to use it, had a confident laugh, and exhorted the military, *his* military, "to wipe out all bastards and thugs."

In the 1970s, Barre came to know of Aidid's own coup plotting against him and locked him away for seven years. Rehabilitation came in the 1980s when the general was sent a safe distance to India as ambassador. Then his own Habr Gedir clan called him back to Ethiopia to serve as their "father of war," to head the armed rebel movement against the Barre regime. The joyful exhilaration of battle never left him.

Aidid had the best claim to power: he toppled the hated dictator, so he had popular support well beyond his clan. And his clansmen inherited a sizable portion of the Barre stockpile that had served the third-largest army in Africa. But first he had to prove himself the undisputed leader of Somalia.

So Aidid directed his Habr Gedir subclan to wage war against the rival Abgal subclan, led by Ali Mahdi Mohamed, a nondescript hotelier who had appointed himself president. In the battle to oust the Barre regime, the two men had been allies, both leaders of the United Somali Congress (USC) and the larger Hawiye clan. But the split was caused by mutual provocation, mutual intransigence, and mutual thirst for power. When Barre fled, Ali Mahdi declared himself head of a new government so quickly that some of his "ministers" had not been notified. Aidid, whose forces had done the job, was livid. And as head of the more aggressive Habr Gedir, he attacked later in 1991 to claim the top job for himself. Blessed with far more firepower, he was able to back his argument with force.

The traditional system that once bound clans to preserve peace, or at least to stem war, dissipated with the clouds of cordite. The conflict divided Ali Mahdi's northern Mogadishu enclave from Aidid's turf in the south, creating the lethal Green Line. Within days, killing was so widespread that nothing short of destroying the enemy subclan would end the complex blood feud.

Most of the population of the city was of Ali Mahdi's Abgal subclan, but Aidid had heavier weapons, controlled the bigger swath, and was reinforced with country-bumpkin supporters from rural areas. The general won major battles, only to lose territory the same night as Ali Mahdi's "infantry" reclaimed it. The constant seesaw reduced the city center to a wasteland.

During the most intense bouts of fighting, from mid-November 1991 to early March 1992, the amount of unloosed artillery fire, aimed by "crews" who knew nothing of the science of hitting a target, made movement impossible. During brief moments of quiet, city dwellers emerged from their holes and damaged homes to hunt for food and water like phantoms, silently gathering the essentials to survive. As hunger increased and insecurity kept out nearly all relief workers and food aid, citizens braved or ignored the resumption of shellfire, taking more chances in open places to pilfer their needs. Snipers killed from rooftops. During shelling no one could bury the dead. Some 14,000 died.

One holy man suggested this solution: "They ought to put a hundred-foot wall around this city and declare it a home for the incurably insane," he declared.[3]

But waging war, even in Somalia, couldn't be done alone. So Aidid relied on a close relation with a financier. Osman Hassan Ali "Ato" was one of the godfathers, a self-made businessman with a large personal militia and significant financial interest in Somalia's lucrative qat trade. When not disrupted by violence at airstrips where it is flown in fresh daily with a fleet of small planes from Kenya, the business is valued at $1 million per month. When there was no other option, I would hitch a ride on one of these planes, paying for my weight in qat and more.

Ato, whose nickname means "skinny," had a likable round face and a slight paunch. When surprised, his playful eyes would open wide and protrude. He lived well, even in this place, but played the game of survival by the same unwritten rules of those on the streets. "If you want security, you must make your own," he told me the first time we met in 1991, relaxing in his expansive home, a long, dark purple print sarong knotted, in Somali style, at his waist. Mogadishu's endless night breeze evaporated the sweat off both of us.

Like every Somali, he *said* he wanted peace. But he hedged his bets with a network of six or seven garages that converted stolen four-wheel-drive land cruisers into battle wagons. Gunmen were paid $150 bounty for every vehicle they looted that could be transformed. There were 20 similar garages in the city, and there were other godfathers. But here was a man who knew well the bottom line and foresaw long clan war in Somalia, so he prepared the war machinery. His operation was run well, as if he had taken his cue from some kind of Palermo Handbook for Mafia Dons. He went to Ethiopia for regular shopping sprees, filling gaps in Somalia's arsenal with the for-sale remains of Ethiopia's fallen Marxist government. He supplied qat to pay the clan militias.

But it was in his garages where the real engines of war were being primed. The canopies of looted land cruisers were shorn away, and custom-made mounts were bolted to the chassis and fitted with American 106mm anti-tank cannon, smaller Chinese recoilless rifles, or Soviet anti-aircraft batteries adjusted horizontally for street battle. In Somalia, they were known as "technicals." Such highly mobile firepower was first used to great effect in the 1980s in Chad's northern Tibesti Mountains by President Hissein Habre against Libya-backed rebels.

The lesson of their success was not lost on the Somalis, whose battle in the thorny interior and sandy city alleyways required mobile force. In President Barre's final days, Big Mouth had created a similar fleet to quell unrest. With the old regime gone, gunmen manning these makeshift Road Warriors rampaged through Mogadishu. Their dependence on fuel—and on the careless, armed young clansmen who roared through the city astride them—gave a vision of the post-apocalypse, a desperate scene taken from a "Mad Max" film in which only born fighters flourish.

Aidid knew that without this support, his claim to power might sound hollow. At our first meeting, he invited me on an inspection tour of the garages, and his narrow face came alive. The warlord's lips curled with happiness as he oversaw the creation of more battle wagons. In one workshop, he spent an extra moment admiring an "Abaas," the cleverly converted air-to-air missile stripped from MiG-21 fighter planes and shipped from Libya to fight Somalia's clan wars.

"This has a very nice effective range," Aidid said, resting his hand lightly on the dull tin housing of the weapon. To me it looked more like a Sputnik-era museum piece than a decisive instrument of war. He rued the day that playing with such toys must end, but that day was still far away.

Aidid took me along to the front line, too, and made the visit dressed in a smart white shirt and trousers. The front shifted along the Green Line from one narrow alley to the next, and we glanced warily down each street as we passed. Today's skirmish was being coordinated by "one of our best-trained commandos, who led the assault on Barre," Aidid explained. "Colonel" Ahmed Sheikh Arabe couldn't have looked less like an officer: he was thin and aging, with one silver tooth and the rest rotting brown. His spear denoted his superior rank, in sharp contrast to the modern guerrilla firepower with which he was protected by his "troops." This was Somalia's version of a "dog of war," a fighting mercenary who enjoyed nothing more than to cultivate his adrenaline rush and to steal what he could.

Close by a burst of machine-gun fire—followed by a quick swoosh of rockets overhead—registered on Aidid's face as a brief flicker, even a detectable flinch. But no more. He was suitably protected by his silver-capped black walking stick, which he pointed at the enemy. "They must surrender, no?" he asked me. I politely concurred. Then as window dressing, he added: "We need peace. People are starving and want food."

The war had encouraged a certain resignation, and even the warlords felt it. If Aidid died then, if any of them died on that front line, it would have been the will of Allah, and inevitable. So there was no reason to fear. But Aidid *did* enjoy this power-grabbing bid, and his death would preclude his further participation in the war—for him, that would be a pity. So the spear-wielding commander ordered his gunmen to fan out along the shrapnel-torn walls. Soon they would destroy their errant adversary and would have to hunt for more enemies.

But that was not a new chapter in Somalia, where "fighting potential very largely determines political status, feud and war are instruments of power politics."[4] The warlords simply extended traditional clashes among nomads over grazing and water rights to a more destructive level.

Aidid may have reveled in his role as war maker, but the result across Mogadishu had no logic—and therefore did not fit any recognizable pattern of past Somali warfare. The vast suffering, in turn, had no meaning for its victims, so the traditional restrictions were easily ignored.

Throughout the civil war, for example, there were few places to hide. One old family in the Hamar Weyn district—unrelated to any of the main clans—

recounted for a Somali journalist how they were visited three separate times in 1991, each one further breaking their will.[5] On the third visit, the father narrated, the bandits took his 16-year-old daughter, pointing a pistol at her head and threatening to shoot unless given money. When they dragged her from the house, the desperate father attacked the culprits. In a hail of bullets that "transformed the house into an inferno," his six-year-old son fell, shirt red with blood. The gunmen refused to let the boy go to hospital. "At last when my wife kissed the feet of the gang leader he decided to let her leave." To deal with the luckless father, the chief called a gang member named the "dentist," who pulled the man's teeth out with mechanic's pliers. The boy died within days. "No trace of my daughter. Until today, I do not know if she is alive or dead," the father said.

The mounting deaths were not the only degradations. Traditional warrior codes dictated that women, who along with children are deemed to be among the "weak," are never to be harmed. They were violated repeatedly.

In a Baidoa hospital rich with the smells of undiluted iodine and un-changed dressings, one depressed Western doctor saw a tough example. The doctor was young and had come to Somalia to save lives: wasn't that the purpose of being there? After sewing the guts back into a wounded young gunman, he told the man's family of five that if they did not give blood, their brother would not survive.

"They let him die," he said. "The bastards wouldn't give him blood."

I spoke to one cadaverous old man who explained why Somalia had been so roundly cursed. His back was bent painfully, adding an uncanny weight to his Stygian appraisal: "It's Allah's will that we suffer so much," he intoned, "because we have not been true to the Koran. We have killed unnecessarily."

In times past, this reason alone might have been sufficient to stay the spear of any honorable Somali warrior. Somali historians say that acts of "unsanctioned violence . . . were discouraged by fear of *cuqubo*, a curse that Somalis believed was brought down upon transgressors as a form of divine retribution. Somalis held that those who perpetrated cruelty on the helpless, holy and revered persons . . . would be unfailingly punished by Allah."[6]

Still, only the militia now prowled these streets. For journalists, negotiating through this obstacle course required patience, humility, stubborn arrogance—taking a cue from the Somalis—and cash dollars. Payments for everything from hired gunmen to hotel rooms were counted in increments of hundred-dollar bills. This was, after all, a *war* economy. Because the risk was so great, I kept my stash—along with my passport—hidden in my luggage at the hotel. Each week in Somalia, communications aside, could easily cost $1,500 to $2,000.

Moving around Mogadishu was like playing a constant game of Russian roulette: the longer you kept at it, the more likely you were to lose. I did not have vicious arguments with all my gunmen, angrily parting with thick handfuls of cash, as I did with Abdi when he nearly killed Sam and me on the Bardera airstrip. Several became good, trusted friends with whom I explored the streets again and again. In the tensest moments, they would sometimes take me by the hand and lead me unscathed through venomous anti-Western crowds of their kinsmen.

Hersi, young and among the skinniest of Somalis—who had been shot through the throat, too, and therefore didn't speak above a whistling whisper—worked with me during many visits. He spoke no English, but maneuvered his white Toyota Cressida through the Mogadishu traffic and along bandit roads with admirable precision and belligerence. In the afternoons, he kept a bundle of qat between us on the car seat, though I found it too bitter and too much effort to be worthwhile.

I trusted Hersi, in part because I had little choice, which was why having a trigger-happy lunatic like Abdi to protect you threatened everybody. Hersi was good. And he had a human face that was otherwise easy to forget in a place like Somalia, where speaking to the "big" people and foreigners was the daily fare. In very dangerous situations Hersi would leave the car to the other two guards and escort me himself, assault rifle ready at full automatic, held as naturally in his spindly arms as I carried my notebook. He had a fantastic blue, yellow, and red flowered shirt that he wore more often than every other day. "*Hair-sssi*," I would hiss from my lungs, mimicking the sinister quality of his voice as it passed over the scar tissue of his throat. And we both laughed. He loved the joking, too.

In Mogadishu tension was steady but prone to surges. Every dusty alley seemed to harbor gunmen, like some near the ransacked Villa Somalia. When they saw us they jerked into action. My guards pointed their gun barrels out the car windows before I even knew what was happening. Hersi swerved hard, my heart tightened like a clenched fist; then both sides recognized the other. Guns were lowered, and we slowed to have a lighthearted chat. The looting today had gone well, they said. We were on our way again.

[Sadly, my friend Hersi would later die in classic Somali fashion. During a visit to Mogadishu in the spring of 1999, I asked a mutual Somali friend about Hersi. "Oh, hadn't you heard? He was killed last year in a gunfight. It was a dispute over land," he said. Then the tone of his voice dropped an octave: "I'm sorry."]

The viciousness of the fighting was lubricated by a growing taste for qat. Teenage gunmen worked this narcotic cud, which left them in an uncaring stupor. Demand for the leaf also rose among civilians who wanted to forget their new reality. The need was described lucidly enough by George, a talkative gunman whom I saw only once. He let his suspicion and fear subside—or rise, according to his mood—each afternoon, letting it run until 2 or 3 the next morning. The demons dissolved with qat's bitter juice, his throat furring up for hours on end. He dipped his hand deep into the pocket of a long, blue raincoat for another stem of qat. The cavity between his jaw and skull was jammed full, with right cheek bulging.

"This stuff will take you to Heaven," he advocated, a stream of green spittle escaping from the corner of his mouth, marking his chin. Yes, just to the haven where Somalis yearned to hide, every day.

To ease the violence, Somalia's remnant police force tried to disarm the bandits. This attempt was as risky as it was bold. The former chief of police, Ahmed Jamma Musa, headed these so-called "neutral" troops, but he had just 1,000 uniforms for 4,000 policemen, and many other problems. A picture of him in police chief's uniform sat like a trophy on a fine wood table at his house. I was surprised to see that even the tall iron gates of *his* compound were sprinkled with bullet holes. I had heard of four separate attempts on his life.

Ahmed Jamma admitted that his police were given only "haphazard on-the-job training. It's not systematic or methodical, but what can you put into the heads of these people? We try to tell them the truth: if they break up into clans, it will be a disaster." But by late 1991, that disaster was already well under way. With commendable foresight, the Red Cross supplied food to the police to inspire loyalty, in the hopes that at least some of the banditry could be brought under control. But no one wanted his clan disarmed. "The only thing to do is cordon an area and seize the weapons," Ahmed Jamma said. "Of course we have shoot-outs, but in 14 days I lost seven men—a reasonable rate."

Ironically, the police were not free from clan strictures and were forced to pay an extortionate death tax. During one search, for example, several looters were killed by the police. Clan elders—backed by their own clan warriors—demanded $7,000 for each casualty incurred, they said, "while you were stealing our guns." The police paid.

Freelance "assistants" caused more problems for the force, since without uniforms they couldn't be identified. One time at a stop near the derelict national theater, I filled my vehicle with gas from greasy jerrycans and let my gunmen fortify themselves with fresh bundles of qat. A roofless Isuzu Trooper roared along the main street, swerving around toppled telephone poles and mangled street junk, before pulling up dramatically behind me in line. There were two cowboys with guns, one carrying a fat wad of new bills, the other skinny as death and wearing a long black wig like a Liberian rebel. "Policemen!" muttered one of my guards, with obvious disdain.

As the civil war raged in Mogadishu, another battle was under way in

Somalia's interior, one that would take tens of thousands more lives by precipitating famine. Months after President Siad Barre was forced to flee the capital to his home turf in south-central Somalia, he regrouped the fighters of his Marehan clan and counterattacked. His forces began moving, ravaging farms and food stocks for six months during three unsuccessful attempts to return to Mogadishu. Barre's three divisions despised the region's "lower" farming clans and abused them accordingly. The Marehan laid waste to the area, turning Somalia's traditional bread basket into a barren ruin of smoldering villages. More than anything else, this tactic was the harbinger of the tragedy to come: it turned food into a strategic weapon and resulted in famine.

The tale of one family shows this "depredation dynamic"[7] at work. Gunmen forced the family at gunpoint to reveal hidden grain caches. Hundreds of their cattle, sheep, and goats were confiscated, and two young daughters were taken "to care for the livestock."[8] A son was shot dead when he tried to intervene. The farmer, until that day a pacifist, vowed to kill his attackers. But the militia returned three days later to find that he kept one grain store hidden from them. To exact revenge, the gunmen bound the farmer's legs and arms behind his back and "kicked me about from place to place like a soccer ball," he recalled. The farmer refused to give in, but the gang head had other plans. The farmer said,

> He ordered his man to prepare a large fire and bring him a long knife. He put the blade in the flames until the knife became cherry red and then ordered his cohorts to unbind me. He said that if I didn't talk within five minutes he intended to put the burning blade to my genitals.

The farmer cracked, and Barre's gunmen "took away our last defense." Without food—like growing numbers in this region—the man tried to walk to Mogadishu. "During those two weeks of hell, I lost three more of my children whom I buried alone, away from the survivors, using only my bare half-paralyzed hands," he said.

The trauma spread among neighbors, too. One woman told of her shock: "I knew this gunman. He stole the grass I was cutting to make soup. I grew up with him and knew who he was. That's what hurts."

The actions of the marauders gave Aidid a chance to widen his power and to conclude unfinished business with Barre. I happened to be with him in September 1991, when he turned one Mogadishu elders meeting into a political rally, using his military strength to win support. I had requested an interview, was led upstairs, and to my surprise was ushered into a bedroom. Aidid was resting in a tank top and wore plastic sandals. We spoke, and then as we were finishing I saw a peculiar preparation. Aidid pulled on his shoes and buttoned up a shirt. Then, though this was to be a meeting with allies, the general removed the pillow from the bed, picked up a pistol that had been hidden there and strapped it on, pulling his jacket over it.

The meeting of elders was held downstairs. The group told Aidid gory tales of the war they were losing in the interior to the west. Baidoa had fallen to Barre's ravaging militias, and further losses could threaten the capital. Aidid listened to the appeals and calculated his advantage.

"The enemy come and cut off women's breasts and bury men alive," pleaded the first elder. His beard was dyed with dark henna, and he wore a squarish skullcap to denote his rank as elder. "There is no government, so we come to you for help. We run from Baidoa because we have no army. Otherwise we would fight and destroy them all." These farming clans were usually despised by arrogant camel-rearing nomads like Aidid. Taking this into account, the bombast increased.

"We know that you, General, are the only one in Somalia ready to fight the enemy. You are the last *mujahideen*," crowed a second elder. The assembly erupted with cheers of "God Is Great!" For them, the equation was simple: they had willing fighters, the general had guns; together they should make war.

"This is my first time to see you, General, and I love you!" shouted another man. The appeal was going well, so his voice grew louder still. "You are the only one who can see the tricks of the enemy. We have just 300 men with guns. The only thing missing is more weapons and a good leader. If we can find them, all enemies in Somalia can be killed!" The elders went wild. The warlord allowed a smile to flash across his face. His pistol would not be necessary.

The elder finished with a flourish: "The future president of Somalia is Aidid—we give our hands to you!"

Leaning on his silver-capped stick, in the unassuming garb of an elder himself, Aidid turned poetic about Somalia's collapse, about how the "revolution" that toppled Barre was hijacked by his enemies, how he would not sleep until those enemies were vanquished, and how he wanted peace for Somalia. It was rhetoric they had all heard before, and it captivated again.

"They call me the dictator and the army man, but if our organization is not politically sound it can't have a strong army. The people should choose who they want, as you have done," he said. Then he made his campaign pledges. "I hear your problems. I will look to my arms store, and meet with the other warlords. We will act immediately and create a good army," he promised, punctuating each syllable. These are the words they've been waiting to hear. "I will get Barre himself as quick as possible, within days!"

It would be months before Aidid fulfilled his promise, but this war council cum rally ensured that peace would not prevail soon. Because for Somalia's strategist warlords, plotting every nuance of their claim to power was done coldly, quietly, aseptically, without pause for human suffering that might result. The weapon was enough.

It was warlords like Aidid and his financier Osman Ato who were the *de facto* government. But like other "leaders" in Somalia, these two trod a narrow line between providing security and directing the bands of looters that contributed to their wealth, firepower, and political status.

Caught in this web, relief agencies that insisted upon saving Somalis had little choice but to accept their "favors." The handful that struggled in Mogadishu in the early days of the civil war to sew up bullet wounds and distribute the trickle of relief food primarily worked in the south of the city, under their protection. Relief workers lived near Aidid's headquarters and Ato's house, for a fee, along what they called "Osman Street." To get by, every agency hired gunmen and their battle wagons—from the warlord's own legions, of course—which they often fudged on their budget forms as cash expenditure for "technical assistants." The name "technical" for any such armed security vehicle was born.

But this was a symbiotic relationship, a distasteful Faustian agreement, made by life savers who had no other way of carrying out their work—and by the warlords who were making their work necessary. Even with the blessing of the godfathers, however, the task of providing relief was dangerous. Somalis themselves no longer trusted their friends, or even their brothers. So to be a foreigner in Somalia—with no one to avenge your blood—was to be an easy target. Sometimes I traveled with relief workers in their vehicles, but even with their staff guards and big machine guns, movement was risky. I would soon learn that neither noble do-gooders, nor journalists like me, were bulletproof.

In Mogadishu, the profits and the stakes of fighting were large, and so required especially ruthless methods to establish superiority. A Somali patriot Aidid may have been—few doubt this about the man. But to him the human cost meant little. The toll was inescapable. In Medina Hospital in 1991, Dr. Rias Soudan, a portly surgeon from Lebanon, operated on 20 victims each day for the French relief agency Médecins Sans Frontières (MSF). Many of them arrived with toe tags labeled GSW, for "gunshot wound." More than anything, he bemoaned the arming of his wards.

"All my patients now keep their guns with them in the hospital," he said. They were smuggled inside, they were hidden under pillows and packed into mattresses. Dr. Soudan reset compound fractures and broken legs on the operating table with a certain force, putting all his weight into rebreaking a limb, silver pins screwed through flesh into bone, bleeding with the twisting pressure. Somalis accepted the pain as a necessary evil, like the corruption of hospital "neutrality." Visiting relatives brought grenades and knives so patients could protect themselves. These wards were no sanctuary.

MSF doctors joked that it would take a month and an army to disarm the hospital. But pressure from a warlord could be quicker, as proved during one hospital "uprising." The chance of dying "out there" was so great that in one incident fully recovered patients refused to leave the relative splendor of free beds, floor mattresses, and food. Benadir Hospital was a soulless place, cramped with casualties and infection, but the patients had formed an *ad hoc* union to ensure that they couldn't be ousted. When asked to vacate to make room for new cases, 20 patients responded by drawing their guns. Three hours of negotiation came to nothing, so MSF called on Aidid to intervene. He sent a truck with 15 of his own armed men. The fighters were asked to wait outside. Hearing of the squad's arrival, the outgunned rebel patients capitulated and laid down their weapons. Space was made for new wounded, further strengthening the strange symbiosis between doctor and warlord.

Gunmen were rarely used so wholesomely, however. One report described the predicament forced upon doctors.[9] During periods of shelling in 1991, "it was routine for groups of armed soldiers to rush into hospital compounds, casualty areas and wards, dictating triage and treatment decisions by holding guns to the heads of physicians and nurses."

The Catch-22 for relief agencies was evident when distributing food aid. As depredations mounted and the hunger gained momentum, I joined an ICRC food convoy to the inland town of Giohar, 50 miles north of Mogadishu. The ties between those who provided "relief" and those who provided "protection" could not have been closer. In September 1991, this was the largest food convoy to leave the capital in nearly a year: fifty trucks stacked with rice, beans, and seed. We assembled before dawn along the stinking waterfront. A plethora of armed guards—lorded over by an anti-aircraft gun—took up their positions. Only in Lebanon, Afghanistan, and Somalia, and later Chechnya, was the neutral ICRC obligated to work with armed escorts.

In those days, that was a secret that the headquarters in Geneva was not happy to advertise, and when I described the gunmen and arms protecting this relief convoy in *The Sunday Telegraph*, I was temporarily blacklisted by the ICRC. But for anyone on the ground in Somalia, it was clear that there was no alternative.

"Trucks with food are like trucks full of money," Stefan Hagelueken, a German Red Cross worker and convoy chief, told me. His ratty hair turned gritty like mine as the dusty kilometers ticked by. But when we arrived in Giohar, the 80 hired security guards mutinied. One was "armed" with a 1928 Thompson submachine gun; the same period tool of Mafia rule in Chicago had shifted its extortion work to Somalia. The "guards" threatened to halt food distribution unless they were paid seven times the agreed amount. "Forget about the starving," was their line, "why don't we get enough?" Tense negotiations took all day. I was taken aback by their attitude. There was no sense of community, no sense of easing a human crisis—just *me*, and what goes into *my* pocket. In the end, the ICRC had to triple their pay.

"They sent us looters, not security," lamented Mohammed Warre, a Somali ICRC worker, articulating a problem that would plague every relief agency in Somalia. Over time, thousands of tons of food would pile up in a warehouse at the Mogadishu port, though the greed of "guards" like these would make it too dangerous to distribute.

Arranging safe passage was a job that would normally have fallen to the United Nations, except that the world body was unconscionably slow in even recognizing that there *was* a problem. The same would occur in Sudan to a degree, but would be repeated with very grave consequences during the 1994 genocide in Rwanda.

The UN stayed away from Somalia for spurious reasons during the crucial first year of crisis, when its help was needed most. At the time of Barre's fall, Somalia was one of the most aided countries in the world. So imagine Somali surprise when the biggest distributor of this largesse, the UN, abandoned the country and then was virtually the last donor to return. The UN's initial bad judgment, however, was but a sad prelude to the screw-ups that would later turn the largest, most expensive UN "peacekeeping" mission in history into a fiasco.

In September 1991, for example, already absent from Somalia for nine months, the UN tried to regain a foothold without consulting any of the agencies on the ground about warlord "protocol." The UN were seen to fête the wrong powerbrokers, and within days three UN-hired Somali security guards were murdered in a "political" hit. Instead of recognizing the reason for this *faux pas*, UN headquarters in New York declared Somalia too dangerous and forbade staff from traveling there. James Jonah, a diplomat from Sierra Leone and the UN special envoy to the Horn of Africa, admitted defeat at the hands of a government that didn't exist: "We were advised by the president [sic, Ali Mahdi] not to go back."

At the end of 1991, UN Secretary-General Javier Perez de Cuellar finally announced his "profound shock" that Somalia was engulfed in a "nightmare of violence and brutality" and dispatched his hapless envoy again to make peace. The belated decision was made in the last days of de Cuellar's reign and was seen as a attempt to add a final feather to his cap. A similar 11th-hour peace team was sent to El Salvador for the same reason, but it succeeded in forging an agreement just hours before de Cuellar left his post.

Jonah's efforts, on the other hand, were dogged by incompetence and did considerable damage. He was forced to land 60 miles from Mogadishu because of trumped-up "security problems," then played the ignorant neophyte. According to one account, he "allowed his visit to be manipulated by Aidid and then issued a hasty statement on the prospects for a ceasefire which only exacerbated tensions. Because of his refusal to hear other factions, the airport was shelled heavily during his visit and was later closed for ten days, enormously complicating relief operations."[10]

These pathetic results only underscored the UN's lack of interest. UN "Somalia" officials worked out of comfortable offices in Kenya, from which they wrote press releases from "Camp Nairobi." They described their important "work" in Somalia and economized on the truth when they portrayed officials as being on "quick-turnaround visits" to Nairobi from Mogadishu, where in fact they *didn't* have offices. The implication was that they were *so* busy working in the Somali capital that they could barely find time to get away.

But as the call for action increased, the jobs of these bureaucrats were in jeopardy. Frustration was so great that the ICRC made an exception to its usual rule of silence. One delegate asked: "How come Unicef [the UN Children's Fund] has 13 people in Nairobi and no one inside Somalia?" A senior UN official responded curtly—and wrongly, relative to Afganistan, Sudan, and Angola—that "in a situation of war, we don't operate."[11] An American request for a UN plane to deliver aid was turned down. Andrew Natsios, director of the Office of US Foreign Disaster Assistance, complained of the UN's failure to "engage themselves," and said that one UN official had described Mogadishu as "unfit for humans."[12]

Somalis were the most alarmed. One former professor put it plainly: "We feel bitter towards the UN because it acted like an irresponsible parent who walks out of the house when his children are turning knives on each other."[13]

I asked David Bassiouni, the head of Unicef for the country, about the UN absence, but he assured me in December 1991 that the UN had "done everything under the sun" to assist Somalia's war victims. Then as an ass-covering measure, he added that *now* the "conditions call for urgent measures. We want to relieve the suffering. The UN is involved in a new effort. Whether the plan will work, we don't know, but rather that than sit with our hands folded." Envoy Jonah added to the false impression of action. He said he went to Mogadishu to "facilitate our ongoing humanitarian activities" but admitted, "These clan conflicts to me are just incomprehensible."

By 3 March 1992, the stumbling UN efforts did finally coincide for a moment with Somali war weariness. Tired of fighting in Mogadishu—a final shelling assault by Aidid in February having failed to defeat Ali Mahdi—the

UN stood over the signing of a cease-fire. Would-be peacemaker Jonah conceded that "we have our own doubts" that peace had been achieved, then added wanly that non-compliance would be a "serious matter." But the warlords had their own agendas, and in fact signed two separate documents that each embellished their respective, spurious titles of "president" and "chairman."

But there was little "peace" in the capital without drama. At the exact moment Ali Mahdi was signing the accord, during the ceremony in Jonah's presence, a group of journalists asked if Aidid would abide by this ceasefire.

"I hope he will observe this one. I hope," he responded.

"What will you do if he doesn't?" was the next question.

Before Ali Mahdi could answer, a mortar sent from Aidid's militia crashed into the next building, sending a whistle of shrapnel, jolting the assembled guests, and enveloping the "ceasefire" party with clouds of dust.[14]

No one mistook the meaning of this precise gesture. It was a final warning shot between warlords that conflict was not over, but only on hold. The battle lines were defined more clearly than ever. It would take famine—the arrival of yet another horseman of the Apocalypse—to crown Somalia's misery.

THREE

A LAND FORGOTTEN BY GOD

Q: *Isn't there a better way to control these gunmen?*
A: *Somebody did suggest one—carpet bomb Somalia*
   with "ecstasy," because it curbs hunger and makes
   everyone love each other. It's not a bad idea . . .

—UN Envoy Mohamed Sahnoun

Still alive, seven-year-old Shukri Mohamed whimpered almost imperceptibly on the hard floor, an emaciated child wraith starving, the slow curl of inexorable death creeping across her body like a spreading cancer. In this barren room her toes were too tiny and too cold, attached to wrinkled feet, attached to rope-thin legs, attached to her own wispy fragile skeleton. She lay as vulnerable as a newborn, barely moving except for listless emotions, skin worn raw at the hip where her bony pelvis grated against the concrete. Speckles of blood stained a soiled threadbare sheet. Fatless skin gathered like thin chamois around Shukri's hollow ribcage, which heaved in its small way like God's tiny bellows, desperate to keep alive a spark, to prevent Shukri slipping away from her existence.

Mother was there, too, staring mournfully into the lost wide black eyes of her fourth and last child. This small room in the Mogadishu University compound was an unlikely spot for such suffering in August 1992. But this was not a retraction of life by the Divine Being; all this pain had been caused by the vicious predations of other Somalis. Its root was the war, depicted on the wall above mother and child as messy graffiti, as charcoal drawings of tanks and assault rifles in full fire, which drew exaggerated drops of blood from hapless stick figure people.

Shukri's jaw was shut hard against Mother's efforts to feed

her; the skin stretched tightly over her cadaverous skull, a blue plastic necklace serving as ornament for a girl-child shriveled by hunger. There had been only one other decoration, distinctly foreign. At the end of her withered arm—so weak and not as thick as my thumb—a red plastic "intensive feeding" band had been tied to Shukri's wrist. Now it was gone.

Mother laid down beside Shukri, and together they began to sing the song of death: Mother, because she had taken off the feeding band—a dead child is so needless—thereby accepting defeat; and Shukri, because she was now almost too weak to breathe.

Mother's pain had been fourfold, a horrific tragedy like so many others from Somalia's famine, which was finally "discovered" by the news media in August 1992. Already the famine had raged for months, sporadically recorded but largely unnoticed. Mother's first child died when she brought her family 160 miles from their village to Mogadishu, in search of food. Then, a week ago, Mother was at the gate of a feeding center when a stray bullet from a distant skirmish struck her baby son, Adad, while he was breast feeding. The lethal round lodged in his belly, like an unlucky arrow shot from God's longbow. Mother buried her third child just days later—"#521, Nurto Mohammed," according to the tiny leftover wristband—who starved to death overnight. Now Shukri was about to follow, one soul departing along with more than 300,000 other Somalis to die of hunger and of war.

Shukri's death would have gone unrecorded but for this writing.

Grief overwhelmed Mother all at once. She covered her face in a red sheet to escape the pain, but her tears soaked through. Her uncontrolled sobs, for a moment, outweighed the disturbed cries that came from the heart of her daughter's wasted body. The scale of Somalia's suffering was almost incomprehensible in human terms. Weary relief workers rounded off the number of dead to the nearest ten thousand. Hundreds of children like Shukri died every day, followed by their sisters and brothers, then by their parents. All left behind a staggering burden of suffering for those, like Mother, who survived.

Mother and child had been going to a feeding center, one of scores in Mogadishu during the famine. Children arrived, bellies swollen with infestations of worms that could be felt through tissue-thin skin. So much emergency food aid is devoured by worms. When Shukri missed two days of rations at a center run by the charity Concern, Irish nurse Margaret O'Mahony went to the university compound to find her. Mother and child were awaiting Shukri's inevitable death. "She was getting so much better, but now it's hopeless," said the nurse, who propped up Shukri's head anyway and began to feed her a high protein gruel. "Can you imagine, back home, losing even one of your children?"

Few *can* imagine it, the fantastic tales out of Africa so ghoulish, complex, and faraway that the minds of those outside do not immediately translate mere statistics into understandable human agonies. The effort of comparison, of a distant African's suffering with one's own ability to withstand such pain or emotional trauma, can invite a disturbing empathy.

But is it necessary? Often, those outside don't *care* to comprehend. Of course, this constant dilemma is faced by anyone on the ground, bearing witness to extreme human experience. For me and many colleagues, the reason to be there at all is to explore the human condition, and to trumpet or condemn. Compelling as any story may be, though, an endless frustration stems from priorities set in the newsroom. First there is the worn rule, "If it bleeds, it leads." Then add this well-known algebra for headlines: One dead American is equal to a handful of dead Europeans. Hundreds of Asians might die to "rate" the same treatment. And bottom of the list, shamefully, are the thousands of Africans who must die before their tragedy will measure up at all.

Does this sound cynical? It should. Look to the distractions and information overload bombarding the average American, for example, and the complexities of day-to-day living that preclude careful following of foreign news. Bad news is constant, and without making an effort, emotive tales even of genocide—and of human endurance—fade into the competing noises of modern life.

But this is an easy excuse that I can't tolerate. Is it possible—is it wise?—to remain so uninterested in the fate of our fellow humans? Or is some fast-food strip town in eastern Oklahoma so remote from the outside world that all those creatures *out there* in Africa and elsewhere aren't really in the same "human" category? Just because I see a tree falling in the forest, does that mean that you should act as though you also saw it fall?

It angers me that there seems so little serious interest in what the sage William Faulkner called the "old verities and truths of the heart" and the "universal bones," whether that spirit is found in Africa or closer by. I wouldn't impose my own crusade, if that is how these words define my wish to spread this gospel. And I don't blame anyone for not pursuing such truths abroad, when there is much searching to be done at home.

But then, in Mogadishu, wearing her plastic necklace, Shukri closed her eyes for the last time. Mother buried her in the sandy university parking lot, next to sons Adad and Nurto. Shukri's desiccation would now become, along with that of so many other corpses here, part of the air we breathed, adding to the powerful airborne fecal cocktail that permeated the nostrils and every pore of the living, so that her death would always be with us.

Beyond the broken walls of this compound and the feeding centers, Somalia's gunmen and warlords still reigned. They patrolled the streets like carnivores. They dictated the rules for the increasing number of relief agencies trying to help, forcing them into the deepening dilemma: How to save the dying without subsidizing the very thugs who caused it?

Such contradictions spelled themselves out on the streets and invested Shukri's feeble departure from this life with no small irony. I returned to my own vehicle, to my hired gunmen, to be protected by boys with weapons. But as I stumbled across the broken asphalt, my boots churning puffs of dust with each step, I saw how I also inadvertently encouraged the war economy.

What did these armed children—kept in check only by my promises of payment—do with themselves and their guns when they were not escorting me from one feeding center to the next? Their young faces were not yet lined with more than momentary cares, despite steady squinting to block the sun's rays. When I returned from Shukri's death and climbed into the car, they didn't say anything. They knew what I had seen behind those whitewashed walls, what dereliction of life haunted the starving behind so many similar high walls in Mogadishu. Some of those who were dying were their family members. But they didn't seem to care.

As we drove off, safe for a moment in our protected cocoon, we were immediately so far from Shukri's dusty new grave that I began to grasp the depth of hopelessness that caused such apparent uncaring among Somalis. How otherwise can I explain the rabid looting by militiamen of 8,000 tons of food from a warehouse near the port? Gunmen fought pitched hand-to-hand battles for two days to win a share and celebrated this windfall by charging through the streets, white as ghosts with the dust of their loot. Relief workers dubbed such an event a "spontaneous distribution," but if distributed properly, it was enough food to feed the capital for two months.

Overnight the price of a sack of maize in the market had dropped from 350,000 Somali shillings to 50,000. Loyalists of Mohamed Farah Aidid, armed with belt-fed machine and anti-aircraft guns, had taken control of the port just days before. And as usual, those with the most firepower did best. No one kept count of the number killed in the mêlée. Likewise, the number of those like Shukri who would also die unnoticed and unnamed, because those gunmen stole that food, could also not be counted.

Looting camels was once "sanctioned by Somali custom" because of their life-giving properties.[1] Fast forward then to post-Barre Somalia, and relief aid had clearly taken the camel's place as the daily currency for the modern urban Somali warrior. Custom saw to it that ripping off food convoys was all part of the game and hardly stigmatized. These were the fruits on offer to a new generation, for whom the camel-centric world of the past had little meaning except for what it could justify today. After all, one camel song noted:

Whether acquired through legitimate means or by force;
As long as [camels] are in the pen;
In neither case are they undesirable.

The fallout, of course, was bound to be violent, as noted in another Somali saying: "To go on camel-rustling mission results in blood-covered heads."

The famine alarm bells were sounded early, back in December 1991 and earlier, but the United Nations was absent altogether, and most relief agencies ignored them. Somalia was not sexy enough yet, or was deemed to be too dangerous.

Admirably, the ICRC took the lead, distributing 75% of *all* the relief food given to Somalia and spending more than half of its 1992 world-wide budget on the mission. Two top American officials were so impressed that they later nominated the ICRC for the Nobel Peace Prize.[2] ICRC surveys uncovered pockets of severe malnourishment in September and December 1991, prompting a warning that "very soon we will see starving in the streets here." I wrote several stories of warning, and so did others, with little effect.

By March 1992—when Aidid and hotelier Ali Mahdi signed their cease-fire—the ICRC had declared Somalia the world's "most urgent tragedy" and predicted that within weeks "people will start dying in their thousands." Realizing that the safest place for food was in people's stomachs, a network of hundreds of kitchens was created that turned dry rations into gooey hot porridge. In this form, resale was almost impossible, and so exempt from the attentions of looters. Half a million people in Mogadishu alone were fed this way.

But even as the famine began to escalate, Aidid began to make good on his promise to central region elders by finally ridding Somalia of Siad Barre. The ousted president's Marehan clansmen had laid waste to Somalia's breadbasket, so must bear primary responsibility for the famine. Aidid launched a final offensive, and by April 1992 Barre was forced to flee to Kenya, where he and 20 aides took temporary asylum in Nairobi's luxurious Safari Park Hotel. As Somalis starved, the man who led them there enjoyed steak, omelettes, and spaghetti without remorse and sipped wine in solitude at the nearby Hemingway's Bar, all at a cost of $1,800 a day.[3] Finally granted exile in Nigeria, Big Mouth, Somalia's "Glorious Leader," died on 2 January 1995.

Aidid's triumph over the dictator resounded throughout Somalia. That badge confirmed his status as chief warrior, enabling him to create a political alliance of southern and central clans—and enhancing his claim to rule. Ali Mahdi's Abgal subclan was furious at their own leader for refusing to take part in the fighting. For a brief moment there was hope, as the strong hand of a single leader was in control. Aidid made promises of peace and had the means to enforce them. But all would depend on Aidid's benevolence, a test that he would sadly fail.

On 23 June 1992, on the day that the general formed his Somali National Alliance, a couple of colleagues and I saw Aidid in Baidoa, the town that would soon be known as the famine City of Death. Our plane taxied past corroding MiG fighter jets that sat parked just as they did the day Siad Barre fell six months earlier.

The warlord was his usual charismatic self, greeting us on the runway. He wore one of his favorite hats, a ridiculous gray one cocked to one side, a gray sleeveless shirt with colorful patches of flowers, and, more befitting his reputation, a pistol. His lips twitched as if with a tic, then spread into that smile, that graft of happy-to-see-you—which he told me he was, with his warm handshake—and wicked.

We climbed into battlewagons, Aidid taking the passenger seat in a bright green, yellow, and red vehicle next to the 106mm anti-tank cannon. In a single motion, the gunmen threw down the qat stems they had been chewing. We departed in a squeal of tire rubber, an invincible convoy that roared through Baidoa like a conquering column of chariots. The streets were virtually empty, the town already a wasteland.

We sat in the covered veranda of Aidid's Baidoa base. With an exuberant toothy grin the warlord pointed to the map beside him. It was almost all colored bright yellow, the color of the general's fiefdom. Peace had come, he said, just in time to save the 4.5 million Somalis who might otherwise die from famine. A woman brought in a tray laden with cups of tea and camel milk. Somalia's history was about to change for the better, Aidid continued, and he would preside over this miracle.

"There is no more fighting, you can go everywhere with absolute security. The war is over," he declared. This man was now Somalia's *de facto* president, head of the strongest of the four militias that had joined hands to rule. There were still some Barre loyalists, he explained, his legs splayed and hands resting together on the cane before him, in perfect balance like an old Chinese portrait that shows both ears and all ten fingers. "But they will not be able to continue the aggressive, fascist policies of Siad Barre."

Then came the promises, the commitment to save lives by controlling excesses of the gunmen—very often *his* gunmen—which would allow a freer flow of relief supplies. Only 15% of the food needs were arriving, he said, and 70% of the people were starving. At least he seemed to recognize that so many of his countrymen were desperate, were already dying. "There are no longer any security problems for humanitarian organizations. They can reach all these areas safely to bring food to all those who are suffering. This is our request."

We managed to get away from the villa briefly to look around. At the rusted gate of one compound, where a Red Cross flag fluttered, men were fighting armed guards with their fists and gun butts. I had seen many feeding centers in Africa and the Mideast, and Mogadishu was crowded with them. So what was the point of going into this one? Men were battling to get in, to grab at the food, to ease their hunger. Aidid's people didn't want us to visit—there was no time.

But the guards let us through the gate anyway—smashing back the men as we squeezed past—and we were immediately confronted with the horrific images of starvation that would soon haunt the rest of the world. Stick-figure children wearing soiled rags or naked sat on the gravelly ground in rows, strangely quiet because of the empty pit of their stomachs, an emptiness that had eaten its way through to their ambition to move, through to their throats to prevent unnecessary noise, through to their hearts to silence any feelings of hope. This "kitchen" had just opened and ministered to a sea of 1,000 starving Somalis, most of whom were already far beyond saving.

Those still with strength lined up at an oil drum converted into a vessel of salvation. Blackened by fire, it held pasty rice. Most just sat and received their ration on the ground, their weakness and misery so complete that they forgot when they last produced tears.

We were allowed no more than 30 minutes there, but I was so shocked that I did not waste time taking notes. Instead I shot frame after frame with my cameras, seven rolls of film in less than half an hour, 250 images, one every six seconds, the details of misery etching themselves onto my mind irreversibly like acid on steel, details that are almost always the exclusive realm of the photographer. Emotion grew within me as I recorded the swollen tummies and useless limbs and the pain of dying so slowly and knowing that you are dying. Then we were forced to leave.

As we ran the gauntlet of fighting men at the gate again, I turned to see one child, who had pulled up the bottom of his dirty shirt to make a pouch for his gruel. In his excitement to cram his mouth full, he had vomited over his arms.

Back in Nairobi I wrote my story, but concentrated on the news of the peace pact and Somalia's de facto president. I mentioned the feeding center but did not file a separate story because for months I had been—like many of my colleagues—predicting famine. Now it was here, and I didn't yet grasp its whole significance. The same happened to the pictures. Strong as my photographic images were, the final edit remained in an envelope on a desk in New York at a major American newsmagazine: the editors meant to use the pictures, but didn't. Nearly two months later, when the "sexiness" barrier had been breached, those editors were swamped by similar images as photographers from around the world poured into Somalia to document the tragedy.

Africa had not been witness to such widespread starvation since the Ethiopian famine of 1984–85, when 1 million people died. Foreign aid then was strictly controlled by the Marxist government of Mengistu Haile Mariam, whose ruinous policies of enforced collectivism led to disaster. As a Cold War client of the Soviet Union, Ethiopia had made no calls for a global response, and even denied the existence of hunger. In Somalia, however, journalists explored as far as armed men could take us—which was far, indeed—to watch the pained wondering eyes of children like Shukri close for the last time.

By then I was shooting for the Gamma Liaison agency based in New York and Paris. If my early images had been prominently published, would they have made any difference, forcing the UN and the US and relief agencies to wake up to the scale of this colossal suffering before the story "broke" in July and August 1992? Only possibly. Several New York Times stories written in July by Jane Perlez from Baidoa are credited with raising the famine flag. But in print, many stories had prepared the world to read about the gathering hunger. In this case, the catastrophe was too remote from the daily imagination outside until the alarm bells were accompanied by television footage.

Finally the shocking film footage of skeletal children dying on screen against a background of ruthless, marauding gunmen—images that showed that it was already too late—ensured that the evil infesting Somalia would capture the world's attention for 15 minutes of conscience-jerking infamy. But Somalia's pain would extend far beyond this brief Warholian allotment. Already 20% of children under five years old were dead, a figure that would increase to one-third: a generation lost. To take advantage of this moment, this accessible tragedy, camera crews paid up to $2,000 to make the two-and-one-half-hour drive to Baidoa, to capture death—LIVE.

The problem was not always lack of food, but the inability to get it to the hungry. This predicament would soon become a hallmark of Somalia's famine. The ICRC paid $50,000 per month for security at the port, and throughout the south they recruited 2,600 mercenaries to "protect" their operations. But even as the number of feeding centers for children in Mogadishu doubled every ten days in 1992, ships carrying food were sometimes turned away from the contested Mogadishu port by mortar fire, as rival militias fought for the spoils even before they arrived.

When relief ships did risk docking, they were greeted with jubilant dancing. As the first sacks of a 5,000-ton UN shipment were unloaded in May 1992, I watched Somalis dockside lay down their guns, press their foreheads to the ground, and praise Allah. But the risks of bringing this food were high, as Médecins Sans Frontières Director Patrick Vial told me: "This first boat is a security test. It may provoke war, it may not. For sure there will be problems with food distribution, but on what scale? If only a few hundred people are killed, that would not be so bad, but thousands could die." Despite Aidid's assurances and new political clout, the situation worsened. Competition among looters was so fierce that one could trace the route of food convoys through the city by charting on a map the casualties as they came into the hospitals.

Pressure grew for action, and questions were raised about how such plain warnings of disaster were ignored. On 22 July 1992, UN chief Boutros-Ghali warned angrily that the world was "fighting a rich man's war in Yugoslavia while not lifting a finger to save Somalia from disintegration."[4] As the death toll mounted, criticism of the UN reached a crescendo. Internal UN feuding spilled into public. Trevor Page, a 30-year veteran of the World Food Program (WFP), pierced the official gloss during a July 1992 visit to Baidoa. He told Jane Perlez of *The New York Times*: "It's so bad because we've let things simmer without paying proper attention. We've had inexperienced people who don't know what they are seeing, who don't know what the implications are, and didn't blow the whistle."[5] Months later, the top UN diplomat in the country would admit that there had been a "tragic delay and now we are paying the price."[6]

A feel for the UN's particular incompetence in Somalia and beyond was evident in a small tale told by Milas Seifulaziz, a very tall, lanky Mozambican consultant with Unicef. When yet another plane was hijacked at the Mogadishu airport, Milas confirmed the news with a weighty nod: "Yes, the airport can be troublesome."

One day I noticed that the left lens of Milas' glasses was smashed, but he wore them anyway, the shattered pieces refracting his vision.

"What happened to your glasses?" I asked, by way of small talk.

"I was in Uhuru Park in Nairobi, when a mammal that looked like a rat charged me," he explained, deadpan. "I stepped back, slipped and crashed down. When I got back here, I sent very detailed instructions to our office. They sent new glasses, but had mixed up the prescription and done exactly the opposite."

Laughable as this small mistake was—a UN staffer working in Mogadishu half-blind because of a bureaucratic error—it pointed to an endemic problem that often afflicted UN field offices, especially in emergencies. Misperceptions reached the highest level: the Security Council, for example, ordered an arms embargo at the peak of the civil war in January 1991, though Somalia was already saturated with weapons, courtesy of American and the Soviet Union—two of the permanent five members of the Security Council.

Despite itself, the UN did get it right in April 1992 by appointing Mohamed Sahnoun the special representative of the secretary general (SRSG). An Algerian diplomat, he was the only senior UN official who understood the unique requirements of Somali peacemakers, elders, and warriors. He worked diligently to earn the respect of every Somali, jutting his long, aquiline nose, narrow features, and hallmark wispy, unmanageable black hair into their power politics. He understood their needs and expectations of those with guns and worked to create an alternative leadership. He was outspoken, and in his frankness was able to briefly improve UN fortunes in Somalia.

But Sahnoun's mandate was impossible. He was responsible for every aspect of Somalia's recovery, from monitoring the cease-fire to broadening the peace, and from handling the emergency to persuading delinquent UN agencies to return to help rebuild. The envoy continually begged UN headquarters for support, but none ever came. For months he struggled without a secretary or computer, and so wrote all his missives by hand. At least he could see the problem clearly: "It has been disheartening for me to visit hospitals and to see wounded people smeared with the very flour that is supposed to save their lives," he said.[7] Where the life of a man was once worth 100 camels in the settling of blood feuds, it had become worth less than a bowl of warm gruel.

Far from stopping the looting as promised, Aidid and allied "businessmen" institutionalized their greed in Mogadishu and the southern port of Kismayu. The warlord and his war machine got their cut. Nefarious business deals had been part of life since Italy colonized Somalia at the turn of the century. But this crisis spawned new business empires: first for stolen goods and arms, then for relief food.

"Always there was looting. Nobody was able to stop it," Mohamed Farah Jumaale, one of Aidid's top political advisers, told me in Mogadishu seven years later. "It was difficult to control the militia. They were everywhere. They are loyal to the clan when the clan is going to fight. But when you are sitting in town and not giving them a salary, they start robbing and are beyond anybody's responsibility."[8]

I saw one damning example in the town of Bardera in September 1992, even though the Great Warlord Aidid himself was ruling from there at the time. Taking a short walk through town with Sam Kiley of the London *Times*—this was the trip where Abdi the gunman was our "guard"—we came to the modest town hospital. It was sunset, a beautiful evening, until the spell was broken: under a tree 20 feet from the hospital door, the fresh corpse of a man lay prone in the sand where he had fallen, face down, wasted with hunger, his body slowly cooling. There was no shroud, just his pale beige-orange shawl with a red flower print, covering his back.

Normally, this new cadaver would have been buried by hospital security men. But while we watched, that "security" joined up with some of Aidid's gunmen, only 50 feet away, and helped them to loot the Unicef warehouse.

Before my eyes, 12 sacks of food were quickly piled onto wheelbarrows and raced out through the main gate, past the dead man and down an alley. The last looter wore a dirty camouflage shirt, and as he rounded the corner, his red thongs flapped noisily against his heels, throwing up a small fantail of sand.

Such increasing unruliness and extortion began to test Sahnoun's patience. Sitting in his Mogadishu office, a pale blue UN flak jacket propped in the corner and crowned with a blue helmet, he said that he had insisted that Aidid see the end result of Somalia's destruction. "I brought Aidid to see the dying, and to show him that the world is concerned," Sahnoun told me, his narrow dark eyes glazed and bloodshot with fatigue. But the display had little effect.

"We see that there is a limit to the authority of Aidid and others, though they do not want to confess their inability to control, their powerlessness," Sahnoun said. The envoy was tired, and especially tired of these self-styled leaders. "It means we have to speak with so *many* people to get anything done. *They* are responsible for these kids dying, and for what is happening to their people."

It is this Somali irascibility that Sahnoun found so difficult to reconcile with their sharpness of mind. Negotiations to bring the first 500 UN troops, approved by the Security Council in April 1992, dragged on for weeks, as warlords angled for advantage. Xenophobia and clanism overrode all. Aidid finally accepted in early August. The symbolic Pakistani force of 500 blue berets, known as the UN Operation in Somalia (Unosom I) began arriving in September. They were armed for self-defense, but these UN troops eventually hired Somali gunmen to guard their positions.

Complicating matters, in August both Aidid and Sahnoun heard over the BBC radio—without first being consulted by UN headquarters—that 3,000 more "peacekeeping" troops would be sent, with or without the approval of the warlords. Aidid knew that such a force would threaten his dominance, and he organized demonstrations against it.

The example of the Mad Mullah's success at driving the British from the interior decades earlier was not lost on Sahnoun, and it still seemed to hold true for the Pakistanis. "The suspicion which greets the stranger is not reserved only for non-Somali foreigners," writes historian Lewis. "This defense mechanism is . . . a national characteristic."[9]

Relief workers summoned a gallows humor about the need for blue UN body bags. "The UN haven't decided on their fire policy yet," said one Somalia veteran. "They should put ten UN troops in an open truck and take a drive around town. When they come back with five dead and five wounded, *then* they should determine their fire policy."

Sahnoun knew that Somalis often described the unwanted UN presence as a new series of "targets wearing blue berets." He sat back deeply into his chair, resigned to the contradictions. "I never thought it would be this tough," he said. "It is vain to try to apply logic to Somali behavior. These are people with nothing to lose, for whom life is cheap. You can see how easily they fire on each other when they argue, even among their own clan."

Sahnoun's gloom was short-lived. Despite his painstaking progress with all factions, repairing damage caused by his UN predecessors, he was dismissed in October 1992. His untimely departure was the final blow to UN credibility in Somalia. Boutros-Ghali criticized him for making high-profile complaints about UN incompetence. In a heartless snub, the UN chief did not respond to Sahnoun's subsequent letter of resignation.

UN staff said that James Jonah, the stumbling former envoy who had by then been promoted to undersecretary general in New York, was largely responsible for leaving Sahnoun without resources and had orchestrated his dismissal out of spite. Sahnoun had been succeeding where Jonah had failed. With Sahnoun's dismissal, morale among UN staff and relief workers was low. Mike McDonagh, the bearded Irish head of the agency Concern, summed up their disgust: "Like millions of Somalis, Sahnoun has become a victim of UN bureaucracy."

The loss of hope seemed total and was nowhere more wrenching than at the barren office of the relief agency CARE in the remote town of Bardera. The one remaining foreigner was Raja Gopala Krishnan, and he felt threatened. He sat in his compound, holding a bleak vigil at a small metal table that barely seated two small metal chairs. There was nothing else in this house but a constant wind and mattresses enough for two visitors. Sam and I slept on the veranda, sweating despite the breeze. Krishnan described his life-saving business as though it was a waste of time, a thankless job because of interference by militiamen.

His long, thin white hair falling down over dark Indian features, he said he was tired of empty promises of security and had complained to the Great Warlord himself, who lived just down the road. Aidid ordered a stop to the looting. But when Krishnan walked in the streets, gunmen would point at him derisively and draw their fingers across their throats. Just days before he was accosted by them while sitting on the toilet. They demanded ten barrels of diesel, most of his stock. He haggled them down, at gunpoint from his looseat perch, to just three barrels.

"Who needs security, if it is their commander who comes and demands diesel?" he asked. There were few people to talk to anymore, and they were not friends. His Somali staff said they expected to be killed.

"People don't like to work here, and why should they?" Krishnan said, a note of mild surprise in his voice. The metal chairs felt hard already, and the drinking water was bad. "If we don't get cooperation to work freely, then why do it? Life is cheap, and only food is dear."

The dusty town was ugly, a terrible manifestation of all that had gone wrong in Somalia, with the tragic marriage of guns and hunger. It was here that the gulf was widest between those who shouldn't die but would, and those with guns who wouldn't. The dead old man in front of the hospital, waiting for burial until the looting was done; the threats against relief workers; the chronic disrespect that underscored the moral erosion of all that was good in Somali culture. It was all here, in Bardera.

We confronted Aidid at his temporary Bardera base, where he was holed up in an empty, ratty palace. I was determined to hear from him what happened to his bold promises of peace and security. Aidid's power was shrinking daily as the cogs of his war machine spun separately out of control.

Aidid bristled when we blamed him for compounding suffering by letting "his" gunmen block the relief effort. He sat on a white cushion on a threadbare rug, under a sign that read "SNA is the key to Democracy." He seemed unsure of himself, his flashing smile still in place but twitching more than usual. Certainly some of the sorghum beans, flour, and maize had found its way onto Aidid's own table. He argued that his gunmen had to eat, too, or else they might be apt to steal. Details of the incidents didn't concern him. "I do not believe food was taken by force by my men, so the agencies must have agreed," he said defiantly. "This is not a crime."

But the evidence of massive crimes was widespread and inescapable. On all roads leading into Baidoa, at the height of the famine in the summer of 1992, villages were abandoned. Woodpiles were left intact, along with all the farming implements to sustain a hard-bitten agrarian life. But people were gone, and the animals were missing. Those too weak to survive the journey to the town had marked the route with their skeletons. Within days, most remains were dried out and picked at, leaving only clumps of hair, horny fingernails and bone.

In the City of Death itself, the famine was manifest in mass graves and in the daily rounds of trucks that each morning moved from one fetid feeding center to another, collecting new dead. Often the only "aid" that the dying received was a plastic 50kg food sack, labeled "Gift from the USA," that survivors used as shrouds to wrap the corpses. How could anyone—how could I—imagine such suffering?

At its peak, the death trucks buried 1,700 bodies daily in Baidoa. Others were carted away in wheelbarrows. Starving men dug graves for their children with pickaxes in the hardpan earth.

There were, finally, rumblings in Western capitals that something would have to be done to save Somalia. The "too dangerous" argument no longer applied, with so many TV crews extracting daily, awesome images of death. In August, the Americans launched a massive airlift from Kenya to bring food. But as the months dragged on, and that food became the prime target of the gunmen, it was becoming clear that much more would need to be done.

As the UN smoldered with internecine blame for its delays and the warlords denied their guilt, Somalia's looters were irrepressible. At a Baidoa feeding center in September, I found children happy to receive a handout of woolen blankets to ward off rain and the chill of night. They barely had enough energy to stay alive, much less to stay warm. But they lingered too long—long enough for the local thugs to hear that 700 new blankets were in helpless hands. An armed gang was waiting as the children filed out, and took nearly every blanket.

Next day these starving sat in rows without their blankets, waiting again for food. Their numbers had been culled: the body truck had already been by to collect those who passed away in the cold night. Many more would follow. While I was there, a mammoth black cloud emerged from the horizon, and when it was overhead rain began to fall. The fatless skin that was taut across the backs of hunkering children mustered sheets of goose pimples, which died down again as the rain completely soaked. The water collected in droplets on eyelashes, and streamed off shoulders and arms, puddling in the dirt. The rain stopped, and the sun came out again to lend a warm, shining light that gave this scene a special beauty.

But the beauty brought death, too, for the children began to shiver uncontrollably. They had no blankets. To avoid a similar travesty—and to outwit the already well-fed bandits—the relief agency vowed next time to cut their blankets in two before handing them out. They were to protect the living, of course, but they fit the size of a dying child.

FOUR

"CLUB SKINNY—DANCERS WANTED"

*Somalia is a land of great beauty and infinite
promise. . . . Tourists are assured an enjoyable
stay in Somalia, where they will find the people
friendly and the country attractive.*

—"Beautiful Somalia,"
Ministry of Information booklet, 1978

Within 30 minutes of landing on the beaches of Mogadishu on
9 December 1992, top US commanders were on the roof of the
airport building, giving live television interviews for network
breakfast shows, explaining this mission of mercy. Have no
doubt, they said: witness the birth of the New World Order, the
first purely benevolent use of the strongest army on the planet,
the military might of the last superpower harnessed to feed people, to save innocent Somalis from the medieval predations of
warlords and gunmen, to rescue a useless Third World nation in
Africa from devouring itself.

President George Bush declared that the troops were doing
"God's work" in Somalia, on a mission at which Americans
"cannot fail."

If ever Somalis required proof of the importance of this
American troop invasion, they had only to note the arrival of
America's top three TV anchors, who squinted into the searing
sun while their minions created a new reality out of the bare
concrete airport roof. Even the studio chairs had been brought
from New York, along with generators, satellite telephones,
makeup kits, and mile after mile of cable that immediately connected Somalia to the rest of the world. That night—prime time
in America—those anchors sat in those chairs, flooded with
light like competing shows at a three-ring circus.

Audiences were not disappointed. Fresh after victory against Iraq in the 1991 Gulf War the American military took the first steps into uncharted territory. Feeling so invincible, this humanitarian mission was to define the noble impulse of the New World Order. But even in the flurry of the first days, there were indications aplenty of the disaster to come.

TV networks had been fully briefed by the Pentagon about the military game plan, so it was no surprise that I was alerted to their arrival exactly as millions of viewing Americans. Dan Rather, of CBS, faced his camera at 1:10 am Somali time, the night wind blowing thick, humid air through his graying hair. "What you are seeing now, live through our night vision camera, is the arrival of the first Navy Seal units on the beaches of Somalia." I looked across the airport tarmac, and reality immediately matched the screen-side vision: a photographer's flash gave away the position of the first landing. I charged for Black Beach under the brilliant full moon, together with 300 colleagues, like a swarm of ants into whose domain had suddenly dropped a succulent bit of fruit.

Relief agencies had been hardest hit by Somali looters, and so made the loudest calls for military intervention. "It is criminal that we have two big ports, good airports and good highways here, and we can't get enough food to these people because the security is so bad," said Mike McDonagh of Concern. "There should be a massive UN operation to disarm everyone, because it's ridiculous that any 12-year-old boy with a gun can disrupt a multimillion dollar relief operation."

Still, the number of famine deaths had already peaked by October-November 1991, and were in decline as the Americans arrived, largely because those most likely to die had already done so. A US-government commissioned report, in fact, found that although the US intervention may have saved 10,000 to 25,000 people (plus 40,000 during the August to December 1992 airlift of relief food), the number of lives lost "due to delays in undertaking earlier decisive action" was between 100,000 and 125,000.[1]

But few were aware that the worst of the famine had passed, like a forest fire running out of fuel. Instead, several high-profile lootings underscored the continuing insecurity and fanned the flames of intervention. The UN and some US officials pushed the untested figure of 80% losses due to gunmen. Boutros-Ghali on 29 November told the UN Security Council that Somalia was no longer "susceptible to the peacekeeping treatment."[2] And then there was the photogenic mountain of 14,000 tons of relief food that had piled up at Mogadishu airport because it was too dangerous to distribute.

Dispatched to reverse such outrages, US troops could easily put the two images together. "The marines have seen pictures of the starving and of the gunmen," one officer warned, "and they are not going to be tolerant of these thugs."

I was in favor of the US intervention, and I think—despite all the subsequent politicking—there was a strong humanitarian root to it. The need was great, and the US was one of the few countries able to do something. Every night for a week before the beach landing, if I heard the slightest sound, I would rush to the roof of the Concern house where I was staying. I stared across the hill toward the airport and imagined an armada of helicopters rotoring toward shore. At night there was no electrical light at all in the city, just the waft of the warm breeze. If I had woken later, first light might be creeping up from the horizon. I was probably the only one in Somalia awake at that hour—or so it felt—waiting for the cavalry, my nation's cavalry.

Still, warnings to stay away were strong and numerous. The US military's gut instinct was to avoid complex clan feuds altogether, despite the pressing human need. US Ambassador to Kenya Smith Hempstone, a former journalist who had traveled widely in Africa, also foresaw a quagmire and warned against "embracing the Somalia tarbaby." Somalis were "natural-born guerrillas. They will mine roads. They will launch hit-and-run attacks. They will not be able to stop the convoys from getting through. But they will inflict—and take—casualties." Referring to the 241 marines killed in Lebanon in 1983 by a single suicide bomber unhappy with their presence, he cabled Washington: "If you liked Beirut, you'll love Mogadishu."[3]

But memories of Beirut figured little during the heat of deployment. Blinded inside their night-vision goggles by our flashes, and nervous and laden to buckling by their water-soaked gear, the first Navy Seals to land brandished their weapons and waterproof map tubes labeled SECRET. I waded into the warm night sea to photograph the Zodiac rubber boat arrival, my boots filling like the Seals' with the sand of the surf. The cavalry had arrived, but its Rambos looked dressed more for World War III than to carry out the task at hand: to serve as glorified relief workers.

"Get the fuck out, or I'll shoot!" threatened one commando, as he trudged along the beach, his wet camouflage trousers coated with sand. "No flash! No flash!" The soldiers sweated under their black and green face paint and settled down on sandy hillocks. There were no armed Somali gunmen about, no battle wagons to confront them, just this irksome crew of journalists.

On the eve of the deployment, some media agencies rented houses for $20,000 a month or more. But the Associated Press did the entire press corps a favor. They provided $25,000 to hotelier Mohamed Jirdah to refurbish in *one week* a large hotel at the "Kilometer Four" traffic circle for use by the journalists. The Sahafi Hotel—its Arabic and Somali name means "journalist"—was born. In time, it was fitted with air conditioning, hot water, and all the accoutrements an exhausted journalist expects for $85 a night. Its bland meals of camel meat and pasta were best enhanced with liberal doses of Tabasco pepper sauce. It was all followed with papaya halves drenched in the juice of small squeezed lemons. The Sahafi provided a bird's-eye view on the dramatic events about to unfold in Mogadishu—and a stage for the camaraderie that would develop.

We had been ready for the late-night action. I was armed with a walkie-talkie radio from Concern. When I radioed back my reports, they called *The Daily Telegraph* on the satellite phone and connected me to London by literally putting their radio handset against the phone receiver. These radios were useful for journalists, to monitor UN activities and security incidents throughout Mogadishu. Most call signs and frequencies were known to us, because in a city with not one working telephone, to be outside the radio net was to be out of the loop.

The invasion itself began as the first brushes of predawn purple illuminated the sky, slowly wiping away the stars and brighter planets. Amphibious vehicles rolled ashore, followed by hovercraft with armored vehicles. Sealed hatches were opened, unleashing a flood of seawater and the first soldiers onto the airport tarmac. Fourteen unarmed Somali airport guards were arrested and tied up with plastic handcuffs.

At the port, two miles up the shoreline, marines stormed the bulkhead. "Fuckin' lie down!" roared one marine to a group of journalists. Some 30 to 40 shots were fired over their heads, and the journalists remained pinned down for 20 minutes.

Nothing could have suited the US "invasion" of Somalia better than to have been swamped by press coverage, particularly since it was Fourth Estate reporting that launched the military intervention. Once Somalia finally came into press focus in mid-1992, media exposure sparked calls for action. Embarrassing as the arrival scenes were that balmy December night, they helped prolong world attention.

US commanders publicly complained that journalists had "come between us and our mission" and accused the press ambushing them on Black Beach. But we were given details on the eve of the landing by Robert Oakley, the US envoy. It was clear that this was a made-for-TV event, and we were issued press guidelines: park your personal armed "technicals" at the upper airport parking lot, keep large weapons completely off your vehicles, and hide hired Somali guards and their guns from view. Some called this an "intervasion."

The Mogadishu air was thick with the usual mixture of fecal dust, sea, and sun-baked rubbish, as the marines set up defensive lines around the airport and port. Sticky in the hot sand, the soldiers lay at the ready, their guns pointed at the growing number of curious children who appeared to see these *new* gunmen, the modern foreign warriors. Then came the first planeload of relief food, 17 tons.

With an engaging mixture of profanity and piety, the marines began work and learned how quickly tempers could flare. As hordes of naughty children swarmed around the planes on the airfield, one good-natured marine held them back. Trained to know when to kill gunmen, or to "put on a happy face" and distribute relief food, he told me: "We're here to bring food to these people, and they love us!"

But as the kids grew bolder, creeping past him and showing no respect for his considerable firepower, I suggested that he might enjoy bashing one of their heads.

"No chance," he replied.

Thirty minutes later, however, his frustration had gotten the better of his goodwill. The marine was wading into the crowd, shouting threats and wholeheartedly chasing after breakaway kids, the transformation from benevolent cop to tough-guy law enforcer complete. To cope with small troublemakers the Americans learned quickly from Somali elders that discipline was best exacted at the end of a whipping stick. To avoid pathetic video footage of brawny US soldiers with thigh-thick arms beating back spindly starving children around checkpoints—one of many stark incongruities, of having hulking corn-fed American grunts on a dusty African relief mission—the marines hired old men to apply the lash.

The Somalis were tough beyond their means, too, the marines found out. During one knife fight between kids outside the port gate, one scrabbler refused to give up his foot-long dagger, even when the marines demanded it at gunpoint. "We were ready to shoot him, and this kid was ready to take on all of us," said one grunt. "He couldn't have been more than 12 years old."

The differences were not just cultural, they were cosmic. "The most powerful military regime could tell a big missile to hit a tiny target and ferry millions of tons of equipment and supplies to a faraway land," wrote one writer. "But for most Americans soldiers, just saying 'hello' to a Somali was impossible."[4]

Still, Somalis had high expectations: that they would be fed, that they would be disarmed, and that the warlords who had brought this calamity upon their beloved country would be silenced. So many welcomed the Americans as liberators. There was a general belief that the Americans—just like the heroes of their swashbuckling John Wayne never-say-die movies—were going to succeed. But the local arrogance also shone through. Somalis rarely deigned to consider themselves Africans, and they reveled in the final realization that *their* situation was so severe that it *required* superpower intervention.

"Don't bring us these Third Worlders, because they are hungry like we are," one Somali told me. "We trust the Americans to come because they don't want anything from us."

A gunman sang gleefully: "We *deserve* the Americans!"

Cheering Somali fans lined the route from the airport to the former US embassy at dusk on the first day, when an armored convoy moved to reclaim the compound and gutted buildings. I watched young pickpockets work the crowds wielding foot-long knives. One man shouted above the din: "With the Americans we are free!"

The forces had yet to divorce military and US government interests from their avowed "humanitarian" work, however. In a ludicrous exercise at the embassy, dozens of marines stormed the gutted building. We formed a gaggle of photographers and followed them every step of the way, as they kicked in doors with pistols drawn and "fought" their way unopposed from one floor to the next. Bulletproof glass had been blasted by rocket grenades, the ambassador's safe was damaged, and the whole place was thickly carpeted with dried excrement. Less than two years after the marines had been diverted from their Gulf War duties in January 1991 to evacuate this plush embassy, they were back in this forsaken country doing "God's work."

But in those first days of Operation Restore Hope, as it was called, the outlook appeared promising. The intelligence team arrived too, to help speed things along. An eight-man posse of spooks disguised as journalists jumped out of a Sea-King helicopter in full view on the embassy grounds. All wore dark glasses, identical Banana Republic khaki photojournalist vests and looked startled when asked what they were doing. "We're from the embassy—State," blurted one. "Communication specialist," said another, as if that were a politically correct version of "spy." Reid Miller, the Nairobi bureau chief of the Associated Press, officially complained that the dressing up of agents as journalists added to the dangers for the rest of us.

The press invasion was huge. Editors in newsrooms from Tokyo to Toronto often fumbled to get it right, to make sense of Somalia's destruction and the reasons for America's decision to use this place as the post–Cold War guinea pig. The AP alone brought in more than 30 journalists, photographers, and technicians for the American military debut.

Spearheading this massive AP operation was Reid Miller, the only real Somalia hand among them. A wizened veteran of wars in Central America and Africa who had been with the AP all his professional life, he negotiated to create a fleet of hired battle wagons, often spending hours behind the Sahafi delicately trying to assuage the fiscal demands of his Somali guards. Reid brought in tons of AP gear, bribing the gauntlet of gunmen keeping watch at the airport gate. Pressures from New York were high to write and edit a constant flow of stories each day, and the demands, of course, were outrageous.

Finally one evening, eyes glazed after many sleepless nights, half an inch of Bourbon left in his plastic cup, Miller was asked to do the impossible by an ignorant editor on the satellite phone.

"You want a story about *the weather?*" Reid confirmed, his surprise turning to raw anger. The half-lit cigarette between his fingers began to shake, spent ash adding to the mess on the floor. Then the explosion:

"The weather? *It's hot! It's always been HOT! It's been hot in Somalia for 2,000 YEARS, and it's NEVER CHANGED!*" Reid shouted, slamming the receiver down. Its violent crash was lost in a stream of expletives, as the remaining Bourbon made its way home.

After conquering the embassy grounds on day one, the marines dug into defensive positions and the mood turned jocular. I watched as they unwound reels of signal wire and cut open bales of sacking for sandbags. When the mood did shift against the American presence many weeks later, the troops would be accused of trying to "steal" this Somali resource: the sand. "Feelin' like a sugar cookie yet?" joked one officer, as his comrades filled sandbags at the embassy perimeter. As two soldiers made their holes more comfortable for the night, their shovels bit into a buried skull. Still moist, it was stuck on a stick to watch—a totem of war that made a good picture. They called him "Boner," and one soldier laughed: "Even marines finish like that."

Crowning the day in Somalia with US-bred patriotism, at the edge of darkness, the marines climbed to the roof of the embassy to raise a large American flag. But this was no Iwo Jima replay: the flagpole cord had long since rotted through, so one marine took off his flak jacket, clutched a stretch of wire between his teeth and shinnied up the flagpole. Old Glory was strung up to flutter in the evening breeze, which brought the deathly smell of the capital to its latest self-appointed saviors. But a crackling radio announcement reminded the Americans of their real business here: "Sniper attacks have been reported."

The embodiment of American strength in Somalia was Robert Oakley, a retired former ambassador to Somalia (1982–1984) and a Cold War warrior extraordinaire with diplomatic credentials that stretched back to before the fall of Saigon. He sat erect and spoke deliberately, his strong features coupled with a pasty complexion that would not be out of place at Madame Tussaud's Wax Museum in London. He was President Bush's special envoy, and his first job was to make sure that the marine landing did not occur in a hostile environment. The dismissal of UN envoy Mohamed Sahnoun in October had ended any chance of a carefully constucted, inclusive peace deal.

So Oakley's predicament was stark, and time was short, since he arrived just two days before the marines. But he made two decisions that would eventually transform the entire US-UN presence in Somalia into a debacle. The first was that, instead of marginalizing the warlords, which many Somalis hoped for and expected, Oakley immediately embraced them, seeking their support for a peaceful US intervention. The second, far more critical decision made by Oakley and cautious US commanders was to leave the warlord arsenals intact and to make no concerted attempt to disarm Somalia. This again was contrary to widespread Somali expectations and desires.

Popular goodwill toward the American intervention was so strong—even Aidid eventually welcomed it—and Somali war weariness was so great that a narrow window of opportunity opened during Operation Restore Hope that had never existed before. Somalis said then, and are convinced even more today, that the chance existed then to lessen the influence of the warlords. If it had been done equitably among all clans, they say, Somalis would have accepted disarmament. Piecemeal efforts with US soldiers proved that it could work, but within months that window would close as US forces were seen to take sides against Aidid and his subclan.

Oakley talked tough, giving the impression of coercing the enemy. Citing the overwhelming military victory against Iraqi strongman Saddam Hussein during the recent Operation Desert Storm campaign, he spelled out the risk of resisting the American landing "They know what can happen. There is a difference between the UN peacekeepers who have been here, and American troops with the full freedom to fire back if they think it necessary," Oakley warned. "Anyone who approaches [the marines] with a .50-caliber machine gun will be in peril. It is very hard for marines to determine between those gunmen with good intentions, and those with bad intentions."

Unlike the previous UN peacekeeping mission, this one was authorized under Chapter VII of the UN Charter, which meant that force could be used to get the job done.

But behind closed doors, the deal was already in the works with the Mogadishu warlords, who recognized that the US troop presence was a *fait accompli*. In keeping with their own historical practice, they were looking for ways to bring the Americans to their side. "It is the proverb 'either be a mountain or attach yourself to one' which reflects the reality of political relations," writes Lewis.[5] When Aidid welcomed the deployment, the price of assault rifles dropped from $200 to $75.[6] Markets ran out of plastic sacks for burying guns, so if the Americans wanted to find everything, they'd need metal detectors.

Throughout the initial five-month US-led mission, called the Unified Task Force (Unitaf), 20 nations sent more than 38,000 troops—25,000 of them American—to save Somalia.[7] General Colin Powell, chairman of the Joint

Chiefs of Staff, later confirmed that the press onslaught was part of the plan: "I wanted the Somalis to see nasty, ugly-looking people coming ashore so they'd decide 'We'd better sit down and talk with Brother Oakley.'"[8]

And sure enough, two days after US forces arrived, Oakley presided over a very public *rapprochement* between the warlords, their first face-to-face meeting in more than a year. This was not a spectacle that we were expecting. Scores of journalists crammed against the net of an old tennis court, waiting for more than an hour in the direct sun. Sweat drained from my arms onto my cameras. And then there it was, on the other side of the net: a faciliated-in-the-USA peace. Aidid and Ali Mahdi embraced, and said they had agreed to peace between themselves, to prevent their loyalists from harassing Americans troops, and to dismantle the Green Line.

Many Somalis were disappointed and saw a cynical dynamic: Oakley refused, for example, to even meet the warlord and former defense minister Mohamed Hersi Morgan, the son-in-law of ousted President Barre. Oakley declared that he was a "cold-blooded murderer" and "massacred his own people" when he was in charge against rebels in northern Somalia in 1988. But in the eyes of many Somalis, Aidid and Ali Mahdi had as much to answer for, if not more, than the notorious "Butcher of Hargeisa" Morgan.

These two were certainly guilty of their own war crimes and of destroying Somalia. But they were also in Mogadishu, where American commanders wanted to land their troops. So Oakley kept them in the political process. The US-brokered peace deal for the first time appeared to Somalis to give an official seal of approval to the warlords' political roles.

Somalis weren't alone in recognizing the danger. Oakley's decision "may have actually elevated their status and power at a time when their authority had been ebbing," wrote Ken Menkhaus, a Somali expert and Unosom consultant. "Thereafter, any attempt by [the UN] to broaden contact with non-factional social constituencies was viewed as a plot to marginalize the faction leaders."[9]

But the quiet landing and the peace deal had a higher price, too, one that smelled of betrayal. For as well as legitimizing the warlords, to win this agreement Oakley also allowed them to keep their weapons in cantonment sites outside the city. As long as no one harmed American troops, the clan arsenals would remain intact. Instead of hunting down the battle wagons that had destroyed Somalia for two years, Oakley effectively put aside the problem so that arriving US forces would not have to deal with it. "George Bush doesn't want a war at Christmas," one UN official explained cynically.

The American decision *not* to disarm came as the biggest single surprise to Somalis. Disarmament had been part of the original mission statement, but it was dropped right before the executive order was issued "at the absolute insistence of the top command who considered it both 'inappropriate for a humanitarian operation' and, more importantly 'mission impossible.'"[10] The military estimated that 45,000 troops would have been necessary to disarm the capital alone.[11] Lt. Gen. Robert Johnston, the marine commander, confirmed this line: "I think the belief that we can disarm Somalia is totally naive," he told us days after arriving. And as Oakley said, 'We can't disarm New York or Washington; how could we disarm Mogadishu?'"[12]

This change of heart caused a row between Washington and Boutros-Ghali, who said publicly that President Bush had promised him disarmament. The new US stance, Medécins Sans Frontières charged, "fitted in with its ambitious timetable to start withdrawing American troops as early as January and its commitment to 'zero casualties,' an approach influenced by the lack of conviction behind a media-driven intervention."[13] Oakley also justified this decision by casting it in a Somali context, to dampen expectations: "There are three things important to a Somali—his wife, his camel and his weapon. In the Somali soul there is the right to have a weapon. So when they hear foreigners are taking weapons by force, they say 'No, never.'" House-to-house searches, Oakley said, would be "absurd," because "the Somalis would see it as rank colonialism."[14]

Part of the reason that Oakley may not have needed to plan too far ahead, nor insist on disarming the warlords, was because the American intervention grew from a mixture of motives. Besides wanting to leave a good mark on the twilight of his presidency, Bush was reportedly affected by powerful images of starving children. "If the US can make a difference in saving lives, we should do it," he reportedly said, "No one should have to starve at Christmastime."[15] Did that mean helping to solve Somalia's long-term problem by disarming a proud, clan-riven warrior nation? Or did that mean only securing food routes so that starving Somalis could live until tomorrow, to face the risks of violence one more time?

"Bush's policymakers envisioned a limited Salvation Army role," one American player said. "And this led us into a political anomaly, the Immaculate Intervention, where we were above the local politicians—an error of major dimensions."[16] For Bush, in the 11th hour of his rule, Somalia also provided an easy way out of action in the former Yugoslavia. "The best thing about Somalia was that it saved us from Bosnia," said a Pentagon official.[17] UN sources in Mogadishu told me that a primary reason the UN pushed so hard for a massive intervention was because Boutros-Ghali thought that it would be a suitable cover for the UN's own pathetic failings and delays in dealing with the crisis at all.

But among Somalis, the fact that Unitaf did not take advantage of its initial goodwill to tackle the central problem was met with dismay. Expectations were certainly too high, as Starlin Arush, the head of one women's group, said: "The women expected the troops to improve security, to control the young gunmen. They have a big fantasy about the technology of the Americans. They thought the Americans would airdrop chemicals from the sky and the gunmen would all faint and the Americans would come down in helicopters and collect the guns; they would identify every spot and collect every gun."[18]

Nevertheless, many Somalis insisted that given the right conditions and political will—which Oakley and the troops could have provided—they would have been willing to be disarmed. "Overwhelmed by guns, we cried out for the help of a greater force," one Somali said at the time. "Without disarmament, the Americans have missed the whole point. Unless they are going to disarm nationwide, they might as well pack their bags and go home."[19]

So here was a rare chance to change Somalia's fortunes, but the American military requirement of "zero casualties" in a humanitarian mission meant that anything risky was left alone. US commanders "did not want to do this operation, and therefore 'Go slow, go safe, no casualties'—the traditional American problem—it worked against us," said Wayne Long, an American UN security officer and for several years later the UN chief of security for all Somalia. "We were playing it *so* cautious that as soon as the command told Oakley—'Gee, I'm not so sure about this'—that *click!* turned the switch on this thing off." The moment of intervention "was an opportunity that was never to repeat itself," Long said.[20]

But Oakley argued in his own book that "the US position was pragmatic in both concept and practice" and was "limited and specific." Any attempt at full-scale disarmament would have "almost certainly have become embroiled in a series of local clashes."[21]

Still, according to one interview, "Oakley later admitted that postponing disarmament created more difficulties for the subsequent Unosom II mission, and he felt that more heavy weapons should have been rounded up during Unitaf."[22]

The little-remarked example of the Pakistani Unosom I troops may have also helped shape Oakley's thinking. Their arrival was carefully negotiated by UN envoy Sahnoun and was approved by both warlords. But Aidid halted the deployment, even as his militiamen laughed at the dated Pakistani equipment. Humiliated—and hamstrung by UN rules that required the consent of all sides —the troops were forced to idle in the desert south of the capital for six weeks. They rehearsed "convoy escorting" and fashioned cricket stumps, as gunmen in the city attacked one relief convoy after another.

"The only contact we have had with them has been a night of folk dancing," snickered Carl Howorth, a relief worker from CARE, which was among
the agencies hardest hit by looters. Aidid had not only neutralized the Pakistanis; he had issued death threats against UN officials and warned against
deploying troops or even setting up relief programs without his permission. If
they disobeyed, he could not be responsible for "accidents." Pakistani commander Imtiaz Shaheen told me how his hands were tied by the UN mandate.
"Now things will change," he said on the eve of the US landing. The marines
had "a combat mission and the UN behind it. Look at me, I have not even a
peashooter."

Five days after they "secured" Mogadishu, American troops took their
peashooters to Baidoa, where they rolled into the City of Death to a cheering
welcome, like victors at war. It was an impressive show: the armored column
rolled into town moments before dawn. Somalis swarmed onto the streets.

Overwhelmed by the reception, a corporal from Alabama told me: "It was
like a hometown parade. They really wanted us to come here, so it's like
comin' home." One soldier taught the Muslim Somali children "Jingle Bells."
He sang, they repeated after him, and photographers jockeyed for the picture
that made the cover of *Newsweek*. "It was the first Christmas song I could
think of to entertain the kids," the soldier said. Another summed up the reason
for his deployment, with a wide-eyed but quiet modesty: "It's peace, sir, that's
what it's all about. At least, I look at it like they'll have a better chance at life."

Despite the Boy Scout Jamboree feel, however, the first "critical" food convoy escorted by the marines in Baidoa was an embarassing overkill. Fourteen
heavily armed vehicles lined up at the airport gate—the soldiers looked nervous but calm—then roared forward, with a dozen press vehicles following
quickly behind. At the offices of the charity World Vision, the convoy stopped
to collect its tiny cargo: a dozen bags of children's food, oil and dry skimmed
milk for a local orphanage. Paul Jones, the agency head, surveyed the noisy
circus of scrambling journalists and soldiers that blocked Baidoa's main
street, turned to me, and said: "I guess we're better protected today."

A marine general quipped that the escort was a "light display of authority" that "clearly and visibly shows you that we can carry out our mission.
This is satisfaction, I can tell you." Adding to the unintended farce, the
marines returned to their base only to find that they had forgotten to unload
their own 20-bag contribution to the orphanage.

The expansive welcome in Baidoa wore off by morning, when steady
overnight rain filled trenches. I had spent the night on a concrete floor—
crammed so tightly with other photographers that I was wedged between
three—and was up early to take pictures. I found a squad on the outskirts of
town. At sunrise their foxholes were deep with brown water, and they were

wringing out their clothes. Boots squooshed with water. One marine from Harlem found that he was covered with ticks. As he gingerly picked them off, we all laughed. He vowed: "I'm gonna tell the brothers never to come to Africa. They can take it from someone who knows—It's shit! I want to go home."

In Mogadishu the peaceful glow of arrival dimmed just as quickly but much more seriously. Within a day of landing, a marine patrol inspected a building across from the US Embassy, from where the troops had received three rounds of sniper fire. They caught a dozen Somalis red-handed, rushing to load green ammunition boxes packed with 40,000 Kalashnikov bullets. Three technicals mounted with anti-tank cannons were under canvas, and an arsenal of rifles, mortars, and rocket launchers stood ready.

"You've got guns, *guns?*" one marine demanded.

"Yes, yes," came the half-comprehending reply. The marines rushed in with their safety catches off, adrenaline flowing at this initial small engagement.

"They're trying to get away, we've got to get 'em!" shouted one soldier. The Somalis were arrested; the marines had made their first contribution to ridding Mogadishu of weapons. But they had stumbled upon a poorly hidden arms cache of Aidid's man, Osman Ato, who arrived personally to sort out the "mistake." Ato commanded the marines to order the press away. When the patrol leader radioed his lieutenant for instructions, he was appalled to hear the result.

"Good job," he was told. Then he was ordered to pull back and leave the weapons to the Somalis. The patrol leader hung up, shocked. "Fuck you," he said under his breath.

The mission had already begun to change, and his men were angry. The politicians were in charge of this TV landing, and they apparently had decided that targeting Ato could jeopardize the "peace" agreement. Two Cobra attack helicopters buzzed the six-story building until nightfall, their multipod rocket launchers loaded and locked on, 20mm nose cannon wagging at the target, and Osman Ato below, safe in the knowledge that within one day of the US arrival, he had already been deemed "untouchable."

But with so many weapons around, the temptation for the Americans not to do some mopping up was too great. Regardless of the hands-off policy, marines eventually did make sporadic efforts to find and destroy arms caches, and confiscated weapons they came across. The untouchables were left largely untouched—so as not to upset the agreed political balance. This irregular policy most affected relief agencies: their hired guards were disarmed at checkpoints, leaving their vehicles at great risk.

For those who doubt that Somalis welcomed disarmament in the early stages—despite Oakley's dire predictions—there were many examples. Somali warlords themselves, meeting in Addis Ababa in January 1993, signed a peace deal in which they agreed to hand over heavy weapons to UN monitoring. And on the streets that month, the soldiers began to "patrol aggressively." In one high-profile raid, 400 marines took control of Mogadishu's best-stocked gun market. They confiscated tanks, armored personnel carriers, and a vast array of rocket launchers and mortars. Officially one shot was fired, to open a padlocked door. The crowd waved and cheered. The sophistication of Somali "gunmen" was evident, too, and should have served as a warning for leaving this job half-done: 70kgs of TNT explosive and 19,650 feet of detonating cord were collected.

Another example came on a hot day in January. I was driving through town when I came across a gaggle of marine combat photographers who led me to where a raid was taking place. It centered on a plumbing warehouse which, by Somali standards, was normal: new baths, toilets, tiles . . . anti-tank shells, mortars, anti-aircraft guns, rockets.

"Hoo-eee! Look at this!" screamed the first sweaty marine to kick in the door. "One-stop shopping!"

Tipped off by a Somali in the crowd outside, they weren't deceived by the shiny new bathrooms advertised on the wall. Inside, between the pallets of broken tiles, they found a bargain-hunter's dream, gleaming in the unsettled dust like treasures finally unsealed after millennia hidden in an Egyptian pyramid: silver-tipped 20mm rounds, the dull brass of long-exposed shell casings, British grenades in boxes labeled with Arabic script. The marines filled six 5-ton trucks, which were taken to their base and destroyed. One marine, his arms laden like a waiter, turned to his officer: "Grenades, sir?"

"Watch it!" was the immediate reply. "If this stuff goes up, my mother only gets $20,000, and that ain't enough!"

And on another day, 900 marines marched through the narrow lanes of the dingy Bakhara market. Except for a few irate men, woken from their siestas by marines crashing through their doors, most Somalis seemed to appreciate the mission. The Americans made house-to-house searches and broke into locked buildings with axes, sledgehammers, and bolt cutters. Most personal assault rifles had been hidden or buried well in advance, but the big-ticket items were there for the taking. This patrol found five large caches on that one day and vowed to increase the number of daily patrols to 30.

In one of the last acts of its kind, the marines found a huge underground network of tunnels on the edge of the city filled with of 1,000 tons of armaments. They were destroyed, the black smoke from their blast leaving Mogadishu under a gray pall for days. Why couldn't this policy, which one colonel said had turned the artillery of "a particularly virulent clan" into "paperweights," have spread to other clan areas and continued?

Instead, Unitaf commander Robert Johnston, in late January, effectively told Washington, "The war's over, we won, it's time to come home."[23]

The limited American mandate and steady political pressure on the newly elected President Bill Clinton to bring the troops home meant that the mission would soon be turned over to UN control. The handover was set for February 1993, but the UN was slow to organize and the date slipped to May. Aidid had bet on American success and had managed to separate the good from the bad—the US from the UN—in the minds of his supporters.

American troops were treated like apostles bringing salvation, and President Bush was the returning messiah when he ushered in 1993 with a visit on New Year's Day. It was hard to believe that a US president was coming to this place, to pay his respects and to receive the accolades of the Somalis. I watched as Bush stepped through a narrow door gap, to shake hands with children at an orphanage in Baidoa for the press.

This was the City of Death, where not many months before I had seen children like these die in droves from famine, had seen them shiver when their blankets were stolen, and had seen their bleached bones form a path along the road. The contrast was stark: how remarkable that the fate of these Somali children were—and would be in the future—dependent in so many ways on the actions of this man who lived 8,000 miles away in the White House. The problem was not the US deployment, in the end. It was what happened to that deployment. Disarmament, if it were ever to be attempted, should have been conducted by those best able to do it, the Americans.

By New Year's Day, it was too soon to tell the final result, so I took heart, along with many Somalis, when the president promised: "We are not going to leave the people of Somalia naked."

Boutros-Ghali's visit three days later could not have been more different. Spurred on by Aidid's rhetoric, there were riots outside UN offices. Aidid supporters threw stones and grapefruit rinds and clambored up the flagpole to replace the UN flag with a Somali one. Under a barrage of chanting against UN "neo-colonialism," Boutros-Ghali was forced to flee by helicopter and had to cut his embarrassing visit to just three hours. Aidid and the UN chief had a long-standing personal grievance, but any student of Somalia—and certainly anyone planning to deploy under a UN flag—should have noted how quickly Aidid could turn his crowds on and off.

But Aidid's goodwill toward the Americans also began to unravel in late February. Aidid ally Omar Jess was ousted from the coastal city of Kismayo under the unsuspecting noses of Belgian and US Unitaf troops by his archrival General Morgan. Overnight Morgan's militiamen had crept into the city disguised as shepherds and farmers. Women and children hid weapons under their clothes. With barely a shot fired, the city changed hands. Aidid blamed the foreign troops for taking sides, and the fallout was heaviest in Mogadishu, where Aidid called for days of rioting. The Kismayo changeover also coincided with an Ato-Oakley confrontation, says one witness. Ato complained that Unitaf was only confiscating his group's arms, making the Somali National Alliance vulnerable. Be fair, Ato said, or protests will begin. "You want to show your muscle?" Oakley is said to have replied. "Go ahead and do it!" The next day, riots began.

For their safety, US troops were confined to base for the first time. Aidid's clansmen blocked roads with burning barricades. Nigerian troops stationed on the roof of the journalists' Sahafi Hotel were targeted by a lone sniper and overreacted, destroying an entire corner of the Egyptian Embassy with a heavy machine gun.

The US was unable or unwilling to stop the unrest, and within hours the lesson was clear: Aidid was still in control, easily able to disrupt the calm at his whim. He no longer trusted US or UN "neutrality." Whatever the reality, Aidid prepared to fight back. The window of opportunity for disarmament shut, as the US and UN were drawn as players into Somalia's political game.

After this turnaround, the Americans hastened to hand over the mission to the UN. Oakley reminded everyone that Washington's intervention was limited from the start and that "violence was a Somali trait." But when the UN finally did take the reins, it had just one-third of its staff in place. And the challenge was unprecedented. The new UN mission of "nation building" was the most ambitious ever devised by the Security Council.

The mandate included total forced disarmament—a task that even the strongest military power in the world had already shied away from. It also envisioned the creation of a new government, rebuilding Somalia's economy, and a UN-financed and trained police force and justice system. Everything from schools to water and electricity to phone systems were to be rebuilt. The UN goal was "nothing less than the restoration of an entire country as a proud, functioning and viable member of the community of nations," according to the US ambassador to the UN Madeleine Albright.[24]

Of course, it was hopelessly ambitious and doomed to fail. But as an expression of the humanitarian intent of the UN—with US support—it fit post–Cold War aims. Some 25,000 UN troops were to be backed by a US logistics team and a US-commanded Quick Reaction Force (QRF). They were given the strongest mandate possible. Under the UN's Chapter VII rules of engagement, applied operationally for the first time ever, peacekeeping would be given teeth. Unitaf had the same authority, but only to open food corridors and protect aid. This expanded mission, called Unosom II, would be one of "peace enforcement," in which warlords could be compelled to disarm.

Under the new rules, warlords and gunmen could be legally eliminated in the UN's greater quest of bringing permanent peace. But the precedent of giving the military top priority—paradoxically at the exclusion of humanitarian work—had already begun. The US spent $750 million on the Unitaf intervention, for example, but pledged only $50 million for rehabilitation.[25] That ratio would be skewed even further during Unosom II.

The problem was that despite the American intervention, the demons that had first split Somalia asunder were still at work, and as well armed as ever. When UN troops took over in May 1993, they expected to be "tested" by Aidid. They were not disappointed.

On the eve of the May handover, Oakley gave a naive and overly optimistic assessment of American achievements. No mention was made of the new legitimacy his own diplomacy had bestowed upon the warlords, or the fact he and the military brass had left them still armed, or that city streets of the capital were quickly becoming as dangerous as they had been before the US came to town. The Americans had "brought Somalia back from the brink of self-destruction," he told us, though I wondered in what direction Somalia was sliding, if not back down. "Death and starvation are almost gone now, and clan warfare—which has taken so many lives—is virtually gone," Oakley concluded.

US officers described their success vaguely as "giving Somalia back to the Somalis." To many, that boast could be taken too literally, for their country had been given back to the *wrong* Somalis, the warlords.

Trying to allay fears that non-American UN troops were not up to the task, Oakley praised the Nigerians who had blasted the Egyptian Embassy to knock out a sniper. That precedent, he said, would prove an "awakening" for critics who accused UN troops of incompetence. Oakley did not mention that, just the day before, a Nigerian soldier had shot his buddy in the leg while they were standing watch. Nor did he mention a previous incident, in which a Nigerian soldier had managed to fire five rounds into the Sahafi Hotel restaurant during dinner, filling the knees and gut of the ever-funny Voice of America correspondent Alex Belida with bullet splinters.

"The Nigerians were doing a slapstick 'Gee whiz, oh no, what do we do' routine," Alex recalled. "They ran off to 'organize transport' for me to hospital. Nothing happened." So Alex found his own way with colleagues. "Next day, a Nigerian officer wearing wrap-around 'I'm cool' shades came to my room and presented me with a potted flower and his apologies. I did not accept apologies. I left the country."

The Unitaf troops had nevertheless brought peace to the islands of security they controlled. Soldiers often enjoyed swimming at Black Beach, despite the prevalence of sharks. Evidence of the famine was dwindling, as rains leveled the graves that lined the sandy roads. But as always, after the Somalis them-selves, the first victims of unrest and insecurity were the relief agencies. Amer-ican and UN troops despaired of protecting all the 585 UN and relief agency installations in Mogadishu, so concentrated on their own sites.[26]

The murders of three relief workers, two of whom were my friends, during the American tenure highlighted the continuing risks. Sean Devereux, the English head of Unicef in Kismayu, was murdered by gunman Abdi Dhere, as he walked the 400 yards from his office to his house. When I had been in Kismayu in January 1993, Sean had told me the ugly story about the killing of up to 100 Somalis on the eve of the US arrival by Aidid's ally, Omar Jess. He told others, too, and for this he was killed. He was as funny as he was serious. He loved children and Somalis. He was a modern-day hero.

Another friend was Valerie Place, an Irish nurse who worked with Con-cern school programs. She had taken me on a tour of her classrooms just days before and had spoken lovingly of the students. Bright-eyed, they attended classes and ate food. They were the hope, if they survived, and Valerie had set them on their way. She was killed on the much-patrolled Mogadishu-Baidoa road, where a gunman stepped into the middle of the road with an AK-47 and fired one shot. The bullet pierced Valerie's chest, and she died within minutes.

Usually when I read of a relief worker being killed, it was as unaffecting to me as a gangland killing in the US or a Mafia murder in Moscow—an event that barely ranked a sidebar story. But I knew these people, and I knew that, beyond their good intentions, they were achieving something. In the aid world, that is an important distinction. When I revisited Somalia in 1999, Valerie's schools were still going strong, while virtually every other trace of big-spending relief agencies had vanished.

Back then, the cost of working safely was growing. "You want security? Here it is," Carl Howorth, then of Unicef, told me in his room. He opened his desk drawer to reveal a loaded pistol. An assault rifle leaned against the wall. We talked about the Americans, my countrymen, and how things were falling apart. I had favored the US arrival, but it was soon clear—Oakley even broadcast the message—that they weren't going to take many guns. Osman Ato's rule that you must provide your own security was becoming valid again. "We didn't need these four months ago, before the Americans came," Carl said, pointing to his weapons. "Now we do."

Marine commanders recognized the problem and told troops to keep wav-ing at Somali kids. "If we're not careful, we will start thinking that we're at war, and we may forget that our mission here is one of peace and humanitar-ian assistance," warned a January bulletin. "The people of Somalia need a friend—not just another oppressor in desert camouflage utilities."[27] US troops were frustrated by leaving a job half done. They blamed politicians and diplomats and gave vent to their unhappiness by belittling their adversary. Somali children were sometimes given the little bottles of Tabasco found in American combat rations. As the children gulped down the pepper sauce, their panicky reactions prompted full laughter. At the airport, graffiti painted onto the wall of one building read: "Club Skinny—Dancers Wanted."

Marine press spokesman Col. Fred Peck, the softspoken man who faced the pack of journalists with aplomb throughout the American mission, had kept a spare M-16 rifle on hand at his US Embassy compound headquarters. He had found the rifle when the marines first stormed the place, and kept it all those months as a replacement, in case the marines confiscated a gun from a journalist's guard.

The assault rifle was in perfect condition, with two full clips bound by camouflage tape and a third empty one as a spare. Peck handled it lovingly, kept it primed, and blew a few last filaments of dust away with a can of compressed air before giving it to me. He should have turned it over to the munitions disposal unit, but his military conscience wouldn't let him. He knew the streets outside were increasingly dangerous, and he shared fears that the UN might not be up to its peace-enforcing mission. He put on his desert-print camouflage shirt and carried the gun to the gate for me himself. We walked around the coils of barbed wire outside and across the trash-blown street to my waiting gunmen. Surprised at this scene, they instinctively readied their own rifles, double-clicking to full automatic.

"Take care of it," Peck said, as he handed me the rifle. "Give it a good home, and only use it wisely."

[I later traded the gun in Mogadishu for a Parabellum pistol, which I smuggled back home to Nairobi, where the crime rate was so high. Before leaving Africa, I gave it to a colleague and former soldier, for *his* protection in Nairobi.]

Peck's final words would have been the best advice for incoming UN forces. Soon enough they would be sucked into a bloody conflict beyond their imagination. A clue of what was to come could have been found in the "Restore Hope Soldier Handbook" provided by the US Army Intelligence and Threat Analysis Center. It said that "Somalis are prone to take an aggressive, pro-active approach to resolving anything perceived to be a problem."[28] Islam, it remarked, "has contributed to a widespread and pervasive sense of fatalism." It also noted that Somalis "admire military strength and power," but failed to include the caveat that had eluded would-be conquerors of Somalia since the time of the Mad Mullah; strength and power had to be used with discretion—just as it was for nomadic warriors of times past—to win Somali respect.

Still, before the handover to the UN, the Green Line was quiet. Violence here had always been the barometer for tension throughout Mogadishu. Marines based on the second floor of the Commercial Bank played Beatles music, while the Somalis crossed Checkpoint 77. The ruined sidewalks were lined with razor wire and cleared through the rubble of destroyed buildings. If the music stopped, the Somalis complained.

This illusion of peace was hard to dispel. The Americans might even be forgiven for thinking they had done their job well.

"It's so safe here now," one marine told me with confidence, "that you can walk around naked with a target on your chest, and no one will touch you."

FIVE

"CAMP OF THE MURDERERS"

*I never saw a Somali who showed any fear of death,
which, impressive though it sounds, carries with it the
chill of pitilessness and ferocity as well. If you have no
fear of death you have none of anybody else's death
either.*

—Gerald Hanley, Warriors

The *muezzin* called to prayer, his high-pitched song of Islamic
faith reaching out at every dawn from mosque after mosque,
creating an echoing holy web between tall white-washed
minarets that drew Somalis for their religious rituals. The violence of the streets was forgotten, if briefly, during this exercise
of the spirit; left at the mosque entrance with the shoes were the
anxieties and responsibilities of feud and injustice, of revenge as
a virtue. Prayers were to Allah, their god, for protection.

And each morning in early 1993, under the same bright blue
sky, UN troops from Pakistan answered a similar call to prayer
at their Mogadishu base. Every day, before lacing up their black
military boots, before click-clacking brass-encased rounds into
the chambers of their assault rifles and strapping on their blue
helmets, these "peacekeepers" also asked their god—the same
Allah—to protect *them*.

This common Islamic bond between Somalis and Pakistanis
was considered by both sides to contribute to a special rapport
in the first weeks after US forces handed over to the UN on 4
May 1993. As part of Unosom II, the Pakistanis were put in
charge of Mogadishu. They greeted their Somali brethren in
Muslim fashion, *as-Salaam Alaykum*, "peace be with you."

At the handing over ceremony, a group of Somali schoolchildren, standing shoulder to bony shoulder in new red T-

shirts, had sung a blessing: "We are Somalis, we are Somalis. We are used to conflicts, but we are also used to solving them quickly." The Americans declared: "We have restored hope to this country."

But General Aidid had been watching the UN's mandate change and was fully aware that he was soon to be disarmed and marginalized—forcefully. Close Somali aides and many Western sources say that if every clan had been disarmed, early on, Aidid would have accepted. But if the previous months had taught the warlord anything, it was that disarmament was not likely to be carried out equally, and would therefore be dangerous to him, the strongest clan chief. Prematurely, US envoy Robert Oakley, despite promoting the December 1992 pact that preserved all warlords' heavy weapons, had declared that "plucking the bird" was his strategy. "You take one feather at a time and the bird doesn't think there's anything terrible going on. Then one day he finds he can't fly," he said. "We did that from the beginning."[1]

Another source of Aidid's ire was the work of April Glaspie, an American Foreign Service officer acting as the UN number two. She had won notoriety as the former US ambassador to Iraq for reportedly nodding to Saddam Hussein on the eve of his August 1990 invasion of Kuwait that the US was ambivalent about any such attack. In Somalia, UN documents note, she worked to marginalize Aidid and his SNA and impose the world body's will in the political and judicial process, both of which went well beyond their mandate. This, and the Kismayo turnover under UN noses, caused Aidid to begin a no-holds-barred propaganda campaign on Radio Mogadishu.[2]

"Radio Aidid," as it was known, accused the UN of "imperialist designs" and "colonialization" and called upon Somalis to defend their "sovereignty." The will to disable those irritating broadcasts had grown, especially among Glaspie and US envoy Robert Gosende. Rumors had reached a crescendo that the UN was preparing to take over and destroy the radio. Many knew that Aidid's main rival, Ali Mahdi, had secretly asked for it to be knocked out. The radio was one of five registered weapons sites, so an inspection was calculated to annoy the warlord and send a warning. But this would be the first inspection of its kind, so it would have been sensitive on the best of days. Nevertheless, Pakistani soldiers were detailed on 5 June 1993 to do the mission. US special forces technicians were also, in fact, sent to determine how best to disable the radio.

On the eve of the operation, Aidid's interior minister, Abdi Hassan Awale "Qaybdiid," received a UN notice that the radio and other weapons sites were to be inspected the next morning: "This is unacceptable," he replied to the messenger. "This means war."[3]

The Pakistani commander had warned US force commander General Thomas Montgomery that the operation would be politically sensitive and dangerous.[4] But Montgomery never told the Pakistanis of the "this means war" response—a charge the commander denies—despite a direct request to do so.[5] Though an independent UN inquiry deemed this to be the "worst time" for such an inspection and an "ill-advised" move, it was approved by Glaspie.[6] A month later, officials still disagreed over whether the inspection was "genuine or was merely a cover-up for reconnaissance and subsequent seizure" of the radio.[7]

The Pakistanis say that if they had known of the Somali objections, they would have taken greater precautions—such as carried more weapons and used armored vehicles. Instead, they arrived in vulnerable soft-sided trucks, protected only by Kevlar vests and the presumed goodwill of their Islamic brothers.

Local Somalis immediately sounded the alarm. The Pakistanis later asserted that they had been treated to a "tour" of the radio station; but the Somalis accused them of smashing the studio equipment with their rifle butts. Either way, an angry mob of Somalis attacked them during their departure. It may never be established who fired the first shots: the UN claimed that gunmen in the crowd fired upon the blue helmets; Somalis countered that the Pakistanis opened fire into the sea of people. The special Islamic "bond" evaporated, and military center of gravity of this "peace" mission changed.

The result of this American-approved "inspection" was the largest single-day massacre of UN peacekeeping troops since 1961, when 44 Ghanians were killed in the Congo.

The first of the 25 Pakistanis to die were rushed to hospital. The unit had run out of ammunition and been forced to fend off a grenade attack using wooden planks as bats. Almost simultaneously, three miles away, a patrol was caught by surprise near the cigarette factory and attacked. Another unit protecting a food distribution center was slaughtered after one soldier, trying to calm a growing mob, was pulled into the crowd and dismembered. Survivors were taken hostage, and one died in captivity.

Italian units were called to help. Their helicopter fire accidentally wounded two Pakistanis. But Italian armor took many more hours to arrive. When the SOS call came, a Somali witness who understood Italian—unbeknownst to the Italians—overheard Gen. Bruno Loi reply to the Italian radio operator: "Leave them."

The real horror, and the cold realization that the UN had grossly misjudged the depths of Somali anger, came when the Pakistanis collected the mutilated remains. Ten of the dead had been castrated and their eyes gouged out. One had his shirt torn away with a dagger wielded by a woman, the ultimate insult in the Somali panoply of injuries, and deep gashes had been carved into his cheeks and chest. Swedish nurses at the UN hospital who received the bodies were so distraught at the sight of the carnage that they had to be evacuated.

"We thought they were our brothers," one Pakistani officer told me later, his voice choking with disbelief. Hearing him reminded me of how quickly any quiet in Somalia could collapse.

When the slaughter took place, I was in Nigeria, covering an election. But the foreign desk of *The Daily Telegraph* saw how quickly things might escalate and authorized me to fly to Somalia immediately. At a cost of $3,000, I flew from Lagos to Brussels, then to Nairobi and on to Mogadishu on a flight carrying qat. The decision was correct, because the US-led revenge was swift.

The triple attack appeared coordinated, sparking claims by the UN that it was a pre-meditated ambush and that Aidid was responsible. But the killing had hardly begun. These first Pakistani deaths served as the grisly prelude to the bloodiest UN mission in history, one that would forever stain the once-triumphal dream of "peace enforcement" and ultimately turn the US into a neurotic lion.

From the start, however, UN and US commanders were ambitious about the Chapter VII provision. With a free hand, they could legally respond to any resistance from the warlords with force. As a vehicle of the New World Order, this mission was going to set the precedent. It fit also with the new Clinton administration's agenda of making the UN a viable tool for resolving conflict. In Somalia, the UN was to demonstrate how to apply force correctly, to right the wrongs of regional and civil disputes. For true believers, Somalia was the altar of universal goodwill, and success would be its self-evident oracle. "We need to demonstrate as a community of human beings that we can come to the assistance of another community of human beings in deep need," US envoy Gosende told me when the UN took over. "If we can't do that in the last quarter of the 20th century, when can we do it?"

But once that pale blue UN flag replaced the American Stars and Stripes in Somalia, this mission was unlike any other. The Chapter VII clause had been invoked briefly during the Gulf War, but not as an operational framework. The UN had legitimized the war against Iraq then, but did not control it. In Somalia, the use of force by UN "peacekeepers" would dictate daily rules of engagement. In part this was because, in marked contrast to its lukewarm support for all other UN operations, the US government had already made an expensive financial and political investment in Somalia, and therefore insisted on seeding the entire mission with Americans.

The New World Order was to have a distinctly American flavor. When I asked about this imbalance, one senior US officer told me, with an arrogant sneer: "You don't want it to fail, do you?"

Though 23 nations contributed to Unosom II's strength, with peak troop numbers at more than 18,000 (the plan had been for 35,000), decision makers were primarily from the US. UN chief Boutros-Ghali had first appointed a Guinean as his new envoy, even having the diplomat's passport inscribed with his new position. But the Clinton administration insisted that an American hold the post.[8] The unfortunate choice was retired Navy Admiral Jonathan Howe, a too-polite career military man and born-again Christian whose appointment was described by one American official as "the miscasting of the century."[9]

Still, Howe had served as George Bush's deputy national security adviser. He always wore a columbia-blue UN baseball cap over slightly graying, close-cropped hair, and a snow-white short-sleeved shirt. Howe's skin was remarkably pale, almost bright like his shirts and without a trace of melanin, prompting snide comments about spending too many years in a submarine.

The staff roster was loaded with US advisers, bureaucrats, and agents seconded from the Departments of State and Defense, the CIA, and other agencies.

The prevailing deference was obvious in the example, according to one inside account, of a senior military officer who had to "fake a heart attack and be flown out of Mogadishu to Nairobi in order to get out of the American firing line . . . so that the Americans could appoint their own deputy commander."[10]

That commander was Montgomery, a short man with the type of paunch that you see on senior officers, when hard training gives way to desk jockeying. He often wore a pistol on a shoulder holster, the black leather buffed to perfection. The troops and hardware that carried out most of the subsequent raids and attacks were also American, drawn from the 1,300-member US Army Ranger Quick Reaction Force (QRF). That force had been meant to be a backup for emergencies, but it gave Montgomery confidence and later would become his personal tool. He liked to be called the "first American general in a blue beret," and when I cornered him briefly the day the UN took control, he made clear that he would brook no interference: "The message we are giving out is that if we are tested, we are prepared for a decisive response."

When that test came on 5 June, the timing could not have been better for Aidid. As the UN mandate widened, Aidid's anti-UN diatribes increasingly included the Americans. Somalis were becoming preoccupied with the "foreign occupation." Weakened by the famine in late 1992, they could have mounted little effective resistance to the first US intervention. But now, with the famine eased and food pouring into the country, Aidid supporters were easily manipulated to unrest when the UN was seen to be taking sides against their clan. The surplus of free food was by then so great that at one Mogadishu feeding center I watched in amazement as women stole sacks of maize flour, then emptied that flour into the sand just to run away with the real prize: the waterproof plastic sacking. Hunger was no longer the issue.

The UN reaction to the killing of the Pakistanis was swift and harsh—there were few other options at that point—and greater than Aidid could have imagined. Before the blood of the dead Pakistanis had even dried, the Pakistani envoy and US Ambassador to the UN Madeleine Albright—later secretary of state—presented Security Council members with a draft resolution that named Aidid as responsible for the attacks and demanded his arrest. As the UN inquiry found: "Without investigation, blame for the attacks of 5 June was laid on the USC/SNA."[11] The warlord had long before been singled out by Washington as the UN's target. The first draft said Aidid was to blame and therefore had to be removed. But recognizing the far-reaching implications of a UN-sponsored manhunt, other council members balked.

"I was not happy with this wording and . . . told them [the Pakistan envoy and Albright] that the council was not a tribunal," said Antonio Pedauye, the Spanish chair of the Security Council at the time.[12] "I proposed to avoid name calling." After listening "attentively," Albright made a call on her mobile phone, and the changes were made.

Meeting in emergency session on 6 June 1993, the Security Council adopted Resolution 837, the slightly watered-down version that noted "grave alarm at the premeditated armed attacks launched by forces apparently belonging to the United Somali Congress/Somali National Alliance [Aidid's faction]." Citing Chapter VII, Unosom II was authorized to take "all necessary measures against all those responsible for the armed attacks."[13]

Conflict had been "inevitable" since 4 June, the inquiry found—the day *before* the Pakistani deaths, when the "ultimatum-like" search notice was delivered. In other words, it was the UN's provocative actions that made the path of violence inevitable and led to disaster, not the killing of the Pakistanis, which was seen as the result of UN moves. Then the Security Council, with Albright's guiding hand, hammered the final nail in Somalia's coffin: "The clashes between Unosom II and the SNA thereafter were a direct result of the implementation of resolution 837," the inquiry noted.[14]

Boutros-Ghali backed up that tough line, in keeping with past clashes with Aidid that dated from his days as Egypt's deputy foreign minister. Boutros-Ghali was then a personal friend of dictator Siad Barre, and under his watch Aidid—as a Somali opposition leader trying to raise support for his war against Barre—was deported from Egypt. Though the UN chief took pride in what he called his "special" knowledge of Somalis, if such an intimate awareness existed, it failed him critically when he allowed Somalia to be the first

Chapter VII guinea pig. Boutros-Ghali should have been the first to warn that Somalis have never been conquered or accepted rule imposed from outside, and there was little chance of changing that.

The wrongheaded provocative buildup was largely due to the mispercep-tions of an inner circle of top American decision makers. Called by some the "war cabinet," they were convinced well before the Pakistani massacre that Aidid was guilty of murder and of blocking UN efforts at nation building. The UN inquiry was very critical of the "inappropriate political advice" that led to the lethal radio search.

"Somalis don't care a damn about the numbers of Pakistanis killed, they just count the dead and see who won," John Drysdale told me. He was a Somali expert with large thick glasses set upon a small academic's nose, who had been persuaded to advise the UN. The Englishman wore an elegant gold paisley waistcoat and remained one of the few foreigners respected by most Somalis, and revered by many. But his advice—based on fluent Somali, more than 30 years experience, and unparalleled access to all faction leaders—was rarely followed, which caused him endless personal frustration. The violence against the Pakistanis, though shocking to the outside world for its brutality, should have been measured in context, he said. "I've seen Somalis torture other Somalis, and they can be cruel as hell when the rage is there."

Drysdale knew Aidid well and was skeptical that the warlord alone was guilty, or that he could have controlled the scale of the Pakistani massacre even if he had sparked it. The point misunderstood again and again, he told me, was that Somalis can coalesce to fight as quickly as they fragment: "Somalis know all about tactics, and are natural fighters. It is second nature to surround and ambush effectively. They don't need a leader to tell them what to do."

For nomad fighters, this has always been the case, agrees historian Lewis. "Armies and raiding parties are always *ad hoc* formations, and while feuds often last for years, and sometimes generations, they are generally waged as guerrilla campaigns. Pitched battles are rare."[15] A Somali writer adds: "Our countrymen fought against those innocent Pakistanis using their logic of clan conflict. In a word they considered the soldiers to be a Pakistani clan," she wrote. "For the nomad, attacking first is a rule of survival. In case of defeat, he is too proud to surrender, according to a Somali proverb: 'A passive warthog goes straight to hell.'"[16]

So was Aidid responsible for a "violent, deliberate and sophisticated ambush," or did the UN charge simply serve as an excuse to flex its peace-enforcing muscle? Aidid's son, Hossein, told me six years later that in his view the slaughter was a "setup" by Osman Ato to topple Aidid. "The Somali side was not innocent," said Hossein. "It was precalculated. The key was to remove my father and take over his place."[17]

Aidid denied responsibility and said he would abide by the findings of an impartial inquiry. But amidst the American-led saber rattling that followed, he was given no chance to exonerate himself. Oakley set the tone for the massive American military response, calling Aidid's denial "bullshit."[18] Howe vowed, rather prematurely it turned out, that "anything we do will be credible, will be fair, and will be just."

The UN's hired "independent" investigator, Tom Farer of the American University in Washington, hurriedly began to gather evidence to ascribe blame. His task would not have been easy under the best conditions. As Lewis notes: "It is always extremely difficult to discover even the immediate causes of a Somali feud; especially when, after the event, many rival accounts are given."[19] Based largely on circumstantial evidence—such as the testimony of one witness who was on hand when Aidid apparently congratulated SNA members for the ambush, and the recovered notes of the interrogation of a Pakistani prisoner—the report concluded that there was "clear and convincing evidence" that Aidid "authorized" the attack. It found that Aidid could be "liable to prosecution before an international tribunal."[20]

Credible as that report may have been, Farer was not permitted to take the testimony of five significant Somali witnesses—one of them a top Aidid adviser—presented by Drysdale. Howe "could see no benefit in the proposition, and restricted Farer to the new fortress-like Unosom compound. The Somali witnesses agreed to meet Farer in the compound provided they would be immune to arrest. Howe gave no such undertaking and the evidence Farer sought slipped out of his grasp,"[21] Drysdale writes.

The more credible UN inquiry—though Aidid did not cooperate as promised, thinking it would not be neutral—later determined that the SNA had indeed "orchestrated" the attacks, but that they were "spur-of-the-moment" and not premeditated. The UN, therefore, should pay compensation to Somali civilians for damage caused in subsequent UN-US air attacks, it said.[22]

But none of this was able to be pursued before Aidid was demonized as a "threat and menace" to Somali and *world* security. The provocations had been made, and the Pakistani blood was spilled in response—so the only option remaining was the path of violence. Aidid was the first to come between the crosshairs of UN peace enforcers. Upsetting the delicate political balance and paving the way for months of conflict, the UN decided to deny Aidid a political future. The UN, not Somalis, were to oust him. The blood feud was on.

The command center for the military operations was the sprawling US-Embassy compound. Behind its 10-foot-high walls encrusted with shards of looter-proof broken glass, the UN would always be separated from Somalis, the people they had meant to save. The compound had been improved with $50 million in cash earmarked for peacekeeping, but few Somalis would ever see the riches inside: working telephone and electricity lines and the sewer, waste, and air conditioning systems that served the foreigners so well. Likewise, few UN staff were ever allowed to venture beyond the walls for long. During much of the mission they would be flown daily by helicopter the short distance from their airport quarters to the compound, completely isolated from the dusty, dangerous capital that swept past beneath them.

As tension increased in early June 1993, the image of Howe—the UN's *envoye speciale* to Somalia—moving the UN civilian offices to this fortified hideaway must rank as one of the most pathetic of UN peacekeeping in *any* country.

Into this fortress, past the armed sentries and miles and miles of coiled razor wire, perimeter security lights, and sandbagged bunkers connected by military radios, Howe rode from his former office inside an armored personnel carrier. Trees that blocked the direct line of fire out of the compound had been bulldozed, potential sniper nests in adjacent buildings were destroyed. He wasn't taking any chances.

Upon arrival, stepping onto the windswept expanse of the compound, the wind whipping at his white short sleeves and pale arms, Howe struggled to carry his own suitcases to his new home: a tiny pre-fab tin box left over from the UN's mission in Cambodia.

Within days, when the UN's counterattack turned into an onslaught, the special envoy moved into the reinforced bunker beneath the US Embassy building itself, which handily doubled as the headquarters for the UN military. Having spent much of his Navy career on a submarine, the admiral must have felt more at home here, within easy reach of the pulse of the military campaign. Howe's hard-nosed attitude was in sharp contrast to his rather calm and nerdish persona. During interviews with me, he often sat relaxed on a bench in the tiny former embassy courtyard, disconcertingly overpolite, like Mr. Rogers about to tell a children's story. It was hard to imagine him commanding a nuclear submarine. He would shrug his shoulders when things were going wrong, and blame Aidid. Safely cloistered, Howe would begin his nation-building mission.

Somalis, now completely cut off from the UN operation that would make so many devastating decisions about their future, referred with disgust to the walled compound as the "Camp of the Murderers."

Outside the walls and beyond, preparations for the coming war were under way. The White House promised more combat helicopters and military hardware. A clutch of AC-130 Specter Gunships, the Hercules planes equipped with 105mm Howitzers on board, had arrived in neighboring Dji-bouti and began flying sorties over Mogadishu. They had proved their utility during the Gulf War, and could strike at night with pinpoint accuracy from up to 14,000 feet. In the capital, the Army's QRF primed its weapons and other UN units made their armored vehicles grenade- and mob-proof with sandbags and barbed wire.

Aidid continued to aggravate with his radio broadcasts.

As Somalis watched the preparations, they readied themselves. Aidid's rivals quietly gloated over his "misfortune" at being singled out for elimina-tion. Appearing before the press on the eve of the UN attack—less than a week after the Pakistanis were killed—Aidid was sanguine. His light blue but-ton-down shirt took the edge off his usually noisy attire, and he sported a new pair of *très chic* rimless glasses. He was engaged in an irreversible confronta-tion, he said, imposed upon him for reasons beyond his control. The Pakista-nis had "triggered an uprising" by "seizing" Radio Mogadishu. He didn't mention that he had tipped off UN suspicion by shifting weapons among his five cantonment sites. Instead he asked the question on the lips of every Somali: "Who are the UN going to fight with all these weapons and troops?"

Though his militia was equipped with artillery and surface-to-air missiles, Aidid's compound showed litle evidence of weaponry. One young gunslinger stood watch wearing a pair of new basketball shoes and a stained shirt. Such loyalists—his Habr Gedir clansmen, concentrated in southern Mogadishu adjacent to the US Embassy compound—were Aidid's most effective protec-tion against outsiders. "If they touch Aidid, the blood will flow forever," a Habr Gedir gunman told me.

Relief work had been halted overnight after the death of the Pakistanis. UN commanders tipped off relief agencies that a "massive strike" would be carried out sometime within the next 48 hours, and implored them to move into the embassy compound. Hundreds of foreign relief workers were evacu-ated, leaving just 13, who painted red crosses on the roofs of their houses and hunkered down. The UN noted ominously that anyone outside their walls would not be protected, if gunmen rampaged through the city or targeted the agencies in revenge. The hundreds of civilian Unosom staff—whose mission, ironically, was to *rebuild* Somalia—were pared down to less than 50.

In anticipation of the showdown, journalists flocked to Mogadishu. Arriv-ing from Lagos via Europe, I was still one of the first to arrive, and was sur-prised to see how quickly the UN "humanitarian" mission was gearing up for war. I found sanctuary at the Sahafi Hotel, where the musty smell of the rooms was by then very familiar. Upon arrival, the first task was always to find a platform to place in the bathroom window so I could set up my satellite telex, the laptop-size machine that enabled me to send stories to London from anywhere, even with just a car battery. This minimized the use of wire agency satellite phones, which were billed to our newspapers at $40 per minute. Then I would wipe the dust off the desk, unpack, assemble my cameras, and go out to my gunmen waiting below.

We made furtive passes through the city, negotiating burning roadblocks and angry crowds. One-on-one my Somali friends—people like my driver Hersi and a handful of Somali professionals—were still close and welcoming. But they made very clear that the public mood was turning ugly and that I would need to take greater care on the streets. Out there, they said, journalists were seen as useless symptoms of the UN disease. As foreigners we couldn't be friends, and so must be enemies.

American forces closed Somali airspace, sealing in those of us expecting violence. The last journalists to arrive by chartered plane, early on the evening of the first attack, were surrounded by US troops, told that they were under arrest, and ordered to depart immediately, on the same plane. One passenger, Sam Kiley of the London *Times*, shouted down the US troops. He'd already spent too much time in Somalia, like most of us, and knew well that only the locals could make the law at the point of a gun. "Whose country is this, anyway?" he taunted. "You don't *look* Somali."

The Americans relented, and their example should have been followed by their commanders. Armed with everything but restraint, the UN was ready to become Somalia's new militia, with Howe as its warlord. And like every previous clan war in Somali history, the conflict would ultimately, arrogantly, be self-destructive. The UN was about to avenge the deaths of the Pakistanis with round two of a deepening blood feud. Legally entitled to enforce peace, the UN was determined to have the final say.

NIGHT ONE

The first Specter gunships began circling over Mogadishu just before 4 o'clock in the morning on 12 June 1993, making a high-altitude roar that filtered down through the firmament to produce a steady, ominous buzz. At the top of the hour came the first shell, a distant pop almost immediately followed by a flat, deep thud; then again, and again. The first-ever UN offensive action, carried out by American forces, began *pa-Daa, pa-Daa*, like a strange and surreal heartbeat that hammered the city awake. The targets were Radio Mogadishu and some of Aidid's weapons sites. After ten rounds, fires illumined the horizon with an orange glow. A few tracer rounds raced across the night sky. It ended quickly, the buzz of the gunships fading away.

I lay down again under a single sheet—I never used the air conditioners, they were too noisy, and the Somali night breeze was cooling enough—but didn't sleep.

Dawn revealed the damage. Radio Mogadishu was destroyed, reel after reel of tape spilling into the rubble. There was a small irony when one man held up some library tapes that had once been given by the Voice of America radio.

One shrunken old woman broke through the angry crowd and told me that the shelling had brought back haunting memories. "It is the new imperialism. It's the Americans who did this, and no one else," said Awah Hassan Osman. Her hands were held out, imploring. "We are all going to die anyway, but if we are going to be destroyed like this, it is better to die fighting than to die sleeping. Now we only have God and ourselves," she said.

Anti-UN demonstrations erupted throughout the city, though I had gone to the radio station early enough to beat the most dangerous of them. Somalis erected burning barricades to show their anger. Just 100 meters from the UN compound—confirming the sobriquet "Camp of the Murderers"—Pakistani troops opened fire from their post into the crowd. The Somalis scattered to either end of the street, too afraid to retrieve the dead. They mobbed our truck, and told us that we—Mark Huband from *The Guardian* and I, as white foreigners whom UN troops would not dare to shoot—would not be allowed to get away unless we collected the dead. With no choice, we veered into the free-fire zone. The body of one man was slumped in the dirt, blood thickening along his leg. A young woman was on her back, lying with eyes open and glazed with disbelief, moaning. Dirty sand stuck to the bloodied front of her red and yellow print dress, though we couldn't see where she had been shot. Other Somali women came at us, begging to be led safely out of the line of fire.

We lifted the wounded woman and loaded her onto the back of the truck, Mark protecting her head from banging on the spare tire. Then we collected the dead man as well, still warm but lifeless, lifting him into the back. We charged back toward the barricade, and I prayed that we would not be swept up in the mob when the body was taken from us. The Pakistanis stared as we drove by, our bloody cargo in the back. We got through, but the Somalis raced down the street behind us. We turned the corner into Benadir Hospital. Mark's tan trousers were smeared red with the woman's blood, like a painter's apron. I don't know whether she survived.

In all the clan fighting that had bedeviled Somalia, this was the first time I ever had occasion to save a Somali from a *foreigner*. I was still dazed by the speed of events, by this whole mission of peace being turned upside down. Somalis were being shot in the streets by UN troops? I was collecting Somalis wounded and dead who had been shot by UN soldiers? Did this unarmed young woman really threaten the Pakistanis, who were high in their protected firing position?

I found this hard to believe, and so did Somalis. But everything was perfectly clear and organized back inside the UN compound. Shielded from reality, the "war cabinet" was pleased. With a knack for coming up with subtle mission names, the Americans shamelessly called this bombing campaign "Operation Continue Hope." Aidid's capacity to wage war had been seriously damaged, they said. A multitude of aging weapons was laid out for our inspection. UN forces captured TOW missiles, artillery pieces, and hundreds of assault rifles. More than 200 loyalists had been detained.

Howe emerged from his command bunker long enough to tell us how happy he was, and that Somalis—presumably Aidid's opponents from rival clans—supported the UN "every step of the way." Howe wore his UN baseball cap, his shirt gleaming white enough for cameramen to take a light reading directly off it. "It is much safer now than before the military strike," he insisted. Radio Mogadishu "will be restored to the Somali people," and he wanted the demonstrators to cooperate "so that we can very quickly go back to peace and security and the good course we were on before these events."

Obviously he hadn't been outside the compound that day.

NIGHT TWO

Overnight on 13 June 1993 the steady buzz of Specter gunships and the *pa-Daa, pa-Daa, pa-Daa* heartbeat were imposed again upon a waiting city. Asleep in my room at the Sahafi, I came awake almost by instinct as the buzz penetrated my consciousness. I grabbed my cameras and ran up to the roof in what was quickly becoming a ritual of journalistic voyeurism, observing from a distance the low-level war that was tearing Mogadishu apart. Zero hour came at 12:50 am. The bombardment sparked a massive cacophony of secondary explosions that streaked across the sky like a patriotic Fourth of July display, to the "Ooh" and "Aah" of the sleepy journalists. Somalis had little to celebrate.

At first light my gunmen and I drove to the impact point, where a column of black smoke churned into the sky. It had been the main workshop of Osman Ato that converted stolen cars into battle wagons, where once I saw Aidid during the civil war affectionately describe the effective range of his big guns. I found Ato angry, surveying the wreckage. All signs of military gear had been wiped away; the earth appeared strangely to have been bulldozed, but there was still plenty to burn. Toxic smoke came from a series of mangled containers and mountains of burning spare parts, tires, oil tins, and orange paint. The waste burned uncontrollably and engulfed us—and dozens of gunmen-cum-firemen—in thick black clouds. People rushed about with hoses and pumps trying to kill the blaze. I choked on the fumes, despite the bandana tied over my mouth. My throat burned.

"There is no reason to laugh and smile," Ato said with a dry humor. He needed batteries for his point-and-shoot camera, which I provided. He photographed the scene of destruction and vowed to sue the UN for $12.5 million in damages. Howe "will certainly get a bonus from his political friends for this," he said. Pointing out three destroyed cranes and a bulldozer, Osman Ato challenged the UN to find any military hardware in the compound. The secondary blasts last night and curious bulldozer work on the ground, however, undermined his innocence.

In the confusion, I was approached by three elegantly dressed Somali women, who had soiled their ring-covered hands to bring me their trophy: the heavy chunk of a dud American 105mm shell, only partially burst. Its torn edge was remarkably sharp, a symbol to them of an American abuse of power. They handed it to me like a poison chalice. "Convey this to your President Clinton," said Faduma Daher Omar, her voice heavy with disappointment. "There is a lot we would like to revenge, but it will take time. We have given a great hospitality to American troops. But instead of food, now *this* is what they send us."

The protests shifted to the main parade ground along Lenin Avenue, where a demonstration of angry Somalis swelled in strength and courage until 1,000 people swarmed down the hill toward the Kilo 4 roundabout, beside the Sahafi Hotel. The Pakistani UN troops were in sandbagged turrets in the next building, four floors high. But their nervousness grew as the belligerent crowd filled the traffic circle. As if waiting for this chance to avenge fallen comrades, the Pakistani restraint faltered. How could the recent mutilations of their own troops not be their paramount emotion? No warning shots: they opened fire on the crowd with belt-fed machine guns, and kept firing as the crowd ran away. Seven were dead, including a two-year-old boy. Another child's brains were dashed onto the pavement; the dying bled, abandoned, in the street.

Photographer Alex Joe, a Zimbabwean shooter for Agence France Presse, ran from the hotel into the roundabout. His powerful images of a pleading boy—his arms begging for help over a crumpled victim shot by UN "peacekeepers," with a UN armored vehicle passing in the background—made the front page of nearly every newspaper in the world. For the UN, the killing was a disaster and shifted sympathy back to the Somalis. Aidid was at Benadir Hospital to receive the casualties. "Now the whole world can see who is right and who is wrong," he said, and accused the UN of "criminal injustice." Anonymous Somali leaflets declared that the "peacekeeping force is indeed a peace-killing force."

One man pulled me aside. He had been loading bodies, and his left hand was dripping with bright red blood. "What can you do when women and children are killed by soldiers with blue helmets?" he asked. "Maybe if we dropped bombs on New York and London—and slaughtered their children—then they would know how we feel."

In the UN compound the mood was somber but defiant. Military commanders said they were not going to let "a few dead Somalis" ruin a day otherwise crowned with the perfect destruction of Osman Ato's weapons caches. But they felt the pressure as journalists began to ask questions. Aren't units that have suffered casualties, like the Pakistanis, normally withdrawn so they are not apt to take revenge? Is *this* kind of bloodshed going to mark the rest of the mission?

Too often the military version of events during Somalia's most heated moments contrasted sharply with those of journalists and other witnesses, the deceptions a deliberate campaign of obfuscation. Our credulity would be tested often by both sides, with the Somalis also trying to convince us of their own outrageous claims. The trend of official UN and US denials of any military failing—and hiding the full truth about operations or Somali casualties—fostered disgust.

One human rights group found that the American rush to pronounce their actions in Somalia legitimate continued a "disturbing pattern" begun by US forces during the Panama invasion and Persian Gulf War.[23] It must have sounded familiar to Pentagon staffers, who heard every word through a direct telephone line: an innocuous-looking telephone that sat on the "United Nations" press center podium. The gaps between the reality we saw and the version we were told meant that our reports often had an underlying scorn. The result, just as it had in Vietnam, left the Fourth Estate subject to official charges of bias in favor of the Somalis.

At first the UN denied that the Pakistanis had fired into the crowd of Somali demonstrators at all. Instead, we were told that "hard-core militia" took over the crowd and shot their own people. When it was pointed out that journalists were *there* as witnesses, we were told that the Pakistanis fired in self-defense only, upon armed men who had infiltrated the crowd and fired upon the soldiers first. This was more plausible, but witnesses had heard no rounds coming from the Somalis. If there were any, they were drowned out by the belt-fed roar of the Pakistani machine guns. The tally of "self-defense?" No Pakistanis wounded; about 20 Somalis dead.

Years later, some Somalis too alleged that this was, in fact, a militia tactic organized by Ato—possibly without Aidid's knowledge—and that the UN had a point. "Somalis fired first at the Pakistanis," said one man, who insisted upon anonymity and was one of the primary sources for the UN at the time. "They used people as human shields. They would gather people from refugee camps to protest and shoot into the crowd. This was an intentional plan to incite and was publicity for the media." Other Somalis vehemently reject those charges.

The UN view was predictable. The front line was made of innocents, said QRF Col. Jim Campbell: "We are facing a particularly callous and cunning enemy who uses women and children as pawns." The UN inquiry took a similar view: "It appears from the evidence that the incident was staged, for the benefit of the international press, to show 'a massacre of non-combatants' by Pakistani forces."[24] Still, relief workers were unimpressed. "These are not the tactics to rebuild," said one senior aid worker. "These are the tactics to destroy. . . . At the moment the blue [UN] flag is becoming a dirt rag."[25]

Overnight, Aidid had been transformed from a "respected" warlord and Somali clan leader into the root cause of all Somalia's past, present, and future ills, a "murderer" who had to be "contained" before the UN could hope to bring peace. This turnaround had begun long before any investigation was carried out into the June massacre. UN troops gave out handbills with pictures and names of the "Most Wanted Criminals" in Mogadishu. One of the four was Aidid, who was given special emphasis as a "Human Killer." Judging by how poorly most of them grasped the nature of the enemy, they probably believed their own propaganda.

NIGHT THREE

Destruction wrought by the third night of bombardment on 14 June 1993 was small, but Somali casualties grew. The American psychological operations (psy-ops) unit was at work again, using mobile speakers to blast Aidid's house with the sounds of moving tanks, machine gun fire, and roaring helicopters. A vehicle compound was destroyed, and when we went out for the routine dawn inspection, we found an eight-year-old boy who had been sleeping at the base of a wall. He was incinerated, his small entrails boiled and protruding, his arms held frozen as though trying to fight off the flames. Somalis huddled around to have a look, as we took pictures. I didn't shoot too many frames, because such gore is rarely published. This boy's death was simply too grotesque to be shown.

By mid-morning another UN mission had turned sour. Military spotters saw an old and rusty BM-21 rocket launcher in a vacant lot and called in an American attack helicopter to neutralize this "top priority." The first TOW missile—a weapon chosen for Mogadishu's urban setting because of its purported accuracy—scored a direct hit. But the second laser-guided TOW whistled away with the wrong spin and lodged unexploded in the earth at a crowded tea stall.

Dutifully following the rumors, I arrived and found that one woman had been killed and 12 other Somalis wounded. Their blood had speckled the wall, and the rocket was unmistakable: it was mostly buried in the dirt, though the small tail fins and tight mesh of sophisticated wires made it unlikely that this was a Somali ruse.

Still, Howe denied that more than one TOW was ever fired from the helicopter, though officials later recanted. Already the grafitti being painted across southern Mogadishu attested to the envoy's unpopularity, playing on his title of admiral. Written upon one wall: "Animal Howe, Go Your Home."

As the UN's credibility plummeted, Aidid was becoming a hero for defying the world's strongest military force. The US appeared to be handing him the patriotic mantle of the Mad Mullah, turning him into a leader whose strength in Somali lore came from the caliber of his enemies. The warlord's Habr Gedir subclan demonstrated in the blinding sun, 1,000 people lining up to pray for victims of what they called "UN massacres." Passionate in their mourning and dripping with sweat, they championed a blue Somali flag, its white star reflecting the sunlight to an unbearable brightness. They clung to the flagpole, fighting among themselves to keep a hand on it, frenetically biting the wood and kissing the threads of the banner. President Clinton was blamed for the carnage, and protesters tore apart small paper American flags with their teeth. Clenched fists were raised defiantly at hovering US helicopters.

Aidid, still accessible and looking rattled and tired, gave a press conference. He told us that he would be willing to talk to the UN if the shelling would stop. Speaking on the rooftop veranda of his house, flanked on the right by a vase of plastic fruit and feather flowers, he struck a brief note of reconciliation. But this concession was not for domestic consumption, for Aidid knew that at home his chance for revenge would come. One of the best-educated Somalis I know, Abdurashid Nur Haile, explained: "During a blood feud, if you are a wronged but too weak to respond, you must be patient," he said. "We will not forget these things."

As the disinformation campaign heated up, the Somalis also began to manipulate press coverage. Aidid's supporters started at the same point as the "official" professionals: by assuming that journalists didn't have eyes. Casualty figures and, later, vivid descriptions of American attacks that were too dangerous for us to witness for ourselves—in large measure because of the threat of revenge attacks by Somalis—were always suspect.

For example, one man told me that 250 people had died at Radio

Mogadishu during the first night of shelling. We couldn't find a single body. And the strange fact that Osman Ato's compound had been so carefully leveled by earthmovers before dawn, quite apart from the massive secondary explosions sparked by the US attack, gave credence to the UN claim that it had been "sanitized" of weapons before any outsiders arrived.

The problem of determining the truth was endemic. The final death toll is still in dispute. Aidid told me that 13,000 Somalis had died at the hands of UN "peacekeepers." After regular denials of any significant Somali casualties from other officials, US envoy Oakley estimated 6,000 to 10,000 casualties, but made no breakdown of dead and wounded.[26] Two-thirds of those were said to be women and children. For those of us keeping rough count, the figure was unlikely to have topped 2,000.

Among the most creative works of anti-UN propaganda ever presented to me was the body of a man found in a sandy graveyard. Somalis dragged it to a hospital mortuary, where I braced myself to see this horrific "evidence" of UN torture. They said his tongue had been cut out and put in a plastic sack (which was true), and that he had been dropped out of a UN helicopter (which was not). They said the old fading tattoo on his arm spelled "UNO-SOM" (which it did not), and that the marks on his chest had been carved by his UN torturers into the shape of a Cobra attack helicopter (which they definitely were not). After this gory display, the corpse was slid back into the mortuary vault, a stainless steel door slammed shut, and a Somali "doctor" told me with finality: "Now they are saying that Aidid is reponsible for the fighting, but who is responsible for this?"

NIGHT FOUR

Zero hour for the final attack was precisely 1:35 am on 17 June 1993, after a two-day hiatus, the destructive *pa-Daa, pa-Daa, pa-Daa* coming in short bursts. The US psy-ops teams were hard at work, their speakers warning anyone around Aidid's compound to drop their weapons, raise their arms, and walk to the main road. "Evacuate immediately, these buildings will be destroyed in 10 minutes. . . . You have 5 minutes, evacuate immediately, *immediately . . .* "

Aidid's house finally came under direct fire—the manhunt was under way. The blasts brought down cascades of gypsum and dust; one round plunged directly through the veranda where I had watched Aidid speak the previous afternoon.

At 4 am a column of Italian tanks lined up at Kilo 4, in front of Hotel

Sahafi. The follow-on ground assault was ready; here was the UN chance to avenge the deaths of the Pakistani. Hundreds of Pakistani and Moroccan troops prepared for the ground assault, flanked by Italian and French troops. American liaison officers coordinated the units, US helicopters backed up the troops, and bomb-disposal experts were ready.

The Italian armor moved and I followed closely, blindly, with two other photographers. In the dark, one tank halted, and my Somali driver lost heart. We had to walk from there, but instead we ran, down Afgoi Road—a place where I had never set foot outside my protected car, because it was so dangerous—through the black with the tanks toward Aidid's compound.

We arrived breathless, and to the right a huge barricade was burning, a massive wall of flames and metal blocking the road to Aidid's home. To me it looked as though an inferno had enveloped the city, but I was moving too fast to think about the risk. Mindlessly we ran toward the barricade—for the photograph only—not knowing what was happening around us, Alex Joe on my far left and Mark Peters, a photographer for *Newsweek,* in between. Alex and I saw the gunmen at the same time and pulled back, but Mark leaned forward and saw too late, and FLASH—his camera illumined the array of rocket-propelled grenades and angry men before us, close enough to touch, assault rifles at full automatic, who were as surprised as we were at our stupid advance. The barrier burned high above our heads and theirs, giving a very immediate sense of how dangerous such a moment can be.

Here was the Old Somalia at war, resuscitated for a moment by the UN attacks, far removed from the illusory vision—stubbornly clung to in the "Camp of the Murderers"—of a New Somalia at peace. After a night of bombardment, and with a UN tank just 40 yards away, this barricade was a potent symbol of resistance.

"No, No America! We will kill you and the UN!" screamed one of the gunmen, menacing with his shoulder-held rocket, loaded up on a nightlong chew of qat and mentally crippled by four sleepless nights of rolling psy-ops tanks and helicopters.

The threat understood, we retreated quickly to the Italians, who were laying coils of barbed wire and battling enraged protesters. "The UN is killing Somalis with American help," they shouted, the sweat beading above glazed and defeated eyes. Somali snipers began to shoot, and the sharp whistle of bullets scattered us to nearby tea stalls, where there was nothing but hanging sackcloth for protection.

South Mogadishu was seething with hatred. The Italians shot a Somali boy and tried to load him into their ambulance, but there was a fight to prevent it. During the scuffle the wounded child was pulled and dragged; the Italians

gave up, turned back to the leeward side of their tanks and fortified themselves with mini-bottles of grappa, their strong unaged brandy. Outside the
razor-wire perimeter, I was threatened by a young boy who taunted me with a
pineapple-shaped fragment grenade. His finger was in the ring, ready to pull:
"Eh, journalista? Eh, bomb-ba?"

Could I blame him for this reaction? He had seen his city bombed by
outsiders, and he was now observing a tough violence firsthand—that was all
he knew. The dead Pakistanis didn't factor into his equation, though the
killing of demonstrators in front of Pakistani troops almost certainly did. The
lore was selective, but even at his age, how could I fault him for falling prey to
the adage that violence begets violence?

I shook off the kid bomber as the Italians prepared to break through the
burning barricade. In the warming daylight the snipers were increasing their
tempo. An American Cobra helicopter roared over our heads, firing TOW
missiles in the direction of Aidid's compound and Digfer Hospital. I looked
up to see one TOW leave its tube and rock wildly, veering off course: another
dud. The gunmen who meant to kill us had fled. The Italians smashed
through the barrier, and we met up with American and Pakistani units on the
other side. At the gate of Aidid's compound the Pakistanis paused—almost
reverently—and then kicked it in.

The compound was empty, the house partly damaged. The elusive warlord
had gone into hiding. US Army bomb-disposal experts, their pistols ready,
moved from room to room looking for booby traps but found only a motley
collection of old weapons. I watched them tear up the bright red rugs with
their knives. Pakistani commander Ikram al-Hasan stood among the ruins and
spoke words worthy of any American spinmeister: the "attack shows that UN
troops have the strength to bring peace and security to Mogadishu," he said,
and kept a straight face. On display upstairs were Aidid's personal accessories.
Bedroom drawers were full of Gillette shaving cream and pots of powdered
custard. There was an old Radio Beijing medallion, Italian Acqua de Selva *eau
de Cologne,* and wooden knives used for protests. Were these the very eclectic
tastes you'd most expect of a former diplomat and accused war criminal?

On Aidid's bedside table I found the secret of his sanity after nights of rau-
cous psy-ops noise: a pair of pink earplugs.

The architects of peace enforcement were ecstatic. Howe claimed a
"tremendous victory," though this unprecedented UN offensive left five
"peacekeepers" dead and 46 wounded. At least 100 Somalis had died, nine of
them patients at Digfer Hospital who were killed when UN troops opened
fire. Officially, the American input was limited to "helicopter liaison," though
of course it was far more. One senior official who participated in President
Clinton's decision to mount the attacks made clear later the depth of Ameri-

can involvement: "We didn't plan to kill him, but the president knew that if something fell on Aidid and killed him, no tears would be shed."[27]

As the battle raged, Somali gunmen took up positions on the roof of Digfer Hospital. Moroccan UN troops responded with cannon fire from their armored vehicles, and American Cobra helicopters fired their armor-piercing TOW missiles. Patients ran and hobbled out the back entrance during the battle. The operating theater was in use at the time of the attack, and bloodied swabs lined the floor. The roof was carpeted with shell casings from the Somali snipers.

The UN at first denied that it attacked the hospital with rockets: a clear breach of the Geneva Conventions. They claimed to have waited seven hours before "securing" the hospital. But when pressed, Howe argued that the "use of a hospital as an armed fortress is a violation of human rights," and the UN assault was justified. He promised that all the violence would be worthwhile: "I'm sorry we had to do it, but we will make a virtue out of it for Somalia."

Described that way, the UN victory began to take on a hue and logic similar to that applied in Vietnam: unjustifiable acts were justified, such that in order for a village to be liberated, it first had to be destroyed. Such brazen doublespeak would mark the UN mission until its end, but this would not be the last damning parallel made between America's war in Vietnam and its undeclared war in Somalia.

Finally targeting Aidid himself, Howe issued a UN warrant for his arrest, just hours after the warlord had disappeared. Aidid was now officially branded a "terrorist threat" who must be brought to trial for reasons of "public safety." His clansmen were "cynical collaborators." Rest assured, Howe said, "our doors are open to anybody who comes in peace."

But Howe himself seemed to note the depth of his own dilemma. "I recognize that we could have a 'Where's Elvis?' campaign, with Aidid popping up on CNN," he said. "But we're not going to hunt for him, or look down every rathole to find him." Despite that promise—and Howe's own involvement in the less-than-satisfactory pursuit of General Manuel Noriega in Panama City[28]—the chase would soon overwhelm every aspect of Unosom II, becoming the mission's new *raison d'être*. The word "manhunt" had never been part of the UN lexicon before. For most Somalis, the perversion from saviors to saboteurs could not have been more complete, or more bitterly disappointing. UN actions would make a mockery of blue helmet peacekeeping methods that had won the Nobel Peace Prize in 1988. Nation building would have to wait, as a target was substituted for policy.

But had the UN already overstepped its mandate? "It is arguable whether resolution 837 really initially envisioned bombing houses, garages, radio stations and meetings," the UN's own inquiry commented drily. "In peacekeeping the force and enforcement action should be regarded as the last resort after all peaceful means have been exhausted. There was no one to teach the basics of peacekeeping to Unosom HQ and contingents."[29]

If there was one lesson from the mutual violence, it was that neither side could retreat now without huge loss of face. There were miscalculations on both sides: could Aidid, or the UN commanders and US "war cabinet," have foretold the ruthless brutality of the other, in pursuing what they both deemed to be limited objectives? There could be no way out now—the stakes had been raised too high, too fast—just an inevitable, violent slide. No one in Somalia was naive enough to use the word "endgame."

During the after-action press conference, American attack helicopters circled above the UN compound, drowning out Howe's voice with their rotor wash. "I love hearing the sound of freedom overhead!" the envoy shouted over the howl. We cringed. "It reminds everyone that the UN is here!" A task force of US Marines had arrived off the Somali coast, and Howe was asked how long he would like them to stay: "Forever!" he shouted again, with barefaced jingoism.

Nevertheless, Howe took pains to describe all UN actions as neutral and claimed to have countrywide support for his all-American anti-Aidid policy. The admiral told us, for example, that he had just been to a meeting with 11 clan leaders—all sworn enemies of Aidid—and received their "total support" and "reassuring words." In a poignant moment before the meeting broke up, the elders and Howe had stood together and sung the Somali national anthem.

"A poet read a poem in praise of Unosom," said spokesman Barrie Walkley, an American with lap-dog enthusiasm. "We are trying to get a copy to you."

"Don't bother," jeered one correspondent. "We've already written our own."

SIX

THE FUGITIVE

What's the use of killing Aidid? Everybody is Aidid. If he goes tomorrow you will have a million Aidids around.

—Ali Gulaid, US representative of General Aidid

Plastered to the outside wall of the United Nations compound, but almost nowhere else because Mogadishu had become so dangerous for UN spies, was the absurd symbol of a manhunt: a yellow poster with a crude drawing of the warlord General Mohamed Farah Aidid. In true Wild West style, it fit the tone of this lawless city. But not its substance; saddle-sore gunmen did pillage the town with scant respect for authority, but they *never* lingered at the saloon bar, quenching their thirst with shots of whiskey, long enough for a well-meaning sheriff's posse to catch up with them. Never mind the inconsistencies: this WANTED poster, a relic of America's cowboy past, was approved. Some 80,000 copies were dumped on Mogadishu from American helicopters, floating down like canary-yellow ticker tape. Designed to entice Somali "citizens" to turn in a hardened war criminal, it read WANTED, reward $25,000, to capture the warlord and "bring him to the UN, Gate 8."

But Somalis had seen the movies and had watched John Wayne conquer the American West in the name of the law, for freedom and the sake of goodness, with a swashbuckling spirit backed up by a Winchester .30-.30 rifle. They had even seen the updated versions: *Delta Force* played at the local theater shortly after the American troops arrived. Later, *Rambo* was so popular that it made three showings.[1]

So the WANTED poster was greeted with knowing laughter, and within hours a counter price was put on the head of "Animal" Howe: Aidid would pay $1 million for capture of the UN envoy. Now that was a reward worth claiming! More Somali laughter—who in his right mind would turn against his clan? What a crazy miscalculation; a ploy by the American psy-ops unit that revealed a gross misunderstanding of the clan support that kept Aidid safe everywhere in his south Mogadishu fiefdom. Psy-ops thought this was Dodge City, but they made poor Wyatt Earps.

In their hunt for the warlord "terrorist," psy-ops must have taken its cue from US federal agents in Waco, Texas, who at the same time were bombarding the compound of cult leader David Koresh with an unbearable mix of marching-band and Nancy Sinatra music, shot through with the piercing tone of a phone left off the hook. In Waco, the result was a mass incineration that left 86 Branch Davidians dead. In Mogadishu psy-ops fared little better.

Loudspeakers had blasted Aidid's compound with the rumble of tanks and roar of helicopters. But Aidid brushed off their clumsy efforts.

Like schoolchildren, the "leaflet unit" dropped harmless notices from helicopters: "Don't let gunmen fire from your house—the UN *will* respond to protect itself," they read, or "STOP the killing, stop the war criminal Aidid." This tactic had gotten off to an embarrassing start. The first leaflets that fluttered to the ground during the original Restore Hope operation won the prize: because psy-ops did not trust Somalis to verify the translation, it read "Slave nations have come to help you."

The second prize showed allied tanks and parachutes with a peace dove. The meaning, the clever psy-ops staff explained, was to "increase the concept of nationality among Somalis, that they are a nation." Doing its part, American forces radio played long doses of heavy metal music, then declared: "You're listening to FM 99.8—Aidid's worst nightmare!"

But few moves could have enhanced Somali nationalism as much as singling out Aidid for punishment. This was the man, after all, who had toppled and exorcised Big Mouth Siad Barre from Somalia and who exhibited all the alluring leadership traits of stubborn arrogance. When US leaders and UN commanders chose to take on Aidid, when they determined that he was so powerful that he had to be hunted down and eliminated from Somali politics, that was strong evidence indeed of his importance. So who better to take on the modern mantle of the Mad Mullah, the martyr who had once challenged colonial rule and has been revered ever since as a national hero?

The mullah's "vain struggle had left in the Somali national consciousness an ideal of patriotism which would never be effaced and which was to inspire later generations of his countrymen," explains historian Ioan Lewis.[2] And it was this attraction of the Mad Mullah that fit Aidid so well: "It was more than anything else his magnetic personality, his ruthlessness and his complete and utter defiance of his enemies, that appealed to the Somali mind and deeply stirred the imagination of a people who with all their traditional democracy, admire, above all else, unswerving strength of purpose and unwavering determination. Tyrannical he might be, but to many Somalis, though not all, his tyranny was directed toward a noble end."[3]

Howe's promise not to look for his quarry "down every rathole" gave way to an obsession to do just that. Aidid and his militia had to be brought to justice for obstructing the most expensive UN "peacekeeping" operation ever. American decisionmakers led the charge, with UN chief Boutros-Ghali providing strong rear-guard support. So Aidid joined the ranks of personalized targets of American ire: Libyan leader Muammar Qaddafi, Panama's Manuel Antonio Noriega, Iraqi dictator Saddam Hussein, and most recently Yugoslav ethnic cleanser Slobodan Milosevic have all been labeled "Hitler" in their time. For Howe, Aidid became incarnate evil, the one individual blocking progress, an obstacle to *world* peace. Could there have been a more perfect target?

Now any degree of violence would be permitted and justified by the self-appointed UN sheriff if it brought the villain to justice. Howe gave the conflict an anachronistic Cold War taste, portraying the battle as one between the forces of Light and Darkness in which defeat would jeopardize the future of the Free World. In a dusty Horn of Africa nation so removed from real geopolitical calculations that, until the famine, few people could have pointed it out on a map—here the UN identified the Devil. Of course these priorities were out of balance, the warped fantasy of people with a skewed sense of mission. UN success in Somalia *was* critical because it would have global implications. But by targeting Aidid—whose name meant, coincidentally, "he who will not be dishonored"—the American-led sheriff's posse set itself up for disaster.

Just as in Vietnam, where cultural incomprehension led to military defeat, here was another dangerous failure to know what made Somalis tick. "Without the remotest knowledge of Somali society or culture, psy-ops attempted to play psychological tricks on Somalis," noted John Drysdale, the Somalia expert who would become the secret liaison between Howe and Aidid during the manhunt. "One thing you would expect from the professionals in psy-ops, and indeed from senior military officers anywhere, would be strict adherence to the old military adage 'know the enemy.' To assume, as psy-ops and the Unosom force command did, that Somalis could be intimidated by powerful-looking hardware and military hi-tech, was a costly error."[4]

The WANTED poster was born of this hapless misconception, which also neglected to account for what gave the warlord his voice and made him powerful. During the hunt, Drysdale—whose rotund belly was kept in check by frequent forays, sometimes on hands and knees, along clandestine rubble-strewn routes to get to Aidid's ever-changing hideouts—told me that "Aidid can't stay in power for one day without grass-roots support. Aidid is not one man, he is Aidid because of his support, his following." In Somali eyes, Aidid never attacked the UN without first being provoked, Drysdale says, which is why his Habr Gedir clan called these UN foreigners "the people with blood on their hands."

Beneath this facile surface of idiotic leaflets, a serious intelligence war was under way. Spies, agents, and double agents were deployed by both sides, playing out a fascinating high-stakes drama of espionage. So for the fugitive, life on the run in Mogadishu's labyrinthine network of alleys and markets was a dangerous game of trying to outwit the American dragnet. He changed his location once or twice a night, never staying too long; he masqueraded as a sheikh, a woman or old man, an Islamic mullah or a hospital patient, disguised in a turban and riding in a taxi or walking—or even as a dead man on a donkey cart. He was available now, or impossible to find; he did business and held meetings to rally support and to plan attacks; he never spoke to groups for more than a few minutes before going underground again.

Aidid communicated with his fighters by low-watt walkie-talkies, evading sophisticated American electronic eavesdropping equipment; he reorganized his intelligence network and weeded out double agents in the pay of the UN or CIA with lethal dispatch; he was relaxed but losing weight; he knew that to secure victory he must be patient and cause enough casualties to force the outside world to revoke this ridiculous arrest order. He was aware that if he lost this battle there would be even more bloodshed because he would be a martyr of his clan. He predicted that if he was killed while holding the patriotic mantle of the Mad Mullah, there would be a holocaust.

To win, the warlord must shed foreign blood and force an American and UN comedy of errors. Both he did, eloquently.

Aidid went on the offensive and popped up on TV like an apparition of Elvis, as predicted by an embarrassed Howe. Two Somali journalists working for NBC News and Voice of America were taken to Aidid's lair circuitously one night, blindfolded and kept down in the back seat of a car. Aidid, whose disguise was replaced for the interview by a striped pressed shirt and tie, told them that he would never surrender. UN commanders had confidently believed that the arrest warrant would "separate Aidid from his people" and that he would fade. But they underestimated the man who spent six years in President Barre's prisons, eating soap to survive—a man who, in fact, admitted to still eating soap to "clean his insides."

On screen, in hiding, Aidid was defiant: "I'm staying with my people to assist them, to live with them, and to share the difficulty they are facing with them," he proclaimed, his face set more than its deep creases required. "I'm not concerned by the search being conducted now. They are trying to arrest me unjustly." Then he disappeared again.

The point man of the UN intelligence network was Lt. Col. Kevin McGovern, a round-faced American deputy—a "good guy" who also happened to be among the most hard-line in the rush to capture Aidid. He made himself quietly available, but I think he preferred the attention he got the few times he spoke at press briefings. McGovern relished the demonization of the warlord, and the subsequent war. "The world has decided the man is a bandit. He is the 'Hitler of Somalia' and will be tried in a Nuremburg-style tribunal," McGovern told me during the manhunt, his deadpan expression sometimes changing to a quirky I-told-you-so smile. His hair was short and graying. To him most of the answers were simple and self-evident. Aidid was guilty of leading a "conspiracy to rule all of Somalia," he said, an accusation that could be applied to every Somali sultan for centuries, and exposed part of the UN's misreading of the essential warlord maxim: He who dies with the most camels wins.

But McGovern had his own problems. "One of the stupidest things was McGovern's driver," recalled a Somali who worked with the UN and was familiar with the network. "He was Habr Gedir-Saad [Aidid's sub-subclan], and he would never give you the correct thing. McGovern didn't understand the clan system. He thought, 'If this one was working for you, he was with you.'"

Yet McGovern was the arbiter of messy intelligence reports, the sifter of various tip-offs and claims from paid Somali spies whom he helped to recruit. It was a thankless task, trying to determine the extent to which every hired informer was torn between "earning" his pay by providing good information and maliciously telling lies for cash. Of course, the margin of error was high, in a city where Somali double agents themselves often spirited along a dangerous track between the hunter and the hunted. "Somalis take great pride in lying," McGovern told me. "They love to be seen as clever and often exaggerate."

This unseen war of spy vs. spy was much more brutal within Aidid's own ranks, as he later described to me in great detail.[5] Hidden from the view of the world, along dark narrow alleys, on dim streets, and in safe houses—always afraid that American helicopters overhead might know something *real*—Aidid's own network of spies strictly controlled information. Only two or three people ever knew of his whereabouts. As soon as the UN issued the arrest order and Aidid went underground, he reorganized his Habr Gedir intelligence network, dividing the city into 18 separate cells to catch informers. "We paralyzed the UN's people immediately by changing our organization. We succeeded in finding 100 of their people, these Somali spies," he claimed. "The Americans were astonished when [the paid Somali agents] didn't come back."

As it became clear that the UN meant to kill their leader, some informers had second thoughts and "came to us and told us everything," Aidid said. "The UN used to say: by day they [Somali spies] work for us, by night they work for Aidid. They were right." Not all who dealt with the foreign enemy were so lucky, and many of those found to be in the pay of the UN were murdered. "They were caught and were killed and mutilated in revenge. Some [UN agents] saw that and denounced themselves, or escaped and ran away, but the people were so angry," Aidid said. "When they saw spies they executed them immediately."

One particularly chilling tale, told by another Somali, described the fate of one young man related to the warlord's family. He was found in a place that Aidid had left just minutes before, directing the helicopter of an American snatch team to the location. An Aidid intelligence cell caught him and took him to his father. The father was merciless, and said: "Please kill him now while I see him, in front of my eyes." The son's captors did so, and mutilated his body.

But not every double agent was caught or even known. Many Somalis had jobs inside the sprawling UN/US embassy compound, and Aidid's spies watched traffic constantly. "They used to pay some Somalis, so we had our intelligence around the gate, and knew the place where they were going—the UN, US Embassy or CIA—so we knew the people," recalled Abdi Hassan Awale "Qaybdiid," the warlord's diminutive interior minister who ran the spy networks.

"Anyone who went there was guilty, and was never allowed to go directly to Aidid," he said.[6] Some Somalis, though, took the money and told lies to the UN and told Aidid's people the truth. Others—loyal to the cash they received, or unhappy with Aidid's world view—told their foreign handlers everything they knew. "They will not tell you exactly what they were doing inside the compound," Qaybdiid said. "Sometimes we couldn't tell whether they were truly working [in a normal job], or an agent or a double agent. In a day you received 10 pieces of information, it may be that one or two was correct."

If Aidid planned to move, or to hold a meeting, guards would often spread false information about the time and place "to change the target," said Hussein Mohamed Abdi "Sanjeeh," one of Aidid's top security people, years later.[7] "There are always some people who work both sides. It was a very big problem for us. We were under surveillance. We really tried to secure our information, to keep everything under control." US commanders say they had Aidid "in our gunsights at least twice," but that "the goal was not to kill Aidid."[8]

As the hunt increased in tempo, the warlord retaliated easily, his clansmen launching hit-and-run grenade and mortar attacks day after day on UN targets at the airport and the embassy compound. Mortar attacks cost him only

$25 each,[9] and more than 250 mortars were fired between June and October 1993.[10]

The hours of darkness were defined by slowly arcing flares as panicky UN troops fidgeted with sweaty palms and strained to catch a glimpse of gunmen scaling the high wall—so bold in the face of coils of razor wire, shards of glass, spotlights, and sentries with fire-at-will orders—before they themselves were caught by a rocket blast. The roar of American helicopters did not stop. This "Elvis" was supposed to disappear forever, so there was no question of restraint, Aidid told me: "The way the UN was acting was so inhumane. They implanted the minds of Somalis with these declarations of human rights and freedoms, then do such actions against humanity. So for us, it was win or die."

This result was obvious at ground zero. "They'd lob mortars at us during the night, and the next day [Aidid's] people working in the compound would inspect the damage and pace off to improve their targeting," said one UN security officer at the time.

Elite US military intelligence units in September made electronic "imprints" and "voice prints" of radio traffic that was used to direct the shelling. Matching these with Somalis working for UN contractors led to the arrest of a dozen Somalis.[11]

"Aidid knew so much," confirmed Wayne Long, another senior UN security chief, who is today responsible for UN security throughout Somalia, "that he would time his bombardment to coincide with the meal schedule at the cafeteria" run by contractors Brown & Root. "He knew the senior leadership all ate there. So every day he mortared at noon, trying to catch everyone," Long recalled. "But it worked. He knew that Howe would walk down there at 12:07 pm, and—Ba-BOOM!—all of a sudden six rounds would come at him. He could have harassed us at night, but he was trying to get the leadership."

Howe's own office was peppered with shrapnel several times, and UN staff died inside the compound from the explosions. Everybody slept with their flak jackets and Kevlar helmets. The admiral was so anxious that he had his hair cut in his bunker and kept a plastic bottle under his bed in which to urinate at night.[12]

No UN troops could patrol the streets. It had become too dangerous, and there was also growing dissent among the 29 contingents of "peacekeepers." The bloodshed hardly made this the relief mission they signed up for. Instead, there were 13,000 UN troops in the capital alone, living on top of each other like packed sardines, hiding behind sandbagged machine gun emplacements, fearing for their lives every time the sun went down. American soldiers, too, forced to celebrate Independence Day behind barbed wire, were disillusioned. "There's a lot of similarities between life for the troops in Somalia and life in a high-security prison," admitted Maj. LeAnn Swieczkowski. "Except that in a prison you eat better, can use a telephone and don't have to worry about getting ambushed."[13]

Someone leaked a restricted UN security brief to me that put the lie to Howe's assertions that "we are closer than ever" to capturing the warlord. Already by 9 July 1993, the situation in the city "remains red" with "potential for terrorist activity," according to the report. "The general population in Mogadishu is slowly losing confidence in the ability of UN forces to protect them. Enemy forces move freely within the city. . . . Aidid has started a guerrilla war using hit and run tactics against UN forces. Harassment attacks against key Unosom facilities will continue," the report warns. "Enemy morale is high."

The Somalis *were* effective, and nothing grated on the sheriff of Mogadishu, Admiral Howe, more than to watch his peace-enforcement mission break down in defeat.

From his 34 years in the Navy, finally commanding a Polaris submarine, and as deputy to President George Bush for national security affairs, the four-star Navy Admiral Howe was aware that Delta Force, the Army's Special Operations anti-terrorism unit, could be the ideal tool to end the manhunt. This supersecret unit—officially, there is no such thing—specialized in rescuing hostages and in clandestine missions deep behind enemy lines. The snatch was an in-house favorite. US special envoy Robert Gosende had first suggested arresting Aidid in May 1993 for violating previously signed peace accords. A CIA assessment shorty afterward deemed Aidid "a threat to peace."[14]

Howe was convinced that eliminating Aidid would eliminate that threat. Using personal connections in Washington, Howe made what one aide to Defense Secretary Les Aspin called "frenetic and obsessive"[15] lobbying for Delta Force at the Pentagon even before publicizing the arrest order for Aidid. On 9 June 1993, Aspin received a request for a team of 50 Delta Force commandos to get the warlord. The request never could have been made by a non-American UN envoy, if there had been one, and almost certainly not by an American civilian in the post. Generals Montgomery and Bir backed the request. But "[Aspin] rejected the idea, thinking that even if Aidid could be found—which the military rated a one-in-four chance—an already skeptical public would consider this a dangerous escalation."[16]

"We just have to remember who painted us into this corner," a US military official in Mogadishu complained about Howe. "This notion of putting out a little cowboy poster with a reward was ridiculous. This was a gross judgment error, a political blunder, and now [Howe] wants the US to solve it for him."[17]

Despite Washington's rejection, the Clinton administration had the temerity to ask the British to send a unit of Special Air Service (SAS) commandos, whose institutional experience of urban guerrilla warfare in northern Ireland was far superior to anything the Americans could muster. Fully recognizing that it would be "Mission Impossible" to find one balding Somali in the maze of Mogadishu—and with a keen historical appreciation of how hostile this territory could become—the SAS refused.[18]

So Howe had to pursue his prey with the assets he already had: the 1,300-strong US Army QRF, which was under sole US command, and for emergencies; and a dodgy intelligence network largely infiltrated by the enemy. Rumors of a high-level informer, in Aidid's circle and cultivated by the CIA, however, began to circulate as early as late April 1993.

In a note tacked on to the Sahafi Hotel notice board, the US Embassy made a vague warning that Americans might be subject to kidnap or assassination attempts. Even before the hunt for Aidid had begun, this "asset" reported that the warlord had uttered a very specific threat to kill a "top American," envoy Gosende told two of my colleagues in May. It wasn't clear if that "top" American meant Howe or Gosende or someone else, but there were so few people in the room with Aidid at the time of the threat, Gosende said, that reporting the details would compromise the informant.[19]

Somalis close to Aidid at the time say today that the warlord never made such a threat—but that they know of at least two relatively important spies who were working for US intelligence. Both men were cousins of Aidid's financier, Osman Ato, who himself had constant contact with official Americans at least until the manhunt. Ato was widely believed to have CIA contacts and was the Somalia representative for the US oil corporation Conoco.

One of the spies was Mohamed Osman "Coon" [pronounced Ah'-oon], a former captain in President Barre's notorious National Security Service (NSS), Somali sources say, whom the Americans knew from that period.

Somalis today say that he was in one of the American helicopters, giving directions during an important US air attack on 12 July 1993 that targeted an Aidid clan meeting and left more than 50 dead and has since been called Bloody Monday. Much later, he bragged to one Somali that he had flown in a US helicopter on that day and had pointed out the target house.

The other spy was Omar Hassan Ganay, a "very dangerous man," Somali sources say, who once worked as a colonel in the NSS. When US forces arrived in Somalia, he was made an "employee" and worked as a liaison officer. During the manhunt, he left the embassy compound each day between 9 and 10 am in a white Toyota Cressida.

"We suspected him, and he never hid his contact with the Americans," recalled Mohamed Hassan Awale, an Aidid aide and spokesman. "But he was not a big fish in the Aidid camp, so no one paid attention to him. He was a bystander. He was harmless.[20]

If Ganay had fooled anybody, his cover was blown during the 12 July attack. He was in the target house at the time, as the clan elders discussed making peace with the UN. Ganay survived—as did Qaybdiid, the interior minister who was a prime target in the attack because he was using his military background to keep Aidid well hidden. The target has since been known as the "Qaybdiid House." When US ground troops swept through the building, choosing a few survivors for interrogation and finishing off others with their pistols, Ganay shouted for mercy.

"We knew he had direct contact with the [US] embassy and the CIA, but we didn't know how far he worked with them," Qaybdiid recalled. "As the [American troops] captured the place, this boy Omar called, 'I am the agent, I am the agent! Don't kill me!' when he was among the bodies."

Shock registered inside the UN fortress, too, after he was brought to the US combat hospital for treatment of severe wounds. Don Teitelbaum, a State Department official working for Unosom, visited them and was shocked to recognize his wounded asset: "You've got to let this guy go," he demanded. "He's one of ours." He was also the "high-level" informant who reported the Aidid threat to Americans in April.[21]

"There was a constant disconnect between the civilian spooks and the military," said Keith Richburg of *The Washington Post*, who kept close contact with American sources inside Mogadishu.

To this day, the two spies, Coon and Ganay, still stay in Somalia—among their clansmen—and only a handful of people know their secret. "They will be remembered for this in history, and will be judged," said Aidid adviser Jumaale. "We know who they are, but we're waiting." But why are they tolerated now? As one proverb goes: "The woman in labor, by the time of the birth, forgets the pain."

Later on during the manhunt, elite American forces would come to rely upon a top-level source they called "Lincoln." Coon or Ganay may have been Lincoln, but because these two were so close to Osman Ato—and because Ato himself was believed by many to be plotting against Aidid to claim the presidency—some Somalis argue that Ato himself was Lincoln. They argue that Ato was using his two cousins as a "bridge" to the Americans. What better way to assume power than to have your rival kidnapped by the enemy?

Clues from Rangers who were briefed on Lincoln are tantalizing. Specialist Jason Moore told *Frontline* that the informant "was nicknamed Abe Lincoln because he was supposed to resemble Abraham Lincoln. He was supposedly one informant on Aidid's team and was gonna tell us when he was at a meeting, what time he got there, and set up a strobe light on the roof to alert us, and then we could go in and take down the building."[22] Ato does vaguely fit the Lincoln description. More telling is this clue: "From what I understand he was [a] financier, he dealt with finances," Moore said. No other Somali I have met, in the context of Aidid, could be considered a financier. But other things don't add up at all: Ato was himself captured in a Delta raid on 21 September, for example, and held for months. And Moore, speaking to *Frontline,* said that despite Lincoln's rank, "he wasn't one of our targets."

Distrust between the Ato and Aidid had been brewing, and one high-level Somali told me that Ato had cut off funds to Aidid at the start of the US deployment—possibly on orders from his bosses at Conoco. US envoy Oakley had been based at the Conoco compound during much of the Unitaf mission, and so was never more than a handshake away from Ato. He used Ato's cars and security.

"Osman Ato was the permanent guy [the Americans] used to work with all the time. They used to meet with him constantly," recalled Aidid security chief Sanjeeh. "He was the person they relied on to give them information about Aidid. He was undermining Aidid with the Americans." The warlord was aware of this, and so he kept Ato at arm's length. Within a year, the two would split up altogether.

CIA agent Gene Cullen has said that one of the agency's problems in Somalia was that all its information first had to be sent to headquarters in Langley, Virginia, where the CIA chiefs would decide what could be passed on elsewhere.[23] This would mean that CIA tip-offs did not necessarily help US forces on the ground—and led some to believe that the CIA did, in fact, have a very high-level source such as Ato. "Many times they got good and correct information, but they didn't do an operation because they kept the info too long," said a Somali involved in the intelligence effort. "This I learned: those mighty Americans have a stupid weak point. They can't coordinate between themselves."

It was Aidid who unwittingly prompted the eventual US Delta Force deployment. On 8 August, four American soldiers were killed when their Humvee was destroyed by a remote-triggered mine. Playing on the threat posed to the entire UN "relief" operation, Howe adjusted his Pentagon request. He now wanted 400 Rangers to "boost" US capabilities in Somalia. Already Howe's obsession led one Aspin aide to note that Howe had "adopted Aidid as his Great White Whale."[24] His nickname in Washington was "Jonathan Ahab."[25]

This time "Task Force Ranger" was approved, and secretly included the full Delta Force squadron 'C' of 130 commandos. They had been training for just such a manhunt since June, and now their mission was called "Operation Gothic Serpent."

The admiral's naval career, coupled with the fact that he was an American, enabled US forces to escalate the war in Somalia far beyond the UN's imagining. But this "boost" also ran the risk of high-profile mistakes. In April 1980, for example, Delta Force had been deployed secretly to Iran—"Operation Desert One"—to free 52 American hostages held by Islamic revolutionaries. Two helicopters crashed into each other at night in the desert, causing US fatalities. That mission was an embarassment for Delta and President Jimmy Carter—one that Delta had since worked to overcome during covert operations in Grenada and Panama and during the 1991 Persian Gulf War.

But success of the Mogadishu hit team would require two things as rare in Somalia as gold dust: brilliant intelligence and good luck. It would have neither and would therefore misstep again and again.

"Once more a president [Clinton] frustrated by diplomacy resorted to the quick-and-dirty solution offered by the CIA and the Mission Impossible men of Delta Force," wrote Patrick Sloyan in *The Washington Post*. "And, once again, it produced a grisly fiasco."[26]

It was the Pentagon's initial refusal to send Delta in June that sparked CIA intervention, according to Sloyan's account. Marine General Joseph Hoar, the chief of the Somalia mission at Central Command in Tampa, Florida, noted that the withdrawal of most US forces downgraded the intelligence capability needed by Delta Force to locate Aidid. "Then it was decided to send in the CIA," an official said. "'But the CIA said there was no point going into Mogadishu unless that snatch team was there,' said one participant."[27]

By late June the CIA team was on its way. Alongside the UN intelligence system, the CIA had created its own network of 20 "principal" Somali agents, and kept a wide stable of lesser informants.[28] Soon the agency was confident that its intelligence was good enough to make chase for Aidid and to bring Delta.

The UN arrest order did not specify what was to be done if the warlord *was* captured. But that issue was apparently easily resolved: "'Using a ship for an offshore trial was a solution to the legal problems,' said one task force participant. 'The CIA would provide the judges.'"[29] Howe eased the fears of UN chief Boutros-Ghali by ensuring him that Delta Force would succeed within days.

In Washington, the Delta role was kept secret, and the Rangers that deployed on 26 August were portrayed as a conventional force with a conventional mission. "This is not an effort to go after one man," the Pentagon told skeptical reporters. "It's an effort to improve the overall situation in Mogadishu."[30] The Delta Force commander, cigar-chewing Maj. Gen. William F. Garrison, even arrived in Somalia disguised as a lieutenant colonel.[31] His presence was a secret, and journalists were led to believe that Task Force Ranger fell under Montgomery's command.[32]

Despite all those official fibs, Garrison knew better than anybody his real orders. His "commander's intent" upon arrival in Mogadishu was spelled out in his after-action report: "The success of this mission is defined as the capture of General Aideed and/or designated personnel," read the report, which I received through a Freedom of Information Act request.[33]

But the public portions of this document do not tell the whole story. Large chunks of the report are blacked out and still classified—sometimes page after page of Xerox was blackened with a sea of ink—but the main "key to success" was left intact, in black and white. That key was "timely, accurate and reliable intelligence."

The first indication that Delta Force had in fact arrived in Mogadishu came at 3 am on 30 August 1993, and could not have been more spectacular—or public. Not far from the Hotel Sahafi, in full view of the curious journalists perched on the roof, and duly videotaped with night-vision television cameras, commandos swathed in black snaked down ropes from helicopters and then burst, firing from the hip through closed doors, into the offices of the UN Development Program. A UN flag was spread across the roof. But five Somali guards and three foreign staff of the program, including a "ranking Egyptian lady in her pink negligee who was pushed to the floor and made to lie on shards of glass,"[34] were mistakenly hog-tied and bundled off. The neighboring compound of the French relief agency Action International Contre le Faim (AICF) was also a target. Walls were broken down with grenades, doors kicked in, and radio equipment destroyed before the special forces recognized their blunder.

The aim of the mission was to nail Aidid—code-named "Yogi the Bear" by Delta[35]—but he was nowhere around.

Damage control began immediately, with fervent rounds of doublespeak from mortified American and UN officials who tried to dispel the Keystone Kops image. As if US forces had nothing to do with the bungled raid, the White House claimed that such search and seizure missions were "UN operations." UN military spokesmen insisted the raid was *not* an attempt to capture Aidid and that journalists would "be in error" if we described every similar operation to come as a snatch attempt. UN spokesman Major Dave Stockwell called it a "textbook example of how these operations should go." Pointing out that the myriad screw-ups resembled scenes worthy of Inspector Clouseau, *Time* magazine noted that "Stockwell must be a big Pink Panther fan."[36]

Colin Powell, chairman of the Joint Chiefs of Staff, said later that he was so angry that "I had to screw myself off the ceiling."[37] But Howe took it in his stride: "The people may have been scared, but nobody was hurt, only frightened. One of them actually told me how professional it was," he said. UN chief Boutros-Ghali was even more sanguine, but inadvertently made a point usually reserved for the growing number of his critics. Pressed to explain the American "cock-up," he replied: "What cock-up? Every day we have operations of this type."[38]

The commandos swooped on the compounds because they had been given wrong information by a Somali agent who had promised that this was one of the warlord's "deep cover" hideouts. Both compounds had been under surveillance for 10 days prior to the raid. "Suspicious" activity included the mysterious fact that barrels of fuel were used up—no doubt by the UN vehicles—and then regularly replaced. Bundles of the habitually chewed narcotic qat were also found.

Another reason for the UNDP raid was a Somali mortar that wounded five Task Force members on 29 August. Garrison "vowed to 'kick somebody's ass.'" He called the UN intelligence cell, asking for "your number one target where Aidid has been reported from time to time"—and got the UNDP house.[39]

A second incident, on 2 September 1993, was another setup, though officially it was not considered a raid. Troops apparently encircled the World Concern compound but, seeing the agency sign, literally knocked on the door first, then asked permission to search the premises. Pink Panther fan Stockwell meekly noted the contrast: "There were no shots fired, no grenades exploded, no doors kicked in, no locks broken." Still, after an incident at Médecins Sans Frontières, aid staff insisted on taking "Task Force Ranger" commanders on an extensive tour to point out all relief offices.[40]

All the while, Aidid's guerrilla attacks were increasing, and so Task Force Ranger persevered. Within days another raid, this time on the house of the former chief of police on 7 September 1993, yielded another embarrassing catch. "The purpose of this raid was to capture Aideed," Garrison wrote in his after-action report; most all other details have been blacked out.[41] Chief Ahmed Jamma Musa was detained for days before a civilian intelligence official recognized him as a UN candidate to head the new police force.

Adding insult to injury, two days after his release, he was wounded during a "routine" weapons search.

"Why did they raid your house?" I asked, when I saw him in the hospital.

"I share my house with a retired police colonel, his name is Aidid Farah," Ahmed Jamma said pithily. "Maybe they read the phone book and believed that Aidid [the warlord] was living there."

On 14 September, yet another comic scene was unfolding. In northern Mogadishu, enclave of Aidid's blood rival, Ali Mahdi—and therefore the least likely place the warlord could be hiding—US Rangers swore they saw Aidid depart the Italian Embassy in a gray Toyota Landcruiser. Exactly 63 minutes later, after the eyewitnesses verified their sighting against a series of Aidid pictures,[42] Delta and the Rangers swooped on a house, cascading from their helicopters onto unsuspecting Somali elders inside. They seized the head of the UN's police committee, Ahmed Jilao, who sported a balding gray pate not unlike Aidid's. He had been chief of Siad Barre's NSS, was once mayor of the capital, and according to one report was in fact an "American asset."[43] When Jilao was accosted, the Rangers demanded: "Are you Aidid? Are you Aidid?" When he answered "No," a witness told me that day, laughing, they hit his head with the butt of a rifle. He quickly revised his answer: "Yes! Yes!"

Jilao and 38 other members of the Abgal clan, including a senior aide of self-styled president Ali Mahdi, who staunchly supported the UN operation, were whisked away in helicopters for questioning. An MSF relief worker photographing the operation from an adjacent building was told to stop taking pictures, and the Americans finally assaulted him with a percussion grenade to make their point. Shortly it became clear who the detainees were, and next day a chastened delegation of American officials visited Ali Mahdi to apologize. They promised to pay the victims for damages. Looters, in the meantime, had moved into their vacant houses, so claims were made for thousands of dollars.

In a cable to Washington, US envoy Gosende wrote, "It would be hard to confuse [Jilao] with Aidid. Jilao is approximately ten inches taller than Aidid. Aidid is very dark. Jilao has a much lighter complexion. Aidid is slim and has sharp, Semitic-like features. Jilao is overweight and round-faced. . . . We are very concerned that this episode might find its way into the press."[44]

"Not catching Aidid is becoming routine," admitted one despairing official, who confirmed that the raid was "just another screw-up." Stockwell was not so forthright, and tried to explain that the target house was in an "overlap area" between rival clans. "I can confirm there was an operation," he said with a stern face, "but the results are classified." No wonder.

When a British SAS officer secretly visited Somalia a second time, his wry assessment hadn't changed since the SAS first refused the American request to send a British hit squad: "Rather you than us."[45] He found the US team disillusioned with their lack of intelligence and "totally inappropriate mission."

For Somalis, the American missteps added to the empirical pleasure of the game. "Their intelligence was completely off. We were laughing, really, at what they did, because those attacks really showed how weak the Americans were, how lacking in good information. They did not know what they were doing," explained one Somali friend.

One reason the intelligence was so poisonous was because, within days of the Delta arrival, the top Somali CIA informant was dead. The plan had been that this source would present Aidid with an "elegant hand-carved cane" embedded with a homing beacon.[46] But the man—who reportedly ran the entire network of Somali spies—killed himself playing Russian roulette. Lt. Col. Dave McKnight, Garrison's chief of staff, "burst into Garrison's headquarters at the Mogadishu airport and exclaimed, 'Main source shot in the head. He's not dead yet, but we're fucked.'" Garrison responded to this bad news by recalling the opening lines of Ulysses S. Grant's autobiography: 'Man proposes and God disposes.'"[47]

So dodgy Somali informants kept the task force on tenterhooks. As pressure for results grew, there was little good news. Weeks into the operation, the fugitive remained as elusive as ever.

"The intelligence environment was excruciating," recalled Wayne Long,[48] the senior UN security officer at the time and a Delta Force alumnus. "The fact was that we weren't very good, we knew that," he recalled. McKnight told Long that their intelligence was good about 30% to 40% of the time—which meant that two thirds of the actions would strike out. Most of that information came from "walk-ins" and not paid agents.

Intelligence was collated in the "war room" at the Delta base. The plan, according to Ranger Jason Moore, was that "Lincoln" would put an infrared strobe on top of a building to mark Aidid's position. "I know that he was supposed to sprinkle himself with juice out of an infrared chem light, because we all go in with night-vision devices, he would glow, and hopefully not be shot," Moore told Frontline.[49] "He was extremely scared about that; we were told, four or five times, that he was real apprehensive and that to make sure that if anybody was glowing in the room when you came in, not to shoot him."

Despite such a source, cynicism grew. "As far as I know Lincoln didn't give us very good information," Moore said. "Everybody was really excited. . . . And after, I don't know, three or four more missions, and still every single time a dry hole . . . we did not trust his information at all."

McGovern, the UN intelligence master, nevertheless told journalists that he always knew where to find Aidid. "They thought their intelligence was better than it was," recalled the Post's Keith Richburg. Conscious that a successful Army career left no room for mistakes, he said, "there was this macho mindset. McGovern couldn't go into a meeting with [head of operations, Col. Ed] Ward and Montgomery and say 'I don't know,' so there was a tendency to talk it up."

For Aidid, the high-profile mistakes set his mind at ease. "Of course, it was clear that if they did not have the intelligence to distinguish me from another, then I had little to worry about," the warlord told me later. At the time, he couldn't have known how correct he was: during one two-week period, Delta Force "nearly became convinced" that the warlord was working in their own airfield mess hall.[50] But the warlord also found time, while on the run, to edit a biography of himself called *The Lion of Somalia*.

Aidid did have some close calls. One came on a night when a helicopter hovered above the next house, very low, for 20 minutes. Somali spies had been given tiny electronic "locator" bugs to direct the Rangers to certain locations using a finding device. Aidid told me that a few of these had been found on some captured Somalis, and one in a room where he was about to hold a meeting. That night the helicopter hovered so closely, Aidid recalled, that his gunmen loaded a rocket-propelled grenade and asked if they could fire upon it. "No, no, if we shoot they will have a clue where we are," he told them. "There is only one, so I will go to sleep. Come for me if there are more." The root of his fearlessness lay in the knowledge that his gunmen on familiar terrain would put up a strong defense.

For American helicopter pilots, that point was well taken. One frustrated pilot noted that the chances of success were small: "You want to know how difficult it is? Let me tell you, from the air all those streets look the same. You can tell the main roads, but that's about it. I mean, look how long it took us to find (Panamanian strongman) Manuel Noriega—and we put the phone system into that place."[51] That 1989 mission took four days in a 20-square-mile city, took 24,000 US troops, and resulted in 500 dead Panamanians and 12 dead Americans.

Among the most forceful hawks calling for the elimination of Aidid was US ambassador Robert Gosende, who had helped point the State Department down this path. On 6 September 1993, he had written a cable called "Taking the Offensive" that called for thousands more troops. "Any plan for negotiating a 'truce' with General Aidid should be shelved," it read. "We should not deal with perpetrators of terrorist acts."[52] But this memo sparked a tough response from General Hoar, head of Central Command, who wrote a classified memo complaining that the UN wanted "facile solutions like, get Aidid and all will be well." If more troops were needed, he said, "then it is time to reassess. . . . Control of Mogadishu has been lost."[53]

In his office on the UN compound, Gosende told me of the not-so-subtle US escalation of the manhunt: "The best effort that anybody could make is being made. There is a feeling this looks too American, but either that or it will fail. These are the choices. Who else will take the leadership? No one is willing to commit violence."

Exacerbating the problem was that most national UN contingents, which all had their own intelligence setups, were loath to share. The Americans were the worst offenders, jealously guarding information gleaned from technology, and even delaying information to each other. They could well have benefited from linking with the Pakistanis, Italians, and others who had more "on-the-street" experience and often a much better understanding of the Somalis. But that again was a two-edged sword: the Italians, whose historical ties to Somalia resulted in an arrogant we-know-best-and-always-will attitude, reportedly helped Aidid avoid capture. The UN removed Italian Gen. Bruno Loi from his command in July because an "unhealthy" distrust and suspicion had developed.[54]

Hope of a peaceful solution first emerged on 12 September, when former US President Jimmy Carter spent a night at the White House on the eve of the signing of the Israeli-Palestinian Oslo peace accords. Talking long into the night, Carter told Clinton that Aidid had written to him to proclaim his innocence. Without Aidid, Carter said, no political settlement was possible. "After Carter's visit, the hard line toward Aidid began to weaken," a Clinton adviser said.[55]

In Mogadishu, too, Gosende was having a change of heart. He wrote another cable on 17 September called "The Making of a Deal; Getting Off Dead Center," in which he called for a new approach. The hunt should be called off with a unilateral cease-fire; African leaders should negotiate with Aidid; exile for the warlord should be explored. Gosende sent it marked NIACT—one of the most urgent priorities—to the State Department, the National Security Council, the US mission to the UN, and the military's Central Command.[56]

The envoy was confident that it would reverse US policy. Mogadishu diplomats even drafted a press release to explain the turnaround. But there was no response from Washington.

Military operations centers instead remained plastered with mug shots of Somalia's worst culprits, the men whose existence was alleged to keep their country embroiled in violence by sheer power of presence. Near the top of that lineup was Osman Ato, Aidid's past financier and former "untouchable," who some Somalis believe was Delta's top-secret Lincoln. The *Post's* Keith Richburg was interviewing him in his living room one night during the manhunt when Ato flipped on the CNN television news.

> The big news that day, the announcer said, was a raid on a hideout of suspected top members of the Aidid militia. The film footage, being beamed live, showed helicopters in the air encircling a villa while a reporter breathlessly told of a major American military operation under way. Ato looked at first serious, then mildly amused. "Wonder where that could be?" he said with a wink as we watched another futile operation, brought live into the SNA living room.[57]

Keith interviewed Ato later a few yards from a Pakistani checkpoint, where troops frisked kids for guns and searched passing donkey carts for hidden weapons. Disguised only in a turban and dark glasses, Ato seemed unconcerned by the manhunt, but sure of the violence that would befall the UN if Aidid were eliminated.

"If the Americans go today and kill Aidid, then Americans will be held responsible for his death," Ato said. If the UN thought that the warlord's clan support was splintering, "they are dreaming. He is far stronger now than when they started bombing the area." Looking up while a US reconnaisance plane passed by overhead, he defined the American predicament: "We can fight like the Viet Cong," he said. "How can that airplane stay in the air without fuel and without money? But I can stay here forever."[58]

As the conflict raged, with casualties increasing daily and the streets of southern Mogadishu cut off by burning barricades, another conflict gathered steam in the UN compound: this one against the press. First under a camouflage net strung up between poles outside, then later standing in front of an expansive UN flag in a sturdier press center, Major Dave Stockwell, the Pink Panther fan, sought daily to reinforce "the line" sent down by his superiors: the *United Nations* mission was making progress, with no problems, thank you; and none of these "routine" search and seizure missions were meant to nab Aidid. Delta Force didn't exist. Even when things went very glaringly wrong for Unosom, Stockwell was thrust before us like a reluctant fall guy. Crew-cut, blond, and smiling but strong-willed, he would have rather rejoined his Ranger unit than try to please an angry, disbelieving press that already *knew* the secret: hard-liners were screwing up Unosom II by clinging to their Mission Impossible, then trying to cover up their failure with a thick layer of bullshit.

One instance, on 9 September 1993, was as instructive as it was shocking. American and Pakistani engineers clearing Somali barricades from a road were ambushed by militiamen with grenades and anti-tank weapons. Crowds of women and children came to watch and took part in the attack. But US Cobra helicopters opened fire on the Somalis with their TOW missiles and devastating 20mm cannons, leaving the road strewn with some 100 mangled bodies, men, women, and children. Howe blamed Aidid for the attack, saying he had a "callous disregard for human life." Aidid in turn, accused Howe and the Americans of trying to "annihilate the Somali people" with this "massacre."

But Central Command's General Hoar was also in Mogadishu that day, and he was appalled. When Stockwell briefed us that night, he repeatedly changed his story according to how well senior officers thought it played on

CNN. Speaking to journalists at the Sahafi Hotel—by radio, because it was too dangerous for us to venture out—Stockwell first said that, in the course of the clashes, it was "regrettable" that women and children were killed. That apparently didn't play well enough for senior officers on the next CNN broadcast, so he was ordered to "correct" himself.

Stockwell contacted us a second time, with a different take on events. Now it was no longer regrettable that women and children had been killed, because they had swarmed the UN vehicles and therefore were considered "combatants." That story didn't sit well with the top brass either, because Stockwell radioed us again to spin yet a new, third version of the facts. We were incredulous. In this rendition, no one was swarming the armored vehicles, but the American pilots were suddenly absolved from blasting the crowds: "All those women and children who were combatants were actively engaged in assaulting us from behind walls, throwing hand grenades and shooting at our soldiers," Stockwell asserted. All those people were targeted, he claimed, because "in an ambush, there are no sidelines or spectator seats."

The feeling of good intentions gone wrong was palpable as elite units weighed the demoralizing effect of defeat at the hands of irregular Somali gunmen—kids, many of them—wearing plastic thongs. Somali tactics were simple and often *ad hoc,* and time and again Aidid's Habr Gedir warriors exploited weaknesses among the UN forces. First the Pakistanis were slain in June, then Moroccans, Italians, and Nigerians were killed with grenades, bullets, and knives.

It was as though the warlord was testing the resolve of each nation in turn. Now Americans were the top priority, though the front line embraced the entire UN clan. Women and children deployed with stones and Molotov cocktails—not forced to join the battlelines, but willing participants, taking casualties as fearlessly as any gunman. Their deaths caused deep surprise in the outside world where women and children are almost always victims. The UN couldn't explain this heartless reality to critics without casting doubt upon their own humanity.

So the daily press briefings began to take the flavor of Vietnam-era media sessions, which back then had been dubbed "Lies at Five." Still, spokesman Stockwell was helpful when he could be, and provided useful post-briefing sessions. He knew that we knew that he had been ordered to fabricate the truth as necessary—to revise recent history—so that Unosom II, or at least the American role, was bathed in the warmest possible glow. Behind the press center, "Brother Dave" joked that he pontificated, imaginary stave of wisdom in hand, to give us a "better" impression of reality. He sent us back to the streets with a daily warning: "Be safe out there!"

He was not a Pink Panther fan, and took the barb with a laugh. But what he didn't take gracefully were violations of the ever-changing "press rules" promulgated when Delta Force secretly holed up at the airport base. On this, he was very quick to anger. Any US soldier could now confiscate film or videotape. One photographer's film had been taken by soldiers at the airport, and the next day he was arrested for photographing Americans firing mortars *into* Mogadishu from positions within the UN compound. These were not images commanders wanted beamed around the world—they hardly fell under the category of "God's work"—so they were confiscated. Brother Dave signed the receipt for the film.

One of the most brazen attacks on the press was exactly that on 18 September. AP photographer Peter Northall was photographing Blackhawk helicopters hovering low over a market area—a favorite practice of US pilots—to clear it of people and blow apart the wood and tin market stalls with the downdraft. Though enjoyed by the pilots, this "rotor washing" was not calculated to win hearts and minds. Peter was targeted with six percussion stun grenades at a range of 30 yards, even after he held up his cameras to signal his business. One burst shattered the windshield of his car, lacerating his guards with glass. The press were to keep out, thank you. Stockwell was merciless, claiming that the photographer had posed "a threat to himself" and that the pilots "acted properly to clear the area."

Even Madeleine Albright weighed in against the press when she visited for a few hours on 3 July 1993. She lectured and scolded journalists for not telling the "real story" in Somalia. She had visited Kismayo, "touring" the market there in an armored vehicle surrounded by Belgian troops and speaking to hand-picked Somalis in the safety of the UN hangar. Still, she exhorted journalists to "do what I did" by venturing onto the streets and talking to "real Somalis."[59]

Deep in Aidid's fiefdom, Somali journalists who tried to remain neutral also had to contend with dictatorial methods. In August, Aidid's clandestine mobile radio station accused Somali newspapers—usually just a few mimeographed sheets stapled together and sold daily—of taking sides with the UN. Shortly thereafter reporters received written death threats. To move around Mogadishu safely even *they* hired armed guards. One 19-year-old was caught trying to assassinate Mohamed Aden Guled, editor of *Xog-Oogaal* newspaper, on the orders of a ranking official of Aidid's militia. He had agreed to kill the editor for a payment of 6 million shillings ($1,500).[60]

When the Delta Force did get it right on 21 September 1993—capturing Osman Ato on their second attempt—the victory was used against the media. Ato was held incommunicado until January, on Camia island off the southern Somali coast, and never charged with a crime.

(Somalis who believe that Ato was the top intelligence source Lincoln say that Ato was "no longer useful" and that his arrest was a setup. True or not, many believe that Ato was held in relatively good conditions, and actually gained weight during captivity. Ato himself speaks convincingly about the rigors of detention and a hunger strike he began. But among interrogations of all top-level detainees carried out by McGovern, the summary for Ato—which I have seen—was positively glowing, while the other Somalis were dismissed as "nasty" and uncooperative. Somalis make special note of a rally held in Mogadishu two days after the detainees were released on 20 January 1994, when he spoke publicly like a changed man: he declared his support for US and UN aims and called for reconciliation.)

Renewing their offensive against the press, the Americans used a letter found in Ato's pocket to illustrate how the media were biased in favor of the Somalis. Sam Kiley of *The Times* wrote the letter by hand, a request for an interview with the fugitive Aidid that got straight to the point: the warlord had already taken the military initiative; would he now welcome the "opportunity to take the political initiative" by meeting secretly the four journalists named below? Sam signed it, Mark Huband of *The Guardian* signed it, along with Paul Watson of *The Toronto Star*—another Mogadishu regular. Though I was not there, Sam kindly affixed my signature.

News of the letter broke first at the UN in New York, where correspondents for our respective newspapers were leaked copies, just before the State Department made its pitch that the press was out to sabotage the mission. Editors of other news organizations picked up the story but swallowed the faulty "evidence of media wrongdoing" spin. I have yet to meet a journalist who would not have signed it, given the opportunity to enter the warlord's secret lair, which even Delta Force had proved incapable of penetrating. US Embassy spokesman Daniel Yett took the remarkable step of informing Mark, a British citizen, that for his treachery he would "not be able to enter any US government building now or in the future." Here was "the law," laid down in a place where it couldn't exist, by those least able to enforce it. I was spared such wasted humiliation, Stockwell said, because he knew that I hadn't actually signed it and "put in a good word for me." But I was as eager to hear Aidid's tale as anyone.

This misinformation campaign helped spread the blame for Aidid's military successes against the Americans, but the failure was much more simply explained. None of the warlord-pretenders of Unosom II understood anything about Somalis. And none of us could have seen that such a feeling of impotence and frustration would have such dangerous consequences—both for Somalia, where the Mogadishu Line had already been crossed, and the goodwill underpinning the New World Order.

Admiral Howe, who approved the WANTED poster and begged for Delta

Force, may have least understood his Somali target. "Our problems are over!" he announced triumphantly to one dumbfounded UN official, as details of yet another fruitless raid came in. "I've got more money—we can make the reward for Aidid $100,000!"

SEVEN

BLOODY MONDAY

*Like it or not, most of you will find yourselves
in a place you never heard of, doing things you
never wanted to do.*

—General John Shalikashvili, chairman,
Joint Chiefs of Staff, to US soldiers
on post–Cold War duties

Through a haze, steeped in memories that roil with anger, I see
the images of 12 July 1993, when both outrage and the need to
forgive battled to control my emotions, when friends died brutally at the hands of Somalis, and when many more Somalis
died murderously at the hands of American forces. These
impressions surround one moment—17 critical minutes, precisely—that would prove to be the turning point in Somalia. It
was a case in which bloodshed compounded bloodshed, a monumental example of vengeful rage exacted without accountability. This moment inflicted murder in the service, unbelievably,
of a sad oxymoron: peace enforcement.

For the Somalis, this act meant war. There was no more middle ground upon which to make peace. The American-led UN
mission was proved to be irredeemable. Peaceniks thereafter
took up the gun. Somalis have come to call this catastrophic
moment Bloody Monday.

But no lessons are likely to be learned, because those responsible for launching the attack—for causing this massacre—
insisted that there was no reason for remorse. They believed
that their attack was *just*.

THEIR SHOES

That July morning in Mogadishu, the shoes of convening elders piled up at the offices of Abdi Hassan Awale "Qaybdiid," the warlord's interior minister. In the second-floor entrance hall, before the carpeted conference room, the dust- and mud-covered shoes were of all types, like the elders themselves, who had gathered in one place to discuss the war between the UN and Aidid's Habr Gedir clan. They were looking for a way to make peace: to somehow end the ruinous blood feud raging between their adamantine warlord and the UN "peacekeepers." Aidid did not approve of this meeting, because his role as clan leader was being questioned. Just the day before, a handful of elders had met UN envoy Howe, who had asked them to look for a peaceful way out. This meeting was the result. These elders may have decided to make a separate appeal to the UN, effectively isolating the warlord. The meeting was publicized in the Somali newspapers as a peace gathering, so it was not a secret—at least not to Somalis.

"That day was a day when a peace agreement could have been achieved," says Hussein Sanjeeh, an Aidid security chief and a survivor of the attack, who had been distributing papers that spelled out Aidid's position. "Among the UN and US and Somalia, we had agreed to resolve everything in a peaceful way."[1]

Defined by centuries of hard parched existence, in which the human presence was ever but the smallest point of life struggling in the midst of an inhospitable threatening desert, the Somali world order is delineated by a series of concentric rings, designed to ensure survival. One is safest when closest to the center, and as one moves further and further from this center—toward an outside world full of of unknowable risks and threats—the less these powers can protect, the less security they can provide. On Bloody Monday, the clan at the Qaybdiid house felt secure, safely encased in its perceived shells of protection, basking in the sweet scent that traditionally permeates such meeting places.

"Everybody was interested in stopping the fighting, to open a dialogue. It was in the interest of all," recalled Qaybdiid, who was one of the main targets but survived.[2] In June, it was Qaybdiid who had received the UN notice of an inspection of Radio Mogadishu. It was he who declared that the letter amounted to a declaration of war, and sure enough, days later, 24 Pakistanis were dead. But now, a month later, the conflict between the warlord and the UN had grown beyond the intentions of either side. It was time to find a solution, to end the mutual killing.

Aidid had been warned by his intelligence that a spy working for the UN had infiltrated the group, he told me later. Some say that the Italians tipped Aidid off. Though unhappy that the meeting was taking place, Aidid tried unsuccessfully to warn Qaybdiid the night before. When finally tipped off in the morning, the colonel confirmed that he knew the face of everybody at his house; then he let his guard down. Aidid had said he would be there, but postponed his arrival. The elders began the long talk of Somali conflict resolution.

But as they sat down on the carpet to discuss their situation—the most aged on cushions and chairs along the walls—they could not have known how quickly the protective rings of their clan armor could be pulled away, exposing them to an incomprehensible fury.

At 10:15 am, one man stepped outside the front door and walked across the compound toward the main gate. He was wearing clothes prearranged as a signal—a suicide mission because he would later be hunted down by Somalis for this treachery. Within seconds of the man's emergence, an American Cobra attack helicopter loosed its first TOW anti-tank missile at the house. "Operation Michigan" was under way. The elders, lost in discussion, saw the flash and their own blood spray bright pink across the wall of the main meeting room before they realized the violation of their protective shield and that—so exposed—nearly all would die.

Qaybdiid was standing up and speaking at the moment of explosion. "I remember the first missile, it crossed in front of my face—*swish!* right in the middle—and then I blacked out," he said, scars on the left side of his face and left ear still visible years later. When he came to, there was chaos. He rushed toward the stairs, which had already been shot away to prevent escape. People were losing parts of themselves as one TOW missile after another blasted into the building and 20mm cannon fire ground up flesh. Qaybdiid remembered that the head of a friend had fallen upright, severed but untouched on the top step.

Sanjeeh remembers the attack as an explosion of confusion. The first missile tore a hole in the walls, revealing a host of Cobra gunships that appeared to be outside at eye level. The Cobras had always invoked fear in Somalia—they roared defiantly across the city, often too low, their narrow profile like a wasp hunting to sting. The 20mm cannon was devastating, sending down a smoke trail of lead bullets that were never meant to shred flesh, but to stop vehicles. The wire-guided TOW missiles—copper tipped, and with a dual explosive to better penetrate targets—could rip away walls of buildings.

"Everyone was surprised. They were out of control running into each other in their madness," Sanjeeh recalled.[3] He is a hard man, whose nickname means "scar on nose," in honor of an inch-long scar between his eyes earned during a childhood fight when a kid pulled a dagger on him. "Some people tried to break the wall, shouting, and nobody was saving them."

Sanjeeh let out a brief laugh when he remembered one scene, when all those people coalesced, and together moved to one window, then to a wall, trying to escape the shooting. "You could really feel the savagery of this action," he said. "There was a lot of bloodshed, and it was vicious, like an animal attack."

Half-conscious, Sanjeeh jumped down the missing stairwell, and when he emerged, the helicopter cannon took aim. Bursts of 20mm rounds tore off his right arm at the stump and shredded his right thigh. Minutes later, American ground troops stormed in and began finishing off the survivors—a charge US commanders deny. "If they saw people shouting, they killed them," Sanjeeh said, counting about 15 who died that way. Bleeding profusely, Sanjeeh played dead until the troops left. "They were using their pistols, to come upon [survivors] who were screaming, and shot them in the head," he said. American spy Omar Hassan Ganay shouted to the US troops, "I am the agent!" and was taken away.

Sanjeeh's scars are still angry. Speaking in his family compound in the Bakhara market in 1999, Sanjeeh pulled up his shirt to show the shoulder stump. With his good left arm, he undid his trousers to reveal a right thigh with a smooth broad patchwork of black and pink marbled scar tissue. He spent two and one-half years recovering in the hospital. While explaining that a skin graft was required from his left side, Sanjeeh's two silver-capped teeth shone through the twilight. Revenge was a deep-seated emotion, one that I, too, found understandable. In the midst of our interview, he broke off to pray at dusk with his family, on woven mats in the direction of Mecca.

"The Americans did this action themselves," Sanjeeh resumed. It was dark. "They always talk about human rights and democracy, so this really surprised me. I could not believe the US could do that. They [the Americans] lied, you know? They came to Somalia for relief—Operation Restore Hope—but they changed it to another thing, a war which had never been seen before."

MY EYES

"Get the fuck out of here, it's too dangerous!" screamed the American soldier, his eyes bloodshot with fear, his men sweating at their defensive positions as Cobra attack helicopters howled above. This was the perimeter cordon sealing off Qaybdiid's house, the latest target of UN "peacekeeping" ire in Somalia now belching smoke.

I had arrived quickly, too quickly, with my driver and diminutive translator, Hassan. From the roof of the Sahafi Hotel we had seen the helicopter attack unfold, first the blast of TOW missiles, then the sustained hammer of 20mm cannon fired from more than half a dozen helicopters at once creating a deadly killing box. Within minutes I jumped into the car with Hassan and driver Duguf and we raced to where the thick column of smoke ascended toward the sky.

Young Hassan had bad teeth, a little English, and a good sense of well-intentioned humor. Duguf was short, built like a bulldog, and tough. He kept a stem of qat in his mouth all the time, like a toothpick, and his skin was very black. He didn't say much, but he was *with* me. I had been working with this pair for a couple months, since Hersi had left the gunman business. The situation had been so calm in recent days that I didn't bother to bring my own M-16 (for another gunman's use—I never traveled armed myself) or, in the rush, even a normal gunman.

We went alone, but already the lump in my throat was there, my own protective instinct of fear growing in warning, telling me I was entering a zone normally forbidden and that I could be harmed.

We arrived at the road behind the Qaybdiid house and found a tense American squad. They were set up at a sandy crossroads, the snipers keeping Somalis at bay down three separate roads. Their commander saw Hassan and ordered him to halt, as I gingerly continued my advance. The Americans warned me away, too, but I had always taken such exhortations with a grain of salt. They rarely visited these streets. And when they did they were under fire. There was Hassan, barely high school age who told stories with long, elegant, magical fingers. The Americans thought Hassan was a killer. Their average age was only 19, just out of high school themselves.

So I ignored the soldiers and crept past and round the corner, leaving Hassan shaking with fright despite my assurances, hunkered down 30 yards from the US unit. What I didn't know in my arrogance was that this mission was to be the shortest ever mounted in Mogadishu: 17 minutes, and I had arrived at minute 15. I peered through an open gate to see the target house ablaze, but from there at the back not worth a single picture.

The Americans disappeared, pulling out as quickly as they had warned me to stay away. And then there was a strange moment of silence, a solitude virtually unknown in this country, and one that immediately forced the lump in my throat to attention and filled all my emotion with terror. The quiet roar of the flames was muffled by my crippled consciousness. Then—with the army snipers gone—Somalis began to rush at me from three sides.

I could see that they were enraged by the concentration of the attack, so I turned and walked, then ran, to get back around the corner to where I knew that Hassan would be able to calm the crowd. I was running then and saw Hassan, but the Somalis were upon him, too, and we were engulfed by the mob. In the last moments they had watched their fathers, sons, and grandfathers die in a fusillade of UN-sanctioned violence, so quickly and finally. In 17 minutes, that single compound had been obliterated by 16 TOW missiles and

2,020 rounds—the American pilots counted them later—of 20mm cannon fire. For all the Somalis knew, I had been deposited there by the US troops. As a foreigner, I was their revenge target.

The mob surrounded me, grabbing hold of my cameras and bag, and my mind raced uncontrollably, knowing instinctively that there would be no running away from this violence, from this seething group that grew larger every moment. It all happened in seconds: I saw Hassan fistfighting, trying to explain that I was innocent; I screamed "Hassan! Hassan! Hassan!" until I was hoarse and we were losing the battle and it was all I could do to parcel out my cameras to buy time, but then I was being clubbed and a boy brandished an 18-inch blade toward my face and as I fended that off a machete smashed into my head. My arm was struck again and again, and the crowd tightened around me; I was fighting and this never was my war but now I had gone too far. . . . I had crossed the line that divides observer from killer and victim.

Death in Somalia is inevitable—who can stop the sunrise?—and I felt my last moments of dawn were giving way.

Duguf was stuck in the mob and waved his 9mm Baretta but it was hopeless, and I knew that I couldn't run—even if I could I would have never escaped. The cameras were gone and there was nothing left to ransom my life, my throat exposed but allowing no sound anymore, and I knew that if I lived this would be as close to . . . as close to . . . the end. Pistol blasts but not shot at me, that bastard with the machete went down, then a Somali man hugged me, his tears soaking through my T-shirt into my thin Kevlar flak jacket, and I was sure he was going to knife me, his arms locked around me and hands behind, but he showed mercy—here was mercy, mercy, *mercy*—and he disentangled me for a split second from the crowd and there was hope, though the tenacious furies followed me, grabbing hold again, then this question pervaded my thinking, cutting through the din of attack: "Where are you from?" Lying without thinking, I blurted out, "I'm British!" and Duguf got to me with his pistol and two Somalis—here was mercy again—dragged me away and bundled me into the car. Hassan was there unhurt, and we raced back to the Sahafi Hotel bouncing along the deeply potholed sand alleys, the blood flowing from my head down my neck and into my flak jacket, the result of Somali vengeance unleashed.

"Jesus Christ! Are you okay?" asked Dan Eldon, a young British/American photographer for Reuters, bounding out of the hotel. No one else had visited the scene yet. Dan and German AP photographer Hansi Kraus helped me to my room and with the first aid kit washed my head wound, the blood staining the sink, my mind shocked by the outburst of violence, and grateful for their help. I looked up into the mirror, to see a pink film seeping out of my hair and down my forehead. I hardly recognized myself, and paused, staring. Very deliberately I took off my shirt and rinsed it. The blood kept coming, thickening in my hair.

The others wanted to go but I gave warning, matter-of-factly: "Be careful out there—it's fucking dangerous today." They insisted that I visit the US combat field hospital, at the UN compound, even though I, too—with a knee-jerk instinct for news, and not yet fully aware of the significance of my escape—really wanted to get back there, to see the aftermath of this blood-bath perpetrated by "peacekeepers." My bleeding finally stanched with a bandage, they saw me off to the hospital.

I thanked them and said, "Take care."

"DANNY'S DEAD"

Only a few journalists had remained in Mogadishu after the exciting edge of the June 1993 attacks on Aidid had worn off. UN forces were apparently in a holding pattern, the lull causing a lapse of interest in our newsrooms. When it was this quiet, the capital was deceptively dangerous, subject to mood swings.

In the days before Bloody Monday we entertained ourselves as best we could. Dan found a scratchy video copy of *Pretty Woman* and played it on the Reuters TV monitors. At 22 he brought to this job far more than his cameras. Dan had a ready smile and a bottomless well of creativity, and was not yet infected with the ugly cynicism of so many of his older, more experienced colleagues. His pictures since the famine and during the war and UN intervention were shot with compassion, if not technical perfection. He self-published a book of them that sold out the first 3,000 copies—to soldiers and journalists—in a month. On the last page he noted wryly that he "currently attends Mogadishu University, studying how not to get your head shot off." He signed off with this acknowledgment: "No thanks to all the guys who looted my stuff and shot at me."

Dan reveled in the unpredictable nature of Somalia and enjoyed the taste of sweet tea with elders, of qat-chewing sessions with gunmen, of trying to understand how these intelligent people were so capable of ravaging each other. He didn't lift his camera to record the worst afflictions. In her eulogy his mother, Kathy Eldon, remembered his graphic descriptions of the pictures he couldn't bring himself to take, rather than the ones he could. "Death, when it came," she said, "would not have been a stranger to him."

Still, Dan was a buccaneering shooter who had worked his way through many crowds and could swear in Somali, causing more than a few would-be camera looters to think twice. His images showed the sacred and profane in stark contrast: gunmen in cathedrals or children at barbed wire barricades who know that life is likely to be short.

At the hotel on the afternoon of 11 July 1993, Dan found me, and with a serious look said: "Scott, could you come here a minute, to identify one of these pictures?" I followed him to his room, at the end of the hall, and there on the screen of his Leafax transmitter was a gorgeous American soldier, naked but for her string bikini, sunbathing on a red, white and blue BUD-WEISER BEER towel. It could be Southern California but for her gun, which lay in the Somali sand, ready for action. Dan broke into hoots of laughter, his eyes dancing. He had spent the day at Black Beach, which—now with shark net—had been turned into a very non-Muslim resort for UN forces. "Check this one out!" he exclaimed lustily, bringing up a new shot of two leggy ladies laughing in their bikinis, walking past a small pyramid of M-16 assault rifles. "Well done!" I said, enjoying the moment. "This is just the thing to grace the summertime desks of those bored picture editors." He couldn't contain his pleasure, and laughed and laughed, a mischievous laugh. The pictures *did* do well in the States. They were the last ones he ever sent.

Dan genuinely loved Somalia and Somalis. They sometimes called him the "Mayor of Mogadishu," a title he wore with pride. But he had seen plenty, and it haunted him.

Less haunted was Hansi Kraus, short and strong, a German built like a tank, like one of the US Marines in Somalia. At work his burly shoulders protruded from sleeveless T-shirts, from beneath the armored casing of his ceramic-plate bulletproof vest. His hair was military-short, and he muscled his Canon 35-350mm zoom lens like an anti-tank weapon. He got his start in Germany during the collapse of the Berlin Wall. Subsequent tours in the former Yugoslavia whetted his appetite for the flavor of war. During one shelling attack in Sarajevo, Hansi saved the life of a severely injured woman by carrying her to his car and taking her to the hospital.

In Mogadishu one night the satellite phone lines were too bad to transmit pictures to London, so Hansi cooked up a special treat for Donatella Lorch of *The New York Times* and me: *tagliatelle verde* with a rich cream sauce. There amid the cigarette butts and spent film cannisters, between the hair dryer taped to the wall to dry negatives and the satellite phone—the whole room bathed in the unfortunate stink of darkroom chemicals—he lit up a gas stove and uncorked a bottle of red wine from the French PX. Donatella, ever-effulgent with her good nature, recorded this taste of Italy with her point-and-shoot "family snaps" camera. She left the next day, and Hansi's stay was nearly over, too. They had agreed to go dancing in Nairobi the next weekend, when he got out, but Bloody Monday disrupted their plans.

On 12 July, Dan and Hansi saw me off to the combat hospital with my head wound and waited at the hotel with the other journalists for a safe escort to the Qaybdiid house. Almost immediately, a member of Aidid's militia was there and promised to provide security. It was an offer we rarely refused, because often it was the only way journalists could visit the scene of an attack without endangering themselves. The warlord's senior officers had proved before that they could protect us. Within minutes a convoy of half a dozen journalists swept out of the hotel gate, leaving behind an angry CNN crew that couldn't break away in time from its live satellite interview.

The remains of the house loomed before the convoy, smoke still billowing from the destroyed structure, a target so perfectly struck that only the slightest collateral damage marred the walls of adjacent buildings. But the crowd was thick and furious, enraged by the scale of bloodshed—they said more than 70 bodies were turned to pulp, their clan leaders and elders now dead, dead, dead. A blood rage boiled inside the Somalis: anywhere else this attack would be murder, a barbarous act blamed on terrorists, a premeditated assassination—a massacre—but here, the Americans and the UN were pulling the triggers, *sanctioning* this destruction.

The journalists arrived as the crowd was seething. Hansi jumped out and fought his way through the gate together with Dan and Hos Maina, also a Reuters photographer, and Reuters TV cameraman Mohamed Shaffi with soundman Anthony Macharia. The mob surged forward and engulfed them; other journalists tried to follow, but their guards sensed the bloodlust immediately and ordered them to get back into the cars. As they retreated, gunmen pounded their vehicles with the butts of their rifles.

The others were left inside. Within minutes stones were raining down, as the Somalis began to exact a grisly revenge. Hansi's bulletproof vest was torn away, his body riddled with bullets and the back of his head smashed with stones. Hos, who arrived just a few hours before to replace Dan, his bags still unpacked at the hotel, tried to run and screamed, "What are you doing, I'm African, Kenyan! A journalist!" "No, no, American!" his pursuers shouted, pummeling him to death, then smashing his head against a wall. The Somalis did not distinguish between black and white, just Somali and "foreign." Anthony Macharia, also a Kenyan, ran away and got close to the hotel before a woman tea seller impaled him in the heart with her knife.

Dan battled his way outside the gate, wriggled out of his bulletproof vest and ran, too. Pilots of an American helicopter on a damage assessment mission spotted him running, and said later they thought he was far enough ahead of the crowd to get away. They radioed back to base to confirm that all US soldiers were accounted for. They were, so the pilots did nothing to save him. No stun grenades—as had been used against journalists before—or a swoop to scare the mob. On the ground Dan's pounding lungs gave way and the Somalis were upon him, stabbing and beating. He was shot but still alive, Somalis tell me later: then the bastard man who had cut my head with a machete—the gunshot wound from Duguf bandaged enough so that he was back in action to "kill Americans"—grabbed Dan by the hair, pulled his head down to get at his neck and "cut like an animal." Seeing the body lying face-down, the American helicopter finally descended, the crowd around the corpse thinning under the downdraft, to retrieve Dan's bloody, sand-encrusted body.

Shaffi escaped, and it was a miracle, nothing less than a gift from God. Chased in three different directions, the others were ahead of him, so he thought they would escape and that he would die. He begged for help at one house from a woman who slammed her door. He tried desperately to get into two different vehicles but was shot again and fell down, trampled by the crowd, then climbed into a vehicle only to find that the Somali drivers wanted to torture him, too. He cried for mercy, that he was also a Muslim, and they finally dumped him at the K4 roundabout, from where he crawled toward the Sahafi Hotel. His voice quivering that night, he recounted the tale: "I . . . I knew I was going to die. I knew it," and then he broke down completely, in streaming tears.

At the US combat hospital, a surgeon was stitching my head when news came of incoming casualties. I was anxious—in my ignorance—that the others were at the scene of the attack, getting the story. If it was *known* that this Somali meeting was attacked without warning, I thought to myself, and the UN was exposed as Somalia's new belligerent militia with the most lethal gun, this bloody war might soon be stopped. My thoughts were interrupted by Jonathan Ewing, a reporter from Washington, D.C., stringing for Reuters who rushed into the operating tent. "Shaffi's injured, but they wouldn't treat him because he's not American!" he screamed. "What the *hell* are they doing here? I had to lie and tell them he *was* American."

The door burst open and Shaffi was rushed in, covered with blood and dirt and moaning. Jonathan stopped, and we stared, slack-jawed. He looked bad. The medics began operating immediately.

Then the call went out again: More casualties were on their way. Jonathan disappeared, then came back from a distant part of the tube-tent hospital. "Danny's dead," he said straight, and my mind couldn't imagine Dan's fear or his pain. "No, no . . . " This was not supposed to happen; no story was worth this, though it was a real risk we so regularly dismissed. We lived with death every day here, but not our death. And this death, the young talent, whose "Mogged Out" T-shirt design said most about the chronic fatigue that all of us experienced covering Somalia.

My wound sewn, I stood up. Shaffi was here, and alive, at least. An army psychologist-mortician came up to me. Did I want to see Dan? We walked down the length of the tent, then through tubular yellow connecting units, like the inside of a sick, segmented caterpillar, and there in the "mortuary," a dark green body bag was laid out on a table in a room eerily yellow, the light filtered through the canvas of the tent. There were scores of Somalis dead today, who once collected would be buried in shrouds . . . but for me this single death was momentous and devastating.

It was hot.

"You don't have to do this."

"I know, but he was a friend."

With clinical precision, the soldier pulled on a pair of white surgical gloves. He was sweating too, through his green military T-shirt. He watched me closely, untied the cord, and pulled away the tape to unseal the body bag.

THE GUILTY

We were steered away from calling the Bloody Monday attack a massacre or a slaughter, but it was difficult not to reach the conclusion that this was murder on a grand scale. It was a war crime, pure and simple. Though witnesses were plenty, the perpetrators made no apologies.

Admiral Howe vigorously defended the destruction of a "very key terrorist planning cell" and claimed that no civilians died except the four foreign journalists. The meeting had, in fact, been called by the Somalis to deliberate over the result of a meeting that Howe himself had held with Habr Gedir elders just days before. Yet Howe's bluster was unrelenting. "I think appeasement is the wrong strategy when terrorism continues," he told us. "There is a time you must stand up and use strength. I hope we can minimize the use of force, and that we'll always use it responsibly." As for the target, he left no doubt: "We knew what we were hitting. It was well planned."

The Somalis understood also that the killing was a deliberate sign of UN resolve, an attempt to decapitate the head of this troublesome clan. For them Bloody Monday became the turning point—the day that Somalis turned almost unanimously against the UN missteps. Unosom II military chief Gen. Cevik Bir from Turkey and his deputy Montgomery—who commanded US troops—were eager to match what they saw as Aidid's 5 June challenge to war. But then any moral high ground or pretensions of UN "neutrality" evaporated, along with the illusion that all this bloodshed was meant to bring peace and help the relief effort.

Already 90% of the Unosom II budget was being spent on the military, not relief. Somalis were now being killed, not saved, and after this attack aid workers were forced to stop their work altogether. The relief community was appalled, and the irony was difficult to hide. "If I were a Somali woman, I would take up my bazooka against the Americans for their crimes," the head of one agency said. UN motives had never been more clear, nor more flawed.

Médecins Sans Frontières charged that attacks on hospitals and non-military targets demonstrated that UN forces "behave as if they enjoyed absolute impunity. Not content with stifling the work of aid agencies, the military has run roughshod over their basic principles by excessive use of force. Ordered there to observe, and ensure the observance of the Geneva Conventions, they have cheerfully flouted them, paralyzing the aid effort."[4] The agency's president, Rony Brauman, accused Unosom II of committing a "humanitarian crime" by sacrificing relief for the "right of vengeance. . . . For the first time in Somalia there has been killing under the flag of humanitarianism."

In the aftermath, agencies in Mogadishu confronted the UN with copies of the Geneva Convention articles and protocols concerning reprisals against civilians and proportional retaliation. Any such attack must offer a "definite military advantage" and is illegal if the harm is "excessive in relation to the concrete and direct military advantage anticipated," according to the 1977 Additional Protocol I.[5] Though the US has not ratified this protocol, it has accepted these portions of it.[6] Instead of assurances of future compliance, however, relief staff in Somalia were told to pack a single bag each, in case the violent fallout from the next "UN operation" forced their evacuation.

Bloody Monday also turned me into a reluctant combatant, an observer sucked into the conflict by virtue of simple presence.

"If you were a soldier, you'd get a Purple Heart for this!" sang one sergeant, inspecting my head bandage, when I stopped off at the press center upon leaving the combat hospital. She spoke with a tone of wonder, and of genuine regret that I would be deprived of this badge, as if the Purple Heart were the kind of thing that every uniformed warrior yearned for. But such auspicious awards should be reserved for "just" wars—and what I had just seen made clear that this conflict was unjust, and reprehensible.

The relief agencies were equally unwitting players in the UN's war against Aidid, even though the blue helmets were making battle in their name. The war-mongering forced all of us, like the Somalis, to choose sides. For Somali witnesses of the useless brutality of the Qaybdiid attack, who also heard the pathetic justifications for it, the choice was easily made. Howe, polite to a fault, claimed that only 13 Somalis died, revising the figure later to 20. All the dead, he explained, were armed men shooting back at the attack helicopters. The Red Cross confirmed at least 54 deaths.

There had been no warning, and there would be none for future attacks. We were told, of course, that this was war. So the element of surprise was too important. UN intelligence guru Kevin McGovern warned smugly that he had a list of ten more Aidid "command and control" centers that would be similarly obliterated. Relief workers should take care; UN forces, they were assured, were doing their best to "protect" the few who remained. But Mogadishu had never before been so dangerous for foreigners. Armed gangs were moving from gate to gate, asking relief agencies by name for American aid workers and journalists.

UN strategists were trying to out-Somali the Somalis, and for them Bloody Monday was the natural reply to the slaughter of the Pakistani "peacekeepers" in June, as well as—and this was clearly stated—revenge for the executions only days before of four Somalis who worked for the UN propaganda sheet *Maanta* [*Today*]. The UN switched its semantics to a war track, too. Instead of hostile forces, Aidid's people became "enemy forces."[7] US Ambassador Gosende told me that it was the UN's turn at the blood feud: "What happens when 24 militiamen are killed by a rival clan? Of course they retaliate and take revenge. Not to do so—it's the same for the UN—would be political suicide."

Not surprisingly, the attack also caused dissent within Unosom II itself. Anne Wright, an American seconded from the State Department to head Unosom II's justice division, resigned. In an internal memo written the day after the attack, she warned against "applying military methods traditionally found in declared war/combat areas without a UN declaration of war/combat." Of the 12 July raid, she noted: "One could argue that in previous attacks the short prior notice of impending attack somehow gave persons in attacked buildings the option to choose between life and death. . . . This is the first incident where no option was given."[8]

The result, she said, was unambiguous. "While the Security Council has given Unosom the authority to 'hold persons accountable for attacks against Unosom forces and to take all necessary measures against those responsible,'" Wright concluded, "Unosom should anticipate that some organizations and member states will characterize a deliberate attack meant to kill the occupants without giving all the building occupants a chance to surrender as nothing less than murder committed in the name of the United Nations."

For Somalis—and anyone who witnessed the attack—this was painfully self-evident. What other word than murder could apply when the spread of victims reached from the supreme elder of the Habr Gedir—90-year-old Sheikh Haji Mohamed Iman Aden—to the women and girls providing tea to the company? "When the victim is sacrificed rather than endangering the appointed protector," Médecins Sans Frontières noted wryly, "one has to concede that the humanitarian political alliance is full of surprises."[9]

Officials had made clear that they considered UN forces to be bound by the Geneva Conventions as a definition of the laws of war. American pilots also have their own restrictions which require any aerial attack to serve a "concrete and direct" military advantage, which does not target civilians nor cause unnecessary civilian casualties.[10] For General Montgomery, commander of US forces in Somalia, this attack was "legitimate" because they were "all bad guys."[11] A Somali "inside informer" working for the CIA fed the information, he told me years later. "This was a council of war. This was where they were making decisions to blow up Americans and [carry out] ambushes," he said. "They weren't innocents, they were people who actively participated in action against the UN. So they were soldiers, on militia operations, so I have no remorse about it at all."

But what about the elders, I asked, and the peace meeting? "What was on their docket that day, I have no idea," Montgomery said. "Were they elders? Yeah, I'm sure there were clan elders. But were they, in our view, non-combatants? No they were not. There were no civilians in there."

The US soldiers who swept through the compound had found "a lot of tactical radios" used in guerrilla-type operations, he said, though that detail had never previously been made public. Instead of taking the communications gear away, however, the soldiers took photos and left. Except for that radio claim about the "key" strategic importance of the Qaybdiid house, I have never heard nor seen any evidence that this attack even remotely met a single criteria of "direct" military advantage. The intended result, of course, backfired: any wavering Somali was now fully committed against the UN, since the dead were largely elders who had left their shoes at the door.

There were other noteworthy contrasts. During the June US bombings of Aidid's weapons dumps, for example, every measure seemed to have been taken to minimize civilian casualties. Raids were carried out at night, and civilians were warned to flee. But the Qaybdiid attack was planned to coincide with the elder's meeting, the target was the meeting, in a crowded area in daytime, without warning, as if to maximize the death toll.

Even during the 1991 Gulf War, in which all of Iraq's military and economic assets were targeted, American commanders spent months planning the air war to minimize collateral damage. Very specific weapons were chosen for specific targets, and bombing runs were plotted so that munitions falling short or long would miss hospitals and schools.[12] General Norman Schwarzkopf often consulted with law-of-war experts and the International Committee of the Red Cross "to ensure that specific military operations would not be seen later as violations," notes the book Crimes of War. "In fact, Schwarzkopf's aides requested so much guidance from the ICRC that its representatives eventually stopped providing it, protesting that they were not legal counsel for the coalition."[13]

But in Somalia, as the manhunt for Aidid escalated, any such precautions fell away. If brought before an international court, UN forces in Somalia would almost certainly have been found guilty of violating the laws of war on Bloody Monday. The legality of numerous other incidents between June and October 1993, including indiscriminant use of air power, also could be questioned. And if Aidid had been killed by US Rangers during any operation, such a killing would have been in violation of US laws prohibiting assassination. Yet undaunted, and armed with the all-inclusive, let's-play-without-any-rules Chapter VII mandate, Unosom II commander Bir had declared—in private on 9 July—that "I will kill Aidid within four days."

If Unosom II could be defined as "at war," then the Geneva Conventions required efforts to collect and identify "enemy" dead. Proper disposal is now mandated by law.[14] But in a telling measure of disrespect, American and UN officers made clear that numbers of Somali dead did not interest them, and they kept no count. My Freedom of Information Act request to the Pentagon for 12 July documents found that even the normally harmless daily "situation report" is not in the standard secret archives and has an unattainable level of classification.

Montgomery's sensibilities seemed to be blunted about the Bloody Monday attack. He was furious about all the criticism and gave vent in *The New York Times*: "It is the inalienable right of the Somali militia to kill and maim United Nations soldiers. But it is treated as a human rights violation if there is any military response against those responsible."[15] No one outside Somalia *understood* the need for violence here, he said.

Months later, when American policy was in full retreat and the manhunt called off, he told Rick Atkinson of *The Washington Post* that the result pleased him: "I think they [Aidid's clan] were set back, or in a state of confusion after July 12. Things were actually pretty quiet for a while." Was *this* the "definite military advantage" required by the Geneva Conventions? When asked whether Central Command chief Joseph Hoar had approved, Montgomery said: "All I'll say is that is certainly wasn't a locally approved plan. It had very high backing."[16]

When the independent UN inquiry was finally conducted, its findings were so embarrassing that the UN delayed releasing the report to the Security Council for a month.[17] Boutros-Ghali asked the commission members to revise and limit the report, but they refused. Finally, one copy was given to the French president of the Security Council, and one other could be viewed only by other envoys of the 15-member council, in a room high upstairs at

UN headquarters. Making photocopies was prohibited, and the sole copy was secured to a desk with a chain so it couldn't be slipped away. Plenty of UN—read US in this case—incompetence, ignorance, and misjudgment were all laid down on paper.

The investigators had agonized over the report because Unosom II wanted to have it both ways: they wanted to be "peace enforcers," but then when they got attacked, they wanted to be unimpeachable "peacekeepers." There were strong arguments, the report said, that every action Aidid took after the UN issued its arrest warrant could be construed as self-defense. "Caught in a dilemma, Unosom II was forced to erect a wall of separation between its peace-keeping and its war-making *personae*—where its civil authorities were often kept in the dark about military actions," the inquiry read. "This dual role . . . worse yet made it possible for Unosom II to be portrayed simply as an enemy of the Somali people."[18]

Stockwell, the UN spokesman in Mogadishu, conceded that this division of labor—and responsibility—was "a little mushy, like nailing Jell-O to the wall."

That could hardly have been the UN's original aim, since on Human Rights Day 1992—which happened to coincide with the American beach landing in December—UN chief Boutros-Ghali declared: "A crucial test [this year] will be our response to massive violations of human rights."

Though we all had eyes and had witnessed the crime, mission commanders defended the indefensible and stubbornly clung to the illusion that more war could somehow bring peace. They thought that Somalis would forget the carnage, forget the spilled blood of their fathers and brothers—forget the lessons of the Dark Side that they had just seen. Unosom II had "regained the momentum" needed to keep the "threat off balance," Admiral Howe said. So without an outward twinge of guilt, he declared the 12 July 1993 operation "flawless."

THEIR EYES

With the Qaybdiid house blown asunder, Somalis began to scour the wreckage for survivors. In two and one-half years of civil conflict, there had never been such a slaughter resulting from one attack. Hossein Ali Salad, a field officer for the International Committee of the Red Cross, searched through the corpses. He looked for identification cards, for anything that might bring order, that might bring definition, tears of mourning and anger mingling as they dropped hotly onto the carnage. Clothing was shredded and bloodied, there was the pile of the shoes and sandals, now crushed under the weight of the rubble. The acrid burning was pervaded by the unique smell of seared flesh and torched hair. There was a horrific shock. But the body parts didn't add up because of the violence of their separation. "Some of them were good friends of mine. I knew lots of them," Ali Salad told me. "One guy—he was so nice—he had no neck, no head, no chest, there was nothing to see but his ID card. I could not recognize my friend."

Throughout the war, another man—among the best-educated Somalis I ever met—had never taken up a gun. But in the aftermath of Bloody Monday, he was ready. "I was so angry. If there was an American that day, I would have shot him. Yes. Not only an American, because on that day all the UN were the same. Later I saw the body of one of the Kenyan journalists near the ICRC, and didn't give a shit about him. I just couldn't."

Though UN commanders said the attack was their turn at the blood feud, this act of revenge went a step too far even in the Somali equation, akin to the crime of slaughtering rival clansmen at prayer. "Some Somalis are still eager for revenge," Ali Salad told me later. "It may be after 100 years, but Howe is now in the history. No one will ever forgive him."

Some of the dead were loaded onto trucks and driven to our Sahafi Hotel, as proof of the ferocity of the attack. The corpses were wrapped in white shrouds, crimson stains spreading across them. They were coated with the white dust of the house. A grapefruit rind lay beside one corpse, inexplicably picked up too in the haste to load the bodies.

CNN acquired a videotape of the attack from a Somali cameraman, who must have entered the target house the moment the last American soldier pulled out. It showed the true extent of the violence, the smoldering piles of meat cleaved with blast-heated shrapnel, the raw primal anger of rescuers overwhelmed by the scene; all the grotesque evidence of an unimaginable crime. But nearly all the footage inside the house was too gruesome to show on the air. Howe called the videotape "suspect" because it made a mockery of his claims that so few people were killed. The final scene showed a crowded street, and an American Black Hawk helicopter hovering over a crowd, then slowly dropping toward the earth. The mob drew back. Partly hidden from view by a parked vehicle, the helicopter touched down to collect Dan Eldon's body.

THE SHOES

The Qaybdiid house blown asunder, the journalists too began to clean up. The bodies of our other colleagues had been dumped in Bakhara Market and along 21 October Road and were guarded by Somali gunmen who had mutilated them. The UN refused to help collect them, so Reuters and AP guards went to the sites and engaged the gunmen. After a fierce gunbattle, the corpses were retrieved one by one, taken to the mortuary and identified. AP correspondent Angus Shaw, a European Zimbabwean, was distraught like all of us. For him it brought back memories of the war in Rhodesia, when he had to search for the fallen and identify dead friends. Later he became a conscientious objector. Hansi arrived lifeless in the back of a Land Rover, his face almost serene.

At the Sahafi we didn't touch Hansi's room for a day. Hansi had his key with him when he was killed, so we had to get the master key. We opened the door quietly, like graverobbers unsealing an ancient forbidden tomb. Hansi's shaving kit was out, his socks hung to dry, Kevlar helmet in a corner. We packed his things. In his photo room there was one camera body, a few extra lenses, and some film. Hansi had been reading a novel about the Marine Corps, some gung-ho front line story of war. When the attack began he had turned the book over open-faced, to mark his place, before rushing to the roof. Anguished, we cleaned up. A can of Orangina soda was open on a ledge, just one-third left.

It was hard to believe that in the city, more than 50 other families grieved. Though routinely cast in our reports as X number of Somalis dead, each casualty was of course as important in their lives and as significant to their kin as these deaths were to us. Somali loss was often more easily accepted or understood, in part because death was seen as inevitable, and therefore no cause for grief. But really that applied only to taking risks in warfare, and did not mean that coping with death came any easier. For Somalis the loss was hard and mourned with as many tears as I cried over the killing of my friends, as many tears as families in the US shed when their sons and fathers died here.

At the Reuters end of the hall, Andy Hill, a circumspect veteran correspondent of Reuters, was broken inside and quietly hurting. He had been forced to negotiate with a heartless, heavy-handed bureaucracy. The bodies were shifted to the airport, and the paperwork was endless. At the US mortuary, Andy had to sign for the loose change, a few Kenya shillings, found in Dan's pocket. If he wanted caskets for any of the dead Reuters three, the American quartermaster demanded that he pay, or somehow "return" them to US forces. They could part with the body bags, that was okay. Don't bring *those* back.

Andy found me and we went to Dan's room. Andy's kind features were solemn. He had spent years in Africa during the 1980s, looking into dark places at very dark things. He felt shamed and even slightly embarrassed that these young men—so full of potential, so full of spark—had died, while he, a veteran of many wars past, a tired witness, had not.

Still, we're all driven by the sheer fascination of observing war, of examining the human spirit torn by extremities, victim of every abuse.

Dan had been the same.

"Scott, you've got to see this."

There on the floor under Dan's photo transmitter—on which so recently bronzed, bikini-clad sergeants had beckoned at us from the screen—was a pair of shoes, set there by the Reuters' guards, to be helpful. They were carefully placed together, as if by their owner, but they were drenched in blood. We surmised that they must be Anthony's; the blood seemed to have poured upon them from above, from his punctured heart while he was still alive, while he was still standing. We stared, unable to take in the terror of such a death, so starkly illustrated by this mundane pair of shoes, splashed with freshly drawn blood.

"I can't send those back," Andy said, breaking the spell. "I am going to take them down to the sea and dispose of them. Along with Dan's automatic weapons."

"Oh? How many are there?"

He listed them. A sizable arsenal, kept for fun. Dan was more Somali than the Somalis. But he never should have died there, on Bloody Monday. Nobody should have.

EIGHT

MISSION IMPOSSIBLE

*It is the nature of campaigns like these that, after
extreme expenditure of courage and energy, they should
lead to what seems a lame and impotent conclusion.*

—Angus Hamilton, *Somaliland*

The makeshift memorial was a spartan affair, with each dead
soldier remembered by his rifle and a pair of boots. An American flag flew at half-mast, its white stars and stripes gleaming
brightly in the brutal Somali sun, the scalding wind making little comforting difference in Mogadishu except to stir dead dust.
These were American casualties, men in uniform killed too far
away from home in a place too obscure, when "God's work"
had turned quietly into a vicious undeclared war. They died 3–4
October, in a raid the Rangers call the Battle of the Black Sea,
but which Somalis call the Day of the Rangers.

There were no flag-draped caskets, and certainly no journalists: this was a "private" ceremony. The media had already done
enough to discredit the Somalia operation, the conventional wisdom went, so we were treated as an enemy. Throughout Somalia's "peacekeeping" war we had not once been allowed to see or
photograph an American casualty—as if such were cause for
secret shame, or didn't exist—though we had easy access to
fallen Pakistani, Moroccan, Italian, and Nigerian warriors,
whose coffins would be lined up on the airport tarmac.

But the Americans were different from the start, and they
made their own rules. Of the 18 who died during America's
most significant firefight loss since the Vietnam War, there were
still five unaccounted for, their desecrated bodies paraded
through the streets by jubilant Somalis. It was a grisly show

that made all American—and many Somali—stomachs turn. Some remains were scattered throughout the city in shallow graves and had yet to be found. They would be gathered slowly, painstakingly, and in pieces by Somali Red Cross workers at the request of the US government. But some strips of flesh would remain here and there, with scraps of uniform and dog tags, all coveted by the gunmen as trophies or held to remind them that the revenge target must always be American.

Days after the fight, tears formed among the assembled units as they heard a military priest say good words, encouraging words about how much better off the dead were now, away from this imperfect and dangerous world, at rest in Heaven. Throats choked with emotion. Every soldier, too young, envisioned himself zipped inside an anonymous body bag.

Maj. Gen. William Garrison, the Task Force Ranger commander, put the disquieting politics of the mission aside and spoke to the hearts of the men still there, who still had orders to find the warlord. He quoted from Shakespeare's *Henry V*:

> Whoever does not have the stomach for this fight, let him depart. Give him money to speed his departure since we wish not to die in that man's company. Whoever lives past today and comes home safely will rouse himself every year on this day, show his neighbor his scars, and tell embellished stories of all their great feats of battle. These stories he will teach his son and from this day until the end of the world we shall be remembered. We few, we happy few, we band of brothers; for whoever has shed his blood with me shall be my brother. And those men afraid to go will think themselves lesser men as they hear of how we fought and died together.

This defeat was not something US commanders or politicians wanted advertised, since it was their misguided insistence on the manhunt that put these troops in harm's way. So more official US mourning took place in America, amid the familiar green grass and trees and white tombstones of Arlington National Cemetery and elsewhere, places where the spectacle of death in the line of "duty" could be dressed up and sanitized, controlled, institutionalized, and made more honorable with local exhortations of valor.

Americans were in Somalia, after all, on a *United Nations* mission of peace meant to save lives, not take them.

Unnoticed outside Somalia, the 312 Somali dead and more than 800 wounded—one-third of them women and children—were buried too, or subject to triage at overburdened hospitals that ran out of blood plasma almost as soon as the fighting began that day.

The battle began simply enough on Sunday afternoon, 3 October 1993. Rangers and Delta Force commandos received accurate intelligence that an important clutch of General Aidid's top lieutenants—if not the warlord himself—would be meeting in Habr Gedir turf near the Olympic Hotel. This was the seventh attempt to knock out Aidid's command structure. Dropping from ropes out of a helicopter, Delta commandos would storm the building. Rangers were to create a safe perimeter. Then a ground convoy would collect the soldiers and their prisoners, and return to base. Like all previous operations, it was meant to be over in one hour.

High above Mogadishu, reconnaissance helicopters watched a Somali agent give the prearranged signal identifying the exact location of the militia meeting: the man stopped his car, left his door open and lifted the hood, then closed it and drove on.[1] Minutes before Delta teams were to lift off from the tarmac, the Somali spy radioed back a confession that he was too afraid to stop at the true meeting place. He was ordered to return. Maps were amended to make up for this mistake, and at 3:40 pm the swoop began.

Aidid's militia was ready—almost too ready. One American investigation later found that militiamen had sent a warning by beating empty oil drums at the airport with sticks.[2] Or could the Italians—former colonial masters, and eager to be friendly with anyone who might be Somalia's next president—have given a tip-off? Aidid maintained that there was no warning, just his ability to marshal a lot of firepower quickly. Apocryphal or not, Rangers reported that when they hovered over the target—in an area of town called Wardigley, which means the "Well of Blood"—instead of fleeing as usual, Somalis seemed to converge below them. Bullets began whistling past immediately.

Aidid's loyalists had stockpiled ammunition and hundreds of rocket-propelled grenades (RPGs) since May, and militia commanders said later that by the Day of the Rangers they had figured out the basic Delta tactics. "It was very easy for us to discover the American way of working," Abdi Qaybdiid told me. As another Aidid commander said: "If you use one tactic twice, you should not use it a third time. And the Americans already had done basically the same thing six times."[3]

But in Somalia, there would be little deviation of the template. Sure, Garrison had conducted fake "lift-offs" and operations daily "that would get eyes moving in different directions," said Wayne Long, the Delta alumnus with UN security. The fact that the Ranger base was at the airport led to a certain inevitability. "Your enemy can watch you move—Aidid had guys out there watching people sunbathing, much less marshaling up for a raid," Long said. "I mean, you can't run a secretive operation in full view of the enemy, 24 hours a day. And that's what we were doing. Talk about UN transparency, there it was!"[4]

An unmistakable sign that the Somalis were catching on to American weaknesses had come just one week before. US helicopters had flown low and slow over Mogadishu for months, as if invincible. I sometimes thought how easy it would be to hit one with a stone. The Somalis, likewise, thought how easy it could be to bring one down with an RPG—and how that might change the American way of thinking about this war.

Normally, shooting an RPG up into the sky is dangerous because of the fiery backblast. But, according to one account, gunmen had received instruction from *mujahideen*, veteran Islamic Holy Warriors from the war in Afghanistan, who were once trained by Americans to shoot down Soviet helicopters.[5] The instructors had come via Sudan, and taught Somalis how to rig their RPGs with a timing device so that they would not need a direct hit. They were taught that the tail rotor was the helicopter's Achilles heel, and they dug holes in the dirt streets to absorb the blast.

Somalis first struck gold on 25 September, when they brought down a patrolling Black Hawk. Three Americans were killed, and Somalis stuffed the body of one decapitated corpse into a food sack labeled "Gift from the USA." Dancing Somalis had sold quick peeks inside the sack.

When Delta stormed the target house on 3 October, Aidid told me later, he was just to the east. Qaybdiid also had been on his way to the meeting, but the attack began while he was still across the street. He rushed away and began directing militiamen to start blocking roads and calling for reinforcements.

"We panicked for 10 minutes, then we started moving," Qaybdiid recalled. Within 20 minutes the roads were sealed, and Aidid had been moved to a safer place. "It was a surprise to us; we couldn't believe they thought they could come easily and drive away safely." But that was the US assumption, time and time again. The American plan required quick insertion and exit, before Somalis could seal them off. But unlike all previous raids, this one was in the heart of what American commanders called "Indian Country," a confusing maze of rough narrow streets and lookalike ratty houses, where the number of Somali fighters was limitless. And it was daylight. Garrison knew that for the Americans, this was an especially dangerous area: "If we go into the vicinity of the Bakhara market," he had once warned his officers, "there's no question we'll win the gunfight. But we might lose the war."[6]

Aidid told me his strategy: "In every district, my people had instructions that the Americans should be encircled immediately. We kept up such a heavy crossfire that they could not be taken away by helicopter. My people moved *en masse* toward the battle, with any weapon they could find."

Despite Aidid's preparations, within 15 minutes of landing the Delta snatch team had done its job, arresting 24 people, including two of the warlord's senior aides, Omar Salad and Mohamed Hassan Awale. A Delta officer on the ground radioed his superior that they were "ready to get out of Dodge."[7] The evacuation convoy finally arrived. But already a new message had screamed across the radio, one that would completely change the face of American and UN involvement in Somalia: the gunmen had lucked out again—a Black Hawk helicopter had been shot down.

Task Force Ranger split up and moved toward the crash site four blocks away, against a growing barrage that seemed to come out of every doorway, alley, and window. But within minutes a second helicopter was hit, crashing half a mile away. Compounding the American troubles, a lightly armored rescue convoy dispatched from the airport was ambushed repeatedly. Fighting was so fierce that within 30 minutes the 100 US troops fired 60,000 rounds of ammunition and hundreds of grenades before they were forced to retreat.[8]

The rescue convoy was ordered to go to the first crash site, collect the embattled Rangers there, then to go to the second crash site. Viewing the scene from the air by real-time video, the top brass saw what appeared to be an orderly progression of the convoy.[9] But on the ground, US troops were barraged with a mind-boggling, disorienting volume of rifle and rocket fire. Every street looked the same, and the delay in relaying directions from the helicopters, turn left or turn right, meant that the convoy became completely lost. The soldiers ran low on ammunition, as their Humvees and trucks became slick with blood. Casualties mounted. Three of the Somali prisoners died in the crossfire. At every narrow crossroads, each vehicle would be targeted anew. One survivor, when asked later how many Somalis he had killed, told me: "I can't keep fucking count anymore."

But it wasn't just the Americans whose no-holds-barred embrace of the fight lengthened casualty lists. "The problem was the Somalis—everybody tried to attack," recalled Qaybdiid. "They came this way, they went that way. If people had left it to the militia and the officers, it would have been no problem."

Every family, in fact, had its own arsenal, from pistols up to a 106mm anti-tank cannon, much of it buried underground. And many Somalis were angry. In the preceding weeks, I had seen American mortar crews—using the least accurate weapon for infantry—blasting rounds indiscriminantly into the city from the UN compound in daylight. Just days before the last Task Force Ranger raid, one of these shells killed a family of eight. Others wounded 34 people in a hospital. So when the 30-minute raid turned into a 15-hour free-for-all, gunmen came from all over the city—even from rival clan areas—to have a crack at the Americans. After the fighting, the Keysaney Hospital on the opposite side of the Green Line was full of dead and injured Abgal gunmen who had also taken part in the battle, alongside their usual Habr Gedir enemies.

Because of the delays with getting the rescue convoy to the second crash site, two Delta snipers were dropped nearby to help protect the survivors. In what was probably the greatest single act of American bravery that day, Sgt. First Class Randall Shugart and Master Sgt. Gary Gordon fast-roped to the ground 100 yards away. As they landed, they saw hundreds of Somalis charging for the wreckage, and must have known that they would not survive. One helicopter hovered above the wreckage and pointed down long enough for the two Delta operators to wind their way through the labyrinth of tin shacks to the crashed helicopter. The pilot was already gone, but they pried co-pilot Michael Durant from the wreckage. Though he was badly injured, they gave him an assault rifle with a full clip. Hopelessly outnumbered, they were all engulfed by the mob.

When Durant ran out of ammunition, he lay the weapon across his chest, defeated. The Delta soldiers were dead, and Durant expected the same fate.

Instead, he was stripped and beaten and taken hostage, to be used as a Somali pawn in the American policy reversal. The US dead from this site would be mutilated and dragged through the streets as trophies. For saving Durant's life by sacrificing their own, Delta snipers Shugart and Gordon received the Medal of Honor—the first time the award had been bestowed since the Vietnam War.

Meanwhile, in the growing darkness at the first helicopter crash site, where Rangers were struggling to pull the body of pilot Cliff Woolcott from the wreckage, seven of every ten soldiers had been wounded. Besides disdaining *ad hoc* Somali tactics, however, US officers had completely underestimated the number of rocket-propelled grenades in Mogadishu. The bombardment continued unabated throughout the night, with grenades exploding every five or ten minutes. The Rangers and D-boys took shelter in four houses near the downed helicopter. The Americans found up to two dozen women and children inside, and locked them into back rooms. Though US officers argued that these Somalis were not hostages, Somalis assert that the captives did keep Aidid's militia from trying to demolish the Ranger redoubt.

But Aidid's concerns were larger than saving those Somali lives, he told me later. Already his fighters had inflicted a heavy defeat on the Americans—with Somalis taking hundreds of casualties themselves—but to slaughter the survivors might invite extreme US retaliation. Aidid had at least one American captured alive. Even if these Rangers were freed, they would be licking their wounds and might be reluctant to take on his militia again. In victory, he could afford to be merciful. As dawn broke, the Americans would be given a window of escape. "I decided to open a corridor for them, but along the way they were under fire from my militia," Aidid told me. "They were finishing their ammunition, and morale was very low. We were listening to their wounded crying. They had already been defeated."

Past midnight a 70-vehicle convoy of Pakistani and Malay armored vehicles, carrying American soldiers, finally made its way to the Rangers. The convoy had been delayed because the original Delta snatch mission was kept secret even from top UN commanders, for fear of alerting Somali informants. So the other contingents were not ready when called to assist. The decision of secrecy proved a fatal miscalculation, but the result of that all-American mistake would be turned by US politicians into a *United Nations* faux pas, one more excuse never to trust UN operations again.

"Special-ops people are hard to deal with," said one former military official. "They are arrogant, they overestimate their own capability, and they're very secretive. This all came back to bite them in Somalia. When they needed help, nobody knew what they were doing."[10]

In the eyes of many Somalis, this engagement proved to be a powerful act of courage and political skill, or *belaayo,* by Aidid. "This word means 'disaster' or 'catastrophe,'" writes British historian Lewis, "but what is disastrous to adversaries is often advantageous to one's self, and it is in this sense that *belaayo* is a term of praise for a man whose actions come near to the ideals of Somali belligerence, independence, daring and panache."[11] Somali casualties were so high and the revenge fever so strong, however, that some Habr Gedir put together a plan to literally overrun the UN's Camp of the Murderers the next night, on 4 October. Though the onslaught never occurred, those ready to take part numbered as high as 17,000.

The city was so dangerous now that no American journalist was on hand to witness the Day of the Rangers. Gangs of gunmen had already gone door to door asking for Yanks by name, trying to get at the US "clan" through any means. For this reason, I too was forced to "watch" from Nairobi. It was the first time that being an American prevented my presence on any story.

The few journalists who remained in Mogadishu were a courageous lot, their instinct to witness history unfold often overcoming their sense of self-preservation. The lessons of the July Qaybdiid attack, when the Somali crowd turned on the press corps, were not lost on this group. Their fortitude in covering the aftermath turned out to herald the retreat of the Unosom II intervention: without images of desecrated US soldiers being paraded through the streets by jubilant Somalis, Americans might never have found out that their country was at war. Like the Tet offensive in Vietnam, the political fallout caused a sea change in America and brought an end to the Somalia adventure.

The myth that American troops were bulletproof Rambos would be broken forever in Somali minds. Shocked by a similar realization—and reluctantly admitting that the relief mission had in fact turned to war—President Clinton would end the manhunt and withdraw US forces six months later. The front lines of "peace enforcement" were to be abandoned. The pullout precipitated the retreat of the 14 other Western contingents, irreversibly undermining the UN's nation-building dream.

The handful of non-American journalists had crowded into two cars on 4 October, their Habr Gedir guards nervous but confident at being able to protect these foreigners from their clansmen. As they approached one of the crashed helicopters, Mark Huband of the London *Guardian* recalled, the first thing that emerged from the crowd was a boy hauling a charred torso through the street. The legs had been tied up with rope, the head was missing. "American! American!" the boy had chanted with glee. The journalists drove further and stepped out in the midst of a thick and angry crowd. "We must have been crazy," Mark said. "But they had some American bodies already, which seemed to satisfy their bloodlust. I am convinced that was the only reason why they didn't turn on us."

A soldier's body was being dragged along the ground when they arrived, the one whose disturbing picture would imprint itself on the American psyche. Like the Vietnam War images of a naked child running from a napalm attack and the south Vietnamese police officer executing a suspect with a pistol, it came to define public horror and surprise at how this mission had degenerated. The American UN spokesman Stockwell said glumly: "We came, we fed them, they kicked our asses."

As if more examples were necessary, the depth of anger was clear when a man arrived with a wheelbarrow and unknotted the cord holding together a piece of rolled-up corrugated metal. "It flicked open and out fell one of the mutilated American corpses," Mark said. "The Somalis all laughed and cheered, and it was a very vicious laughter, a killing laughter." When another body was dragged along the street, wearing only stained green underwear and gouged with knives, the roar of the crowd was deafening. Finally the high risk forced the journalists' guards to spirit them away. "There was a constant expectation that the crowd would turn: is it us they want?" Mark recalled. "We gauged their emotion, and when they had that body there was the sickening reassurance that they wanted him, and didn't want me."

The journalist who took the pictures that spread double-page or even in pullout format in American news magazines and were pasted across the front cover of nearly every newspaper in the world the next day was Paul Watson, the Canadian correspondent of the *Toronto Star*. He had been in Somalia for months, covering the unfolding debacle as though on a personal crusade. He was so well known—which didn't mean that he was necessarily protected, as the example of the murdered "Mayor of Mogadishu," Dan Eldon, showed—that he had a nickname among Somalis: Gamey. It meant "he with one arm," referring to Gamey's arm stump, which he used to great effect when making a point during an argument. His humor was boundless and included lewd jokes about the best use of his stump.

Gamey boldly insisted on climbing out of the car twice—against the warnings of his guards—to ensure that he had the pictures of the bodies that would tell the story of Somali rage and American impotence, that would undermine the UN intervention. Though not a professional photographer, he won the Pulitzer Prize and Robert Capa medal for those images. TV footage shot by a Somali cameraman was broadcast worldwide almost immediately. Next day pictures of hostage Michael Durant, bloodied and frightened, being questioned by an interrogator, further traumatized American public opinion. The strength of media images of the famine first precipitated US military involvement. Now press images would precipitate the first US retreat since the Vietnam War.

CNN proved faster than the usual intelligence channels, and President Clinton was forced to react. As more details of the lethal raid emerged, the call to pull out reached a crescendo. Aidid vowed to "double and triple" Somali efforts to kill and kidnap Americans. The cover of *Time* magazine reflected the question on the lips of many who still thought US troops were feeding starving kids in Somalia: under the visage of fearful hostage Durant, it asked, "What in the World Are We Doing?"

President Clinton himself seemed surprised and out of touch with the turn of events, though he had personally authorized the Ranger and Delta raids. He told families of Rangers killed that "he was mystified that the raid had been tried . . . because Washington was shifting its policy."[12] The administration had been considering changing the manhunt in favor of reconciliation, and barely two weeks before that last Ranger raid, Secretary of State Warren Christopher presented a classified state Department paper to Boutros-Ghali that urged exactly that.[13] The UN chief wrote back on 30 September that he was "obliged to make every effort to bring Aidid to justice," and anything less would "lead to the rapid decomposition of the whole Unosom operation."[14]

Clinton was upset at the death toll: "This is stupid," he said. "How could they be going after Aidid when we're working on the political end?"[15]

As with any war—small and insignificant as this one seemed to be—casualties were always a risk. "Too many innocent people are getting killed," Durant told two Western journalists taken to see him in captivity. "People are

angry because they see civilians getting killed. I don't think anyone who does-
n't live here can understand what is going on here. Americans mean well. We
did try to help. Things have gone wrong."[16] Video footage shot by a Somali
cameraman of Durant, his face marked with bloody lacerations, made a deep
impact. These images brought back recent bad memories of the Gulf War,
when captured US airmen were paraded by Saddam Hussein on Iraqi TV.

"It curdles the stomach of every American to see that," Clinton said, then
gave a less-than-honest description of the US role in Somalia. "It makes me
sick and it's reprehensible since all the Americans ever did was go there and
try to save children from starving, reopen the hospitals and the schools and
give people a safe place to sleep."[17]

The American withdrawal was couched in terms that would serve as a sop
to both the UN and the US public. Boutros-Ghali saw the weakening US
political will as cutting and running just when, as the strongest link in the
"peace enforcement" strategy, the US needed to show resolve. The pullout
was gauged to convince the US public that troops would not stay more than
six months, though to protect the retreat, they would need to be doubled in
strength. To justify this new policy and explain the erosion of the old one,
Clinton radically overstated US achievements: "In our nation's best tradition," he said of the Restore Hope famine relief effort, "we saved close to 1
million lives."

"And make no mistake about it," the president warned. "We came to
Somalia to rescue innocent people in a burning house. We've nearly put the
fire out, but some smoldering embers remain. If we leave them now, those
embers will reignite into flames, and people will die again."

Echoing the language used by President Richard Nixon in 1969, when he
said that a premature withdrawal from Vietnam "would result in a collapse
of confidence in American leadership," Clinton added: "If we were to leave
today, we know what would happen. . . . Our leadership in world affairs
would be undermined at the very time when people are looking to America to
help promote peace and freedom in the post–Cold War world. All around the
world, aggressors, thugs and terrorists will conclude that the best way to get
us to change our policy is to kill our people. It would be open season on
Americans."[18] Somalia's "thugs," of course, had come to this conclusion long
before.

Days after the firefight, Robert Oakley—the US president's envoy who
negotiated the safe arrival of US troops in December 1992—was called in to
handle the gunboat diplomacy. I was back in Mogadishu too, now that the
battle had dampened the urge to target Americans. The Somalis had won. The
manhunt would be called off, the US would be allowed to build up with
5,000 more troops and to withdraw without more casualties, though—above

all—hostage Michael Durant had to be released. Oakley made clear to Aidid that mistakes had been made in shifting the UN mission from rebuilding to revenge, and ever since has been fond of describing Aidid as a "bottle of nitroglycerine" that could "blow up in your face at anytime."[19] Intelligence deputy McGovern paraphrased Oakley's threat to Aidid for me: "Give Durant back, or we will give you one hour to leave the city center, then blast it," Oakley had said. "They would love that in the US, because no one cares if you *die* or your clan *dies*—you're seen as murderers."

Ten days later, Aidid released Michael Durant, expecting that the Americans would return the favor by persuading the UN to release Osman Ato and other detainees. From the dusty photographer's "gallery" 50 yards away from the helipad, I watched as Durant was wheeled on a stretcher to a waiting helicopter. He clutched his purple beret and looked over with a smile of relief. He was free. But the Somalis were held for two more months.

The tough talk became much tougher after the hostage release, when Aidid had given up his American "shield." Clinton changed his tone of reconciliation overnight, and Stockwell left nothing to our imagination. The new boost in American troop numbers would "reestablish security, street by street" and "open lines of communication" for relief workers. "We're not bringing in tanks to feed children," he said, ominously. "We want to scare the Somalis badly, and be prepared to kill them if we have to. It is provocative, yes, but it is the cost of doing business." Aidid's militia—their lethal record already well established—were not afraid of having a fresh batch of targets wearing American flag shoulder patches.

In preparation for renewed conflict, the psy-ops unit even printed fresh leaflets declaring that the "bandit Aidid" was blocking peace.

The diplomats tried to put a sugar coating on the militant talk. The mission had become "distorted" because the UN and US had "already decided on an individual and upon an entire subclan for guilt," Oakley said. The US strength was only meant to "protect" foreign troops already there, and he promised: "I will use it in the cause of peace, not in the cause of war."

But the newly deploying American troops felt the need for revenge. "What are we planning with so many troops?" one soldier asked me. "It's going to be heavy, whatever it is." Their enthusiasm dissipated, however, as their aggression was held in check. The recently arrived commanders—head of the gung-ho faction ready to retake the streets—were given a lesson in humility by the veterans. Stealth, surprise, overwhelming force, and the best mind-numbing tricks that psy-ops could muster: everything had been tried, except for an effective hearts and minds campaign. So the new US troop buildup was in fact symbolic only. The Americans had enough firepower in the country to level every Somali town, but they sat helplessly. At one barren crossroads, they didn't even bother to remove the tangled metal barricade set up by children just down the road, in plain sight.

It was December 1993, exactly one year after the marines first stormed ashore in a military intervention that felt like a hometown parade, in which the lucky first wave felt that the Somalis "loved" them. I wanted to get a taste of the US legacy, but in the torment of retreat, it was a bleak picture.

From the gunner's turret, the sweat dripped down from Army Sgt. Wildman's leather helmet strap into his eyes, exacerbating his irritation with another wasted day. His eyes were tired with inactivity, the sun baked his Kevlar helmet and the brain inside. Other soldiers were now laying down triple coils of razor wire in the sand near the American "Victory Base." A US sniper watched the sporadic traffic along 21 October Road, with "skinnies"—and that damn barricade—in his crosshairs. Wildman shouted orders to the Somalis passing through the checkpoint to keep moving, but they just stopped and stared. What could Wildman do? The depressing endgame was now all too evident, and every day the unused weapons would have to be meticulously cleaned of sand and rust. It was obvious that the US military was going to leave with its tail between its legs.

"This could have been finished six months ago, but the politicians screwed it up," Wildman said. He was pissed off. His unit was prepared to die in combat—this was their professional choice—far from the marbled halls of the US Senate where even one casualty could change everything, especially if it was dragged through the street by vengeful Somalis. "This machine was built for one thing, and that is to destroy," he said, head and shoulders up above the armor of his M1A1 Abrams tank. He had planned to make a career of the Army, but Somalia convinced him not to. His helmet was decorated with scrawled barracks poetry: "Man was framed to go to war, women to please the warrior," it read. "All else is folly."

Ground-level as his instincts may have been, Wildman drew an important distinction that many of his senior officers—and politicians, certainly—did not: that there is a very fine line between "peacekeeping" and "peace enforcement" that separates sitting from killing. "What do people expect when they send infantry into an urban setting?" he asked. "Of course we kill people and take casualties. That's all we know and are trained to do—not to be policemen."

Another sergeant was more candid, but could not give his name in line with the newest press rules. His friend had lost a hand in combat, another went home in a body bag. "We don't even know why we're here, or what good we're doing. That's the most depressing thing," he said. "'Why, why, why?' we ask. We're supposed to bring peace and democracy to these people, and they don't even want it."

Later I took a routine night flight in a Black Hawk, part of what chummy military spokesmen referred to as "Eyes over Mogadishu." The city raced past underneath, as we held night-vision goggles to our eyes, to watch the eerie luminescent green and white grid unfold. This was as intimate a view of Somalia as many soldiers would get, and it was positively comprehensive compared to that of most, who were constantly confined to base.

The pilots hovered low over a few buildings, and we watched the green people below become engulfed in sandy rotor wash. The market was a particular target of this Black Hawk diplomacy. The scrappy tin and wood structures ripped apart in our downdraft as if blown apart with explosives.

Petty "vengeance" also found its way on to the streets, where American sharpshooters pushed their aggressive rules of engagement to the limit. After the Day of the Rangers, the snipers killed more than 14 Somalis, some of them children who were found later to have a toy pistol, or *nothing*. By the rules they were not to be "engaged" unless they directly threatened foreign troops. "They were shooting at anything by the time they left," UN spokesman George Bennett told me. The Americans insisted on using high-powered .50-caliber guns usually used to stop moving vehicles and accurate up to 1.2 miles.

But rules were made to be broken. One Navy officer recalled how elite Navy Seals deployed secretly in Mogadishu got around the strict engagement rules. At night, they placed a large crew-served machine gun in the middle of an intersection as bait. One Somali would come to check it out, then call over another to help him carry it away. The moment the second person touched the gun, the Seals could "legitimately" kill the men. Nine Somalis were killed in this manner, the officer said, before it was stopped and "swept under the rug."

In the most embarrassing public incident, which eventually caused sniper teams to be withdrawn, a sniper fired upon what he said was an armed man in the back of a "technical." One round hit the target, the second killed a pregnant woman. US spokesman Col. Steve Rausch said that the "hostile environment" prevented a full investigation, but that "US forces acted properly and dutifully carried out their mission by engaging a Somali armed with a machine gun." This, also, was "a tragic part of doing business."

By this time I had come to expect such cowboy tactics in Somalia. For these young Americans, this mission was all a game, often a fun game in which the tools of their military trade could be used with abandon, "doin' good." For many, time in Somalia was like playing a super-realistic 3-D video game. The targets were often very distant—whether at the end of a sniper rifle or brought down with the twitch of the joystick.

Even when fighting was hand-to-hand, when the Task Force was trapped and being cut to pieces, these soldiers had a particular detachment. As Mark

Bowden, who spoke to scores of Rangers to reconstruct the events of 3–4 October, explained: "Their experience of battle, unlike that of any other generation of American soldiers, was colored by action movies," he wrote in *Black Hawk Down.* "In my interviews with those who were in the thick of the battle, they remarked again and again how much they felt like they were *in a movie,* and had to remind themselves that this horror, the blood, the deaths, was real."[20]

For Vietnam War veterans, all the fears, restrictions, and frustrations of this dishonorable retreat inevitably kindled a sense of *déjà vu.* "Brother Dave" Stockwell once joked with a gallows humor: "We're building a helicopter pad on the roof of the American Embassy so we can have a replay of the fall of Saigon."

Also similar to Vietnam, when the military came up with blood on its hands and began to wonder "What are we doing?" the media were blamed for their discouraging—and disparaging—reports. In Somalia, without the press, US military heavy-handedness would have continued unnoticed except for the accumulated Purple Hearts. Now on the verge of the US retreat, the policy seemed to be to hold things together with surface tension. Some troops, unaware that their problem in Somalia was largely of their own making, wanted to shoot the messenger. I was accosted by one angry soldier when he heard that I was on a photo assignment for *Time* magazine: "Did *you* take that picture of our man being dragged through the streets?" he demanded. I said no. "Good. 'Cause I'm going to kill the fucker who took that. It made us look like shit!"

For these soldiers who risked and lost their lives trying to capture the fugitive, the most galling moment—a tough lesson in *realpolitik,* unbelievable to many—was the sudden rehabilitation of its nemesis Aidid, the great "threat" to world peace. The UN Security Council dropped the arrest warrant, and the warlord came out of hiding like a hibernating dragon now suddenly woken, angry and stronger after a long rest. Aidid had hidden for 97 days from 30,000 troops, including the most elite snatch experts in the world.

The proof was Aidid's flight to peace talks in the Ethiopian capital, Addis Ababa, in early December 1993. He had refused to travel on a UN plane, but accepted a lift on an American transport, which had so recently been used as part of the air armada to hunt him down. Oakley requested the plane, and a joint detail of American troops and militiamen protected the armored convoy as it carried the warlord from his lair to the Mogadishu airport. The sight of Aidid stepping off the plane in Addis Ababa, the Stars and Stripes plainly visible on the fuselage, ignited a firestorm in the US, and more than anything confirmed the end of the war.

With the manhunt over, Aidid could claim victory. The Americans were forced to accept that he *must* be part of any solution to Somalia's crisis. No longer the thug, murderer, or ruthless terrorist, he was now being feted again as "Mr. Wonderful." The White House began to refer to him as "a clan leader with a substantial contituency in Somalia."[21] The chastened and furious Delta Force and Ranger detachments left Mogadishu without ceremony.

As Aidid's career was resuscitated, the architect of the star-crossed manhunt, Howe, left Somalia quietly in March and never returned. After first hearing of his dismissal on the BBC, he sent back a pathetic three-paragraph goodbye message from UN headquarters in New York. His aides had to pack up his personal effects and send them on.

Resigned to an ignominious pullout, the last American soldiers counted down the hours before departure. This was the first US seaborne withdrawal since Vietnam, because commanders didn't want potshots taken at evacuation planes.

To help lessen the blow, US officials later suggested that Aidid was getting "significant" help by Iranian and Sudanese advisers and cash from Libya. The Somalis weren't the only ones to make mileage from the US defeat: Somalia was my "greatest victory," claimed the Saudi Arabia–born terrorist Osama bin Laden, whom the US blames for blowing up US embassies in Kenya and Tanzania in July 1998. Somalis laugh at this claim that bin Laden helped them and say—unanimously—that they never even heard of bin Laden until he began boasting about Somalia years later.

The final days of the US retreat were heavy with symbolism and punctuated by a little gunfight on 24 March 1994 that reminded everyone why it was best to leave. The shooting erupted during a simple dispute over an identity card at the airport gate. Egyptian soldiers first clubbed the offending Somali with truncheons and drove him away. The victim's brother reacted, with his assault rifle. Bullets sang overhead and the American guards drew their pistols and ran for cover. I had been passing through the gate on a routine visit, so I ran too, sweat spreading under my bulletproof vest. This was just another day in Dodge City: the Americans' last.

The Egyptians opened fire with their machine guns but missed the gunman. A brief cease-fire ensued, and the crowd of young men at the gate began to throw stones and blocked the road with chunks of rubbish. US Army Col. Ed Ward, the head of UN operations, happened to be in the area; he strode forward, without flak jacket but with forearms thicker than most Somali thighs. Rolls of flesh bunched, glistening, at the back of his shaven head. He imposed his will through sheer menace of presence. "Yeah, it's fun throwing stones, isn't it?" he asked, as he herded the Somalis one by one out of the airport gate. "I used to do it when I was a kid, too. Different airport."

The Somalis began to throw trash, and a soaring tin can entered my range of vision from an unexpected angle. Thinking it was a rock, I flinched wildly. Ward jerked a chunky thumb at the Somalis, and said: "Obviously, this is always going to be a violent city." One on one, the application of force could work. But collectively, the world's most sophisticated military force had been outmanuevered by a ragtag band of warriors.

The US combat helicopters were shrink-wrapped with molded plastic, armored humvees and tanks painstakingly pressure washed three times each to pass US customs inspection. Before stepping onto the ship, soldiers dropped the loaded M-16 clips from their assault rifles into a box. Painted on one was the promise: "Death Dealer."

On the streets and surrounding the growing number of abandoned bases and UN "strong points," millions of sandbags rotted in the sun. But that was not the only legacy of the American role in the bloodiest UN mission in history. When asked about concrete contributions, US spokesmen pointed to the 28 mobile clinics that treated 5,000 Somalis, 50 tents—which had to be saved by UN officials from destruction because US soldiers deemed them "too dirty" to take home—and 1,000 cots. They noted the 600 miles of rehabilitated roads and a new "safe" road for tanks in Mogadishu that skirted Aidid's turf. Some school supplies had been donated, benches and a few school buildings were built, and orphanages were opened with US-supplied food. Soldiers built an awning at a feeding center for the Irish agency Concern and a playground of used tires.

In truth, President Clinton's assertion that one million Somalis had been saved by the Americans was an exaggeration by as much as 100 times. The manhunt alone took at least 2,000 Somali lives, and as noted earlier, the *delay* in decisive famine action reportedly cost 154,000–240,000 lives.[22] On the American side, there were 44 dead—30 of them in combat—and 175 wounded.

The departure was not pretty, either. Boxes of intravenous fluid—which would have been critical to help stem a budding cholera epidemic—were cut open, and the plastic IV sacks slashed with knives. The soldiers didn't know where to donate other leftovers. One said that he had never seen any Somalis, except those in the camp picking through the American garbage. "We don't have any special friends to leave gifts behind so we're taking our extra sneakers and old T-shirts and clothes, packing them in a bag and leaving them outside our tents," he said.[23]

On the other, destructive side of the ledger, the list of US "achievements" was far longer. Besides the large number of Somalis killed in fighting, parts of the university, the vaccine factory, cigarette and match factory, ministry of livestock, Mogadishu radio, and other buildings were destroyed in the name of security. A tiny offshore island south of Mogadishu was obliterated by artillery and tank gunners, whose job was to blast it with the mountain of American ordnance deemed too unstable to take home. Reuters correspondent Aidan Hartley—who had covered Somalia longer than any of us—laughingly recalled how one gunner let loose into a sand dune with his .50-caliber machine gun. "It's just like eating potato chips," the soldier shouted. "You can't stop!"

By this time, of course, every soldier was convinced that Somalis were naturally violent, and that if the US had succeeded in saving anyone, it was only so they could kill each other. "The mission was worth it, up to the point where they became strong enough to fight us," a departing intelligence officer told me. "We should have left them. They are happiest when they are shooting each other. For us that is barbaric, but here it's okay."

The ironic result of all the violence—Somali and US-led together—was that the streets had become so dangerous that relief agencies, too, were packing up. Despite the altruistic hype of the New World Order, Washington had decided to turn the lights out on Somalia, and who wanted to stay alone in that dark room?

For relief workers, the military expedition was a disaster, and the withdrawal confirmed what they had long suspected: that US forces were by then more interested in saving face than in saving Somalia. Prophets of doom forecast renewed anarchy, so all parties sought spiritual guidance. The Islamic Imam who looked after the divine interests of rival subclans in Mogadishu announced that Somalia's fate was "up to Allah." An Indian tank commander, one soldier of the much-maligned "Third World UN army" staying on, told me that they had already tried to reason with Somalis before, to no avail: "We asked them, 'Why don't you water your crops?' They said, 'Allah will provide.' These Somalis, they rely too much on God."

Deeply cocooned in his Mogadishu bunker, Kevin McGovern, master of UN intelligence, let his mind cogitate on this wasted outcome of peace enforcement. Somalia was no better for the failure, and the world—beset by an ever-growing number of regional ethnic and religious conflicts—would be worse off. Stung in Somalia, the Americans would be reluctant to lead such a "benevolent" adventure again. McGovern was disheartened, more than anything by the lack of resolve.

"The weak link was the assumption that we could do this easily, but we were not ready to take casualties," he told me, his usual smug demeanor set aside for a moment. It was true: when Somalis fought against each other, they did battle against warriors whose readiness to die was as established as their own. The Americans were not willing to die—certainly not here—and that hesitation was all the advantage the Somalis would need.

"We could have stayed after Aidid, but this 180 degree reversal has given him victory. We could have used more overwhelming force. In every instance—except the attack on the Qaybdiid house—we used limited force," he said. A pause. "I'm disappointed we lost people, because now it is for nothing." He held his hands quietly in his lap, as he probed the repercussions of defeat.

"It was a bloody war, an up-front and personal kind of war," he said, his voice controlled, as though balanced by reason. When things went wrong politicians took control, meddling as they were now. "This was not Iraq, where people were killed thousands of meters away. Here the images were up front and in your living room, so that people asked, 'Is this place really worth sacrificing our soldiers for?'"

He stopped again. A great flaw was the lack of clear political objectives, of a viable endgame. And now, the resurrection of the warlord was shameful.

"The man is a killer, a criminal. The US was outfoxed because we let him do it," McGovern said dismissively. But the real problem was one of perception. His voice hardened: "I don't think people even realized that this was a *war*."

When I arrived at the airport for the final send-off, the US guards were in no mood for niceties. My translator, Bashir, was searched, and then the marine hassled my Somali driver like a small-town traffic cop. "Slow down, slow down!" he bellowed. "If I see you do that again, I'm going to work you over."

But the real Hollywood show, complete with a choreographed happy ending, was under way inside. Standing on the Mogadishu tarmac, in full combat dress and surrounded by journalists in the last moment of departure, Montgomery too called on superior powers to save Somalis from themselves. Trussed up in his flak jacket with two black stars stuck to his front, the "first American general in a blue beret" put an unlikely spin on this "peace" deployment: history would look at the "great successes" and "accomplishments" of the US mission, he predicted, and "it will be a marvelous story."

There was no mention of the lowpoint that stuck in the collective Somali memory, the daylight raid on the Qaybdiid house, which was Montgomery's call, in which US forces without warning carried out a massacre of at least 54 people under the banner of UN "peace enforcement"—a massacre that by most any measure qualified as a war crime. And this was no retreat, the general claimed: it was a "tactical redeployment."

The troops "are very proud of what we have done here," Montgomery insisted. "We are the best of the best."

Flanked by two American snipers, soldiers on the roof of the exposed hangar roof lowered Old Glory without a salute. Montgomery made this final offering: "I pray to God for the Somali people. I pray that they will find a way to raise themselves above this anarchy and turmoil, and to build some kind of society based on love, instead of on the gun."

A potentially poignant moment came when a 12-year-old boy broke through the coils of razor wire and ran toward a marine helicopter, waving, just before it lifted off. Despite clouds of sand, a huge soldier jumped out of the back, and gave the boy a hug. But Abdi Hakim—nicknamed "Shortie" by marine sentries, who had given him a fake ID card and the title "Front Gate Honcho"—was not saying goodbye. Instead, he complained that he had been promised 80,000 Somali shillings, or $20. He ran back, empty-handed. It was a whine I had heard many times before—and voiced by ruthless and greedy gunmen, it was the reason US troops had arrived in the first place. "They cheated me, they owed me money," he told us, crying, as the helicopter lifted off.

Left behind also, in the control tower, amid a fistful of American hunting magazines, was a faded page from *Newsweek*. It was printed with one of my pictures of Aidid at a rally, as he paused for a moment from full rhetorical blast. Taped to a wall, Aidid's face had an X target marked out across it.

Even the final act was cloaked with symbolism. An American flag was left flying atop a row of amphibious vehicles as they rolled into the sea. The last words of the last officer, in the last vehicle, was a warning to the crowd of journalists. "I suggest you get out of here while you still can!" he said, and sealed his hatch and was gone.

My translator, Bashir, was late for Friday prayers, and unmoved. "The Americans can burn in hell," he said, with venom in his voice. "Thanks be to Allah, they leave us."

NINE

BACK TO ZERO

[O]nly vengeance fully satisfies honour.
—Ioan Lewis, *A Pastoral Democracy*

Somalis knew well that they were being left behind. Author Mariam Arif Gassem pointed an accusing finger at her own nation: "While the world as a whole, without distinction of race, creed or religion was sympathetic with our agony and willing to reach across vast distances to assist us, we the Somali people were not ready to help ourselves," she wrote in her book *Hostages.* "The world has with pain learned that Somalia is indeed a difficult patient who refuses to be tested, fed and cured."[1]

The result was "self-inflicted social suicide," as Gassem called it. And after the Americans left, it was this "cultural propensity" that led to an initial instinct among Somalis for revenge.

They say they will never forget the carnage inflicted by US-led UN forces, and looked toward time-honored methods for revenge. "Debts in blood lying between groups may sometimes be allowed to remain outstanding without any immediate reprisal being made, and they may even seem to an observer to have been forgotten," explains historian Lewis. Time is no guarantee of safety, and could create "prolonged and bitter hostilities when an incident occurs months, and sometimes even years, later."[2]

UN envoy Howe was top of the hit list, though the larger American clan may be marked, particularly by Aidid's Habr Gedir. But for those who doubt the depth and scale of such possible revenge, there is the chilling tale of Somali Smith. It was told to me prophetically by a foreign man, who knew the victim and played a role in the story.

In 1947 the British district commissioner of Las Anod, in northern Somalia, was a Colonel Smith. He carried out a court order to seize camels from a bandit of the Majerteen clan. Some Somalis were killed in the ensuing fracas. In 1967, having been abroad for many years, "Somali Smith" asked a friend—my narrator—if it would be safe to return briefly to the country with his Somali wife. They decided that, after so much time had lapsed, it probably was. But the day after his arrival, at the door of his hotel room, Somali Smith was stabbed to death by the son of one of the men he had killed in the 1947 raid.

The incident is so famous that it is referred to in a well-known poem that concludes: "There is no sympathy between Smith and the man who took his beautiful camel out to graze / There is no sympathy between the orphan and the man who killed his father."

I was cautioned about the moral of this story, and its visceral repercussions for Howe, who lived at the time in Washington, D.C., home to the largest Somali community in America. "Howe will be tracked down to his house in the States and have a problem for the rest of his life. He and the top UN generals are considered murderers," my narrator warned. Revenge would be carried out by relatives of the slain, and Howe might not be the only target. "Americans will not be safe from assassination, or even able to walk the streets of Somalia for 20 years. They've just killed too many people."

When I brought up this risk with Howe, in the concrete confines of the UN/embassy courtyard, he was slightly taken aback. Howe told me: "This mission is the will of the world. I hope those people realize that we are doing good things for Somalia, and that we are an instrument of UN policy."[3]

But that is not what many Somalis believe. Their thinking follows that of Jimmy Carter, who wrote to President Clinton after an East Africa visit to say that he had found unanimous agreement "that Admiral Howe has been a disaster, with an almost fanatical belief that he must win some kind of military victory in Somalia."[4]

So for those like Hussein Mohamed Abdi "Sanjeeh," the scar-nose Aidid security man who survived the Qaybdiid house massacre minus his right arm, justice is inevitable. He wanted "a chance to go to [the war crimes tribunal at] The Hague, the international court. It's a war crime, really. I'm very glad that I'm still alive, to be witness, and to take revenge," he said, his good arm resting in his lap years later, the whites of his eyes clouded by a life of steady pain that began when he was caught between the eyes by another boy's knife.

"If there is no court, I will do something, some other way," he vowed. "I will pass on to my son or my daughter that the Americans have done this or that, and it will be very bad news for the future of Americans and for my children," he said.

"For me it is our revenge. And Howe will be the first. If I don't find Howe, I will find his family, and revenge his son. Even his clan. I believe that all Americans are part of this clan altogether," he continued. "Not all Americans [will be targeted]. I don't mean that I will avenge all. But if I don't find them, I will avenge their sons and their daughters."

As of this writing in winter 1999, Admiral Howe, a retired four-star US Navy admiral, lives in Jacksonville, Florida. He is executive director of the Arthur Vining Davis Foundations, among the largest grant-providers in America that, their literature states, are a "philanthropic institution strongly committed to honorable service to society."

Sanjeeh is not alone in harboring a deep urge for revenge, and one casualty has already been recorded. A civilian American pilot who regularly flew relief shipments to the northern Kenyan town of Wajir was killed at the end of August 1993. He was hacked to death, a UN source said, because he was American, by a Somali soldier of the Kenya Army whose father was among the victims of the American Bloody Monday assault. Despite a tradition in Somalia of adhering to specific laws of war that can lead to peace, paying blood money has never been a guarantee of calm and "hardly outweighs the gain to name and honour which is brought by retaliation."[5]

As Somalis turned to thoughts of revenge, Americans turned to thoughts of blame. Who was responsible for wrecking the ship of peacekeeping? Who propelled that ship across the Mogadishu Line, by turning a relief mission into a war? Who began to kill Somalis, when they were meant to have been saved?

Certainly, Somalis were guilty of atrocious acts. But so were Americans. It is for this reason—not just in Somalia, but because of potentially illegal aspects of engagements in Iraq, Yugoslavia, and elsewhere—that the US government is one of the few nations that does not endorse the creation of a supreme world court or a permanent war crimes tribunal. Somali warlords such as Aidid and Ali Mahdi have enough blood on their hands—and did so long before UN and US troops ever arrived—to face a war crimes tribunal.

But Somalis also have a keen sense of justice. And they know that since almost all the US military efforts were under the guise of the UN anything-goes Chapter VII mandate, there may never be a legal reckoning under the Geneva conventions or laws of war. In this face-off, as Somalis see it, even the purest motives mean little when measured against dead kinsmen.

For his part, Montgomery defended any mistakes with the simple Bible-echoing line: "There is no such thing as an immaculate intervention." Testifying before the US Senate Armed Services Committee in May 1994, Montgomery said he supported the manhunt because Aidid was the "center of gravity" for anti-UN attacks. "And that if Aidid is removed from the scene, the consensus opinion was that the SNA militia would have a hard time continuing to conduct operations," he said. "I did indeed think that it made sense to take Aidid off the scene."[6]

Though Montgomery might have been the natural fall guy when the mission fell apart, he claimed that he did not act without direction from above. To prevent him, in the words of the *Post's* Keith Richburg, from "spilling the beans, because they [the top brass] were all in on it,"[7] he was given a third star and promoted to a comfortable NATO job in Brussels before he retired. By the fall of 1999, his official Somalia After Action Report had not yet been declassified.

The "future of Somalia is clearly in the hands of the Somali people," Montgomery told the Senate. "That is the bottom line of what we did there. We gave the Somali people another chance. . . . The story of US forces is, I firmly believe, a positive one."

General Garrison, who led the Delta Force and Ranger Task Force to the Battle of the Black Sea—and had nothing to do with approving the manhunt itself—coincidentally retired the same day that Aidid died, in August 1996. But he also sent a handwritten letter to President Clinton in which he made clear that America's costliest firefight since the Vietnam War was his operation. "The mission was a success," he wrote, because the targets were apprehended. But as to the outcome: "The authority, responsibility and accountability for the Op rests here in MOG with the TF Ranger commander, not in Washington."[8]

Testifying also before the Senate committee, he said that he had all the fire support he needed, such that "if we had put one more ounce of lead on south Mogadishu on the night of 3 and 4 October, I believe it would have sunk."[9]

But of course, the military focus on a manhunt was the political product of high-level assumptions and decisions. Along with "United Nations" representative Howe—the manhunt king—US envoy Robert Gosende also pushed hard to remove Aidid. He was sacked immediately after the Black Sea battle for his tough stance, and later reemerged as a public affairs officer at the US Embassy in Moscow. April Glaspie, also among the hard-liners, later joined the UN Relief and Works Agency, which works for Palestinians in Gaza, the West Bank, and refugees across the Mideast. A colleague of hers—referring snidely to the fallout of her diplomacy with Saddam Hussein and Aidid—joked that "she has trouble with men."

Moving up the food chain, Secretary of Defense Les Aspin, who had conveniently turned down a request for more armor, was forced to resign and was the obvious political casualty. His decision to reject armor in September 1993 was made when the Clinton administration was under pressure to act in

Bosnia, when Congress would have been loath to approve any more hardware for Somalia. Though sending tanks then would have been seen as a dangerous escalation, Aspin nevertheless became the whipping boy after the battle.

Madeleine K. Albright, the US ambassador to the UN who presented the "Aidid manhunt" resolution within hours of the slaughter of the Pakistanis, would soar to become secretary of state. But before assuming that post, at the UN she would be instrumental in ensuring that the US fudged on its responsibility to help stop the 1994 genocide in Rwanda. Then, as Clinton's ranking hawk, she would continue to single out unsavory leaders—Iraq's Saddam Hussein (1998) and Yugoslavia's Slobodan Milosevic (1999)—for personal demonization and then military attack. Albright's point of reference in these campaigns was her status as a "daughter of Munich," one whose Czech family had fled Nazism. The result was a hard-nosed rejection of any policy of appeasement and the belief that crucial moments of diplomacy required tough lines drawn and a credible military threat to enforce them. Top Russian officials called her "Madame War."[10]

The UN inquiry into the disastrous escalation of fighting in Somalia, however, found that the Security Council resolution calling for Aidid's arrest—the vote that Albright wanted to be as tough as possible, even before any investigation into the 5 June killings—guaranteed further violence: "The resolution resulted in a virtual war situation between Unosom II and the SNA, as the two sides attacked each other over a period of four months."[11]

At the top, President Clinton authorized all Task Force operations, but later, inexplicably, said that he was "mystified" that this 3–4 October raid had been carried out. He was vilified by Larry Joyce, a retired lieutenant colonel and Vietnam veteran, whose Ranger son, Sergeant Casey Joyce, had been killed in Somalia. "The thing that haunts me, is if it was so important to capture Mohamed Aidid when the Rangers went over there, why was it so unimportant on October 4?" Joyce asked.[12] The US military escort for Aidid to talks in Ethiopia especially galled him. "Now the same amateurs who orchestrated that fiasco are dishonoring every American soldier who died in Somalia and are insulting every family member who lost a loved one there."[13]

As the realization grew within the administration that Somalia had become the biggest military misadventure since US "peacekeepers" were sent to Lebanon in 1983, the president's role was masked until the debacle was safely overshadowed by other presidential concerns in Haiti and at home.

The truth for Clinton was even tougher to take, an adviser reportedly said, because "as a young anti-Vietnam activist, [he] had written that he 'loathed' American Army tactics that often killed women and children in Vietnam. 'Now he felt responsible' for the same tactics." The same report described how an "elaborate damage-limitation program managed to fog the public perception of Clinton's responsibility."[14] One Clinton confidante conceded that "Somalia was the one thing where we were really responsible for what went wrong."

And if there was still any doubt about institutional responsibility, US politicians and officers alike perpetuated the greatest myth of all: that the UN was to blame for "dragging" America into a *United Nations* Mission Impossible in Somalia and for "moving the goalposts" without alerting the US. That myth—for it is nothing more—holds that it was the UN that laid down the treacherous Mogadishu Line, and this view has stuck fast in the popular American mind.

Clinton struck out at the UN, accusing it of incompetence and endangering US lives, and implied—already just days before the Ranger firefight—that the US was drawn into the deep waters of nation building against its will: "The United Nations cannot simply become engaged in every one of the world's conflicts," he told the UN. Later he said to reporters, "If the American people are to say 'yes' to peacekeeping, the UN must know when to say 'no.'"[15] In Mogadishu, spokesman Stockwell took up the theme, telling me, "No US officer approves of these cowboy tactics."

The UN inquiry, however, found that "many major" operations "were totally outside the command and control of the UN, even though the repercussion impacted crucially on the mission." In this way, the UN was "handicapped in prosecuting that war" because the US QRF and later Task Force Ranger were not under Unosom II control. "If these operations were not under Unosom II the question arises as to whether they were authorized by the United Nations," the report noted. "If they were not, then the SNA's right to defend itself was even more appropriate."[16]

The "Vietnam Syndrome" of a strong (but goodhearted, in this case) Goliath defeated by a weak (and evil) David was overcome by the 1991 Gulf War. But now it was coming back, dressed up as the "Somalia Syndrome" and causing collective amnesia at the Pentagon. So what better excuse than to blame the UN? Calling the bluff, the *Economist* termed this slippery blame shift "a chutzpah level high even by American political standards."[17]

Far more damage, this time in foreign policy, was the impact that humiliation in Somalia had on American willingness to engage in multilateral peace operations abroad. When the Clinton team first entered the White House in early 1993, it aimed to revitalize the UN as a tool for world peace.[18] With high hopes, the new president ordered a review of US policy toward peacekeeping operations. The first draft was approved in July and "supported an enhanced use of multilateral operations, elevated the UN as a major actor on the world stage, and committed the US to support such operations in all of their political, military and financial dimensions."[19]

But events in Somalia caused that ambitious agenda to be reined in. It "blew up in our faces," the State Department's policy director told Boutros-Ghali. That draft was "put on the shelf forever. Somalia will have a devastating impact on the future of UN peacekeeping operations. No more big ones.[20] When the final Presidential Decision Directive 25 was signed on 3 May 1994, it was a draconian version that imposed a host of strict conditions on any US peacekeeping participation. There had to be American interest at stake; the mission had to be clearly defined in size, scope, and duration; peace among all local parties had to be fully evident; and there had to be sufficient political will and an identifiable "exit strategy." What had started as a broad guideline had been "laboriously reworked after US casualties mounted" to become a "statement of caution."[21]

It was a recipe for future inaction and it was signed, conveniently for gun-shy politicans, less than one month after the start of the genocide in Rwanda—just when calls for action to stop the killing there were gathering pace. US envoy Richard Holbrooke also had a hard time finding support in 1995 for sending US troops to the Balkans, and even in making peace. "Phrases like 'slippery slope' and 'mission creep' were code for specific events that had traumatized the military and the nation: Mogadishu, which hung over our deliberations like a dark cloud; and Vietnam, which lay further back, in the inner recesses of our minds," Holbrooke wrote in his book, *To End a War*. The failed manhunt was paramount: "The scars from that disaster would deeply affect our Bosnia policy. Combined with Vietnam, they had what might be called a 'Vietmalia syndrome' in Washington."[22]

The new American skittishness likewise made the UN wary of taking on US troops for peacekeeping, for all the attendant baggage that accompanied their deployment and their insistence on "zero-dead wars." Though 58,000 Americans died in Vietnam for reasons that, 25 years later, were deemed to be wrong by the decision makers who kept American troops there, the near-bloodless success of the massive Operation Desert Storm campaign against Iraq in 1991 raised popular expectations to the point where even a handful of American casualties could force a policy reversal. After all, how many Americans shoot *each other* in the US each year? The number of Americans lost in Somalia, noted one critic, was "fewer than the number of New York taxi drivers murdered every year."[23]

That irony was not lost on the UN, which found the US to be an unreliable ally. Kofi Annan, then the UN undersecretary-general for peacekeeping, noted wryly that "one has only to kill a few Americans and the US leaves."[24] The US reversal was even more galling for UN chief Boutros-Ghali, one of the staunchest proponents of Chapter VII intervention and a hard-line obsessor of the manhunt. He complained that the pullout would "condemn the people of

Somalia to the resumption of civil war and all the horrors that would result" and "represent a humbling" of the UN. "All my experience tells me not to trust the US. You are unpredictable and change your minds too often."[25]

The Australian general who led the UN force in Cambodia in 1994, for example, said that a key to success was "no American combat troops." Why? "No GIs means no teary widows on the evening news, fewer flak-jacketed heroes of the Fourth Estate . . . no teenage staffers on a 'vital' congressional delegation—none of the stuff that gets in the way of operational decisiveness."[26]

Already the date for a final UN military withdrawal had been set for the end of March 1995, one year after the American pullout. Somali anger at the failed nation-building mission focused on the "Camp of the Murderers," because even as US troops bid *adieu,* the UN still had a job to do. Unsavory as that task might be, however, US officials had set the precedent for living with style behind very high walls. Even as violence consumed the streets, they had gone about creating a modern city in the midst of chaos, to more comfortably weather the battering storms that tore daily at the lives of Somalis stuck *outside.* Money was lavished on the UN compound, while a fraction was spent to ease the suffering of Somalis themselves. As fighting intensified, many Somalis working inside were told to leave and were replaced by imported Kenyan workers, who were considered less of a security risk. The isolation of this Eden was complete.

No expense was spared for the comfort of foreign staff, who had deigned to take up such a hardship post and do battle to save Somalis from themselves. There were immaculate new street signs and lights, the only ones that worked in the city, and a satellite communications system linked to ten earth stations that kept foreigners in touch with distant homes. Senior officers parked in reserved spots. Shopping was a top priority. At a PX run by Israelis, single malt whiskey, fine French wine, and cases of ice-cold beer were sold next to packets of Doritos and Chips Ahoy cookies. There was aloe vera sunburn ointment, zinc oxide for white noses, and dark glasses. Bootleg replicas of Dan Eldon's "Thank You for Not Looting" T-shirts were on sale next to leather and nylon shoulder holsters.

Third World soldiers spent their hard currency earnings on elaborate stereos and big-screen television systems, the duty-free booty of their time in Somalia. (The Bangladeshi squad arrived in the country with one shipping container full of gear, for example, and left with 14.) The video store did brisk business in pornography and action thrillers, since every gunslinger, Somali and otherwise, wanted to be Rambo. Pizza with any mix of toppings was served up at Bogart's Take Away for $6.50. Dollars only, please.

Military units fought to win the coveted "Quarters of the Month" award, manicuring tiny flower beds that bloomed from the cultivated sand in the shape of their national flags.

The sprawling former US Embassy compound was leased to Unosom II for one token dollar, but that was the only evident saving. Of the billions spent in Somalia, most was swallowed by the military. Barely 4 percent found its way into the local economy.[27] The built-in 9 percent profit for Brown & Root, the American contractor building the camp, was by itself reported to be far more money than was spent rebuilding Somalia. The new UN sewer system alone, with a price tag of $9 million, contrasted starkly with the $7 million spent outside the compound on Somali "infrastructure repairs" in one entire six-month period.[28]

Eventually, this glittering prize was all to be handed over to the new Somali "government." But officials recognized that the imbalance might give the wrong impression. "We've also got ideas for recreation—tennis courts, squash courts, swimming pool, a mini-golf course. But we're not quite there yet," one said. "We thought that was really gilding the lily a little bit. We don't want to be seen as looking just after ourselves when, after all, we're not going to be living here that long."[29]

Outside the walls, recognition of the fiscal injustice grew. Unosom II had created 11,000 Somali jobs. But the unprecedented Band-Aid of $2.5 billion was wasted as Somalia returned helplessly back to year zero. Somalis were enraged and asked, "How can anyone can justify spending $10 on 40 cents of aid?" They pointed with disgust at the shining creation. Dr. Mohamed Ali Fuje, a hospital director, told me it reminded him of London's Oxford Street. "It is very clean, and very beautiful, but when I go outside it's another world."

On the eve of the March 1995 UN troop withdrawal, the anger among veteran officials was also strong with contempt. They knew the Somalis had outmaneuvered them at every turn, and a dispirited gloom descended upon the final days. From the Somalis, too, there was no letup. Where else but here would a contractor hired to pump out UN septic tanks empty the first, and then refill the second with sewage, so that he would constantly be called back? Where else would a group of people, promised by one UN official that they could each have "one plastic jerry can" full of gas, *each* fill their cans first with boiling water, to stretch the plastic and maximize their gift of fuel?

For days, I had watched huge Somali lorries loaded with looted plywood, planks, and canvas wind their way out of the compound, past Pakistani UN checkpoints at the airport gate. It had become a free-for-all that galled many UN staff who were helpless to stop it. Anger was vented in small ways. Rotting old Somali Air Force planes were taken away to be UN museum pieces.

One dawn, I watched armored bulldozers smash up UN vehicles, so they couldn't become battle wagons. New furniture was burned. This pathetic sight was topped only by the madness of one frustrated UN official, who stayed awake all night drilling holes through the bottom of each of a thousand plastic cups that were to be left behind. Somalia would be left alone, but he was damned if it would be left with usable UN coffee cups.

At dusk, I patrolled with Pakistani troops as they tried to clear the airport of looters. They would sweep in on a group of women and children looters with their headlights on, and round them up into cars and pack them off to beyond the fence. There were frantic scenes as tearful women shrieked and fought with the armed Pakistani troops. Overloaded, many had to sit where they had collected their loot, waiting for succor. Holes in the fencing gaped, letting looters out with their booty like a pricked balloon slowly loses its air.

When Egyptian troops abandoned their camp at the airport, they tossed every conceivable "gift" over the fence to the waiting looters who had crept in with fake identification cards. As I was taking pictures, one child wore a stolen camouflage flak jacket and a new blue beret, replete with enamel UN badge. He saluted me comically, as the crowd fought for Egyptian throwaways.

With more assets in the country than anyone else, the UN payoff to avoid angry hassle was heavy and covered huge amounts of back pay, extra pay, and tidy severance packages. In its last weeks, Unosom II paid $1 million *each day* in cash to Somali workers, virtually depleting the dollar reserves of Kenyan banks. But still that was not enough to pay for "security." One morning, hundreds of Somali UN workers staged a sitdown strike on the airport tarmac, stopping a planeload of hundreds of evacuating Pakistani soldiers from leaving. It was a scene not unlike one I had seen two and one-half years earlier, when Pakistani UN troops unable to deploy—thanks to Aidid's conditions—spent their days carving cricket bats and *rehearsing* escorting food convoys.

To try to ensure that there would be no further embarrassment and bloodshed, and because he said "it's the right thing to do," President Clinton ordered a marine amphibious unit to protect the withdrawal. These Americans would be on Somali soil only a few days, and to avoid lethal "accidents" this time, they came equipped with the latest riot-control gear—the kind of thing that might have saved many Somali lives if deployed during earlier street battles. One UN security officer often asked Howe, as Somali casualties added up because guns were used for crowd control: "Where are your water cannons?" The UN envoy, he said, didn't see any reason for them.

For Operation Quick-draw, the Americans carried "bee-sting" hand grenades that sprayed hard rubber pellets and nozzle goop-guns that blasted immobilizing glue. Where was all this non-lethal gear when American forces were blasting the Qaybdiid house or killing kids with .50-caliber sniper

SOMALIA

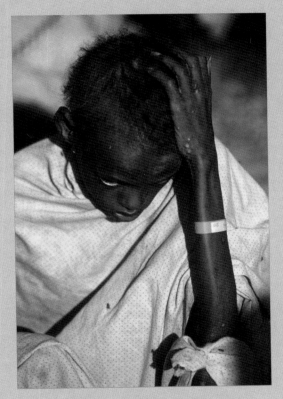

A simple child that lightly draws its breath . . .
What should it know of death?
    —William Wordsworth

Photographs by Scott Peterson

Gunmen: "If all Somalis are to go to Hell, tribalism will be
their vehicle to reach there."
    —President Mohamed Siad Barre

Hunger: "I do not believe food was taken
by force by my men. This is not a crime."
    —Warlord Mohamed Farah Aidid

US cavalry: "God's work" at which Americans "cannot fail."
—President George Bush

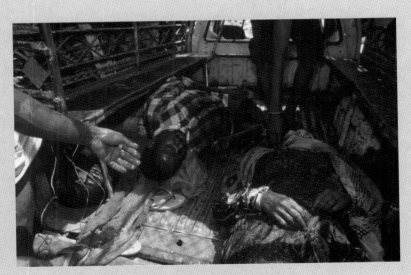

Victims: "What can you do when women and children are killed by soldiers with blue helmets?"
—Somali man loading bodies

Gen. Mohamed Farah Aidid: "We know that you, general, are the only one in Somalia ready to fight the enemy." —Somali elders

Shukri Mohamed: "Can you imagine back home, losing even one of your children?" —Irish nurse

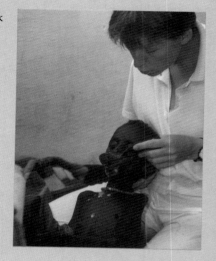

Adm. Jonathan Howe: "We're not going to hunt for [Aidid], or look down every rathole for him."

Maj. Gen. Thomas Montgomery: "History will record the 'great successes' and 'accomplishments' of the US mission and 'it will be a marvelous story.'"

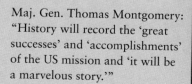

Protest: "During a blood feud, if you are wronged but too weak to respond, you must be patient. We will not forget these things."

Casualty: "The best thing about Somalia was that it saved us from Bosnia."
— Pentagon official

Black Hawk: "If we had put one more ounce of lead on South Mogadishu . . . I believe it would have sunk."
—Maj. Gen. William Garrison

Departure: "The Americans . . . came for relief but they changed it to a war which had never been seen before."
—Aidid's security chief

SUDAN

Prayer: "Where will our people run to? Their only chance remains to run to God."
    —Bishop Paride Taban

Famine: "Now we are like flies. Wherever there is food, that is where we go."
    —Displaced man

Rebel: "To say that the war is coming to an end is a gross misconception."
    —SPLA chief John Garang

Arab horsemen: "Anyone who betrays this nation does not deserve the honor of living."
—President Omar al-Bashir

Wounded guerilla: "There are many reasons for sorrow in Sudan, but your faith is stronger than your enemy."
—Archbishop George Carey

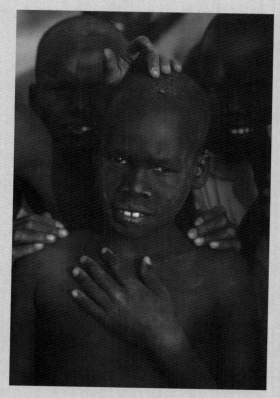

Lost boys: "We are the forgotten people.
Why do you let us die?"

RWANDA

Resolve: "To kill thousands of people in a day means that you are very serious about what you are doing."
  —Tutsi commander

Hutu soldier: "The grave is only half full.
Who will help us to fill it?"
          —Radio des Mille Collines

Rukara carnage: "The people sang hymns and
cried and prayed."
          —Survivor

Innocence: "I believe in Santa Claus."

Tools: "The crocodiles in the Kagera River and the
vultures over Rwanda have seldom had it so good."
    —UN Security Council diplomat

Hutu corpse, Zaire: "This dying may have been divine retribution, but the Hutu refugees did not see it that way. They didn't believe they were guilty."

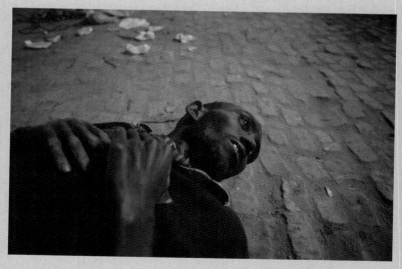

Tutsi near death: "All over the world there were people like me, sitting in offices, day after day, who did not fully appreciate the speed at which you were being engulfed."
—President Bill Clinton

Refugees: "How can we think of passing food through the window while doing nothing to drive the murderer from the house?"
  —Médecins Sans Frontières

Tutsi children: "Lord, we stand here outside your church, where we have seen things that most people never will. . . . "

"Also, [Lord] we ask that you provide us with understanding, so that when we go away we will know how this can be your will. . . . "

rounds, or the Pakistanis were firing upon—and being fired at—by Somali crowds?

The UN troops being "protected" didn't think they needed this American help, but they had no choice. To guarantee safety, US commanders followed a tested formula: They paid groveling visits to Aidid and Ali Mahdi, winning public guarantees of support for a peaceful withdrawal. What happened afterward, they didn't care. "It is like a symphonic rondo," explained UN spokesman Bennett. "Because it started with the Americans, it must finish with the Americans."

On the roof of the Sahafi Hotel, as the UN was leaving, we sat and enjoyed the sporadic whistle of gunfire overhead. The predicted civil war had not yet re-erupted—this shooting was entirely normal. We laughed when Carlos Mavroleon, an ABC television cameraman (who died in Pakistan in late 1998) described a recent ride back from Baidoa with his gunmen. They got a flat tire and stopped. One of the gunmen jumped out heatedly and menaced the driver with his assault rifle. "No, No, Abdi!" Carlos shouted. "Don't shoot the driver! It's not his fault."

Knowing laughter, I thought back to the day when another Abdi worked as *my* guard, and was also rather too ready to kill. Some two and one-half years later, the streets were still as violent as ever, the cycle of action, reaction, and revenge unsheathing itself. In the days before the final UN pullout, looters and gunmen swarmed into the airport like starving ants gorged on syrupy adrenaline. The New World Order was once again in the hands of the warlords and their militias. Albright's highly touted "assertive multilaterism" seemed to be in its death throes. Aidid confirmed this return to "normalcy" by taking a personal tour of the airport in a particularly well-appointed technical. He was triumphant, the burst of heavy machine guns reassuring. Now there was nothing to interfere with the medieval machinations of Somali politics.

I went back to Somalia a few months later, to see how a nation gets on after it has been officially abandoned by the outside world. The sense of *déjà vu* with my earliest trips was startling. But the lawlessness had become routine. Somalis just absorbed it and made the daily struggle to get by their permanent business.

At the edge of the abandoned UN compound, the massive metal gates had been bent with forced entry, and then the moonscape began. The once-glittering US Embassy grounds had returned to wasteland, with scraps of torn plastic blowing against the wall, or caught in leftover coils of razor wire, whipping past the few looters who dug deep to extract every stretch of copper wire and every last segment of water pipe. Even the concrete foundation blocks for prefab houses and offices were gone. For the $160 million the UN spent on this compound, if nothing else, at least some foreigners had the pleasure for a few months of ordering take-away pepperoni pizza and of watching their excrement flush away into a modern sewer system.

But as I surveyed this wreckage, I couldn't help wondering what the result would have been if as much effort had been put into understanding Somalis as was put into the state-of-the-art UN sewer. Such a waste. And such a shame.

To me it was incredible that Somalia seemed so cursed. One well-used joke is that when God created Somalia, he cried. And I was coming to think that it was true: how could it be possible that so much blood had spilled here? I had seen so many tears—from the civil war, through the famine to the American-led war, to the tears of watching the Western saviors with their food and money and "civilization" wave goodbye. For good. And the result of that microcosm of experience—I've just spent nine chapters describing it to you—was nothing. Nothing here had changed at all.

What happened to all the blame? Where was all the anger that had been generated by the violence? Where were the joys of the children who were briefly in school again and being fed, or living for a while in peace, at least? What about the "all-important" politicking, all the human and emotional effort spent to bring hope, and for what? Will anyone outside remember this traumatic moment of human history in ten years time? What about even today?

Nothing, nothing had changed. It seemed that Somalia's particular relationship with all four of the Horsemen of the Apocalypse would continue, and Somalia would remain an isolated organism worth examining only for what it tells us about the Dark Side.

Somalis were still battling for food. Gunmen were still battling for their clips of bullets and their daily bundles of qat, to escape the hideous reality of *nothing*. And the warlords plotted still, looking to control this street or that, struggling to exemplify all the Somali characteristics of war and peace—embodied in one warrior-king. *Déjà vu.*

In the early morning at the UN compound, most gunmen had yet to sleep off their night of chewing qat. They were lethargic, so freelance looters moved in to cart away a lamppost, or empty food tins, only mildly harassed. I watched these miners at work, with pickaxes, searching for booty. They looked exactly like their predecessors at the beginning of the war, soiling their hands to dig up the buried cables and wiring that had once bound Mogadishu into a working, viable place.

My presence with a camera alerted some gunmen, and they rounded a corner with their rifles ready. As we made our escape out the main gate, they ran after us. My guards were nervous—nothing new about that: remember the gun market?

As we left, near a former UN checkpoint, I saw an old man hunkered down, his narrow dried hands busy near his feet. He had no reason to fear the gunmen who were chasing me. They were *his* people. But I could see that he was at work. Methodically, he made a growing pile of Somalia's most abundant resource: sand. He didn't need it, nobody did.

But he *had* to steal the rotting green plastic sacking, all that remained from 14 million sandbags.

My mind flashed back to all those dire warnings I had been told long ago: don't do business deals with Somalis; they are all gangsters and thieves. They would steal anything.

Still, such stereotypes of Somali violence were not perceived by foreigners alone. Speaking softly, as though giving voice to some terrible muse, one gunman conceded: "We need another ten years of civil war and thousands more dead, then maybe we will be ready to stop," he told me. Any hope for Somalia's future was squashed between his finger and the trigger of his gun.

"This is the way we think, and you can't change that," he said.

"It is us."

PART II

SUDAN

ENDLESS CRUSADE

Every soul shall have
A taste of death.

—The Koran, Sura III:185

TEN

DIVIDED BY GOD

Our religion says that it is wrong to mistreat cats.
How could we torture humans?

—Abdelaziz Shiddo, minister of justice,
defending Sudan's human rights record

The biting sharp stink of sweaty saddle leather was more acrid in the heat, and blended well with the charged air of Islamic fervor. Battalions of chanting Arab warriors sat astride horses and camels, cracking hide whips, menacing with long swords and their 1,000 spears glinting in hard sunlight. They wore full battle regalia, white turbans and flowing robes, on the southern edge of the Sahara desert. In Sudan in March 1992, this town of Ed Daien, nearly 1,000 miles southwest of the capital, Khartoum, is as close to the front line as you could get without taking up a sword or Kalashnikov yourself. For this is a civil war between north and south, a war that is both ethnic and religious, one fought between Arabs and Africans, Muslims and Christians. It is one in which violence has steadily increased as if to comply with ancient prophecies of apocalypse.

The rally was a medieval show of strength by those bent on imposing Allah's will—Islam—from the north across all of Sudan; and then much further, deeper, into Africa. The horsemen had gathered *en masse* to greet Sudan's President Lt. Gen. Omar Hassan el-Bashir. When his small plane touched down on the airstrip, the rhythmic clanking and shouting noise of battle doubled. Urging these citizens on with his stick, the general made his way past the lineup for 20 minutes. Presidential pride grew with this show of support, renewing hopes of triumph in the Holy War against infidels in the south.

The stocky president mounted a platform, his green military

uniform out of place among the throngs of robed Sudanese footmen, who choked in the clouds of dust whipped up by the horses and camels. He roused the mob with promises of victory and held aloft the dual badges of his junta, a copy of the Koran and an AK-47 assault rifle—the proverbial book and sword.

"Whoever thinks of subjugating us," Bashir warned, a bright paperclip incongruously holding the tongue of his belt to his wide belly, "they will find a nation that loves martyrdom."

A unit of Sudan's new Islamic militia, the Popular Defense Forces (PDF), paraded past. This was the vanguard for PDF forces that with reserves would soon number 100,000—both zealots and conscripts—the Islamic "shock troops" that that year were beginning to replace the regular army on the front line. This platoon was young, carried Korans, and wore worn khaki uniforms donated by Iran. The PDF was heralded as God's scourge on the rebels, who dreamt of going to Heaven to join the ranks of the martyrs.

Carried away in their excitement, the president and his commanders jumped up like schoolchildren at play. They chanted *Alahu Akbar!*—God is Great!—and hugged each other as if the war was already won, as if God were pleased. The crowd was lost in the roiling dust, as roars of approval blanketed the town. Here were the true believers, on a mission that harkened back to a golden age of Islam after its seventh-century founding, when Islam knew few borders. The faith was then spreading from its source in Arabia at Mecca and Medina—the Hejaz Red Sea coast of the peninsula that is now Saudi Arabia—carried by Islamic armies marching to conquer new territory. But ever since the *muezzin*'s call to prayer first swept through Egypt and today's northern Sudan in the ninth and tenth centuries, a barrier arose at the southern edge of the desert, where Arab blended with African, and where the parched land gave way to impenetrable jungles and swamps.

Sudan's conflict today is a modern extension of the Crusades, of the collision between Islam and Christianity. As it was then, this war is still wholly primitive in its disregard for civilians. This is a battle in which there are no prisoners of war. And of course, these days it carries on with 20th-century weapons. Not every northern fighter is a bearded Muslim zealot swinging a sword for God's will. And not every southern rebel is a Christian soldier marching as to war. In fact, when the civil war first began more than 45 years ago, religion was hardly a factor. But over time, religious aspects have turned into red lines, even a *casus belli*. In the past decade, the war has been transformed that way.

The revival of militant Islam in northern Sudan in the early 1990s reflected a growing reliance on fundamentalism throughout the Muslim world. Across the same pathless terrain that halted Islam's spread in Sudan centuries ago, the mission has been taken up afresh, with horrifying results.

Religion may be window dressing—a means of mobilizing troops and cash for both sides, though citing holy imperatives has produced a special breed of fighter in Sudan's frontline trenches: one whose protection is often left to God. For the populations hammered by this conflict, religious sense has also, not surprisingly, deepened. A more religious war was always just the next step.

This conflict differs from other Africa afflictions because there has never been a defining moment. No threat of famine has been so dire, no battle so decisive, no mass killing so graphically recorded that it ever caused lasting outrage—or action, or even more than passing interest—in foreign capitals. Unlike Somalia and Rwanda, where saturation media coverage of atrocities sparked attempts to find solutions, war in Sudan is so wide and often so incomprehensible that it almost defies intervention.

Instead, UN and relief officials feed and retreat. The conflict simmers and erupts and simmers again, almost by its own volition, and—despite years of aid and massive influxes of relief food—Sudan is worse off today. The death toll still surges. After a devastating famine in 1988, the UN the next year created a huge umbrella organization called Operation Lifeline Sudan, an ambitious relief behemoth that has ever since sought to feed and care for those suffering in north and south. But the organization has been restricted by its own cardinal rule: it must have the approval of both sides to operate, and so has been easily manipulated.

Aid donors are difficult to motivate and know their work is a drop in an ocean of suffering. Children are saved, it seems, only so they can fight in the war.

For me, this is what makes Sudan the most desperate and corrosive of all conflicts in Africa, stretching from the Western Sahara to Mozambique. I'm convinced that Somalia will sort itself one day; even Rwanda may find a post-genocide order that puts off the next round of mass killings for a decade or two. But in Sudan, the fortunes of war have swung to and fro too many times already, perpetuating violence by giving unwarranted hope of victory to each side in turn—just enough to encourage fighting to go on. Largely out of sight, Sudan's war has killed 1.5 million people—one out of every five southern Sudanese. That's more bodies than in Somalia and Bosnia combined; it's nearly double the toll of Rwanda's 1994 genocide.

Most of the rest of the 4.5 million to 5 million people in the south, from a mixture of African tribes dominated by the Dinka and Nuer, are either refugees or displaced from their homes. They live, as one relief worker put it, "like they might as well be dead."

Wracked by successive government and rebel offensives, drought, and war-induced famine, the victims foresee no end of suffering. The north is a barren band of desert that produces nothing but sugar, cattle, and camels. Khartoum fights to control the tropical jungle wealth of the south, with its gold and oil deposits and rich, loamy soil. So, for northerners living in a windswept sandbox carpeted with thorn trees, southern secession is not an option.

At the Ed Daien rally, in the shade of a large tent, a great feast was laid before the president, military officers, and holy men. Farther south—even in this town, to a degree—the chronic famine simmered, as it had for years, fluctuating with the delinquent rains and the front lines. We ate heartily anyway, for this was an important visit. Countless bowls were filled with spicy vegetable and bean dishes; expansive platters were laden with meat. Smoke-flavored camel's milk bit the tongue, and was passed around in greasy metal cups—all of it capped with supersweet milky tea in delicate glass cups. The generals' round bellies strained at the buttons of their military uniforms as they reached for more. They wiped sweating brows with the sweaty backs of their hands, or with dampening handkerchieves.

As if to make up for this gluttonous display—for not too far away, many southern Sudanese were living off a diet of roots, bark, and lily pads—gifts from Khartoum were given to local leaders with much fanfare. As the only Western infidel present, I was presented with an orange-dyed and decorated leather camel saddle, with the blessing of the president. Lines written in Arabic with an El Marko pen described the occasion, and Islam's central theological tenet: "There is no God but Allah, and Mohamed is His Prophet."

But on the way back the celebration had worn off for at least one member of our party. Sudan is famous for its collapsing infrastructure, and old military gear is no exception. As we flew to Khartoum in an aging C-130 transport plane, the president slept across from me, 10 feet away, stuffed belly sagging happily. But next to him, Sudan's Air Force chief sweated through his uniform and chewed the end of his wooden cane—mouthing prayers that nothing would go wrong.

In Sudan, most Muslims adhere to mystical and esoteric Sufi orders that were spread for centuries by ascetic holy men who traveled to even the remote desert regions of the country, providing miracles and looking for converts. Deemed today to be the "inner dimension" of Islam, Sufism is the "inward" path, the "science of the direct knowledge of God" that is seen by "the eye of the heart."[1]

The Muslim holy book, the Koran, rejects "compulsion in religion"—that is, imposing Islam upon non-believers. It also delivers a message of tolerance of Christians and Jews, whom Muslims consider to be People of the Book who simply follow different prophets. But in practice in Sudan, these precepts have proved to be little protection for non-Muslims.

Divisions between the north and south have been part of Sudanese history since biblical times, when the territory was known as Cush, the faraway end of the earth from whence the Nile mysteriously sprang. Herodotus himself was captivated by the Nile, discussing its flow and floods, and contemplating its sources during a visit to Egypt around 454 BC.[2] The name Sudan was drawn pejoratively from the Arabic phrase *Bilad al-Sudan,* which means "Land of the Blacks." A Roman commander in 23 BC moved south from Egypt and stopped, determining that the kingdom of Meroe before him was "too poor to warrant its conquest."[3] Nevertheless, Sudan's history as a religious battlefield mirrored the victories and defeats of Christianity and Islam in Europe and the Middle East.

For centuries, three Christian kingdoms held sway in the north, with monks hiding in the desert during Muslim onslaughts until 1505, when Islamic armies finally took control of the region from the mouth of the Nile at Alexandria, on the northern cusp of the continent, south to below Khartoum. The depths of southern Sudan were not penetrated until after 1820–21, when Turkish and Egyptian forces—battling on behalf of the Ottoman Khedive—took over northern areas of Sudan, and then stopped at the usual natural obstacles. The harsh Egyptian rule sought to exorcise Sufism and replace it with Cairo's orthodox Islam.[4] But for many, the real prize was in the south. "The few Arab adventurers who engaged in slave raids were not interested in Arabizing and Islamizing the southerners, as that would have taken their prey from *dar al-harb* (land of war) and placed them in the category of *dar al-Islam* (land of Islam), thereby protecting them from slavery," notes historian Francis Deng.[5]

The Sudan was a popular hunting ground for African slaves, and Arab traders did brisk business in human cargo. Under Egyptian rule, slaving surged in the heart of Dinkaland, and Khartoum turned into a major slave center. Southern tribesmen were powerless to defend themselves. Lulled by promises of an end to slavery and abolishment of taxes imposed by the Egyptians, several northern and southern tribes united in revolt under the charismatic Islamic holy man Muhammad Ahmed ibn Abdallah. He called himself the Mahdi, the "one who makes salvation," and carried off a popular belief that he was the messiah. In 1881 he led a rebellion to rid Sudan of the Egyptian army and its British commanders. His Sudanese Arab army, bolstered by the southerners who believed the Mahdi meant to end slavery, swept across the country, finally capturing Khartoum in 1885 and killing British General Charles Gordon on the steps of the governor's residence. Gloating over this victory, the Mahdi stuck Gordon's head on a stake for public display.

For the southern tribes, though, the Mahdi's triumph gave way to a resurgence of slave trading and forced conversions to Islam—an early version of the uncompromising Islamic state that would emerge in Sudan a century later.

The Dinka retreated again. But this time, protected by the natural barriers of the south, they began clandestine attacks against the Arab marauders. Guerrilla fighting in Sudan was born.

That pattern of resistance is still being played out. Battles then, as now, were decimating. One British officer in the 1920s noted that the Dinka "lost hundreds of thousands of cattle; men, women and children in thousands were slaughtered, carried off into slavery, or died of famine; but the survivors kept alive in the deepest swamps, bravely attacked the raiders when they could, and nursed loathing and contempt for the stranger and all his ways."[6]

The Berlin Conference of 1884–85, which had dismembered the Somali nation and diced up the continent with little reference to tribe or nation, also demarcated the impossible borders for Sudan. North and south were bound together in one country, the largest in Africa, and allocated for British rule. Within those borders were all the ingredients of antagonism: some 56 ethnic groups divided into more than 572 tribes speaking more than 100 languages and dialects.[7] Southern Sudan alone is three times the size of Britain and took nearly two decades to be "pacified" by the colonial administration. When the south was finally brought to heel, British policy was divisive. Following the time-honored practice of divide and rule, Britian encouraged north and south differences and legally enforced them to prevent any rise of nationalism. They also aimed to one day join southern Sudan with a British East Africa colony.

Mutual suspicions were exacerbated in what amounted to two separate states. In the north, which was quickly developing with foreign trade, Muslims observed their Friday holy day and spoke Arabic. In the south, where the British even then openly referred to maintaining a "buffer" against the further spread of Islam, the Christians respected their day of rest on Sunday, and missionaries set up schools to teach English. In 1908, a British missionary warned about a "bloody Mohamadan Crusade which will have as its object the sweeping of the entire Continent of Africa and every vestige of Christian civilization."[8] In 1921 the British further widened the gap with the Passport Ordinance Act—very similar to South Africa's apartheid-era Pass System—which closed some areas to travel and controlled migration back and forth. Dinka in the north were asked to return south, so that "a more complete separation could be enforced."[9] Within two decades, it was an open secret that British policy was for total separation.

So the stage was set for civil war, and hostilities were already under way with the rebellion of the Southern Corps in 1955, just four months before independence, set for the New Year's day 1956. Southerners had been excluded from any role in drawing up the new constitution and were shut out of the government. Subsequent military governors "devoted much of their time and energies to spreading Arabic and Islam," noted one historian.[10] In

1961, religious gatherings for prayer outside a church were forbidden, and priests were arrested for a protest, charging that Islam was being imposed upon them and declaring that no one "be he King or Emperor, can make us go contrary to God's Commandments and our own conscience."[11] Hundreds of missionaries were expelled under the Missionary Act of 1962, which is still in place.

As for the civil war, some 500,000 deaths later in 1972, a fragile peace was finally agreed which granted self-rule to the south within a united Sudan and, significantly, religious freedom. The modest education and infrastructure gains made during British rule, however, had already collapsed.

Eleven years later, the 1972 peace deal completely unraveled. Jaafar el-Nimeiri, the military dictator who signed the original agreement, was becoming increasingly tyrannical and religious. He unilaterally abrogated the cease-fire and, in an even more shocking move, imposed Islamic *sharia* law across the country. Thieves in Khartoum began losing hands and legs in gruesome public amputations, and the capital's entire supply of liquor was destroyed—an act led by Nimeiri himself, who drained bottle after bottle of booze into the Nile. A special arena was built in Khobar prison for viewing amputations.[12] So in 1983, the non-Muslim southerners dusted off their weapons and reignited the guerrilla war, in part to oppose this imposition of Islam. (By one account, the rebels had in fact announced the end of the truce three months before Nimeiri's dramatic declaration of the so-called "September Laws."[13])

Even today, that one period of relative harmony, from 1972 to 1983, is remembered as "the last peace." Deliberately hidden from the outside, and therefore forgotten by all but the most persistent, the fighting has since taken an extraordinary toll as Sudan seems caught in a self-defeating seesaw battle against the gravity of history.

In the Book of Isaiah, the Bible describes the woe of Sudan, the "country of whirring [insect] wings" that was "always feared, a people mighty and masterful."[14] Such ominous Biblical prophecies do not lend themselves to peace and may condemn the Sudanese to eternal conflict. The Book of Ezekiel describes the people of Cush taking part in an apocalyptic war against Gog, a chief prince who came from Magog. With the help of God, the "great army" in full battledress destroyed Gog's legions. "With plague and bloodshed" and "every sort of terror," God would pass judgment on Gog.[15] In Revelations, the nations of Gog and Magog—led by Satan—were to fight a climactic battle of Armageddon against the Kingdom of God.[16]

The modern flavor of Sudan's apocalypse, however, has been a virulent interpretation of Islam in the north, with human rights abuses that betray the absence of any higher piety. And in the south, it has been manifest in splits among the rebels along tribal lines, causing an especially vicious fratricide. The fighters and their victims know little of historic prophecies, though: as far as they are concerned, the end is already here.

Late one night in 1992, in Sudan's desiccated capital of Khartoum—the famous confluence of the Blue and White Nile Rivers, from where they blend together and flow deeply north, toward Egypt—an old Englishman broke Islamic law and decapped a bottle of Johnny Walker Red. There were three finger-widths left of the whiskey, enough to bring 40 lashes of righteous government cane down upon his withering back. He had a tattoo on his arm and told tales of his time as a British SAS commando. "Nothing is as bad as Sudan is now," he said. During journeys spanning a decade and through two governments, this was a refrain I heard every time I visited Sudan. And nearly every time I returned, for whatever reason, it *had* gotten worse.

Many years after the spearing to death of General Gordon in 1885, the last redoubt of the English adventurer was the Sudan Club. But even this watering hole—with cloudy swimming pool and increasingly decrepit services—was soon without alcohol. As conditions deteriorated under the Islamic regime, there were few Brits left who were capable of restoring the Sudan Club to its former drunken glory, as the clearinghouse for grumbling about every native injustice, spilled over countless bottles of chilled beer. Every British official was expected to be a member. At least the shade trees were still there, to filter out some of Sudan's gratuitous dust.

Britain's early footprint on Khartoum is still plain to see, when it is not shrouded by a massive dust storm, or *haboob,* that rolls in from the desert and blots out the sun. The city plan was arrogantly laid out in the design of the Union Jack by British commander Herbert Kitchener, who rebuilt the city after recapturing the *Mahdiyya* in 1899. But little else remained of the British presence except the wrinkled expatriates, some of them former soldiers engaged in an inexplicable love affair with Sudan.

"In any other country there would be a revolution," my drinking SAS commando explained. "But people here are so battered now, they're finished."

Foreign aid had kept Sudan afloat for years. And of the $1 billion Sudan received in 1985, $350 million came from the United States.[17] But the festering war had hurt President Nimeiri, to the point where avoiding a public outcry was paramount. High casualty figures were denied and the dead and wounded from the front were secretly brought to Khartoum hospitals in the middle of the night to mask the numbers.[18] Nimeiri's elected successor in 1985, Prime Minister Sadiq al-Mahdi—grandson of *the* Mahdi who took Khartoum from the British a century earlier—recognized that peace in Sudan required giving wary southerners some self-rule, and exempting them from

Islamic law. Many others in the north, also, found *sharia* unnerving. After painstaking negotiations with the rebels, a peace deal was ready. But word of this "treachery" soon reached a cabal of hard-line military officers.

On the night of 29 June 1989, just hours before he was to suspend *sharia* law—and end the civil war—Sadiq al-Mahdi was overthrown.[19] General Bashir, with the blessing of fundamentalist clerics, began an Orwellian transformation that aimed to create a police state, replete with Allah. Purges of the army started immediately: within months 3,000 to 4,000 officers and some 11,000 soldiers were expelled.[20] Universities were "cleansed" of liberal elements, and unzealous civil servants—apparently 80%—were replaced. Militant hard-liners wearing party badges and armed with sticks and iron bars beat students for three days at one campus of a "heathen school" because they did not "Arabize" their curriculum. Prayers in school were made compulsory, torture became routine. In the old town of Omdurman, part of Khartoum across the White Nile, 30 churches were closed.

The pile of Amnesty International reports in my Sudan file, detailing detention and human rights abuses against vacillating Muslims, from poets to veterinary lecturers, grew thicker with each passing week. Even the director of the government antiquities department was locked up, reportedly because he found more Christian than Islamic ruins.[21]

The UN Human Rights Commission was so concerned that it appointed a special rapporteur. Gáspár Bíró, from Hungary, found that "torture is particularly widespread in the secret detention centers known as 'ghost houses,'" ten of which were in Khartoum alone.[22] The regime's torturers extracted confessions from dissidents and suspected rebel sympathizers, he said, with beatings, burnings, electric shocks, and rapes. Testicles were crushed with pliers; one man was reportedly forced to stand on a hot plate.

In conflict zones, a favorite technique was the "tying of a plastic bag containing chili powder over the head of a prisoner, which makes him almost suffocate." Chili peppers were rubbed in open wounds, and in one alleged case, chili powder "had been poured into the genital organs of a woman."

The regime was outraged by the UN report, and officially called it "blasphemous." Bíró was branded an "enemy of Islam," and Bashir screamed that the rapporteur's aim was "to erase the faith of Allah . . . from the surface of the earth."[23]

In the spring of 1991, the *sharia* laws were made more sweeping than ever before. Ministry of Justice translations of the Criminal Act of 1991 spelled out the severity of several maximum sentences. Armed robbery was punished with "death and crucifixion," apostasy warranted death; adultery, execution by stoning.[24] By that measure, a southern Sudanese Anglican bishop got off lightly. In 1993 he was sentenced to a public flogging after being convicted of adultery.[25] The bishop received 80 lashes with a rod, though the official inflicting the lashes gripped a copy of the Koran under his arm to limit the force.

Fellow churchmen were "deeply shocked," and found the punishment "barbaric" and "medieval." "There is a theory that it was staged because the Europeans were there and the Muslims wanted them to see the power of Islam," said Canon Timothy Biles, rector of Beaminster in Dorset, who was in Sudan at the time. "A Muslim told me, 'Violence for Allah is greatly to be praised. We are exactly like your God in the Old Testament.'"

Thousands of people lined up outside foreign embassies to get away, though newly required "exit" visas were difficult to come by. For the first time in Sudan's history, there was a government of *action*.

General Bashir soon made clear too that there would be action in the south: no mercy for rebels, just victory for Sudan, and for Islam. *Sharia* law would be enforced. "I vow here before you to purge from our ranks the renegades, the hirelings, enemies of the people and enemies of the armed forces," he told a rally in Khartoum, holding a Koran and a Kalashnikov, soon after taking power. "Anyone who betrays this nation does not deserve the honor of living. . . . There will be no fifth column. The masses have to purge their ranks."[26]

Adding punch to his promise was a religious decree, or *fatwa*, that declared a *jihad* across southern Sudan. The war had been incited by "Zionists, crusaders and arrogant persons," the *fatwa* read. It concluded that "those Muslims who deal with dissidents and rebels and raise doubts about the legality of *jihad* are hypocrites and dissenters and apostates for the Islamic religion. Their lot is to suffer torture in hell for eternity."[27]

Returning to Sudan in 1992, I found that, far from growing weak with chronic dissatisfaction, the government had entrenched itself. A further example of its resolve—and of the extreme phobias of this Islamic junta—had taken form with the creation of "peace camps" in the inhospitable desert far outside the capital. Officials proudly described how they planned to bring "fresh air" to 1.5 million squatters—the majority from the south—by moving them away from their "dangerous" lives of squalor within the city limits, where they lived in cardboard huts on mountains of trash or next to industrial waste dumps.

In Khartoum, these people made up half the population. Ethnically and religiously diverse, they had fled war in the south and drought everywhere. Aware that the fall of Nimeiri in 1985 was precipitated by unrest in such volatile settlements, Bashir created a *cordon sanitaire* around the capital. As far as he was concerned, every squatter was a potential rebel sympathizer. That was not the case. But the government treated these people so brutally that, by the time the authorities were finished, he was probably right.

With bayonets fixed in November 1991, soldiers moved through the shan-tytown hovels, protecting army bulldozers in a phalanx as they forcibly evicted the squatters. The dirt block, mud, junk, and cardboard "homes" were flattened. In one area, Unicef had just spent $1 million installing more than 200 hand pumps for fresh water. So residents took on the soldiers with sticks and stones. At least 20 were shot dead in the ensuing melée.

The remaining victims—some 425,000 people in five camps—were dumped in the sand an hour's drive west of Khartoum and told to get on with their lives. No preparation had been made for their arrival. Appalled Western relief agencies and embassies scrounged together 20,000 blankets, then were reduced to issuing burlap sacks for "housing." The resulting shelters emerged from the desert like the hopeless camps thrown together during the 1984 famine in Ethiopia. In Africa, there is no worse comparison.

Even a well-controlled official visit turned into a farce for a handful of Western diplomats and donors, who were taken to prove that the "housing" plan was benign. On the way, a young man walking toward the long sand track to Khartoum—half a mile from Peace Camp—crested a sand dune, jerked up his arm, and collapsed from heat exhaustion in the path of the British ambassador's vehicle, in which I was a passenger. We slowed down and drove around the fallen man, the ambassador caught his breath, wrenched his neck around to see this casualty, his face ashen with concern. No Sudanese official expected us to see this.

In Peace Camp, security officers carried Uzi machine guns, electric cattle prods, and truncheons. They were young and pimply, mostly out of uniform and clearly instilled fear in the unfortunate camp dwellers. Islamic relief agen-cies were the only ones permitted to work. The nearest food was at a market four miles away, a vast desert journey in the heat.

"If they rise up in the middle of the desert, they can howl all they want," the outspoken American ambassador, James Cheek, told me. "If they want to march on Khartoum, they will die of exposure on the way. We're not applying a Western standard of judgment to these horrid conditions. Any Sudanese—Muslim or Christian—would be appalled more than us, because these are their own people."

Still, the government was proud of its work. The home-demolishing pro-ject was spearheaded by the housing minister, Sharaf Bannaga, an academic who handed me a business card for his previous job: a UN regional develop-ment planner. The urban plan for this project, after all, was a Greek-designed World Bank proposal meant to—humanely—ease overcrowding in Khar-toum. It was no secret that Bannaga had hoped to win a medal of distinction at the June 1992 "Earth Summit" in Brazil for his contribution to "environ-mental protection and urban renewal."

Beside the squatter "cleanup" operations and public works projects to fix Khartoum traffic lights and encourage rich Muslim businesses to paint and repair traffic circles, the regime channeled its enthusiasm into establishing fundamentalist credentials.

During the 1991 Persian Gulf War, Sudan backed Iraqi strongman Saddam Hussein, along with Libya, Jordan, and Palestinian leader Yassir Arafat. Alarm bells sounded again in Western capitals in December 1991, when Iran's President Ali Akbar Rafsanjani visited Khartoum with 200 senior officials and the commander of Iran's Revolutionary Guards. On a live radio broadcast, Bashir told the nation that Iran's 1979 Islamic Revolution led by Ayatollah Khomeini "carried hope to Muslims and encouraged us to declare an Islamic revolution in Sudan." He also offered to let Sudan serve as a springboard for spreading Islam throughout Europe and Africa.

When my SAS commando had polished off the three fingers of Johnny Walker, the well-lubricated truth began to flow. We had met during my very first visit to Sudan, waiting in a grimy and stifling office for approval to travel outside Khartoum. He gave me a compendium of loosely gathered intelligence, sort of a report card on the bad behavior of the Islamic regime. Young men were being forcibly "recruited" as holy warriors during roundups at busy markets, he said; all the "dregs of the Middle East" had washed up in Sudan, and this new generation of Islamic terrorists was being trained in secret desert camps; there was even a sinister video making the rounds that showed two hands wearing protective gloves displaying a cracked cannister— for sale—supposedly packed with weapons-grade nuclear material: was it from a former Soviet Republic? From South Africa? As always, rumor here spread easily, and mixed with tales of torture at "ghost houses" that made the hair on my neck stand on end, even when enjoying a cold drink, and wafted by the warm evening breeze off the Nile. Extracted from all this, some facts remained.

"Sudan has nothing," declared my friend and informant, toying with his whiskey glass and staring at its emptiness. His aging arm tattoo was almost lost between overtanned skin and sun-bleached arm hair. "Sudan can offer nothing, except a base for fundamentalism."

With the end of the Cold War freeing the minds of Western intelligence agencies, Sudan became a new target for vilification. NATO generals began to fear the creation of an "Islamic bomb" that could hit Europe. Tucked away in Sudan, which in those first years of the Islamic experiment let any Arab enter without a visa, Khartoum hosted every conceivable resistance group or guerrilla force—just about anyone who might be or was branded a "terrorist" by the US. So in 1993, the country was added to the American list of state sponsors of terrorism, joining an elite club with Libya, Syria, Iran, Iraq, Cuba, and North Korea.

The presence of more than a dozen training camps, and of hundreds of Iranian Revolutionary Guards "advising" the Sudan army and PDF militias, rattled moderate Muslim states such as Egypt and Saudi Arabia, which feared violence from their own extremists. Among the guests was exiled Saudi Arabian millionaire Osama bin Laden. Under pressure from the US and Saudi Arabia, he was kicked out of Sudan in 1996 and was forced to live in Taliban-controlled Afghanistan. He had been linked to the bombing of the American barracks at Dhahran, Saudi Arabia, in June 1996 and to the destruction of two US embassies in Kenya and Tanzania in August 1998.

For southern rebels, the Islamic renaissance meant that the civil war could only drag on further, and be even more difficult to win.

Behind the military face of the regime was a cabal of Islamic hard-liners who had formed a fundamentalist political organization, the National Islamic Front (NIF) under the control of the erudite, charming, and ruthless leader Hassan al-Turabi. Though he fainted while watching an amputation for the first time, as attorney general in 1983, this Sorbonne- and Oxford-educated lawyer was the architect of President Nimieri's embrace of Islamic law in the 1980s—and, by extension, the resumption of the civil war. The NIF was a minority, its hard line grating against north Sudan's quieter Muslim tradition. In the 1985 election that brought Sadiq al-Mahdi to power it won less than 20 percent of the vote. So Turabi waited.

As the *éminence grise* of Sudan's Islamic transformation—branded by some the "Pope of Terrorism," a title that made the man laugh—Turabi was the forbidding intellectual driving force, the genteel face of a not-so-pretty "revolution." When I first visited him in Khartoum in March 1992, he was nonchalantly strolling on the sidewalk outside his nondescript residence, without bodyguards and apparently secure as Sudan's premier firebrand and holy man. He wore white flowing robes with a simple small design embroidered in light blue, his white turban and short gray mustache and beard framing benevolent features, buck teeth, and big ears.

He spoke very quickly and articulately, almost faster than I could think, with wild gesticulations, chortling and giggling at his own jokes. He had pat answers for every question and could justify anything. Of course, he denied having anything but marginal spiritual influence in Sudan. The NIF was *not* behind the coup, he claimed, citing the too-perfect fact that he himself was detained briefly afterward. Many believed that he had kept an official distance from the regime so that Bashir—and not the NIF—would be blamed for this rather brutal transition to an Islamic state.

"Of course I'm happy," he told me, with his thin, undulating voice. "My work of all these years is finally coming true."[28] This Islamic resurgence was part of an unstoppable worldwide awakening, and secular Arab governments, such as Egypt's, had reason to fear. "Yes, we're fighting a *jihad,* and we've always been fighting a *jihad* in the Sudan," Turabi said. He cited the French Revolution to justify bloodshed: "Did the West develop democracy without violence?"

The *jihad* was raging with renewed vigor in the south and west of the country, he said, and made no apology for imposing his perfect and fair Islam upon southerners. "We want to plant a new civilization in the south. It is our challenge."

It was this renewed sense of religious purpose that had rekindled the long-standing rivalry between Arab and southern tribes and imparted fresh brutality. But ethnic differences were a cause, too. "Until recently, calling the southern Sudanese 'slaves,' *abeed,* to their faces was a common practice," notes historian Deng. The term "is the exact equivalent of 'nigger' in American popular usage. When northerners are caught in the act of such an insult, they often give as their defense, 'We are all slaves of God,' an uncanny admission of a deep-seated slave mentality."[29]

Turabi had a similar dismissive attitude regarding southern spiritual values, which he let show when I next met him six years later, in August 1998. He was still his same effusive self, but his arguments were confused, a stream-of-consciousness effluence that jumped around like random-access memory, and with an unstoppable flow like a record album that kept skipping in the same place.

Power sharing and development money were all the rebels really cared about—not *sharia,* Turabi insisted. "You know why? They are 'partly Christians'—not Christians with an old history, a legacy of colonial and imperial and Roman and denominations and fighting. They're African," he said derisively, "who you could find yesterday in the bush. They don't care much about Christian doctrine . . . It's a fact."[30]

It was clear by 1998 that the revolution—Turabi's Islamic revolution, tailor-made for Sudan and meant to be an envied model for all the Islamic world—was ailing. His personal influence, too, was waning. Despite being in power for nearly a decade, the economy was still teetering, and Sudan was utterly isolated—though trying to change that. Opponents were more tolerated, it was true, and the tortures of the early years at "ghost houses" had largely disappeared. But the civil war still plagued Sudan. Despite dramatic early gains, it was just where it had been in 1989, in virtual stalemate.

The government had just offered a vote for self-determination in the south, and Turabi spoke as he never would have done when I first met him, when his revolutionary blood still ran hot. But his confidence had been shaken by a 1992 attack in Canada, in which a Sudanese exile and karate expert left him temporarily paralyzed and blind. Continuing stagnation at home sapped it further. Instead of enforcing a "new civilization upon the south," he said, "unity of this country must be based on free will, not the north coercing others."

Turabi was also more candid about the role of Islam on the front line. "Armies are violent, armies are horrible," he said. "Soldiers, sometimes they go wild. Mostly in a hard battle—they win it, and they just go and crush things, rape women. [We use Islam] to control the army."

For himself, he said, "Religion guides me, it moves me and controls me." But it can help too where secular arguments alone won't produce wagons full of volunteers to charge the enemy. Religion, Turabi conceded, was useful "just to sell your cause."

Despite purging the army after the 1989 coup, Bashir did not trust his military. He created the PDF militia to augment and eventually replace the armed forces, though they have the checkered combat record of amateurs. These units were sent to the front with only cursory weapons training and a booklet of Koranic sayings. The aim was to mobilize Sudan's entire population of 18 million Arab Muslims; women in shapeless Islamic dress learned to handle assault rifles. Government spending on the war jumped to 60% of the gross domestic product, a figure the International Monetary Fund put at $2 million each day. On average, the treasury has been drained by $1 million per day for years.

The PDF practiced the mindless tactic of mass onslaught, which provided innumerable martyrs but rarely brought victory. Diplomats in Khartoum joked that these were "atrocity battalions," because when they pushed the Sudan People's Liberation Army out of an area, then they "mowed down all the civilians. It is probably the only role they are qualified to play," said one. General Bashir ensured high-level attention: he presided over mass rallies, like the one I saw in Ed Daien; over PDF graduation ceremonies that boosted the numbers of these stormtroopers; and he pardoned prison convicts who had been transformed by training into *mujahideen*.

With Islamic battle cries, the PDF waged war in its own way, burning villages and killing civilians. Along the battlefront, unlucky innocents were often caught up in the conflict, and the abuse of fellow human beings was systematic. Southerners of course knew these acts as ethnic cleansing. Certainly blackened shells of huts and abandoned villages, left behind by northern troops, were no different from the "cleansed" towns of Croatia and Bosnia in the early 1990s, and Kosovo, in the Serb-run rump Yugoslavia in 1989–99. In the Balkans, war crimes trials have dogged a handful of the perpetrators, even some of the big fish like Yugoslav President Slobodan Milosevic have been indicted by international tribunals. But in Sudan, such accountability—even if only recorded on the paper of tribunal documents—is as unlikely as an outbreak of permanent peace.

Sign of a different trouble emerged in 1995, with reports that draft evasion was widespread and that the defense minister had told parliament that of 10,000 Sudanese men ordered by letter for training, only 89 people showed up.[31] But not all troops had to be dragged to the front, and not all PDF shock-troops are ex-convicts and anxious conscripts. Among them are the True Believers, the holy warriors who know their mission, and in whose name they do battle. One family I met in Khartoum in 1998 was a perfect example.

Tipped off by a Sudanese businessman, I knocked on their metal door, and the family invited me in for sweet tea. On the wall of the home, in a well-to-do neighborhood with potholed dirt roads across from the airport, a black-and-white portrait of a young Sudanese martyr hung alone, in pride of place: Al-Fateh Omar Hussein, an ambitious university student not yet graduated, staring out of the picture in jacket and tie. A color tint had been airbrushed in the studio to make the picture live.

Instead of working as an engineer, Hussein volunteered to fight in the war. He fought for God, his family said, and to defend his Muslim religion and the unity of his country. Tears of mourning at Hussein's death in 1993, when he was 24, had since turned to tears of pride for his family. Beyond the official *jihad* sloganeering is sometimes a true religious impulse. Though often mysterious and inaccessible to the outsider, Hussein's story illumines how such belief in the Sudan could translate into waging war.

The rebels also invoke their Christian faith in battle. But few in the south use their religion, like Hussein and other northern zealots, to justify and ensure their own deaths—all for the glory of their God and to reach Heaven, as promised by the Koran.

"He was really on a mission, and determined to be a martyr," remembered Hussein's sister, Amel Omar Hussein, setting down her thin glass teacup. But the young fighter caught malaria during his first tour and was evacuated from the south, to the delight of his family. Hussein was angry. "Don't be happy for me. I don't want to die in bed," he told them. "I must have done something wrong in my life, because God has not selected me to be a martyr."

Before Hussein had left for his second tour of duty, he acted with even more conviction. He gave away all his clothes, and then his money, and made a cassette tape for his mother of him reciting Koranic verses and singing songs. He knew he wasn't coming back, and he reminded the family of the line in the Koran: "Don't think those who died for the cause of God are dead."

"This is the highest aspiration of the Muslim, to die a martyr, a *shaheed*," said Amel Hussem, who spoke fluent English and worked for a Western multinational company. The blood of her kin seemed unlikely to be spilled in some *jihad*, but she understood her brother, and his motives. "This is why they are not afraid to die, because they go from life on this earth to Heaven immediately." It was for this reason that martyr's bodies are not washed before burial, and prayers are not said. The body is simply wrapped in a shroud and buried. Not many militiamen are volunteers. The high casualty rate meant that school-graduate conscripts often tried to escape their training. But for young men like Hussein, the PDF helped form and carry out his wish to be a martyr.

"Nobody pushed him to join," says his sister. "Even my mother resented the idea at first. But since we were kids, I can tell you that he was different. Our grandfather brought us up reading the Koran and to live in the right way, and that inspired al-Fateh. When he left us he told us, 'I have one thing to say: be close to Allah, and live with him. That is all I ask of you.'"

Hussein's mother, Zeinab Abu al-Gassin, admitted that she did not want her son to join the PDF because there was a "50-50 chance" he would not return. Food was scarce down there, and militiamen marched long distances, always risking rebel ambush. They hunted birds to eat and drank bad water.

"I love him so much, and he has done something very special for his country, for his God—he sacrificed his soul," said the mother, with obvious pride. "Not everyone is a martyr. It is God—He selects who He wants near Him."

Most of Hussein's personal items—a prayer book, Koran, and the notebook of poems and short stories he wrote—were parceled out among friends on the front line. But for his mother, some details of his death retold by witnesses bore important signs of religious significance. Hussein died during a 17-hour melee near the Sudan-Uganda border. He ignored advice and ran from his trench to help a man critically wounded by a rebel mortar shell. But another shell tore away Hussein's leg and carved his chest with shrapnel.

"When he was hit, he shouted, 'Alahu Akbar!' God is great! and clenched his fist above his head," said the martyr's mother, holding her arm aloft to illustrate. "His body was hot to the touch for 12 hours—that was a signal." Several members of the family in Khartoum, all sleeping in the same room, claim that they woke at the exact moment of his death, and had a vision of Hussein, calling out their names. They believe that 70 members of the family will also "be forgiven" and eventually meet Hussein in Heaven, "because of the sacrifice of his blood."

Such stories circulated in Khartoum during the jihad, to inspire wavering Muslims to fight. For militants, it was food for the soul. Tales of the debabin, or "tank blowers," for example, recalled the purity of one especially youthful PDF unit that stopped a tank assault on the Juba garrison in the south in early 1998. They tied explosives to their bodies and threw themselves under the tank tracks. That action led to the creation of a new PDF battalion that wears red headbands in battle to denote their readiness to die.

From the Western point of view, such reliance on religion often translates into a "religious war," which many northern Sudanese insist that their civil war is not. "The tricky thing is that in Islam there is no separation of church and state," one told me. "So what is seen as nationalism in a Western sense, here it is seen in religious terms."

Hussein's sister elaborated, reminding me that imposition of Islam upon the south—the fate that the rebels are fighting against—is contrary to Islamic doctrine.

"The aim is not to bring Islam to the people of the south, but to use religion [to fight] the war," she said, echoing Turabi's admission. Before this regime had re-energized the civil war, "generals ordered to the south would take off their epaulets" and refuse to go. Then in the first heady years of Islamic rule, senior government officials often boosted their careers by a front line stint with the PDF. On this precipitous career track, many have died. A former minister of industry lost his life to a land mine, and even Hassan al-Turabi's youngest brother—a recent college graduate—was killed in the war. President Bashir's brother, a medical doctor, was seen in action on Sudan television.[32] One arts student, Abu-Dijana Ali, "always wanted to be a martyr" but survived his first tour in the south. Dreaming of helping the *mujahideen* in Afghanistan, he instead found death in a second PDF mission.[33] In speech after speech made over his body, his determination to die was set forth as a model—a model that Hussein prayed to match.

And for such zealots who believe that death is the only bridge to Heaven, dying for the faith is the noblest aim. Martyrs' families are well cared for, school fees are paid by the regime, and streets and even PDF brigades are named after those who embrace Allah's will.

"Religion in this war is not the core subject," says Hussein's sister. "But when they say it is a *jihad* to defend your family, your government and your people, fighters will be motivated by the religious reward. For human nature, killing is very hard, and it is not acceptable unless there is a very high reward. Today, the reward is very high."

"We are not supporting the antagonistic party," injects Mother al-Gassin, sitting under the portrait of her beloved and martyred son. "We Sudanese are with God, and with peace."

Despite this faith, Khartoum was not beyond pursuing extra spiritual help. When government forces captured a rebel headquarters at Torit in 1993, a minister who visited the town told Sudan Television that he saw angels coming down from the sky to pay their respects to the "martyrs of the *jihad*." This divine intervention was even more profound, he said, because wild monkeys marched in front of the advancing soldiers, acting as minesweepers. The government was taking the advice of one academic who suggested the use of jinns, spirits lower than angels that appear in human or animal form and can influence people. Bashir was quoted in the army newspaper requesting a feasibility study on "how the jinns could help in planning strategy."[34]

Reliance on such non-Islamic methods did not pass the notice of many Sudanese. Of course, officials dropped to their knees for the Islamic *Rak'ah* cycle of prayers five times a day, as required. But even this was part of the façade, said one holy man in the north: "All this government has to claim it's Muslim, is that it prays."[35]

Despite the perennial appearance of chaos along the battlefront, the north's prosecution of the war is not haphazard. A decade earlier, in 1989, I chanced upon proof of sophistication. I applied for permission to travel to Juba, the southernmost garrison. Juba was the capital of the south too, but had been besieged by the rebels for years. I have been to Juba twice: first as a tourist and freelance journalist in 1989, and then in 1993. My first journey was made on a whim, almost as a dare to myself. I needed approval from a top military chief, and so in Khartoum visited a long, low building on the southeast corner of the Union Jack, just across the railroad tracks. I was amazed when the general led me down a long hallway with glass walls on either side. Behind the dustproof barriers, banks of computers and communications equipment tracked the war throughout the south.

This nerve center must never sleep, and belied the messy military situation hundreds of miles away. The officer was bedecked with epaulets heavy with rank. His office was packed with three separate Codan radio sets, a host of walkie-talkies, and three telephones, one of them red. In my hotel, by contrast, the one phone line was hopeless, even for local calls. I convinced the officer of my good intentions as a tourist, because journalists were rarely allowed into Juba. Military units there had too much to hide, and too few places to hide it. Most relief workers had evacuated, but there was still plenty to see—even for a greenhorn like me.

I joined a crowd of parishioners in the Catholic church on Sunday morning and enjoyed their hymns sung to an African beat. I was surprised to find them there at all, practicing their faith. "Today the enemy of these people are both the Sudanese army and the rebels," Juba Archbishop Paulino Lukudo Loro told me. "Without the church and relief organizations, these people would have died."

It seemed to me that they still might. I visited a large camp at feeding time, and found a husk of a man who showed me his rusty metal bowl. His two-week ration of maize barely filled it. He said he was dying here, and people nearby nodded in agreement. "I'm very hungry." Not far away, in another part of the camp, a 55-gallon diesel barrel had been set over a fire to make the daily batch of porridge. As two women stirred the mixture, waif children, some wearing rags and others naked, lined up for hours with their dirty bowls—plastic and tin, they were their instruments of salvation. The gruel was deposited with a big ladle. One toddler hunched over with hunger and worm-bloated stomach. Flies swarmed his head and fed rapaciously at the sticky lip of the boy's dish. The slop ran out, and 30 children were still left standing, clutching their empty bowls, the apprehension of more pain in their guts slowly coming over them.

Wasn't the 1988 famine supposed to have ended? What about this micro-famine happening in front of me?

At night on that first trip, I would ruminate alone by candlelight on what I had seen. It was hard to believe, hard to absorb, such suffering. I wrote, read Faulkner's *Absalom, Absalom!*, and lived in a barren house for five days on less than a kilo of rice—left by relief worker evacuees—after tediously picking out the bugs before boiling. I, too, was hungry—on such a small scale, of course, compared to these chronically malnourished. But it still hurt. Then I, too, was evacuated from Juba.

The nation of Sudan is so vast that its civil war was often masked by sheer opaqueness. In my mind, Juba was a microcosm of this ugly war, where shadowy forces battled away from prying eyes. The entire besieged population of 250,000—estimates have ranged from 30,000 to 500,000[36]—alternately served as a human shield and as a lure for relief agencies who fed the civilian population. They fed, also, by association, the encircled army. Still, there was room for playing games. Apocryphal or not, one tale told of 40 fundamentalist students arriving in Juba to "see the war." Ignoring warnings, they climbed into a truck and drove toward rebel positions on the outskirts. When they returned, each one's right hand had been severed, a not-so-subtle rebel rebuke of Islamic law.

When I returned for a second visit to Juba in February 1993, the arrival again felt like a sinister fun fair ride. To keep out of range of rebel anti-aircraft fire, our unmarked government transport plane started down in a tight corkscrew pattern, soldiers and tons of ammunition and food stuck to the floor of the cabin with the strong centrifugal force of gravity. There were no windows. I sat with a handful of other journalists on a rough wooden crate labeled "Sudan Ministry of Defense, Item #8." The plane lurched on landing, bounced the tarmac hard again, and again before we ground to a halt.

Every year the war affects Juba and the countryside in different ways, as it ebbs and flows across the south. Fortunes of fighters might be buoyed by a fresh influx of weapons or by shifting rains. The general pattern for years had been simple: during the dry season, government armored units went on the offensive, raising the Sudanese flag above a handful of major towns and villages. And during the wet season, when army supply lines bogged down in mud, the rebels would retake the same towns and villages, tear down the government flags, and consolidate their hold on the countryside. As the rebels acquired more hardware, this cycle began to break down. But every year the attack and counterattack uprooted huge populations, adding to the burden of suffering southerners and rendering relief efforts almost impossible.

During this journey, I arrived in Juba when things were turning worse. The usual pattern had been disrupted by massive government gains, rebel infighting, and rebel retreat. The Sudan People's Liberation Army (SPLA) had in July 1992 retaliated by launching a suicidal assault on Juba, which in the decades of war they had *never* controlled. Juba had always been the rebel goal: like Jerusalem was the prize centuries ago of the Crusaders, then the rallying cry of Muslims, and then again—as 3,000 years before—the Jews. The SPLA had suffered serious setbacks, but staged a surprise attack. For a few days that summer, the rebels infiltrated Juba, destroyed food stores, and took control of two-thirds of the city. Fighting was fierce, hand-to-hand, and the rebels shelled the airport to block reinforcements. The army finally drove them out, leveling a densely populated suburb to create a free-fire zone. On Khartoum radio, President Bashir dismissed the failed assault as the "last kick from a dying animal."

Though the SPLA launched the attack to increase morale, "Operation Jungle Storm" instead led to 40% casualties. Army retribution in Juba began immediately. Government forces moved house to house and shot dead hundreds of young men suspected of supporting the rebels.[37]

During our visit, the roads leading to the town were lined with deep trenches and foxholes. The faded words "The Islamic Association for the South of the Sudan" were stenciled on the door of several trucks, including my own, which was also riven with bullet holes. There was an eerie silence—in fact, a disarming, terrifying silence—but little outward indication of the awesome fear and trauma that hid below the surface, like a vicious beast kept in check only by the proven brutality of its torturer. As with the aftermath of engagements in so many African conflicts, Juba seemed disarmingly "normal." The main cathedral was almost deserted and stood alone, casting a pall like a tombstone.

The remaining priests looked at me with tired resignation when they saw the internal security "minder" from Khartoum, who never let me out of earshot. Father Nicholas Adalla, very young and recently released from detention, appeared exhausted and was thin from months of hunger.

"We priests are few, but we preach freely," he said. He knew the risks of straying too far from this line. My minder, his fat belly testing the weak buttons of his shirt, took notes in Arabic of our conversation. That chat was colored by a reality that Adalla was long used to. I would be able to leave Juba, but Adalla would not. Was there any truth to complaints by the Vatican that churches here are being closed? That Christians are ever harassed? That your survival in the face of wolves, as one faraway—and safe—bishop said, is a miracle of God's grace? There was a long pause, then a vacant look, and Adalla said slowly: "I don't think so . . . we may not be able to say anything."

This was too much for the minder, who herded me away. When I asked his business with me, he said simply, "I am a citizen." But then he chased me past rows of pews until we were outside, where again all was disarmingly quiet. One can't tell that the war is *just there,* beyond those trees and that field. Juba and the ring of rebels around it is a tiny, self-contained killing field, where persecution is second nature, a place so secluded—but at least identifiable on a map—that it is cut off from the usual norms of human behavior.

Now I could see the accuracy of the words I heard in 1989, when Marc Desverney, the head of a French medical team told me: "We can't figure out that we are at war. This is not a real war situation, but we can smell it."

Here the smallest infraction—intended or not—could endanger life. Like a community that had been deformed by years of isolation and incest, violent emotions were compounded like bad traits carried from one generation to the next, with every mutation of war intact and enhanced. The same is true for most of the rest of southern Sudan, so utterly remote that much of it is described on maps with vast patches of nothing. In those rebel-held wildernesses, people also died for nothing. The entire region, so open and apparently boundless, felt unbearably claustrophobic.

Turabi himself, godfather of the Islamic regime, made a visit to Juba and sought to squeeze out the last vestige of fun. Residents were admonished not to "waste time playing football," because it was a "manifestation of conflict."[38]

Reality was hard enough to forget already. The scores of feeding centers in Juba were as much a part of the landscape as the distant hills, and will probably remain for as long. The famine is chronic enough, and is therefore easy to neglect, considering the whole panoply of Sudan's misery. The handout then was half the minimum ration to sustain life. Anything else had to be foraged among the rings of government and rebel mines that defined the city limits. When told that the ration would be cut yet further, one man pulled me aside: "We are the forgotten people. Why do you let us die?"

The crucifix stood 40 feet tall, the rallying point for the High Mass in Khartoum where Pope John Paul II in February 1993 would bless his battered Sudanese flock. Its dark aspect was sinister like a crime, a towering monolith, a black Christ with exaggerated features and huge bleeding hands riven with spikes. The pontiff was there to remind Christians that God was still with them and knew of their troubles. But John Paul's presence was like that of the crucifix: an overdrawn alien caricature in the heart of militant Islam. Few here will forget the remarkable image of the pope bending to his knees and kissing the ground of northern Sudan.

The pope was warned that his visit would be turned into a propaganda stunt. He visited anyway, for only nine hours, and drew tens of thousands of displaced southern Sudanese onto the streets. I had already been blacklisted by Khartoum and was unable to get a visa, because of my travels with the rebels. But aware that, as part of any pope visit the host country must allow in *every* journalist who applies, I siezed the chance to return to Khartoum. Beyond that trip, I remained on the blacklist for five more years.

Mass was held at "Green Square," a former rubbish dump that had been cleared for a previous visit of the president of Iran. Under the stadium steps at dusk, before the pope arrived, I watched two Muslim men on the cleaning staff kneel on a large rug and offer their prayers. Similar acts of Muslim faith were being carried out across the city, as the mosques erupted with the *muezzin*'s call. There are many fewer churches now than there once were—centuries ago, during the era of the "Three Kingdoms," Sudan was renowned as the "land of many beautiful churches." Still, the pope had come to stand beneath this crucifix and deliver a message of hope.

The setting sun refracted red through the dust. There were hymns, and the pontiff arrived walking through the crowd, showered with makeshift grass crosses and garlands of flowers. The stage was ringed with soldiers, and the crowds were kept back with whips. The pope likened the suffering of Christians in Sudan to that of Jesus on the cross. The crucifix overshadowed all.

"In this part of Africa, I see clearly a particular reproduction of the mystery of Calvary in the lives of the majority of the Christian people," he intoned. He appealed for a "new relationship between Christians and Muslims in this land," but also criticized the fundamentalist regime: "We must realize that to use religion as an excuse for injustice and violence is a terrible abuse, and it must be condemned by all true believers in God."

The crowds murmured approval, for if this were not the pope himself, the man would be arrested for blasphemy. John Paul called for an end to the persecution and "the terrible harvest of suffering" of Christians in the south. This Eucharist, he concluded, was being celebrated for all Sudanese. For those trapped by war, "I have written your name on the palms of my hands. Yes, on the palms of the hands of Christ, pierced by the nails of the Crucifixion. The name of each one of you is written on those palms."

As predicted, President Bashir used the papal visit to deny that any offenses at all were committed in Sudan, and certainly not by Muslims. His case was boosted by live local TV coverage of the pope's visit, which absurdly claimed that the pontiff endorsed *sharia* law. Allegations of government "ethnic cleansing" and torture of dissidents and Christians were "grotesque fabrications," Bashir said. Imposition of Islam on non-believers was "simply unthinkable and categorically inadmissable since God Himself has clearly and unequivocally stated in the Holy Koran that 'There shall be no compulsion in matters of faith.'"

Invoking the Koran, Bashir told the pope directly that, for Muslims, "Christians are the closest to them in love."

Catholic bishops in the south had foretold it. But they also know all about public professions of religious goodwill by the regime and private exactions of brutality. The rebel leaders, too, claimed their religious faith as Christians just as shamelessly, but rarely adhered to mercies spelled out in the Bible.

So Sudan's bishops warned the pope in a secret letter, before he ever left Rome: "While you are in Khartoum, you will be given a red carpet welcome and you will hear many solemn official speeches," they wrote. "You should know, Holy Father, that these are the same people who persecute, torture and kill pastors, priests, sisters, catechists and evangelists. You will be shaking hands dripping with the blood of Christians."

ELEVEN

WAR OF THE CROSS

There is a season for everything . . .
under heaven;
A time for tears, a time for laughter;
a time for mourning, a time for dancing.
A time for loving, a time for hating;
a time for war, a time for peace.

—Ecclesiastes 3:1, 4, 8

My thick files on Sudan are laced with maps, upon which scratches and smudges mark front lines that mash together and withdraw, where the calculus of battle is delineated by an endless array of arrows that show multiprong offensives, massive population movements, and armored columns in motion. These carefully kept parchments are now meaningless, except for what they described at the moment they were drawn. Like any war gaming board, only a few landmarks remain constant. Even when scrawled like this, the fluid actions seemed distant, and belied any suffering. On paper, the rumble of shellfire was easy to deny; the suction noise of tanks deploying in mud was impossible to imagine.

Sadly, not one of my maps portrays Sudan at peace, because no one yet knows what that peace might look like. As in Somalia and Rwanda, chronic antagonism has become part of the topography of the place, adding up to an endless compulsion for war.

Fighting to ensure that future maps of Sudan will at least show the largely Christian south intact, and not lacerated by front lines or engulfed by a malevolent green-shaded Islamic north, rebels faced their nemesis every day, year after year. The Sudan People's Liberation Army (SPLA), led by Colonel John

Garang de Mabior, "defends" the south from the rapacious government *mujahideen*. Ngangala and Lobonok are like many other front lines, for they were in constant flux like my maps. Only the local layout of stones, trees, and strategic hills varied; to the Divine Gamesman, they were nothing more than a temporary cluster of arrows darting in every direction, like the steady, random emissions from a radioactive isotope.

This is the view from southern Sudan, an almost unparalleled view, as it turns out. For if these battlefields weren't described here, their value as confrontations would be almost zero. Militarily, they mattered some. But in the broad mosaic of war in Sudan, they are only pieces that fit into a much bigger picture. And so if not recorded here, some of the most valuable details of the Ngangala, Lobonok, and Aswa fronts—even much of an important religious pilgrimage—would have been forgotten.

For almost every battle and every event I saw in Sudan, I was the sole outside witness. This was because I almost always prefer to travel alone. And also because of the extreme logistical difficulties of getting to such a place. The job was dangerous, too, and often involved pain: sporadic or no meals, sporadic or no sleep, and the constant hassle of charming rebel "officials" into approving my plans. Still, focusing on these few events, we can learn the emotion and mind-set wrought at these places at least, and so can better appreciate the wider, larger human experience so rarely observed in Sudan.

Cheers erupted from the hills overlooking Ngangala in April 1992, as SPLA artillery shells scored a direct hit on enemy trenches below. Young rebels laughed from their perch behind a rocky outcropping, for they knew that, for this moment at least, the advantage was theirs. As they blasted the village, we were near enough to snipe at anyone who dared move. As the clouds of smoke rose, Khartoum troops dashed through the haze to safer foxholes. This firestorm had held them for two weeks, pinning down 1,500 soldiers. Their 122mm howitzer had fired its last round five days before, but finally there was return fire from one double-barreled anti-aircraft gun. The SPLA estimated that 350 dead had been buried in the trenches.

The 20 government trucks meant for retreat lay burning across the battlefield. The troops were part of a massive government offensive that President Bashir in Khartoum vowed would finally finish the war and defeat the rebels. But along this front, the push forward had bogged down. Only a few years after the government had transformed this war into a sacred Islamic duty, the scene I saw before me must have been a setback. Crouching next to me, a rebel fired a rocket-propelled grenade, mortars blasted off behind us, and heavy machine guns fired rather haphazardly.

These troops were cocky. "They are dying every day, 15 or 20 of them," boasted rebel commander Oyay Deng Ajak, using powerful binoculars to direct mortar fire. His uniform and epaulets were in marked contrast to most of the young, barefoot and rag-clad rebels, who were toddlers when the civil war resumed in 1983. Oyay himself was not even born when the conflict first erupted in 1955.

Still, there was no need to think about that. Today the killing was easy, a chicken shoot. "This is the end of the big Khartoum offensive," Oyay bet optimistically, with a broad smile. "We still have the men and the ammunition, and will push on to Juba."

But the SPLA was instead driven back from Ngangala, and a string of other towns. I adjusted my maps as necessary, charting the changing tide, and journeyed again and again to the south to understand. One and a half years later, in November 1993, my sense of *déjà vu* was complete: I found myself again with Oyay, hiding in another foxhole, this time at Lobonok. His situation was the same, though set back from before by quite a few miles. He still watched the enemy across no-man's-land with his binoculars, and he remained optimistic that the SPLA would conquer all the south. The tree immediately in front of our position had been shredded by heavy gunfire, forming what must look—to the other side—like an arrow pointing to our exact location. This spot was regularly shelled. The government had officially declared the war a *jihad,* which brutalized the fighting.

"They come here to die, not to be captured," said Oyay, gazing across the minefield before us. "I know it's not humanitarian, but we leave most of the bodies so that when they attack again they will see the skeletons and be demoralized."

When they stripped the dead—often taking the bloody uniforms, despite singed bulletholes, and boots for their own use—the rebels burned the small Korans carried by soldiers. Some died with red "Key to Heaven" ribbons pinned to their shirts. When the army and Islamic militias made an offensive, they ran hard in human waves, chanting *Alahu Akbar!* in numbers meant to overwhelm the rebels. Such a tactic had been used during the Iran-Iraq war of the 1980s, with zero strategic result. The human wave was also used by the SPLA in the first assaults of this war, though heavy losses curbed the practice. Years later, much wiser, the SPLA stuck closer to their trenches. Though not all southerners are Christian—many follow animist and other pagan ways— the SPLA also protected themselves spiritually, by carving small crosses into trees around their positions, a token of hope where nothing else, after so many years of inconclusive battle, seemed to suffice.

Decades of war have thrown southern Sudan back into a new Stone Age, in which the one symbol of modernity is the assault rifle. Attuned to calculating the weight of killings with a spear, the ease of gun slayings complicated things. "Whereas the power of a spear issues directly from the bones and sinews of the person who hurls it, that of a gun is eerily internal to it," explains anthropologist Sharon Hutchinson. "Outside of a minimal effort required to hoist and fire it, a rifle's power was seen to be completely independent of its human bearer—'all a person does is aim it.' And thus, the force of a rifle, [the Sudanese] reasoned, demonstrates nothing definitive about the human being behind it."[1]

Normally, killing would result in a "highly dangerous and contagious form of pollution" that would require an earth priest to bleed away from the killer. But "as firearms burned deeper and deeper into regional patterns of warfare, many people began to wonder whether the spiritual and social consequences of . . . gun slayings were identical to those realized by spears." As a result, rebel officers tried to convince their followers that there was no blood curse in fighting the north because that was a "government war."[2]

The rebel base camp at Lobonok was not far behind the front line, a random cluster of grass huts built only to last until the conflict shifted again, taking the young fighters forward or back. Many southern villages and camps are made of grass and built upon the same premise: at any time they may be forced to uproot yet again, and move on. The entire population of the south, whittled down to less than 4.5 million, manufactured absolutely nothing. Even if the war stopped today, the south would not be able to feed itself for years. Instead of seeds, southern Sudan has been sown with hundreds of thousands of land mines.

At the Lobonok base and across the great poverty of this region, the only hint of the industrialized world beyond are scraps left over from brief contact with the outside. Some SPLA soldiers have uniforms, but everyone else wears a discordant collection of T-shirts and rags that often first arrived in bundles of used clothes collected for the "poor" of Africa at church bake sales in America and Europe. The Sudanese represent a myriad of US high school sports teams and are seen to be frequent visitors of far-flung holiday resorts from Disneyland to Lapland.

Many young warriors marched into battle clad in wildly incongruous outfits: bright children's ski jackets with crude designs; polyester powder-blue flare-bottom trousers, thrown away by some American in the late 1970s, when *Saturday Night Fever* style quietly gave way to Levi's 501 jeans; flannel pyjamas with childlike teddy bears and sometimes even bathroom slippers. The handouts were worn until they became threadbare, until shoulders and knees wore away and the last fibers disintegrated. "It's exceedingly primitive," one foreign visitor said. "You get the impression they could have been doing the same thing for the past 100 years and could still be at it for the next century."[3]

Rifle clip, grenade, and ammunition pouches are fashioned from the leather of captured army boots too mangled to wear. Small backpacks are made from the sacks of relief food. These rebels may one day be defeated, but they will never be annihilated. Still, Oyay feared the increasing fervor of the enemy. He was reading a well-worn copy of *Holy Terror*, a book about Islamic fundamentalism passed among SPLA officers at the front.

"Look," he said, pointing to a quotation from a hard-line Islamic judge. "This is what we are fighting against now: 'Those who are against killing have no place in Islam,'" it read. "'Our Prophet killed with his own blessed hands. . . . If the survival of the Faith requires the shedding of blood, we are there to perform our duty.'"[4]

The Stone Age persists in southern Sudan and has worsened because this conflict really is forgotten. Southern Sudan is cut off from everything except war. But the scale of need has slipped beyond anyone's ability to solve the problem—much less improve lives—without peace.

So rebel areas are poisoned with the same silence that I found so disarming in Juba, that pervades empty churches and abandoned mosques, muffling every murmer of the dying like a suffocating blanket. Left to the predatory instincts of men with guns, who seem to operate free of any moral judgment, the south has reverted to the timeless rhythm of wet season and dry, of advance and retreat, of hopeless day followed by terrifying night.

The breadth of this wilderness is ominous, and only fully understood in the hours of darkness. The night sky is alive with a shimmering canopy of stars, the Milky Way like a bright wedge splitting the universe overhead in two. Dreaming is easy while rooted to this damaged land, but the spell breaks as the first blush of morning erases the stars and dims lingering planets. The sun is still far below the horizon, but the purple before dawn turns orange, red, then yellow. By 5 o'clock in the morning at one outpost, I heard the youngest SPLA recruits lining up to chant songs of war. Child soldiers were often collected in sweeps by rebel factions to fill their ranks. Their chants that morning made the hair on my neck rise. For in any other country they would be in school and would be choirboys or Cub Scouts. But here in Sudan there is only the war, and that is what they do.

Still, though the conflict has affected every life in the south and tens of thousands die each year, "covering" the war adequately as a journalist is virtually impossible. To hear the silences of this place—to be where the choirboys load their assault rifles before dawn—requires patience and fortitude. Often one can travel for three weeks and never manage to crawl beneath that muffling blanket for a glimpse of reality, or even to *feel* that here is war. Or one can land in a chartered airplane at some remote spot and be under fire within minutes.

From the government side only the rarest, controlled journey to Juba or Wau is ever permitted. Most of the rest of the war is off-limits. But in rebel-held areas, where the number of kilometers of paved road is barely more than the number of fingers on my two hands, logistical difficulties define each visit. I flew as often as possible in relief agency planes, but most aid agencies now work under the OLS umbrella and in keeping with UN rules, which require journalists to have an almost unobtainable visa from Khartoum before it will carry them. Flight costs are very high, too. Many times I had to drive overnight from Uganda or Kenya, running the gauntlet of tribal militias and bandits that control the lawless border areas. Once inside the south—powered by my own food, water, and gas and willing to sleep under the stars or in grass huts after squashing spiders and white scorpions—one's ambition was limited by the shifting war zone, sometimes aggressive rebel "minders," rains that turned dirt roads into quagmires, and by one's own fear of being in there, alone.

For relief workers, access to Sudan's neediest people is just as difficult and as restricted. The government must approve all OLS aid flights, and often entire regions—always those worst hit by the war, or where famine is brewing—are kept off the flight plans. Areas inaccessible by road are forgotten, since the small number of relief workers rarely can cope even where they *do* have access. From outside, they must bring every bite of their own food, every drop of their own petrol, every vehicle and radio, and they must expect to lose everything and be able to evacuate immediately by plane. All sides manipulate aid workers to their advantage and have killed them to make their point. The dangers that corrode the south can overwhelm any visitor, just as they have done to southerners for decades.

When Sudan's civil war reignited in 1983, the rebel forces created secure rear bases in Ethiopia. The Marxist dictator Mengistu Haile Mariam welcomed the opportunity to back the rebels, as a counterweight to Sudan's support for Eritrean and Tigrean separatists who were fighting him in northern Ethiopia. For years the SPLA maintained offices in Addis Ababa. In a string of so-called "refugee" camps just inside the border, Ethiopians trained the guerrillas, gave them a radio transmitter to beam liberation propaganda into Sudan, and air-dropped weapons to rebel units inside the south.[5]

John Garang became head of the movement because his personal friendship with Mengistu meant a steady supply of weapons, large training camps, and an internal security network that ensured his dominance. To placate his host's Marxist sensibilities, Garang coined the SPLA's revolutionary name.

But he also learned lessons from his ruthless quartermaster: Mengistu's East German-trained security forces reportedly killed two SPLA dissidents on Garang's behalf. Another potential rival, the SPLA's first representative to Britain, was lured back to Addis Ababa and killed.

Under Ethiopia's tutelage, the SPLA was transformed from a motley crew—a "mob," as Garang once said—into a 110,000-strong army.[6] But it also picked up some unsavory habits that would blemish the SPLA for years to come. Besides human rights abuses, trainees were "entirely dependent on relief food" that flowed unaccountably in the "refugee" camps.[7] Recruits were indoctrinated and told to live through the barrels of their guns. The formal SPLA "graduation song" had disturbing connotations:

> Even your mother, give her a bullet!
> Even your father, give him a bullet!
> Your gun is your food; your gun is your wife.[8]

And there was an SPLA twist: "All military training is, in a sense, dehumanizing. It prepares people to kill others," notes African Rights. "But the SPLA took this to an extreme. It inculcated a callous attitude towards civilians, not only in order to help its fighters to survive, but to spread the idea that the only option for a self-respecting man was to join up. . . . Of course atrocities happen in many wars. But from the beginning, the SPLA failed to show a determination to eliminate such actions."[9]

In the first years of the war, the coalition of rebels took control of large areas of the south, so few questioned the dictatorial practices of the leadership. Slowly, Garang's Dinka tribe also began to exert superiority over the movement. Dozens of non-Dinka dissidents were kept in confinement by the SPLA for years, and the conviction grew that if the SPLA ever won the civil war, the triumph would collapse into a battle among tribes.

I met Garang in a swept dirt compound, more than a year after the 1991 fall of the Mengistu regime, when the SPLA and 100,000 southern Sudanese refugees were forced to move overnight into Sudan. We were in the rebel headquarters at Kapoeta in April 1992, and the war was going badly. Rebel gains from a decade earlier were being rolled back by Khartoum troops, one town after another. A rival southern faction had broken away in August 1991, and just days before our meeting they accused Garang of secretly "directing a campaign of disinformation and lies under heavy influence of drink and fear." I had expected to find the rebel leader hiding deep in the trenches around Kapoeta, or fleeing in defeat.

Instead, wearing a pressed camouflage uniform and swaggering slowly like a confident cowboy, he greeted me quietly, took a seat in a red folding chair set out in a clearing, and splayed his legs. His eyes looked tired, though they were the only outward sign that recent events had been disastrous: the SPLA had split into factions, and the Islamic enemy was then almost within shelling distance. Garang carried a round gut, and—like most Sudanese of the Nilotic tribes—his skin was very black. A few gray hairs infested his thin beard, which he scratched thoughtfully with a curious shoehorn with a hand-shaped end, a totem that once belonged to a government commander. Garang attended Grinnell College in Iowa, then took a doctorate in economics from Iowa State University. As an officer in the Sudanese army, he passed the US Army's Infantry Officer's Advance Course at Fort Benning, Georgia. Ironically, he graduated from the Khartoum military academy in the same class as President Bashir.

But we are a very long way from Iowa.

"To say that the war is coming to an end is a gross misconception," Garang began, feeding me a line that has sustained the SPLA for years. "Even if all the towns here are taken, as guerrillas we will never be finished. We retreat now, but will lay siege to them during the rainy season—in the end more of the enemy will die."

He seemed bored, legs spread like a dog airing its testicles, around a small table that was draped in a red cloth, clinking with glasses of juice brought by one of his lieutenants. He had said this many times, described how his movement could never be crushed, how it never could have survived so long without the unqualified support of the people. In Maoist terms, he said, repeating another time-worn dirge, the SPLA rebels were the fish "swimming in a friendly sea" among the population. There was no such thing as a rebel headquarters "because we are never really there." The Islamic fundamentalists were fighting in vain.

"From the start they had an artificially high morale," Garang said, thumbing through a ledger labeled BSC, for "Bright Star Campaign." Here was the record of weapons, of barrels of diesel, trucks, and rounds of ammunition captured from the enemy—captured with no small sacrifice of SPLA blood. "Bashir worked up his ego to believe that this time he would have victory, that he would walk over us, so he drummed up public emotion. But there will be wailing in Khartoum as Arab boys are brought back dead. People will ask what happened."

Since peace was a pipe dream, Garang's game plan has been utterly destructive. "This war will not end with an agreement between the SPLA and Bashir. The problem is the Islamic regime in Khartoum, which is a threat to Sudan, to Ethiopia, to Egypt and the whole region. The Bashir government came to power to *prevent* peace." The only explanation for its tenacious grip, he said, "must be a special relationship with the Almighty."

Garang claimed that he wanted unity between north and south, a united secular Sudan free of religious and ethnic intolerance. For him, that can only be achieved militarily. Some say he envisions the SPLA overrunning Khartoum, to the cheers of Sudanese lining the streets to catch a glimpse of their liberators. Others argue that his talk of unity is just cant, meant to engender support from some Arab tribes in western Sudan that despise rule from Khartoum as much as he does. His real plan—if the SPLA were strong enough—would be to control the south, secede from the north, and declare an independent state.

Evidence for this tack came in April 1997, when the government offered a peace deal exactly along the lines noted above. The fate of the south would be determined by a referendum among southerners, and the choice—secession or federation—would be respected by Khartoum. By that time, Garang's SPLA faction had recaptured much of the south, and Bashir's *jihad* had lost steam, even among hard-liners. Separate nations may be Sudan's only solution, because neither side will ever be strong enough to win, or weak enough to lose. But Garang dismissed the offer outright, as a ploy.

The SPLA, however, was facing its own frustrating conundrum, which was being exacerbated by its abuse and neglect of civilians. Far from following Mao's precept, the rebels were swimming in a sea they themselves had made distinctly unfriendly, with other fish that knew only hatred for them and their domineering Dinka tribe. Problems began when the SPLA was forced to abandon its bases in Ethiopia in spring 1991, so that Garang could no longer handily control dissent. The end of easy provision of relief food to his fighters, which poured into the Ethiopian camps in the 1980s, proved to be the unraveling of rebel discipline. Following the same "depredation dynamic" at work in Somalia, the guerrillas began to practice what it had preached: to brutally forage its needs from among the population.[10]

One result was predictable, though its scope was not: "The most telling verdict on the SPLA's humanitarianism comes from the fact that hundreds of thousands of southern civilians preferred the trek north, into the heartland of the northern militias, to trying to survive in areas controlled by the SPLA," African Rights notes.[11] More than 1 million people have made that choice, and most of them have gathered penniless around Khartoum.

Another result was the acrimonious split of the SPLA into tribal-based factions that alone caused more killing among the rebels than the Khartoum forces could ever have hoped to achieve. The rebels failed totally to win hearts and minds as waves of murder, rape, and tribal looting swept across the south from mid-1991. Suspected dissidents were kidnapped from camps and towns in northern Kenya by SPLA operatives, and thousands of refugees fleeing government bombing were forcibly prevented by uniformed soldiers from leaving Sudan and used as a "human shield" along the border with Uganda.

Garang, still king of the largest faction—and the only one to continue the war against Khartoum—reacted to his weakening power like any tyrant: by tightening his grip. He said wartime was no time to experiment with democracy. One former SPLA security chief, Ochan Top Ruak, alleged that "thousands and thousands" of dissidents had been killed. There was wide use of the nickname "Pol Pot" for Garang, after the genocidal Cambodian despot.[12]

The guerrilla leader was unmoved. "What is the price of freedom?" he once asked. "Wars are known through history. The Allied forces fought for freedom, for things they valued. London was virtually leveled. There was lots of suffering. Six million Jews perished. History is very cruel, and wars are very bad. Civilizations die."[13]

Still, by 1994 Garang seemed to have recognized the new way of the world. "We shall restructure ourselves," he declared. "Our civilians have suffered a great deal. We have now put the citizen at center stage. He is the one that liberation should serve, not the one that should suffer from liberation."[14]

During my own visits, it seemed that the tattered remnants of *this* civilization might die, in large part because of misguided dictatorship at the top. One of Garang's aides leaned over and whispered into his ear a report about Bor, a town along the Nile at the heart of Dinkaland, where tribal clashes had been fierce and government forces had moved in. Bor was Garang's hometown, but the Khartoum troops had found it deserted. The SPLA had made a "tactical withdrawal" and ordered everyone out. But now the rebels had returned to encircle the garrison. This was a small detail, one of hundreds that the rebel commander logged into his thinking each day, adding up to a very particular image of the war. Even he couldn't keep the whole picture in his mind, intact, for reality in this conflict reflected the physics of the Heisenberg uncertainty principle: the more accurate the measure of fighting in one location, the less accurate it was in another.

Neglecting for a moment every other contested spot in Sudan—most of which he could reel off, town by town, one burnt village after the next by the dozen; the politics of tribe, the rains, and the disintegration of his people—Garang thought about Bor. He has been at this game for too many years to worry about every injustice, to fret about not being omniscient. He found the Bor report humorous.

"Our fighters can even fish in the lagoon there, but what can Khartoum troops get? Nothing," he told me with a snicker. "Their only hope for logistics relief is from the steamers."

He knew that the likelihood of such relief was small, as small as the chance that the mythical winged horse Pegasus might spirit you away from any tight spot. Still, he said, he let the possibility of a Khartoum waterborne escape come to life in his nightmares.

"At night I dream of boats."

I drove alone into south Sudan from Kenya that April 1992, in the sparkling new four-wheel drive Mitsubishi Pajero owned by Catholic Bishop Paride Taban, a churchman who for a time was among the most respected by SPLA leaders, who could point out brutal excesses constructively, without too much fear for his safety. His Pajero was shiny white, a perfect target for government planes. Some modifications had been made in Nairobi, and someone else drove it to the Kenya border town of Lokichokio, where I was in need of a lift. Like everyone in the south, I had problems getting safely from one place to another, and so happily did the favor of driving it in.

Even in Bishop Taban's vehicle, which was later painted a less targetable dark blue, my journey to Torit was complicated by insecurity. A shadowy militia of the small Toposa tribe was trying to cut the road to Kapoeta. This was their area, not Dinkaland, so when they held up a vehicle they often asked first if there were any Dinka aboard. The Toposa were armed by Khartoum to harass the rebels, and some walked for days to Juba to collect AK-47 assault rifles. These they could trade for ten cows each, or even take them to the "enemy" SPLA and exchange them for G-3 rifles. The Dinka feared them. Tension came and went, but right then it was very high.

The reason was simple enough, it seemed: there had been a party recently in Kapoeta, at which the SPLA officers got drunk. Toposa made off with hundreds of the Dinka commander's cattle. Cows are as sacred to the Dinka as camels are to Somali nomads, so the reaction was swift. Every Toposa village within miles was burned. When I arrived, the Dinka were expecting retaliation. The feeling of imminent attack was palpable. The *fear* alone was sufficient to unleash gremlins in my mind, which raced. The year before, the SPLA had posted soldiers every 5 kilometers along the road. But now, there was no one.

For safety, I joined a convoy of relief food traveling the same road. I was warned that if we were stopped, we would probably not be shot, but we would lose everything. I hid my camera bag, rucksack, clothes, and watch under dozens of 50kg sacks of food in the next truck. I wore a disposable sarong tied up with a rope—my belt would have been be the first thing to go, I was told—a pair of plastic thongs and an old T-shirt. As the column revved up, I lit a cigar and breathed deeply, in prayer, to prepare for this drive. I plonked my wedding ring into the ashtray.

The dirt road was still gouged by the many convoys of the past rainy season. The bishop's 4WD drove well, but the only cassette tape was a collection of tinny gospel songs. They were company enough. The last two convoys up this road had been attacked, and we met up with one at dusk. I got out along with the Kenyan drivers to inspect the damage. The attack had been brief but severe: three bullets in the door had shattered all the windows and killed the driver, spraying his blood throughout the cab.

It turned dark, the cigar was finished, and all that was left was patience. The convoy seemed to crawl along, almost tempting anyone in the bush beyond the cast of our headlights to fire a few rounds or jump into the road and order a halt. I shifted uneasily in my sarong, and my heart seemed to stop beating; our luck had been too good. Surely now we risked attack. Another hour passed, then a cheer went up from the lead vehicles, as the first buildings of Kapoeta loomed into view. The roar of rejoicing ran the length of the convoy, like the release of a too-deep breath that had overstretched the lungs.

The rest of the journey, from Kapoeta to Torit, I drove solo the next day. The rains were over, and I saw *no one* on the dirt roads. It was as if the land was empty. The solitude of this *war zone* was again disturbing. How crippling it must be to live here, fending off the demons day after day.

Bishop Taban was at the cathedral in Torit, and there were just two candles lit when I arrived in the night. The well water in the clay urn in the corner was still warm with the heat of the day, with the flat earth flavor of well-drawn water. I helped myself and we sat down. The bishop's bulbous face reflected oddly in the light, belying the inner strength that he had built up during years spent handling the spiritual needs of a devastated people. He knew the explosive blasts of attacks by government Antonov planes, when bombs were simply rolled out of the back of the aircraft, to land randomly below. But he also knew what it was to be a victim of the rebels: when Torit first fell to the SPLA in 1989, Taban had been running a school and a dispensary and providing food for the poor. He and three priests were arrested by the rebels and accused of prolonging Torit's resistance and—absurdly—of feeding the army. The clergymen were held under house arrest for three months.[15]

So Taban knew the anguish of his people, a generation wasted by war, and of their anger at the additional immoral hardship imposed by their self-declared leaders. The problem afflicted everyone trapped here, though, and the leadership was just a symptom of a wider degeneration. "None of us in south Sudan live with integrity," Taban said, his large cross hanging by a long chain down across his belly, visibly bright in the candlelight. "People in the villages want to be independent of northerners, but we have muddled our words and wrongly equate 'Arab' with fundamentalism, which is not always the case: 'The only good Arab is a dead Arab,' they often say." Little room was left for compromise.

One candle guttered, and it was late. Bishop Taban's broad hands rested lifeless on the arms of the chair, for he could little afford to waste energy with useless movement. "Khartoum's attitude is the same today as it has always been," he said. "They have never believed that the SPLA is strong, that this successful fighting can be done by people they consider to be slaves."

Days later, after visiting the Ngangala front, the drive back out was as frightening and unorthodox as the drive in. This time a vehicle belonging to a relief agency in Torit had overturned. The windshield was smashed and the roof caved in over the driver's side, so I drove it out for repair. Hunched over and with our heads against the collapsed roof, two Sudanese companions and I ground to a stop in a cloud of steam. It was night again. The radiator cap had been lost in the crash, but within an hour we found a rebel base where there was enough water to quench the engine's thirst. I fashioned a new cap out of wire and the thick brown plastic packaging of an American combat meal.

At Kapoeta we heard that no one had made it down the road to Kenya since my convoy arrived a week before. The choices were unappealing: wait for a plane, which could take a week and might not have space for me; or drive. We calculated that even the Toposa must sleep, and if we drove fast enough we would catch them off guard. At 2 am I ate a cold tin of beans—the third in as many days, for there was nothing else—climbed into the battered cab, and again plopped my gold wedding band into the ashtray. My eyes watered and strained to see the road, as the stinging cold wind whipped, without a windshield, like a wind tunnel through the cab. The headlights were askew and almost useless. We were all frigid, and reason gave way to the charge ahead. The Toposa remained asleep, and six hours later we crossed into Kenya, a new sun rising over low hills, free finally of the dangers that haunt southern Sudan.

Kapoeta fell one month later, in May 1992, to government soldiers who relied on Toposa guides for their assault. The attack was a complete surprise. The UN and relief workers who had advised me of road conditions the night I ate my tin of beans were given one and one-half hours warning to evacuate by panicky SPLA officers. Tens of thousands of people marched toward Kenya in flight and were bombed repeatedly by government planes.

Such endemic uncertainty is what has turned southern Sudanese to their religion. The rituals of faith are maintained, the vastnesses engendering a certain monastic purity. Spiritual strength in this place is honed and burnished almost by default. Under these bright heavens, trying to determine one's station in God's universe is what fills the gap between birth and death. Inevitable war seems only to fortify this reflex. So a visit to these forgotten faithful by the head of the Anglican Church, the Archbishop of Canterbury George Carey, at the turn of the 1994 New Year, became reason for spiritual regeneration.

Bishop Taban was ecstatic, for no spiritual effort was wasted when measured in counterpoint to Khartoum's *jihad*. "He's showing that he is ready to shed his blood for the people," Taban told me about Carey's visit. "They will forget their suffering and their empty stomachs."

This was a pilgrimage laden with symbolism, of contrasts between war and peace—of guns and crosses—and of both sorrow and hope. Archbishop Carey's message behind rebel lines was not unlike Pope John Paul's in the capital: "Your agony, your fears and your tears are known to God." The prelate was also to have visited Khartoum, but at the last moment the Bashir regime insisted on controlling his schedule. Carey refused to be manipulated, sparking the immediate expulsion of the British ambassador, Peter Streams. Britain responded by expelling the Sudanese ambassador from London. But the diplomatic row could not have been further away from the events unfolding in southern Sudan.

The archbishop's modest convoy drove north from the border town of Nimule as bush fires raged unchecked alongside the road. I was in the sole media vehicle. The fires covered the route with acrid black smoke and, though unrelated, were a reminder of the destruction already wrought by war. At Aswa Camp, home to nearly 30,000 displaced Dinka, crowds mobbed the archbishop as he walked the final stretch. Sweating in his heavy maroon robes, the pale Englishman looked uneasy holding his long stave and crucifix aloft in the midst of the throng, as dust and filaments of soot clung to his skin. The Sudanese wore small crosses fashioned from grass in their hair, and pranced wildly. One man used his 4-foot-long cross as a scythe to sweep clear the path before Carey. During the prelate's address in a dirt compound, scores of amputees balanced on their crutches and listened intently. Seen from knee level, because of their missing legs, they appeared to levitate above a forest of poles.

Another group held a placard that described a tenuous existence: "We may not be here during the next few days, because Sudan will have completed their military destruction of the south." The prediction was accurate enough: the next time I visited Aswa, less than a year later, this camp would be a battlefield. As if in premonition, the bottom of my chair was marked with the name of one desperate establishment. It read: "SURVIVAL HOTEL."

The only permanent concrete building for many miles—built, ironically, by the Islamic Dawa agency in 1983 as part of a campaign to spread Islam—was a hospital on the other side of the Aswa River. It was full of casualties, supported by a Norwegian surgical team. Carey and his wife, a nurse, walked the grimy corridors, their nostrils filling with the smell of iodine and dried blood. They did not linger with the worst cases. The archbishop rubbed the back of his finger across the forehead of one feverish boy. Upon entering another room, he apologized to a young mother: "Sorry to disturb you." Thus prompted, Tabitha Ajok took off her hat and beamed at her new twins, born days before, on Christmas Eve. "A boy and a girl?" asked Carey, and smiled through the layer of dust on his face. "Good, that's lovely."

When he departed, the crowd chased after the archbishop's convoy. A young priest in Roman collar ran until he choked on the dust and ash, his chest heaving.

Carey called these the "longest four days of my life," and years later, a church official said that this Southern Sudan visit was the "most important" they had ever made. Quite apart from having to cope with the diplomatic row and physical risk, the archbishop came down with a stomach bug that was troublesome on long flights in the five-seater plane on which I too was a passenger. But there were light moments, too: Carey and his wife were given a treebark bedsheet. And Mrs. Carey was presented with one extraordinary garment. "What's this?" she asked, then received it graciously as her own laughter was swallowed by the knowing laughter of the assembled holy men: the outfit was designed to be worn with bare breasts. To preserve the goodwill with which it was given, it may still be hanging in a closet at Lambeth Palace in London.

I happened to be the only journalist traveling with the archbishop, though others appeared at day stops. At night, our small group would be taken in by some of the local clergy, fed, and found places to sleep. There was also a complete fascination with my satellite telex machine, which I used to send stories to *The Daily Telegraph*. They could not get enough of this exclusive story, since access was so limited. The archbishop and his crew marveled that this little gadget, plugged into a car battery or on battery power, could communicate from anywhere on the planet. This satellite technology had revolutionized my work in Africa. We used it to send messages that all was well to Lambeth Palace, via the *Telegraph* foreign desk.

As Carey continued his journey, SPLA commanders feared that the diplomatic row, and government anger at the "illegal" visit, would spark retaliatory air strikes. The route was guarded by rebels wearing rags and carrying assault rifles. The contrast with so many symbols of peace was stark. But there was reason to worry. Relief workers expressed surprise that the itinerary was published in advance: they *never* discussed flight arrival times or destinations over the radio except in code.

But southerners were used to such fear and would not have their enthusiasm so easily dampened. In Akot, Carey was greeted by naked Dinka boys with round patches of powdery dust marking their black bottoms. Old women adorned with stained and cracked ivory bracelets raced to catch a glimpse of this spiritual headman from outside. There was nothing but poverty, and an indefatigable spirit. In Yambio dozens of elderly Episcopal priests lined up outside the church, clutching their Bibles and *Books of Common Prayer* in the Zandi language. Their Bibles were worn through, the pages blackened on the edges from overuse, like their stained dog collars and threadbare robes.

"We have to hold our Bibles until the end of our days," one priest told me. "We will be fighting a religious war as long as there is Islamic law in the north. We are forced to fight." A senior priest, soiled like one who traveled constantly, added that the regime "has succeeded in building a fence around the southern Sudan, so that *nobody* from the outside world knows our fate."

Standing at a simple wood altar on a brick dais, Archbishop Carey was clearly moved by his apostolic journey. This was a moment of joy, a Eucharist in the wilderness. "The Church in the West is lazy and slow. We can learn so much from your enthusiasm for God, and your love," the prelate said, as an ant crawled slowly up the sleeve of his robe, toward his miter. "We are seeing Christianity here struggling with issues of confrontation, facing the fact that it could so easily be obliterated from Sudan if you lose your faith," he said. "There are many reasons for sorrow in Sudan, but your faith is stronger than your enemy."

Here were the antagonisms of "life and death, isolation and deprivation, hunger and pain. But alongside the human misery there is an outstanding Christian enthusiasm, a tangible sense of God's presence with you . . . and a conviction that God will not let you down. If there is a crucifixion in Sudan, there is also an undeniable resurrection."

Ecstatic at the rousing sermon, one old priest lifted his rheumy eyes and proclaimed: "God has protected me for 80 years, and now he will protect me for 80 more!"

Any divine intervention on the side of this aging holy man could only be assisted by foreign governments, however, who might see Khartoum's belligerence as a threat to their own stability. President Bashir's insistence upon waging a *jihad* eventually did wake neighboring Uganda and Kenya to the possibility of an Islamic threat on their doorstep. Rwanda and Ethiopia, too—backed in the late 1990s by the US and driven in their concern by American Christians in solidarity with the "persecuted Christians" of south Sudan and their "religious" war—also entered the fray.

"You do what you need to do, and we will help [SPLA allies]. But it's a very dangerous game," said one American strategist. "If [Sudan government officials] don't change their internal policies, their human rights policies, then they're digging their own grave. This is just one step short of saying that we will provide the bullet."[16]

But Khartoum took several confident steps too many, by expanding its policy of waging war through proxy militias. It secretly armed a fanatical "Christian" militia, the Lord's Resistance Army, to hassle Sudan rebels and north Uganda alike. President Yoweri Museveni of Uganda reacted by providing even more weapons to Garang's rebel faction and by serving as a willing conduit for other foreign support. The US and Israel, fearing that a Khartoum victory in southern Sudan would create an unstoppable Islamic movement in Africa, were believed to be primary actors. By the end of 1994, the renewed support began to make an impact among SPLA battlefield commanders.

"Everything has come in the last three months, and it's all hardware," said Dan Eiffe, the head of the relief agency Norwegian People's Aid (NPA), in late 1994. He had watched the weapons arrive. "This has become Museveni's war," he said. The Americans were funneling support through Uganda, and more openly gave a first-time gift of $11 million to NPA, which was well known to be an SPLA supporter. Before this assistance policy began, however, not all the goodies had made it to the war zone. "Visible gloom" had spread in the SPLA offices in Nairobi in August 1992, for example, when news came of the arrest in America of a Ugandan presidential aide—and the seizure of 400 TOW anti-tank missiles and 34 TOW launchers that he had illegally tried to purchase for the SPLA.[17]

The new rebel support showed. Many guerrillas had new uniforms and seemed well supplied. Rounds for 12.7mm heavy machine guns were unpacked from gray ammunition boxes labeled "Parts for Typewriters." Eight-foot-long 122mm rockets for banks of Stalin Organs were marked "Equipment for Construction," their new cold steel sweating in the heat. The rocket fuses came in crates for bulldozer parts. The equipment could not have come at a more critical time. Already one front had shifted south all the way to Aswa and straddled the river. During a visit in November 1994, I saw Khartoum troops had dug in on the north side around the hospital building, where Archibishop Carey had so recently blessed the war wounded. The camp for the displaced Dinka had been abandoned. SPLA positions were largely hidden by tall elephant grass and the rotting abandoned camp huts.

The two armies then were locked into a stalemate and had been battering each other daily. We were just nine miles north of the strategic border town of Nimule, where these rebel units defended a critical supply route. I was with a handful of colleagues, all old Somalia hands. We were on a stony outcropping that served as a lookout. Shouting into his field radio, Cmdr. Obudo Mamur Mete ordered the firepower with enthusiasm: "Heavy machine guns—900 rounds *each*; 120mm mortars—10 rounds *each*; 107mm field artillery—10 rounds *each* . . . " And the list went on.

Dripping in the heat, Mamur gripped the radio handset: "If you are ready, then *blast off!*" he shouted.

The burst of cannon and tick-*BOOM* of impacting shells filled the valley, and the Khartoum troops were caught off-guard. For three hours their trenches filled with dirt thrown up by the shells, their base camp adjoining the hospital began to burn, and then finally they responded with tank rounds. Long into the battle, Mamur looked through his field glasses and announced that the government troops were "fleeing back from their trenches." But the defiant return shelling continued; the two T-55 tanks had not been abandoned: their gunners spied our observation post and fired one, then another round from their main gun, the line of impacts steadily closing in. Neither of those blasts managed to silence the birds that were chirping steadily in the trees around us.

We jumped into foxholes, and mine seemed to be a very narrow but deep enough pit, reinforced on the inside with rings of stones. Donatella Lorch of *The New York Times* (with whom I had shared a *tagliatelle* dinner in Mogadishu before the American "Bloody Monday" attack, in which our dinner partner, Hansi Kraus, other friends, and scores of Somalis were killed) had unwanted company in hers. "Hey, do you guys mind if I come over and visit you?" she called out. "I have two snakes that are keeping me company here. I don't like snakes."

But the third round was a direct hit from the 100mm shell, detonating on a branch above our heads. The air pressure dropped suddenly, then with the explosion the sky disappeared in a cloud of hurtling fragments and dirt. My deep gut tightness gave way to the enveloping smell of cordite, and over the ring in my ears I heard the shouts of our wounded. Exposed for a moment while dashing to a better bunker, James Schofield of ABC-Australia was hit with a chunk of shrapnel that entered his left buttock and ripped through his thigh to exit above his knee. He was bleeding but could walk well enough to rush to the rearward bunker. He laid back on the damp, musty dirt floor, and we were pinned down by more shelling.

The birds never stopped singing.

Inside the bunker, Alex Belida of Voice of America—who had himself been shot in the legs by Nigerian troops in Somalia, and so could understand exactly what James was going through—and Donatella tried to calm James, who was breathing heavily. Dan Eiffe of NPA had helped arrange our visit. "Dan! Is it possible they'll launch an infantry attack on this place?" James asked, breathlessly. "No, no. No question of that," Dan replied, a little too hurriedly, and bent over double in the small bunker.

Two rebels were also wounded, and appeared stoically unfazed. They even waited outside the tiny bunker—I could see them from my half-protected perch on the second step. Moses Lemi Moi was hit with a piece of shrapnel that shredded the fingers of his right hand. In eight years of fighting this was his first injury, though he surely would have died if the shrapnel had not lodged in the full clip of the assault rifle he was holding. "It's no problem, I'm fine," he said calmly, wrapping his hand in Alex's red handkerchief.

Simon Mading Atem was hit in the groin, his second serious injury in ten years as a guerrilla. He had done battle with the SPLA since he was 16 and had seen many friends die. We eventually got to the main road. Eventually we were able to walk out, the adrenaline and shock carrying James forward. Moses' hand was bandaged. SPLA medics poured iodine into James' wound and bandaged his leg. Mamur helped James into the back of a jeep. Simon sat quietly in the back of the vehicle, his blood seeping through a worn gray uniform and coagulating on the plastic seat. He must have wondered why he was there, wounded . . . for what? But if he was angry he didn't show it. He was another casualty, another hash mark on some universal list of broken Sudanese bodies that surely must be tallied somewhere.

At the Nimule hospital, I reassured James and held his hand tightly, as the first dressings were changed unsparingly, and the anesthetizing adrenaline rush of the front line gave way to the throbbing pain of the wound. He was evacuated by plane the next day. As for me, when I left Sudan my pallor had turned to the sickly yellow of hepatitis that put me down for several weeks. Donatella later wrote that she thought I was "immune from fear," and noted that taped above the screen on my computer were the words: "Hesitate, and Die." But about our flight out of southern Sudan together, she wrote, I was "subdued and pensive."

"You know," she quoted me telling her, "I prayed for all of us out there."[18] And I certainly had.

Alex had left his cassette recorder running throughout the Aswa shelling and later—under the rubric we coined during the trip, "War Correspondents for Peace"—he put together a memorable tape. One song blended the front-line blasts with the Vietnam War-era tune "Down in the Bunker," by the Steve Gibbons Band. It featured Donatella coping with the snakes, mixed with these lines:

I've been cast into the mould of new times,
I've been gassed, behind enemies lines,
I was the last one from two thousand and one young squaddies.

I thought to myself, it's got to be a dream
That's when I noticed this hole in the green,
And the girl in the bunker, revealin' her beautiful body.

Well, there were handicaps, all around,
But I had to get into that hole in the ground,
Though the grass was covered in blood, the green was muddy.
I took my aim, but I missed the shot
And it landed right down in the spot,
Where the girl in the bunker was flashin' her beautiful body.

The second song imposed the impressive *rat-a-tat* and *ka-boom!* of the front onto the somber and haunting ode to "mankind and brotherhood" by Ace of Bass, called "Happy Nation." It still is, for me, a powerful reminder of the impact of war in Africa.

For commander Mamur, our experience was just another day of conflict. "This is routine to us," he said. "What is happening here is also happening all over the south. They don't want us to survive." We both knew that the maps would change but the predicament would not. Prayers will be sent skyward from both sides of no-man's-land, appealing for a dispensation that will almost certainly never come. Mamur would be easy to find: he will be in another foxhole next year, and the year after, directing artillery barrages against the enemy until his luck, too, runs out.

Pathetic testimony of south Sudan's decimation was played out on a bridge above the muddy and small Aswa River.

The stones below were worn, bleached by the sun and used, when the war was far away, for washing clothes. The Archbishop of Canterbury's convoy stopped to appreciate the view. Carey walked to the edge of the bridge, leaned forward with a point-and-shoot camera, and snapped a picture. He turned to Meker Deng Malok, one of the church guides, and they walked back together.

"Do you have a camera?" the archbishop asked hopefully, putting his arm around his thin companion.

The reply was wistful: "I used to."

TWELVE

THE FALSE MESSIAH

Lucky are the people in Yugoslavia and Somalia,
for the world is with them. It may be a blessing to die
in front of a camera because the world will know.

—From a letter smuggled out of southern Sudan,
August 1992

The legend of tribal holocaust had passed down from generation to generation in southern Sudan, from one of the most
influential prophets of the Nuer tribe, Ngundeng Bong. Pos-
sessed of one of the sky-spirits common in Nuer religion, this
prophet had foretold of a fierce final battle of Nuer conquest
that would result in total defeat of the Dinka. Drums would
sound, and tribesmen would sharpen their spears to prepare for
slaughter. A messiah would emerge, the prophecy predicted, to
lead the Nuer into battle from the village of Nasir.[1] Victory was
preordained.

Such prophets are a relatively recent phenomenon—Ngundeng died in 1906, after erecting a 60-foot-tall pyramid, ringed
at its base by elephant tusks—and according to one account,
this one had the "pathological qualities" of a "genuine psy-
chotic."[2] Nuer prophets had gained their prestige by initiating
raids against the Dinka. Big raids required a sacred blessing,
and sacrifices were made in advance.

The Great Tribal War in southern Sudan, as ordered by the
prophet, was indeed launched from Nasir. In November 1991,
some 30,000 Nuer were united under a modern messiah, and
renewed—through telling and retelling of the "ancient"
fables—war against the Dinka. "As far as history and tradition
go back, and in the vistas of myth beyond their farthest reach,
there has been enmity between the two peoples," explains E. E.

Evans-Pritchard, a British ethnologist in his studies of the Nuer. "Almost always the Nuer have been the aggressors, and raiding of the Dinka is conceived by them to be a normal state of affairs and a duty."[3]

So in 1991, Nuer warriors marched on the Dinka heartland at Bor and Kongor to recapture lost cattle, chanting their battle cry: "We will make you Dinka drink your own blood!"

The raiders killed so many that the death count was stopped after reaching 2,000. People were speared and shot, bound with ragged belts and knotted cord, strangled, and burned. Three boys were tied to a tree and clubbed to death. Men were castrated and disemboweled.[4] The region was depopulated as 100,000 Dinka fled south into the swamps to survive or die on a diet of leaves and water lilies. Food stores left behind were put to the torch, and tens of thousands of head of precious cattle were spirited away by the marauders.

Even if the "Nuer Messiah," renegade SPLA commander Riek Machar Teny-Dhurgon, never intended such a vicious onslaught, once under way it could not be controlled. The Nuer, in the words of Norwegian priest and relief worker Dan Eiffe, who helped count the dead, "killed anybody who could shout."

The 1991 Bor Massacre revived an antagonism that, for many southerners, completely overshadowed their fear of the Islamic north. Suddenly the enemy was inescapable, and coming from *within* the south. Only decades before, this had been the norm, though the reason for war was always to acquire the enemy's revered cattle. "Fighting, like cattle husbandry, is one of the chief activities and dominant interests of all Nuer men, and raiding Dinka for cattle is one of their principal pastimes," notes Evans-Pritchard. Though Nuer "have a proper contempt for Dinka and are derisive of their fighting qualities"—fighting with Dinka "is considered so trifling"—boys looked forward to the day they could join raiding parties as men, "to enrich themselves and to establish their reputation as warriors."[5]

Like the story of Jacob and Esau in the Bible, the ethnologist explains, another Nuer myth justifies this order:

> Nuer and Dinka are represented in this myth as two sons of God who promised his old cow to Dinka and its young calf to Nuer. Dinka came by night to God's byre and, imitating the voice of Nuer, obtained the calf. When God found that he had been tricked he was angry and charged Nuer to avenge the injury by raiding Dinka's cattle to the end of time.[6]

The result, noted one 1907 British intelligence report, was that "to this day the Dinka has always lived by robbery, and the Nuer by war."[7]

But these two largest African tribes of Sudan had lived together in relative peace during the decades of Sudan's independence. Though united under the SPLA until 1991, the rebel leadership then split along tribal lines. Col. Garang and his Dinka officers were accused of dictatorship, tribalism, and rampant violations of human rights and were guilty on all counts. Riek led the breakaway faction, which drew most of its support from Nuer SPLA units and civilian militias. But almost immediately, Riek secretly agreed to a mutual "hands-off" policy with the archenemy, Khartoum. The war for the south turned into a divisive three-way battle royal.

Making the Bor Massacre fit the legend was easy. Riek based his breakaway rebel "movement" at the fabled Nasir. Faction leaders and intellectuals may wage war for political reasons, but for those doing the killing and most of the dying, the conflict was about satisfying a vengeful tribal bloodlust. One who lived long among both tribes saw the same simple tactic from Somalia to Sarajevo: "If you ask these people to fight for democracy, that is too much," said Bernadette Kumar, of Unicef. "The way to make them fight is to revive the old differences. There is nothing like a line of ancestral murders to motivate a fighter."

Riek's faction tapped deeply into that loyalty. The civilian forces that joined him for the Dinka hunt were called the "White Army," an informal group of thousands of Nuer men whose name was derived from the "white" metal of its spears and pangas. They were united under the powerful prophet Wutnyang Gatakek, who drew heavily on Ngundeng's legacy.[8] During the Nuer-Dinka wars of the early 1990s, they often entered battle surrealistically wearing sheets or with their skin smeared with white ash. Along with the prophecies of success against the Dinka, the White Army was spurred to fight to "retake their cattle" and replenish Nuer herds. But such promises of victory apparently did not extend to cattle: besides sparking reprisals, stolen Dinka cattle spread diseases, causing Nuer cattle to die by the thousands.[9]

The violence of the Bor Massacre was no surprise, even if the scale was. Historically, Nuer raids on Dinkaland were brutal affairs. Earlier this century, "Older women and babies were clubbed and, when the raid was on a village, their bodies were thrown on the flaming byres and huts."[10]

Southern Sudanese folklore warns against dangerously manipulating the spirits of the tribes and especially deplores allowing one's tribal spirit to wage overly brutal campaigns while the enemy spirit is "sleeping." One account explains how a victory won without restraint could turn into catastrophe: "The fear has always been that if a tribe tries to gain too much, its spirit will begin to tire just at the moment when the opposing tribe's spirit awakens. . . . If too much has been taken or destroyed, the vengeance of the counter-attacking spirit will be intense."[11]

The Dinka lost little time avenging the deaths at Bor, ensuring a recurring pattern of raids that would turn villages and food stocks to ash and further desecrate the south with tens of thousands more dead. Garang's SPLA faction retaliated with force and summarily executed all Nuer they captured. Near Bor, one group of 19 Nuer men were tied up in a cattle shed and speared to death.[12] As the atrocities mounted, both rebel factions were corrupted by their own violence. The sense of inevitable war felt almost as natural as a gravedigger picking up his shovel, fingers again fitting very worn grooves. The fact was not lost on the UN's special rapporteur for Human Rights, who found: "Indiscriminant attacks on civilians by both factions seems to have become part of the strategy; thousands of civilians . . . were deliberately targeted."[13]

The man who sparked this tribal bloodletting was Riek Machar, the gap-toothed rebel officer who matched the qualifications of the expected Nuer messiah, the leader of legend who had come to liberate his tribesman from the predatory Dinka. It didn't hurt that Riek was an immediate descendant of a renowned prophet of the Neur divinity Teny—hence Riek's third name.[14] At his Spartan compound in Nasir, Riek stoked the dual imperatives of his rule. On the wall of his bare mud hut, there was a primitive painting of an African snake. But sitting on his desk, almost alone and surely for everyone to see, was a thick *Good News Bible* embossed on the cover with gold lettering. The close proximity of the snake and the Bible—both tokens of southern Sudanese spiritual strength—would be necessary if he was to fulfill the prophecy and totally defeat the Dinka.

I interviewed Riek soon after the Bor Massacre, before the tribal spirit of the Dinka had woken and counterattacked in revenge. Unlike most towns in Garang's territory, Nasir was on the short list of UN relief flight destinations approved by Khartoum, so getting there wasn't too much trouble. We sat on chairs of thick wooden slats fashioned from ammunition crates. Riek was confident and wore a big broad smile of welcome. He had a Ph.D. in management from Britain's Bradford University and said he was fighting for what many Sudanese believed could be the only solution: secession of south Sudan. He was the deputy commander-in-chief of the SPLA when he broke away. He claimed that he controlled one-third of the south. From there I couldn't tell: he might not even control the trees nearest to the horizon, or the other side of the Sobat River that flowed past Nasir.

"I'm not a messiah to anybody. If they say so, I say no. This is not a religious war we are fighting," Riek told me, sitting at this *desk* in a mud hut in the bush, a practiced humility in his voice. Speaking easily, he said he turned down lucrative job offers with insurance companies upon graduation to return and fight for his people. "The secession from the north is in their blood, [my fighters] are fighting for issues, not tribes." He discounted tribalism as "from a different age," though boasted that he has "not seen a Nuer who doesn't support me." In the same breath, he added, "if there is a tribal element, the Nuer would destroy all the Dinka."

Riek justified the Bor Massacre, saying that it was meant to show Garang that he must negotiate a peace with the breakaway group and couldn't overpower them with force. He claimed that he felt acute "embarrassment" because "so many civilians were caught in the crossfire." No male prisoners were taken alive by either side. Three generations of Nuer were fighting, and if they lose the entire race would be wiped out, so the reponsibilities weighed heavily. "The atrocities committed are things [the Dinka] asked for," he said. He claimed he had dictated what happened: "Fighting at Bor did *not* get out of control. I was in total control of how far the troops went."

Though isolated at his remote Nasir base, Riek was married to an English convent girl called Emma McCune. Her fine features and hair tied back with a bandana were a sharp contrast to the rough life hewn out of the bush with a Sudanese warlord. They met in 1989 in Sudan when she was setting up schools for a charity. She found Riek "deeply romantic" and wrote: "I knew this was what I wanted—to be with the man I loved in the country I loved."

Driving to the wedding ceremony in June 1991, the unlikely couple had to push their Land Rover out of the mud. It was a suitable reminder of the hard life that she seemed to be adapting to with relative ease. Along with every southern Sudanese, she suffered nightly plagues of mosquitoes, scorpion and rat bites, and the company of huge wall spiders. Deep trenches dug behind their hut were to hide from bombing raids or Garang's artillery. During trips to Nairobi she worked to rally support for her husband's breakaway bid. Garang called McCune a British spy, and she admitted that "there are some people out there who would gladly put a bullet through my head." She died— five months pregnant—in a car accident in Nairobi in November 1993.

Emma McCune may not have witnessed the most extreme acts of her husband's tribal war. But she was still aware of the impact it had on her adopted country, where her body was buried. In the visitor's book at a friend's house, she wrote under the "Address" column: "From the wasteland of southern Sudan."

Arrogance stood at the root of the Dinka-Nuer conflict, as it had underscored the rivalry for centuries. Dinka refer to themselves as *mony-jong*, which means "men of men."[15] In the Dinka's thinking, they "represent the standard of what is ideally human and therefore best," notes historian Francis Deng. "Others may have superior technology or great wealth in monetary terms, but all things considered, Dinkaland is the most beautiful, the Dinka race the perfect example of creation, Dinka cattle the ideal wealth, and Dinka ways the best models of dignity."[16]

And in the face of attack, brutality was normal. The tradition was passed on in cattle camp, where Dinka boys learned to tend their herds and how to fight at the slightest provocation. One Dinka man explained the game: "The type of sport we do is war. The idea is to defend yourself and show your manhood. I try to hit your head with a stick, you try to dodge."[17]

The Nuer were equally as arrogant and ready to fight. "Cattle are their dearest possession, and they gladly risk their lives to defend their herds or to pillage those of their neighbors," notes Evans-Pritchard. "Nuer say that it is cattle that destroy people, for 'more people have died for the sake of a cow that for any other cause.'"[18] As a tribe, the Nuer have also demonstrated a definite superiority in battle over the more numerous Dinka during the 19th century. Then, the expansionist Nuer pushed east into Dinka-occupied lands, which resulted in a "massive absorption of Dinka and Anyuak lands, cattle, and people."[19] Though fighting was "incessant from time immemorial," it "seems to have reached a state of equilibrium before European conquest upset it."[20] British forces sent no fewer than ten expeditions against Nuer tribes from 1902 to 1928 before the Nuer "finally submitted" to British rule. Dinka tribes required just seven expeditions.[21]

So the drama unfolded, lost either in the tall elephant grass of wide borderless plains of the south or among its rocky hills. Riek's aim of forcing Garang into submission was thwarted by his own soldiers' abuse of civilians and lack of outside support. One journalist who traveled with Riek described fumbling in the bush with a ragtag band of fighters who seemed to have forgotten that war was about more than their own survival. Garang attacked the town of Ayod, for example, and Riek tried to reinforce his garrison there. But, as Rory Nugent recounted,

> [T]here is less than a barrel of diesel on hand. Without a dime in the treasury, and no way to buy fuel in Ethiopia or Kenya, [Riek] has to wait until his border units are able to steal it. Meanwhile, his troops will have to move by foot, the big guns remaining in storage. Complicating everything is an inadequate intelligence network: no one can be sure about the enemy's position. None of Riek's scouts have watches, maps or compasses, making it virtually impossible to sort out the various sightings.[22]

Intelligence reports were dismissed because officers were "positive that the scouts, lacking compasses, had confused north for south, not an uncommon occurance."[23] Medical supplies were so short that for one doctor a pair of pliers from the motor pool was his only operating tool. He had been using leaves to wrap wounds and amputating limbs with a razor blade and a bayonet; with no painkillers to dispense, a width of tire tread kept tongues in one piece. He called the $6.95 folding saw brought to cut firewood a "life saver," and he meant it.[24]

Such conditions did little to foster noble intentions among the tribal fighters. Riek said that any attempt to alter the ancient order was fruitless, even as his Nuer soldiers built a fire before charging out to face a Dinka assault: "'Tradition,' he explained calmly. They must sacrifice a cow before they go into battle. 'There is nothing I can do about it. That's the way it has been for centuries.'"[25]

What Riek could control were his political friends, but his secret alliance with the Islamic regime in Khartoum was seen by most southerners as a sellout. Despite Riek's emphatic denials, UN and relief workers who lived in Nasir confirmed that government delegations visited regularly and that air force planes air-dropped weapons and ammunition for the breakaway rebels. The deal was mutually distasteful to both sides, but they also had mutual interests. The enemy was Garang and his Dinka-led SPLA faction. Riek believed that Khartoum would help him rid southern Sudan of this menace. And Khartoum was happy to supply Riek with weapons; enough, at least, to fuel the fratricide with supreme efficiency.

In Nasir, Riek denied that he had sold his soul. "I am very conscious what I am fighting for, and I've fought Khartoum for years," he told me, defending himself. He was so cool that he was almost believable. "I do not want to see a weak SPLA—if Khartoum attacks, we will be united against them." But any chance of that had dissipated during the Bor Massacre. The Nasir faction had been joined by one pro-government militia, and during the spring 1992 dry-season offensive, the implications of Nuer treachery were even more clear. With Riek's blessing, Islamic troops skirted around Nasir to strike at Garang from the rear. The attack was just one of the five-prong action that President Bashir claimed would be the "final offensive."

Within months the government had recaptured two-thirds of the south, and SPLA control was cut down to portions of the countryside. Garang no longer held even a handful of towns. Throughout the fighting, not one war casualty was admitted to the Nasir hospital. Riek's troops sat idle as Khartoum pushed back the Dinka. The results of Riek's sell-out to Khartoum could not have been more glaring. The Dinka suffered mightily. Severe retaliation, by both the SPLA and government troops against civilians, plunged southerners into deep depression. The New Sudan Council of Churches, the

group of Christian churchmen in rebel-held areas, appealed in a pastoral letter to the rival commanders, pleading that "the time has come for peace."

> The South is like a body which cannot despise any of its parts.
> Our brothers are like the two hands of the body. Both are needed.
> And when something comes to crush the body, the hands must do
> something. If they fight themselves, the body will be crushed.[26]

The plea was met with knowing nods and then, like so many others,
ignored.

One town after another fell victim to the clashing tribes, to the point that
displaced, abused, and exhausted civilians could be forgiven for their sense of
betrayal at the simple, promising prayer nailed to the wall of a Catholic
seminary in Pageri: "Bless this house, Oh Lord, we pray; make it safe by night
and day."

The danger in southern Sudan, as the rebel tribes ate themselves from
within, was compounded by a terrifying local fact. In the shadows of the
dense jungle, or hidden amidst the fields of 10-foot-tall elephant grass, there
was no longer any place of sanctuary. The once-trusted rebel movement was
now two, and in conflict. And from the north, the perennial threat. One was
alone down there, and only ever sure of what was within one's limited field of
vision. Beyond the next tree, beyond the perimeter of one's immediate spot,
any manner of evil could lurk, and often did. The equation was only one-half
of the Heisenberg uncertainty principle that had afflicted Garang when he
had thought of the Bor front and dreamt of boats. Because civilians, by the
simple nature of their circumstances, have an accurate measure only of *their*
location. Often it extended no further than a few feet. All else was rumor
fueled by rumor. And therefore the devils of war that swept through the south
could prey upon civilians without warning, feeding on paranoia and taking
control.

The trap in southern Sudan was this crippling fear. It gripped the heart like
a vice that tightened at the sound of shellfire. It strangled at a whistle-burst of
bullets. Anyone on the road was an enemy. Night may have been the only
moment of freedom because in the darkness the hunter is as blind as the
hunted. Every southern Sudanese learns to live with this fear, seeking solace
with family and tribesmen whose mutual fate is at least jointly endured. The
poisonous knowledge of the horrors that *could be* festers like an incurable
wound at the back of every mind.

In all this confusion, Sudanese squirmed because there were no "good
guys" anymore. "They should let us determine our leaders, not those two
monsters—*Doctor* John Garang and *Doctor* Riek Machar," one Sudanese

spat out scornfully when I asked his view. "In the SPLA, the ones making all the mistakes are these so-called Ph.D.s—poverty, hunger and disease."[27]

Such graduate-degree brilliance led to the creation of a Famine Triangle in 1993 marked by Ayod, Waat, and Kongor, the burnt area between Dinka and Nuer territory. Relief workers who could get there described it as a "new Somalia," where people gathered in towns with airstrips to pray that their prayers for food would be heard, and that UN relief flights—"the flyers from heaven"—would not stop.[28] Extreme famine again returned in 1998, this time to Bahr al-Ghazal province, again because of tribal and militia fighting and human rights abuses that decimated local food stocks.

In the triangle in 1993, at Kongor, I watched naked boys and wrinkled starving grandmothers, on hands and knees, paw through the dust for loose kernels that spilled from sacks of relief food as a plane was unloaded. Inside an airless "clinic" it was almost too dark for photographs, but the scene was stark and strangely beautiful. Mothers and their starving children were resting on the floor, which was spread with a blue tarp. The children moved listlessly, their large eyes protruding. Because of the small windows, the light on them was so low that only their silver bangles glowed—all else was deep shades of purple and blue. Aid workers expected the town to change hands at any moment, so they flew in daily, then left. Rebel "officials" seemed to think the need for fuel was greater than the need for food. During my brief visit, I was surprised to see a small charter plane from Nairobi land at the airstrip, unload 300 gallons of diesel, and fly back. Total cost: $8,000.

Deeper inside the Famine Triangle there was a shocking absence of children under five years of age. They had died. Boys over the age of 11 were missing, too; they were press-ganged to fight for their tribe before they had even learned to write their names. In Ayod, skulls "litter the drop zone" where the UN dumped pallets of relief food, and in one school classroom an ominous message had been scrawled across the blackboard: "1993 is the year for the Dinka and the Nuer to fight to elimination."[29]

Civilians constantly were caught in the fracas and disappeared. Like the civil war waged against the north, the rebel split was a war without prisoners. During purges, one SPLA spokesman tried to convince me of their revolutionary purity: "Surely in the liberation, people die," he said.

For Bishop Taban, the old rebel habits and suspicions that once kept him under house arrest for three months were returning. After so many years of suffering, he felt, nothing has been learned. He was a man in perpetual motion now, trying to head off disaster by negotiating between the factions. "They say they are liberating the people, instead they are killing them," he told me in Nimule, on his way to another session of talks. "It's got to stop, or the Church will wash its hands of them."

Taban's plea had only increased in urgency since he had sent a radio message to a relief organization a few years earlier: "This war in the South has become a fratricidal war," he pleaded then. "Where will our people run to? For wherever they run in the South, their imminent death is waiting for them. Their only chance remains to run to God."[30]

Peace remained as elusive as ever, and reports of atrocities multiplied. At Yuai, Garang loyalists attacked a UN clinic and feeding center with mortars and rocket-propelled grenades, killing 40 people waiting for food. And Riek's units were just as irreverent. A leprosy hospital was ransacked, and the patients killed; near Ayod, some 18 children were locked into a hut and burned alive; the three who escaped were gunned down.[31]

This killing was so callous and becoming so routine that the differences separating man from mindless beast could rarely have been so narrow. How often are animals so cruel to their prey?

Such disturbing thoughts worried and frightened me, but they consumed the bishop, who balanced them with his own strength of spirit. In an address called "What I have learnt as a Christian and as a human being in the Sudan situation," he described grappling with such an extreme emotional spectrum:

> I have seen how people can fall so low in selfishness, cruelty, lacking of any respect for life and of other races, of other religions, of other tribes or groups. I could not have imagined this before I witnessed it. On the other hand, I have discovered what I did not know before, how high people can grow in love, pardon, bearing suffering without hatred or even bitterness. People still smile and laugh in the midst of sufferings.[32]

The rival factions attended endless truce talks and proclaimed numerous cease-fires that fizzled within days or even hours. Hubris and tribal animosity blocked any agreement. Even in Washington, during a high-profile reconciliation conference in October 1993, Garang and Riek tussled over their official titles at the bottom of the cease-fire agreement. Riek insisted that he was the chief of the main SPLA faction, so no document was signed. Both men accused the other of serving as a "paid agent" and "collaborator" with Khartoum.

Deep in southern Sudan, so far from the posh Washington hotels where Garang and Riek fussed about the finer points of making peace, the victims were disgusted. One priest explained the solution: "We need new leaders to replace the old blood who are so entrenched that they don't know what is wrong and right." A teacher in a miserable displaced settlement was scathing. He had been on the move for many months, from one camp to the next. For him the tribal killing had become an end in itself, a corruption of self-respect.

"It is war I don't want, but I don't think anyone is interested in ending it, neither the warring factions nor the world. Khartoum and the SPLA will all try to get more arms, and there will only be war, war and war until nature stops it."

Rebel soldiers were angry with their leaders, for being distracted by tribal infighting when there were *real* enemies so close at hand. And popular rage at the tyrants responsible was fierce and understandable. Even an outsider like me found both rebel leaders drenched—during their long and messy opportunistic history—in blood of their own letting, often the blood of their own people. I could only imagine that they had just become used to living inside their own skins, somehow ignoring the crimes they saw, that they ordered, or that were committed by loyalists, fanatics, or other killers in their name.

How do these men sleep at night? What good have they brought to their people, in the end? Certainly, the appearance of Khartoum wanting peace at the end of the 1990s—after decades of war—may yield a separate state, or at least self-rule. But couldn't the "liberation" have been conducted a little more efficiently? Wouldn't so many lives have been spared if the "movement" hadn't been run by a cabal of old-school revolutionaries, whose passing commitment to Marxism, Stalinism, or any other convenient ideological marker simply made it easier to maintain their repressive grip on power? Of course, the front line is rarely any place for democracy. But was ideological purity (read: quashing any show of dissent), and a doctrine of pillaging the "sea" in which you are supposed to "swim," any way to run a guerrilla campaign—if you want to win?

The tyrannical Garang commander Kuol Manyang—who, after capturing Torit in 1989, kept Bishop Paride Taban locked up for months, on suspicion of "feeding" the enemy, and who committed *many* far more serious human rights abuses—once spelled it out for me: "I'm not very interested in casualties," he admitted. "War is war." This is a man who, as a result of a story apocryphal or not, was widely believed to have shot dead his own mother.

Are these people—who since the 1991 Garang-Riek split have proliferated into half a dozen warlords terrorizing southern Sudan today, almost certainly war criminals to a man—are they the hope for the future? I make no apologies for the ruthless strategy of the north, which expertly conducts crimes unseen, on a massive scale using proxy militias and its own troops; my sympathies are always with those unable to live their lives as they choose. And in the south, Garang may well be the best of a bad crowd.

But what I have seen in those war zones is a human spirit—one that these top men seem remarkably without, despite their glowing rhetoric—struggling to survive. I am disgusted at the unaccountability of these "leaders," for the curses they have brought upon their own people. And I'm not even Sudanese.

This chapter is dark, I know: that is how I deal with the crimes of Sudan.

Some Sudanese have better ways. They embrace their religion, or they just let their imaginations escape when they can, to find solace anywhere.

I was enjoying a party on New Year's Eve 1994 in Pageri, a town that within months would be overrun by government troops. I watched a dance there of such eloquence that I will never forget it. The party was a mix of Sudanese and foreigners. And as the chilled beer flowed, and as the canopy of stars over Sudan traced their concentric paths slowly around Polaris, one Sudanese man wearing a white doctor's coat and tire-rubber sandals took up a silver flashlight—one of the cheap tinny ones made in China, that are ubiquitous on this continent—and he danced.

This Dinka moved as if entranced, as if out of mind, holding the flashlight up and swinging it around, a silent partner and cradled tool of pleasure. His shin bones were narrow, with narrow Dinka muscles, and he lifted his feet backward, sharply up to his buttocks like a bird. The dance music pounded through the village, with the cacaphonic shouts of celebrants. The sweating cluster of bodies made their own heat.

Yet unassuming, alone except for his flashlight, this dancer moved with grace and abandon, a picture of love, affection—and calm. Eyes half closed and with a gentle smile on his lips, he found his epiphany. To this day in my mind—and his, I hope—that spell remains unbroken.

THIRTEEN

DARWIN DECEIVED

It's really very simple. Either we feed them or they die.

—Philip O'Brien, coordinator,
Operation Lifeline Sudan

"This war has created a certain mentality," the Catholic priest said, speaking under his breath even at home, in Khartoum in 1998. Dusk had turned to darkness, and it had rained. We used no lights, but the remaining water puddles reflected whatever ambient light they could find—like the flare of a match being drawn to the good father's cigarette. "We Sudanese tell a joke about it."

> There was an Egyptian who was blind and begging. God appeared and said: "What can I do for you?" The Egyptian, of course, replied: "Please open my eyes."

> There was a Lebanese who was deaf and dumb. And God appeared and said: "What can I do for you?" The Lebanese replied: "Please give me the power of speech."

> And there was a Sudanese, who was crippled and paralyzed. God appeared and said: "What can I do for you?"

> The Sudanese answered: "Please give me a wheelchair, but make it an automatic, so that I can beg more and more."

The priest and I laughed knowingly. But he was dismayed, too. "It's a sign of hopelessness," he said of the joke, for he knew that behind it lay a critical aspect of Sudan's war, and any chance of peace. After all, the art of manipulation—to draw a lifeblood from donated relief food—has long been an unscrupulous scientific pursuit in Sudan. Government garrisons have been kept alive for years by relief food, while rebels have shamelessly fed off the aid.

Nowhere else in Africa has food so directly contributed to the continuation of war. In Sudan, it has become the most powerful weapon, and so afflicting hunger has been the key military strategy for both sides.

The rebel SPLA has sought to starve garrison towns—worn down by years-long sieges—into defeat. Relief convoys and barges have been regular targets. The government has co-opted an increasing number of Arab and African militias to wage a slash-and-burn proxy war that makes it impossible for rebels to govern, and impossible for civilians to live. In Maoist terms, the strategy for more than 15 years has been to "drain the sea" so that the "fish"—the rebels—have nowhere to hide.

By definition, such strategies result in human rights abuses and cause famine. But the fate of civilians seems rarely of consequence. Though such total disregard is in keeping with the hard-line military history of the government and rebels alike, the implications have been staggering and worthy of war crimes charges. But in Sudan, like almost everywhere else in Africa, human rights and who violates them factor little.

So in some cases, the relief efforts of the UN and outside world may have saved hundreds of thousands of lives. But it is easy to argue, too, that they have also prolonged the conflict, causing many more deaths through more war, or yet another man-made famine.

But what if the fighting had been allowed to resolve itself militarily—left to its own modern-day, Darwinistic "survival-of-the-fittest" fate? Would more lives have been saved? That may be very likely, though such a solution would require difficult moral mathematics and seems contrary to any humanitarian impulse. Still, examples of abuse in Sudan are endless, exactly as in Somalia. And as sure as the sun rises each day, foreign agencies still work to save those victimized by war, even when that work may extend suffering. The dynamic is common in Africa. But in Sudan, spurred on by the unquestioning injection of aid, combatants long ago came to believe that relief was their right, and they act that way.

Witness, for example, the case of the human shields at Yuai, which brought relief food closer to one warlord's front lines. In late 1992, breakaway rebel chief Riek Machar "encouraged" people to move to the Famine Triangle town of Yuai. Conditions had been improving for them where they were already, with UN relief flights arriving regularly. But thousands of Nuer tribesmen picked themselves up and walked to Yuai, a barren patch of earth without a single hut at the time.

That move put this population virtually in the firing line, and though it had sprung up overnight at the behest of the faction leaders, the UN determined that it could land its planes there to help the growing numbers. In January 1993, Riek moved his headquarters there too, deliberately endangering the people further. The displaced said they had little choice: "Now we are like flies," said one man who moved to Yuai, after rebel promises of aid. "Wherever there is food, that is where we go."[1]

The UN at Yuai first served 3,000 people, but the arrival of food, medicine, and the presence of foreigners became a magnet until the population swelled to more than 15,000. Garang's forces first attacked in April, killing hundreds of civilians and burning Yuai to ashes. Survivors rebuilt, but Garang attacked again in June, slaughtering hundreds more and again leveling the town. A UN visit to the place in September 1993 found only 100 desperate people.[2] Riek was gone too. I'm not sure there could be a starker image of how easily—and temporarily—relief agencies can be manipulated.

But by the 1998 famine, such reactions had nearly been institutionalized. Migrations in search of food rations were "such a common phenomenon" that the wanderers were called "C-130 invitees," after the Hercules transport planes that air-dropped food.[3]

When food came, the soldiers always got their share. Though such figures are disputed by the UN, some relief agencies charged that up to 80% of the food sent to south Sudan in 1993 was being stolen by the army and factions. During the 1998 famine, the rebels alone were diverting between 10% to 65% in the hardest-hit Bahr el-Ghazal region, and taxing 10% to 20% of the food of non-sympathizing families.[4] As far as the rebels were concerned, they were simply exercising a form of pragmatism that had been followed by famine victims for centuries: since the weak child will die anyway, it is better to feed the strong child, so one might survive.

But the problem for relief agencies went deeper. After so many years of crisis in Sudan, they experienced a deep lack of respect—at least from the leaders of the people they were trying to save. An early warning came in 1989, when the SPLA shot down a well-marked Médecins Sans Frontières plane, killing three French doctors and a Sudanese WFP worker. The rebels boobytrapped one of the French bodies, but instead of exploding as intended on the flight back to Khartoum, it blew up and started to burn as the corpses were being loaded onto a plane bound for Paris. The whole truck burned.[5] That bombing should have served as a warning to relief agencies working in the south that no side in Sudan's conflict was fighting a "righteous" war that respected the integrity of their own people, much less any other.

Also take the September 1992 case of UN workers and a journalist, killed when they by chance got caught up in the fighting during the defection of another Garang commander, William Nyuon Bany. The execution order had apparently come from Colonel Garang himself: the foreigners were to be "eliminated." Details of the order were given to the UN by a rival faction, however, with a vindictiveness meant to undermine future relief missions to southern Sudan. No one was sure if the orders were genuine, though even if not, few doubted that the relief workers were killed because they saw too much. The splits and crippling fratricide among southerners were embarrassing to all rebel leaders. What better way to be rid of foreign witnesses?

And who would notice if, somewhere in the south, lost and muffled by the same suffocating silence that absorbed the faint sound of so many dying Sudanese, these four foreigners were murdered? Two of the bodies were presented to the UN by Garang's people. Their heads had been shaved execution-style, then they had been dispatched with a single bullet each.

Repercussions were significant, but by no means damning. Fearful UN and other aid workers withdrew for months from the area of the killings. The results of the Unicef investigation were never made public, nor—in the interest of maintaining "neutrality" in Sudan operations—did the UN ever publicly condemn those responsible. But an internal Unicef report leaked to the press did not hold back: "Throughout this sad episode, the SPLA response can best be summarized as callous, obstructive and deliberately committed to misinforming us," the report said.[6]

The killings woke the UN and relief agencies to their disturbing dilemma as nothing before: their care for the innocent starving was heartlessly used by the self-appointed "leaders" to better fight their wars.

Most mired in this Catch-22 is the UN's Operation Lifeline Sudan (OLS), which has a mind-boggling responsibility in its scope and ambition. It serves as the official umbrella mission for some 35 relief agencies in southern Sudan. Since 1989, OLS has made possible the distribution of tens of thousands of tons of relief food in the south, negotiating "corridors of tranquility" to deliver food to the hungriest. At one time, it was believed that 1 million southerners completely depended upon OLS food supplies and 3 million more needed assistance. Some relief agencies doubt those figures. In 1995, the chronically famine-struck Bahr el-Ghazal region received only 19% of its OLS-assessed needs, while one agency noted that "most people in south Sudan survive chiefly by their own efforts and are not dependent on OLS."[7]

As a "humanitarian" mission, OLS has argued that it is a neutral provider and should not judge those who commit atrocities—it barely scolded the SPLA for executing its own staff members. And it did not publicize the amount of food that made its way into the bowls of combatants. Though politically weak, however, OLS is not inert, and it moves to "assist" wherever Sudanese create a humanitarian problem by drawing weapons upon each other.

As a result, there are not many relief operations that have lent themselves so easily to systematic abuse. Few agencies are blind to the problem. A 1993 assessment by Médecins Sans Frontières pointed out the dangers: "One of the most bitter tragedies of Sudan is that the dilemmas facing humanitarian organizations today are almost exactly those faced repeatedly over the last ten years. . . . But while the generals and guerrillas have learned their lessons, the UN humanitarian agencies have not."[8]

Among these lessons are that the UN has been overly compliant. "Operation Lifeline has continued. But gradually it has become an instrument of war, rather than a force for peace," MSF noted.[9] With promises of food, government or rebel factions can coax civilians to areas under their control and hold them, thereby adding weight to constant arguments for more.

Yet another famine in early 1998 in Bahr el-Ghazal provided fresh proof of this dynamic on a huge scale, in which the government, its militia agents, and rebel forces—not drought—all seemed to conspire to bring hunger to Sudan. Another Garang defector who had been held for years in an SPLA jail for dissent was commander—now warlord—Kerubino Kuanyin Bol.

Motivated largely by his hatred of Garang, during 1997 Kerubino had been allied to Khartoum, his militia attacking his own Dinka people and destroying their food stores. Then, after infiltrating many of his fighters into the government garrison at Wau, the warlord overnight in January 1998 rejoined the SPLA and led an attack to capture Wau from inside. But after the initial skirmish, Kerubino's troops began looting instead of fighting, and were driven out. Dinka civilians in Wau were slaughtered in revenge, and survivors were expelled into the countryside. Arab militias paid by the government to destroy local villages rampaged through the countryside. And as the human need soared in the spring, Khartoum did its share by halting all relief flights to the area for two months.

The result was as predictable as it was man-made. In Bahr el-Ghazal alone, some 1 million lives were threatened. Across the south, the UN estimated that 2.6 million people were at risk of starvation, fully 10% of the entire population of Sudan, and one-half of that in the south. The government flight refusal was a "greater obstacle to relief delivery than actual military activity," Human Rights Watch noted.[10] The cost of the relief operation crested at $1 million per day, about the same the government had been spending on the war. Despite all the confusion, the root cause of the crisis was simple: "It is fair to conclude that, but for these human rights abuses, there would have been no famine in Sudan in 1998," the group added.[11]

For this reason, I believe, Kerubino should be added to the growing list of Sudanese war criminals.

Not much had changed since the early days of OLS, and in fact, there was little to suggest that all that relief pumped into Sudan in the previous decade has done any good. "For most programs, little is known of the program delivery, let alone impact," admitted a candid 1996 OLS review—the first conducted since OLS began. "Even less is known about what people actually receive, who receives it, or about the coverage." Lack of data, it said, made it "difficult" to determine how much "unnecessary hunger" and high death rates had been eased by OLS efforts.[12]

"This is extraordinary," charged one rights group. "Relief operations have consumed billions of dollars. All are justified on the grounds that they are saving the lives of ordinary Sudanese people, especially women and children. But they cannot produce systematic evidence that they have succeeded." Other drawbacks can't be quantified, but have real impact, it added. "Most insidiously, humanitarian power influences the way people think: it makes them expect solutions from outside. International aid has *managed* Sudan's political decay rather than *halted* it."[13]

Corroborating examples abound. I came across one case in which southern Sudanese behaved as though they were *overfed*. In early 1994, the SPLA ordered 70,000 bewildered Dinka from the Triple 'A' camps to walk for four days to a roughhewn spot near the border where there was no access road. These people had been completely dependent on aid agencies for survival and relied upon established hospitals, clinics, schools, and regular food distribution. That was where Archbishop Carey blessed war wounded and addressed a sea of amputees. And the place had been blessed: after months of persistent infusion of relief food, the camps had been awash with the stuff. Every grass hut had its own store of two or three full sacks. But the SPLA wanted more.

On my way to this new "camp" by road, I came across a food truck from Catholic Relief Services (CRS) stuck in a culvert. Its story would turn out to be an unsavory parable of relief manipulation. The culvert, formed by a flash flood, was 30 feet wide with steep dirt sides. Several trucks had made it through, but this one was stuck, making the road impassable. This was where the SPLA had ordered its people. I was surprised to see the amount of labor marshaled by CRS to overcome that culvert: to meet emergency needs in the new camp, 50kg sacks of relief food were being unloaded from 20-ton lorries, carried by paid porters across the culvert, then loaded onto smaller vehicles on the other side. I spent the night nearby with Todd Cornett, a CRS field officer. He had slept there in the open for four nights, to make sure the food didn't disappear.

When we first saw the new "camp" the next morning, our jaws dropped. It was an inhospitable patch of dusty scrub and thorn trees. The first food arrived by truck—before the treacherous culvert in the road was blocked— but the distribution was delayed. The Dinka—who were quite healthy after two years of being cared for in the just-deserted "Triple A" camps—were unwilling to unload the relief food. Grown men, most of them able-bodied, stood idly by as women and children tried to wrestle the 50kg sacks of sorghum and lentils off the trucks and into piles. The food was provided free, and obviously carried at great cost and effort by the charity.

Cornett was exasperated. "They came crying to us that they needed this food desperately now, now, now or their people would die," he said, disgusted. "But they can't even find 20 men among 70,000 people to help off-load it." Eager to keep to their own schedules, the Kenyan drivers unloaded three of the trucks themselves. Finally, with the incentive of extra rations for those who worked, a small, slow crew of Sudanese began to shift the sacks.

Another truck arrived. Again, strong men watched, and no one moved. Despite the promise of extra food, the previous porters had vanished. "They just expect everything to be handed to them," Cornett said, as he stomped off again to convince the Dinka chiefs to act in their own interest. I was angry, too. I could see the corrosive effect this was having, the tension it created in the camp. I had come all this way—a flight first, a hard drive, and then a night in the bush, with no way out yet determined—to write about the plight of displaced Dinka. Now I had to craft a knife-twister about Dinka notions of aid entitlement.

Over time the camp built up. But in February 1995, the people here showed how docile they had become to SPLA authority. They were ordered to move yet again: "The hospital is empty," said a surprised relief worker. "The patients literally picked their bandages up and walked out."[14]

The south wasn't the only trouble spot. At the UN offices in Khartoum, there had been more than a little soul searching when I visited in August 1998. "It's unfortunate that OLS is only doing salvation work, but not finding a solution," Philippe Borel, the UN coordinator for Sudan relief operations, told me. He was a veteran of Angola, where I first met him, and many other emergencies before. In Angola too, the UN airlifted food to government garrisons that were encircled by Jonas Savimbi's Unita rebels. I flew many times to those forlorn besieged towns in the Angolan interior, and they were like islands of suffering afloat in an unremitting hostile sea. The UN there was also accused of "feeding the war." And if your aim was to help people, playing the politics was a tricky business.

The problem in Sudan was that values had changed to a Hobbesian sense of survival at all costs—certainly at the cost of anyone else. Borel spoke of a young girl in Ajiep, who was under a bush and thin as a skeleton, collapsed just 400 meters from a feeding center. No Sudanese helped her. "The people don't want to look. This young girl couldn't walk. This is *one* person. How many could be out there?" Borel asked, clearly agitated. "It's survival now. You get your food or you die. They don't live anymore on land, but in hell."

OLS, he said, was simply "giving serum to an agonizing problem. We are only treating the symptom, not the disease."

In Somalia years after the crisis there, Somalis would tell me straight: "Aid is bad." They had seen how it had further corrupted their warlords and gunmen, and turned it into a high-profile prize that was worth fighting for. Many Rwandans and other Africans told me the same thing, about how well-intentioned outsiders could upset fragile social systems—even when they were collapsing. In Sudan the dynamic was just the same. Borel recounted a conversation he had with a Tutsi woman from Rwanda, who thought that all foreigners bearing "humanitarian" gifts should depart. "You should leave Africans in peace," she said. "It's better to have a good war and people break down, than to have them artificially maintained so they can come back and fight."

The danger of turning "survival-of-the-fittest" into an ethic, Borel explained, was that in African emergencies, "only the carnivores will survive." In Rwanda, food aid to the refugees who committed the 1994 genocide enabled them to rise and fight again. "We let a lot of people survive who were gangsters and criminals, who made it because they are the strongest, the worst—because they could eat the food."

So is the solution to end aid altogether? My instinct is yes, to halt aid, to end this chronic giveaway and end any chance of creating dependence. But every case is different. In Somalia, for example, the paradox is not easy to solve: aid meant that the war and warlord *status quo* continued, creating the conditions for the 1992 famine; though later without any aid at all, more Somalis would almost certainly have died during that famine.

In Sudan, there are good arguments for a total shutdown. Afterall, starving civilians get by on fewer calories than the UN believes can sustain life. One report noted with surprise that, despite receiving just a fraction of the nutrients they needed, "most people in southern Sudan do manage to survive."[15] But despite OLS faults, wouldn't so many more die if the aid to government garrisons were cut off? And if there was no relief food to be diverted by the rebels, wouldn't they be forced to steal *all* their needs from their starving populace?

The best case of all may be Rwanda, where perpetrators of genocide in camps in Zaire were allowed to rebuild their military strength, to fight again. But then what of the innocents in those camps, corralled like sheep in a pen by notorious killers who enforced their will with intimidation and murder?

There are no easy answers, of course. This is a question that has also vexed relief workers since the first rope-thin African wrist held up a grimy bowl in a war zone and saw it filled with a cupful of maize. But the case of Sudan is especially complex "because the parties to the conflict are not solely motivated nor sustained by emergency relief," notes Human Rights Watch. "The 1988 famine demonstrated that war could persist at an extremely low level of food assistance to famine victims and a staggering number of civilian deaths. . . . The 1998 famine is making the same point."[16]

So the requirements of south Sudanese are calculated with scientific precision by UN teams. Lists of villages and changing malnutrition rates are maintained in thick ledgers. I saw these volumes at the Famine Triangle town of Kongor, where grandmothers had pawed through the dust for a few kernels of corn. Needs for hundreds of thousands of people were worked out to the nearest kilogram of cereals and beans and to the nearest liter of vegetable oil, based on the "facts" laid down on these pages. The only wildly changing detail was the column marked "held by," which described whose fiefdom each village fell under from month to month. When whole villages were obliterated, burned, or abandoned, they were simply struck from the list.

But this science of need did little to convince the war makers to restrain themselves, for their calculations were every bit as detailed, and also depended upon aid. Put simply by African Rights, the ready supply of food and willing relief agencies "enables the commanders to ignore their responsibilities to the civilians under their control, on the grounds that others are taking care of feeding them."[17] Wielding this weapon, warriors can concentrate on the enemy, and not waste time with the luckless minions in their territory.

In the north, Khartoum takes full advantage to squeeze relief organizations for cash and food. Exchange rates in the past have been so unfavorable—making the cost of a gallon of engine oil $1,200 in 1990[18]—and relief so lucrative for the recipients that the Sudan government budget for the same year forecast better growth through faster implementation of aid projects.[19] "Some countries are more palatable than others," one UN official told me. "In Sudan we work in a political war environment, and the costs are enormous."

Still, the Islamic regime was surprisingly susceptible to pressure from outside, providing an example of what might be achieved if the right buttons were ever pushed. The American military intervention to feed Somalia in December 1992—uninvited by Somali warlords—prompted a temporary moment of cooperation from Sudanese officials. They were frightened by talk that Operation Restore Hope would serve as a model for dealing with them. To head off a similar unwanted "invasion" in south Sudan, Khartoum's policy changed overnight. Never mind that such an operation would be nearly impossible in the vastnesses of Sudan, where even pinpointing the problem itself was a monumental task. Still, the number of government-approved UN flight destinations in rebel areas jumped from seven to 41, and agreement was reached for the first time to allow "safe" corridors for barge convoys and trains to "service" 40 more isolated areas.[20]

This access revealed the extent of the hunger across the south, where entire populations were found living on leaves and roots. Rates of severe malnutrition in the Famine Triangle were "among the highest ever documented" and rivaled peak rates in Baidoa, Somalia.[21] The government even promised to commit 153,000 tons of its own food stocks to "cover all requirements" in the south.

As the US intervention in Somalia soured, and it became clear that such a humanitarian adventure would not be repeated in Sudan, Khartoum returned to its old tricks. Approval for some rebel-held towns was withheld, and bombing resumed. Nevertheless, with barely a wimper of complaint, the UN, relief agencies, and donors again scaled back their minimum expectations.

The drama of civilians locked in southern Sudan is perhaps best described in the saga of the Lost Boys. Their odyssey carried them 1,000 miles in six years, tracking across an expanse half as large as Europe. They were first gathered as child recruits for the SPLA. Their example—child soldiers being fed unwittingly by relief agencies during their training in Ethiopia, and later facilitating their journey to safety to Sudan and then Kenya—to me served as a chilling reminder of how deeply relief workers can get entangled in someone else's war. It also served, once again, to illustrate how ruthless Sudanese warlords can be.

In the late 1980s, more than 17,000 southern Sudanese boys were separated from their parents, most of them lured to rebel "refugee" camps in Ethiopia for "education." The exodus of boys from Sudan became routine and was promoted by the SPLA. Some boys went willingly, others were collected during rebel sweeps of villages. Though fed in the Ethiopia camps, they were completely controlled by the rebels: UN and relief workers were forbidden to stay in the camps overnight, or even to linger beyond 3 pm, for "security" reasons.[22] That was when military training began.

Boys older than 12 years were given full military courses. Boys as young as seven were trained only during school "breaks." The battalions created by these children came to be known among the rebels as the "Red Army." They were deployed alongside regular SPLA units, but with little success. "In the first few years, the Red Army fought and was always massacred," one former rebel officer said. "They were taken off the front line. They were not good soldiers because they were so young." Nevertheless, when Ethiopian dictator Mengistu Haile Mariam was on the verge of being overthrown by Eritrean and Tigrean rebels in 1990 and 1991, the SPLA provided Red Army units to fight in the Ethiopian army. Again, few survived.

The journey of these Lost Boys began after the fall of Mengistu in May 1991, when the entire SPLA network was forced to flee back to Sudan overnight with 250,000 other refugees. When the minors described their traumatic journey, it takes on the hue of a biblical exodus, with the tenor of great lamentations.

It's unlikely that these kids would have died *en masse* if food was not secured for them by the officers who controlled them. But speculation in this case is a wasted exercise, for already the boys had been deprived of their lives and stunted by their experience. Here is an example of military and humanitarian needs blending into one simple question: to help, or not?

The route was plagued with threats and war, obstacles natural and man-made. One group of 12,000 boys—out of the original 17,000, with never a single girl among them—finally emerged at Pochala, a village on the Sudan side of the riverine border. This was where I caught up with them in January 1992. Their tales were fantastic. As this group—this town-in-motion—trekked on, I would see them twice more, and watch some of these boys come of age. Already they were well-stained travelers whose capacity for affection and other human traits had often been left behind, somewhere on the road. They had nothing, fled with nothing, and knew nothing of love nor hope. They said they were "born in war." When asked about their thoughts on the future, many children began: "If I am not dead . . . " or "If I am alive in the year 2000 . . . "[23]

At first blush, many Western boys might welcome a collective journey with boys-only peers, like a glorified Cub Scouts expedition. But when I first came across the group in Pochala, their conditions were bad and their mental capacities had been brutalized. Simon Manyang Malei Majok, 14, explained the reason for their agony: "We are suffering because of war. Some have been killed. Some have died because of hunger and disease. We children of Sudan, we are not lucky."

In Pochala the boys threw together a motley array of grass huts, or *tukuls*, but even here the fighting was never far away. Seen through the haze of smoke from raging bush fires, the camp spread away from the crocodile-infested Akobo River like the far-reaching tentacles of a thirsty root system. Every boy had planned for the inevitable: a foxhole outside one's hut was as indispensable as the cooking fire, and thousands were dug with care by small hands dirty with war. They attended makeshift outdoor schools, tried some cultivation, and did all the milling and "kitchen" work—usually reserved for their mothers—themselves.

The camp was smothered in the acrid camp smell of constantly burning cooking fires, of legumes of some type on the boil, and of wafts of excrement and other human mess—it's the same penetrating camp odor you find from Liberia to Eritrea to Angola. As I picked my way through, boys gathered around like curious children do everywhere else. But they were silent, and happy enough just to observe—unlike most African children, I found, who feel they must *participate* in your presence. Plastic crucifixes hung from some necks. Most boys wore the same rags they had worn for a year or two, and others were naked, their clothes long since rotted under the constant pressure of equatorial sun or steaming heavy rain.

I stayed with a relief agency that was providing food, but this was no ordinary camp. There was an eerie, deliberate absence of anything military—not even toy guns or spears, in this traditional warring society, in a continent thick with children with weapons. Rebel officials and "teachers" took too much care explaining that these boys knew nothing of fighting, and only of their studies. This is what they told the agencies, and now I too was receiving "the line." The fact that this odyssey began so many years ago, however, pointed to to an utterly cynical calculation that this war might never end. The next generation had to be ready.

The practice of using children as fighters, as cannon fodder or as slaves behind the front lines, was so reprehensible that even the SPLA seemed to have recognized how damaging this image of these boys under arms could be. Garang denied the existence of the Red Army, but even in this admission fudged his own responsibility. He claimed that he did not know what his commanders have been "doing with kids."[24]

Others were full of spin. "We want the boys to be educated," Elijah Malok of the SPLA "relief" wing told me. "We must educate them as a group, to dispel once and for all to the world the idea that they were ever soldiers." The excuses for such a huge group of boys were elaborate, but none were plausible. Boys have historically been separated from their families and grouped together for cattle camp, I was told, to pool education resources. Or this: southern Sudan had provided "gun boys" to assist colonial officers for more than a century.

But in Pochala there appeared to be little difference between the Lost Boys and the young SPLA "soldiers" with guns who stood watch at the edge of the camp. I had seen boys commit themselves to armed conflict across Africa, so this was no surprise. In some ways, it was probably seen as fun. After hearing stories of heroism and war, wouldn't joining the ranks appeal? But these boys had no choice, and certainly any sense of fun would have evaporated long before. So in this camp, there *was* no difference between the boys and the boy soldiers. The UN human rights rapporteur accused the rebels of the "practice of running children's camps as a human reservoir for combat."[25]

In front of a camera though, they smiled shyly like any other group of kids, and laughed when I handed out a few translucent plastic film cannisters. One boy held one up to his eye, distorting his vision like a fun-fair toy. His grin grew as wide as it goes, and he seemed to have forgotten for a moment his panicky escape from Ethiopia. And there was much to forget.

Across the murky river, in that dark jungle on the other side, lay the bones of friends, and the spirits of many other boys who were lost. Some were swept away, drowned in the torrents of the Gilo River during an emergency mass crossing; others were eaten by crocodiles; a handful were ravaged by lions, survivors watching the grisly feasting. Many others succumbed to disease, knobbly young knees and legs without the luxury of muscle or strength giving way under an unbearable burden of hunger and thirst. There was gunfire, and always a menacing terror.

But having made it to Pochala, the boys' long march had hardly begun. Already their dreams were thickened with violence, with terrific visions that entered unbidden into their thoughts.

It was from that far side of the river that more and very real demons came. Soon there was a small raid on Pochala camp by 200 marauders. There was little damage, but fear of another attack in late February 1992 prompted the SPLA to order the boys to march to "safety" farther south, to Narus.

The International Committee of the Red Cross (ICRC) was responsible for the boys' care at Pochala, and were ready to assist the boys' evacuation. They had prepared 6,000 "basic items kits" with food, pots, pans, utensils, blankets, and plastic sheeting to aid their survival. A tented warehouse near an airstrip was packed with a mountain of the lifesaving gear. The ICRC had dug wells along the route to the next destination of Narus and had set up three transit camps, where the boys could rest and get medical care. The idea was to entice the boys and other refugees away from the border area. Once the route was prepared, the ICRC just waited. There was no sense of collusion with SPLA war aims—the SPLA had largely given up on its Red Army plans, it seemed— and the ICRC concentrated on the solid work of saving lives. There was no sense either that these kids were being saved to fight in the next war.

"It is now or never—if we don't get these people out, then we must feed Pochala for another year," the ICRC's Claire Podbielski told me. "They are well-fed now and ready to move, but we do realize that we will lose some people along the way."

Ordered to leave by the SPLA, the boys picked up their sack-fashioned backpacks and again began to walk. The ICRC transported 180 sick and disabled children, and the Lost Boys strung out for miles along an unforgiving road, nursing sores on their legs, protected by SPLA soldiers and relying for life on the elaborate ICRC arrangements. Tanker trucks full of potable water ensured that thirst did not kill—during the escape from Ethiopia, the boys recalled, some died of dehydration, and others could no longer sweat. Still, one night Toposa tribesmen killed five boys and two SPLA soldiers. Halfway through their flight, news filtered back to the boy refugees that government forces had captured their empty camp at Pochala. Because of Riek's "hands-off" sell-out pact with Khartoum, they were able to storm across the river from Ethiopian territory. After one month of walking, the boys arrived in Narus. For saving the lives of these waifs, the Khartoum government expelled the ICRC from Sudan.

I visited the boys again at Narus in April 1992, passing through on my way to see Garang and the front line. They had set to work again, more exhausted than ever, building a new camp. It was dusk, and my convoy would wait no longer. A low layer of smoke hovered over the camp as the thousands of boys applied themselves like ants in the service of an unforgiving queen.

The sanctuary at Narus was brief, though. Khartoum troops swept down from the north and east in spring and summer 1992, taking advantage of Riek's treachery and pushing Garang back one town at a time. Kapoeta fell, and the boys became part of a massive exodus of tens of thousands of Sudanese refugees into Kenya, the rear of their long column bombed by the Sudan air force as a final farewell. The children told vivid stories and suffered visions and flashbacks—day and night—of people screaming, in pain, from exhaustion, and dying before their eyes.

Psychologists tried to help, though for the UN they could only quantify this extreme exposure to war: up to 74% of the boys were survivors of "close" shelling or air bombardment; up to 85% had witnessed somebody starve to death; up to 92% said they had been shot at; and 97% said they had witnessed a killing.[26]

I have seen children in Sarajevo—beautiful children—whose lives have been transformed by the three-year Serb siege and constant shelling that started in the early 1990s. And in Mozambique, I've spoken to boys as young as nine—called "institutionalized children"—who were captured by Renamo guerrillas and trained as assassins to kill their own parents. But as a group, Sudan's Lost Boys are among the most badly war-traumatized children ever examined.

The new camp this time was just inside the Kenya border, but even here the boys were drawn to the war by "teachers" and rebels who tried to lure them back to the ranks of the fighters. I visited the boys there, too, though their coming of age was becoming ever more apparent. Staying overnight with an aid agency, I walked over to the camp before dawn, to take pictures during the sunrise light. The boys were already awake, and I could immediately feel their sense of relief and safety. They had slept in makeshift tents. Saplings served as tent frames for clear plastic covering, or were draped with UN-blue tarps.

At dawn, boys peered out of the tents to inspect the day. Some began wrestling among themselves, and the competition—football and other athletic games that drew up the dust in clouds—continued after sunrise. Aid agencies had rushed to care for the boys, who had now crossed an international border, and so were officially refugees.

The odyssey finally came to an end two and one-half years after it began, in August 1992, at Kakuma Camp, 60 miles inside the Kenya border. Here the army of boys could learn to read and write without the presence of guns. But the SPLA grip was still strong: when the boys were moved to Kakuma, some 1,500 disappeared in transit, either willingly or forcibly taken back as "recruits" into southern Sudan. Despite the rigors and danger that awaited those who returned to the south, the Rev. Benjamin Madul, a Catholic priest who accompanied the boys for much of the journey to Kenya, explained a new frustration: "Many want to go back and fight. They have seen their mothers and fathers killed, and there is a lot of hatred among them."[27]

As just as this war may be against domination by Arab Muslims in the north, tribalism and abuses have undermined its cause. Are civilians so expendable that rebel factions can run roughshod over them to fight among themselves, while the real enemy—which has deprived southerners their freedom for decades—gloats? Do faction leaders think that their people are so ill-informed, and so accepting of their self-seeking opportunism, that they will ever forget this suffering at the hands of their self-appointed "leaders"?

For the Lost Boys, life at Kakuma Camp was relatively calm. But they were quickly turning into young men, who could better recognize the crime of their stolen childhoods. A melée erupted during a 1994 soccer match. One boy was killed and 100 were injured, as pent-up emotions and violence flowed easily.

"The boys are getting big, and there's no one to look after them," said Stefan Savenstedt, who managed the camp for the UN.[28] "I think we'll have more and more of such problems."

But returning to the always-encroaching wilds of southern Sudan seemed no solution either, for this land was too freely impregnated with the centuries-old menace of conflicting religions and battling tribes. There appeared nothing left to rekindle hope, nor any mercy shown for those—like the Lost Boys—who will inhabit the future. In my time in Africa, scrutinizing fallen man in the continent's obliterated war zones, I had never seen a spirit among people so ready to rebuild, nor one so relentlessly violated by the so-called "defenders" of Sudan.

This is the conundrum, sadly, that those who bring aid may never reconcile. For when will the danger of respecting people more than they respect themselves be learned?

PART III

RWANDA

THE MACHETE WAR

There are no devils left in Hell. They are all in Rwanda.

—A Roman Catholic missionary,
quoted in *Time*, 16 May 1994

FOURTEEN

A HOLOCAUST

*To be a Tutsi or a Hutu today means remembering who
killed your parents 15 years ago and imagining who
might kill your own child in ten years time.*

—Médecins Sans Frontières

The rain swept down hour after hour, so the climb through the
jungle soaked to the skin, then turned cold. High up the mountain, deep in the dark verdure, suddenly I was among Rwanda's
famous gorillas. They chewed slowly, their foreheads sloping
down to broad nostrils and thin lips of wide aperture that
chewed and chewed. This family was not worried: the silverback male had beat his chest or sat like an immovable boulder
of flesh, gracefully emasculating the vegetation, for hundreds of
tourists. Now they sat hunched and nearly hidden, droplets of
water gathering like balls of bright mercury on whiskers, coating black fur like dew.

This was Rwanda for tourists, and when I first traveled there
in early 1990 the tiny country was a welcome sanctuary, compared to the rigors of its chaotic neighbors. Like many Western-
ers, my imagination had been captured by the story of Dian
Fossey, the American researcher on whose life the film *Gorillas
in the Mist* was based. And like many, until I'd seen the movie I
never imagined that such a magical kingdom existed.

Rwanda was the "Switzerland of Africa," a land of 1,000
mist-shrouded hills and immaculate paved roads. At the airport
in the capital, Kigali, a life-size statue of Digit—Dian Fossey's
favorite silverback ape—was sculpted from soap and greeted
visitors from his glass cage. In the left hand of this monstrosity
was a small flag with a yellow banner labeled SULFO, for the
soap company that created it. In his right, Digit carried a big

green bar of the stuff. His feet were almost a yard long to keep him from toppling over; the sign read "*Protegez Moi.*"

Never mind that Rwanda was among the poorest countries in the world,
or that less than 2 percent of its population got as far as high school. Here in
the center of francophone Africa fresh baguettes were baked each morning,
luxuries such as phones *worked*, which they rarely did in English-speaking
African countries, and frothy brown Guinness beer was available. One tall
billboard in the capital, Kigali, advertised its potency: male and female hands,
decorated with gold rings and red nails, clink together pints of frothy Guinness under the promise "The Power of Love."

For road-stained travelers like me, Rwanda seemed a haven of order and
hospitality, a place to see the gorillas and to relax before venturing into Zaire
or Uganda. Those with a longer view knew that Rwanda and its equally small
neighbor to the south, Burundi, had been subject to occasional violence
between tribes. But the festering conflict between the majority Hutu and
minority Tutsi seemed an easily forgotten historical footnote on the dance
floor of the Kigali Night club, where the young and wealthy gyrated closely,
sodden with booze, entwined slick with sweat under twirling lights.

Still, there was one hint of potential trouble. It was true that Dian Fossey
was murdered as she slept at her research base in the Ruwenzori Mountains
in 1985, in apparent revenge for her efforts to save the gorillas from poach-
ers. But even this couldn't dim Rwanda's glow, thanks to the reassuring words
of one "expert." Because Ms. Fossey was dispatched in a border area with a
machete, he wrote, "the way she was killed is more Zaïrois than Rwandan:
the Rwandans are a peaceful people who abhor violence. If a Rwandan
wanted to kill someone he would use poison."[1]

But there was another problem in Paradise, which became evident enough
during a gentle poke around. Verdant as these hills were, choked with growth
out of fertile black and red soil that was drenched with rain, I was shocked to
find, beneath all the undergrowth, a hidden famine. Rwanda was the most
densely populated country in Africa—second in the world only to
Bangladesh—with 800 people vying for space on every square kilometer. The
average woman gave birth to nearly *nine* children.

An exhibit at the National Museum back then told the story. Outside the
museum, a chain gang of prisoners in striking pink tunics were planting row
upon row of trees on a hillside. Inside, the population growth chart made me
wonder what kind of world those trees might inhabit in the future. In two
decades the population had doubled, and the thick red line rose steeper and
steeper and then took off altogether in a series of dots beyond the year 2000.

People were starving, and growing desperate. Compounded by the fluctuating tension between Hutu and Tutsi tribes, it seemed that these "peaceful

people" were on the verge of a Malthusian war for land and for food. One report at the time noted then that "there is a large majority who have nothing to eat for one, two, three, even seven days successively." People were selling the windows and doors from their houses to buy food, and children were too exhausted to stay awake in class. When caught, those who had stolen from the fields were beaten to death with spears . . . and even machetes.

Still, Rwanda was the most overtly "religious" country in Africa. With more than 80% of the population professed believers in the Roman Catholic faith, the hungry turned to the Church for help. In Butare, to the south, Sister Gratia handed out bean seed in 1990 to some of the 500 who gathered at her doorstep each day. She knew their problem: Rwanda's soil was overworked and couldn't produce enough. When her beans ran out, she faced those who remained emptyhanded and told them to come back tomorrow. Then she turned to me, a white wimple framing her face. "When the earth is ill, then the people are ill," she said, her words more prophetic than she could have known. "People are just slowly suffocating. It is a time-bomb ticking."

Although I was staying at a cheap guest house, I wrote my story at the 5-star Hotel des Mille Collines, where scores of tourist groups had left their company stickers on the glass entrance doors. I borrowed a big manual typewriter, carried it downstairs, and set it up on a table next to the gently lapping pool. Guests were enjoying a generous buffet breakfast, with slices of fresh pineapple, coffee, and all manner of eggs.

I beat out my story noisily—the heavy clack of the manual keyboard was especially satisfying, I remember, like I was *creating* words, not just quietly *submitting* them to a computer—added a roll of film of Sister Gratia handing out beans, and sent it all by courier from the reception desk to *The Sunday Telegraph* in London. "Famine in the Green Hills" was the headline the paper used.

One cynical analyst ominously explained the Malthusian dynamic at work in Rwanda: "When you put two rats in a cage, they go to separate corners and leave each other in peace. But when you put 30 rats into the same cage, they eat each other."

Accurate as that may be, Rwandans are not rats, and such pressures alone don't account for Rwanda's later embrace of the Dark Side, which here is called genocide.

But that was in early 1990, when there was still peace in Rwanda, and a baguette or two.

Testimony of Alex Bizimungu, Tutsi: I am waiting, terrified but hidden, standing for many days in the small gap between an open door and a wall at my home in Kigali. Spiritual strength has ebbed in me, as it has across my country since the night of 6 April 1994, when the president's plane was shot down. The assassination of President Juvénal Habyarimana was taken by extremists of the majority Hutu tribe, soldiers and civilians alike, as the signal to unleash the holocaust.

Now my world is this gap, the wooden door on one side, and the hard wall on the other. I dare not lean, or rest, for if my position is given away I will be sacrificed with all the others. This gap, and all the horrifying sounds: ten strides away I can hear a militia checkpoint, where Hutu men are killing Tutsi, or anyone who arouses suspicion by evading their drunken gaze, or by staring at their bloodied tools. Machetes, clubs, screwdrivers and knives, bicycle handlebars and piercing wheel spokes; belts laden with grenades and assault rifles. They use anything that can draw the life fluid from a body.

These were the killers, so relentless here, so close to me.

When the plane was shot down I was at home, but within an hour soldiers were at my door and the door of every Tutsi, knocking, then banging, demanding a tithe to save our lives, or shooting if there was no answer. They took all my money and my TV set, then left me. I was so afraid, and tried to hide with some neighbors. We were found by a gang of five civilians and a soldier, who carried knives and machetes. I was there. They wanted to kill me, and said they would come back. The extremist Hutu militia, the militant wing of the ruling party, experienced a surge of power like they had never known before. They called themselves *interahamwe,* which means: "those who attack together." They had set up the barrier on the road outside outside my house.

From my gap the next morning, I heard a soldier. "I come for Alex," he said, and I knew that things were very bad. But no one revealed my hiding place, so I wait . . . and listen. With my ears I can "see" the Apocalypse unfold. I stood there, silent for 21 days, my vision limited to this narrow, impossible gap. The houseboy, a Hutu, just as silently brought me some food, quietly resisting the utter extremism demanded outside. My legs slowly began to swell. I couldn't move them, or lift my knee in this space; I could not run away now if I wanted to, even if I had to. They swelled, legs of iron, the pain keeping me awake, as my consciousness jumped between images of fear. Only ten strides away, the trauma was well under way, and I could hear every crunch of machete into bone, the pop of heavy clubs bursting each human skull.

I have been so afraid, trapped in this gap. I have only my ears and my mind—my imagination gorged on adrenaline—to envision this carnage.

"Our Father, who art in Heaven, hallowed be thy name, thy kingdom come . . . "

What was that? The militiamen are raiding the next house. My neighbors will die. I heard the father's cries as his children were shot dead before him. I knew them all well. The *interahamwe* cut the father down next, then dragged his shrieking wife and sister into a hole, killing them with a single grenade.

"... *and forgive us our trespasses as we forgive those who trespass against us, and lead us not into temptation, but deliver us from evil. Amen. Amen. Amen* ..."

My gap seemed to grow smaller. Everyone I knew, everyone who knew my name, is being slaughtered. What was happening out there, in the minds of those murderers?

There was no food anymore, so the Hutu killers were fortified with looted beer and soft drinks and were sick. They had taken to the killing with a terrifying ease—with the trademark obedience that once set Rwanda apart from its unruly neighbors. I could hear when new prey came into range. They howled and barked and charged toward it, with menace in their throats and weapons swinging. In the safety of a group such as that, any cowardice was too easily overcome. *Holy Father,* can this be happening everywhere across my country? Is Rwanda entirely convulsed? Are we so drunk with blood that no one can stop? What sin of such pure Evil has been committed that we are being visited by this soul-destroying Hell?

Oh God, my God, my legs ...

After three weeks of this purgatory, there was a lull in the killing, the militiamen were elsewhere for a moment. So I crept as I could like a cripple to the next house for different shelter. The bodies lined the road in putrefying piles; could there be anybody left to kill? Disbelieving, I found my wife in the next house. She is Tutsi like me, but years ago, to get ahead as a nurse under the Hutu regime, she bought the false identity card of a Hutu.

Her face was lined with a fear that I have never seen. She told me that all Kigali has been seized by the same terror that was on our doorstep. There were barricades everywhere, massacres of thousands of Tutsis were being orchestrated by local authorities, defiling even the churches and parishes. No one was trying to stop it. Foreigners fled first and UN soldiers, too, were running away. The extremist Hutu radio station broadcast constant pleas to exterminate all Tutsis and their Hutu sympathizers, to kill until none remained. For a Hutu even to show mercy, she said, was to invite death. All those rumors that had circulated for years. Now it was coming to pass.

My wife hid me in a tiny crawl space in the rafters, and for three more weeks I waited. I could hear the last shred of killing, though my area was cleansed long ago. I was nearly alone, then completely so when my "Hutu" wife was forced to flee with the Hutu army, or risk being killed herself by the advancing Tutsi rebels. I am scared. I don't know where she is, but I think she is dead. There was much fighting where she went.

No one else even knows who I am.

". . . Holy Mary, Mother of God, pray for us sinners, now and at the hour of our death."

Beyond Alex Bizimungu's neighborhood—indeed throughout the maze of roads that spread weblike across the steep hills of Kigali, and onto every corner of Rwanda—the killing was massive and unprecedented in scale and speed. The genocide that afflicted Rwanda for three months in 1994 was the bloodiest episode recorded in modern African history, and was more ruthlessly efficient in causing death than were Nazi Germany's gas chambers. Some 800,000 died, most of them in the first month of the bloodletting, though some estimate the death toll at greater than 1 million. The nature of the killing, with so many thrown into pit latrines or buried and dissolving in dank mass graves, makes an accurate count impossible. They were murdered eyeball to eyeball by friends and neighbors. Often the only difference between killer and victim was the tribal distinction marked upon their identity cards.

A mathematical calculation of Rwanda's national suicide makes the speed of any other recorded catastrophe or single act of war pale by comparison. The two atomic bombs dropped upon the Japanese cities of Hiroshima and Nagasaki killed 200,000 people. The toll of the entire four-year war between Serbs, Croats, and Muslims in the former Yugoslavia during the early 1990s also just topped 200,000.

Previous genocides and mass killings this century—of Armenians by the young Turks of the Ottoman Empire in 1915, against 6 million European Jews by Germany's Third Reich in the 1930s and 1940s, and by the Khmer Rouge in Cambodia in the 1970s—though in the end taking far more lives than Rwanda's killing, proceeded at a slower burn for several years. The mammoth death toll of 20 million Soviets achieved by Stalin stretched over two decades.

No system of genocide ever devised has been more efficient: the daily kill rate was five times that of the Nazi death camps. Extremist Hutu officials, army commanders, and militia thugs conspired to eliminate all Tutsis and moderate Hutus and to draw every Hutu into complicity. For years they had prepared for this moment of genocide, organized for it, and manipulated a political system that required total, unquestioning obedience to authority. So throughout the country, the heat of anti-Tutsi propaganda turned participation into a life-or-death imperative. Hutus were programmed to kill.

And the result was specifically Rwandan, or "very Swiss," as the French historian Gérard Prunier, notes: "Anarchy, rape, arson and murder were all carried out according to plan and under supervised authority. People were throwing repression to the winds; yet at the same time even the Apocalypse had to be in accordance with official guidelines."[2]

The daily death rate *averaged* well more than 11,500 for two months, with surges as high as 45,000. During this peak, one murder was committed every 2 seconds of every minute, of every hour, for days: an affliction befitting the Apocalypse. Transfixed and aghast, the rest of the world watched, fiddled, then hid its eyes and did nothing.

Unless you had been a very close observer of Rwanda before the genocide, in those first days it was not clear what was happening, nor how organized it was. When I returned to the dusty file of my own yellowing news clippings, initial stories confidently described a "free-for-all" and "chaos." There there was a gradual recognition as the death toll grew into the tens of thousands and hundreds of thousands that this was a feat of social engineering. The word "genocide" comes up often during conflicts in Africa, every time before speciously. But I'm ashamed to report that the first story in which I mentioned genocide—just 350 words quoting the British charity Oxfam, on 28 April, saying that the "pattern of systematic killings of the Tutsi minority group amounts to genocide"—has this sad epitaph scrawled across the top: "Not used." The paper didn't run it.

The morning after the president's plane was shot down, I joined several other journalists on a charter flight to Kigali. While we were *en route,* Kigali airport was closed, so our small plane diverted to Mbarara, in southern Uganda. Plan 'B' was to attempt to go overland from there, through a strip of territory controlled by Tutsi-led rebels and a United Nations cease-fire line. But that night in Mbarara, for me, was one of intense trepidation.

As an Africa correspondent, I was devoted to the BBC World Service radio and its Africa news. I listened religiously. That night, while preparing to sleep, I turned on my radio and froze when I heard the report of the violence from Kigali. Lindsey Hilsum, a former BBC correspondent then based in Kigali as a UN press officer, had immediately reverted to her old job: the streets were piling high with bodies, she said. There was killing, chaos, an orgy of Rwandan blood that had erupted like a grenade blast inside an overripe melon.

There are degrees of fear, just as there are degrees of danger. Some are more acceptable than others. And at that moment, I felt real fear—and I wasn't even in Rwanda yet. For the first time I could remember, I looked deeply into myself, and started asking questions. Did I really want to go to that place, to witness those things? Could I observe such a human collapse, absorb it in my own mind, but also keep enough distance to protect myself? With so much killing, was it possible for me to be there and *not* be killed? My fear deepened, vexing me further because I had long before learned how to control it. I lay down in my barren hotel room. But the thought of events in Kigali kept me awake, clutching my pillow and praying throughout the night.

Never before had I had such a strong reaction, not even during that first front line in Eritrea. But never, either, had I imagined landing in the midst of such a maelstrom. This time I had more than enough experience to know what risks, what horrors, lay ahead.

The next day, 8 April 1994, we waited anxiously at the border, listening to the BBC until finally permitted to drive across by the Rwanda Patriotic Front. It was raining hard and getting dark. We were going to stay on the floor of a "guesthouse." All of us were tense. We slipped in the dark down a steep muddy path to our quarters, with a precipice on one side. Then Mark Doyle, a BBC correspondent who was soggy with whiskey—we all were by that time—threw his arms out straight like a man nailed to a cross, lost his balance and toppled head first over the edge, into the night. Despite ourselves, we couldn't stop laughing as he scraped his way back through the bushes below.

At daylight, we were told that overnight the rebels had launched an offensive toward Kigali in a bid to restore order. "To kill thousands of people in a day means that you are very serious about what you are doing," said the RPF Vice Chairman Patrick Mazimpaka.

We were not allowed to follow the rebels across the UN-monitored cease-fire line—which the RPF had just violated themselves—to make our own way to Kigali. But we did tour the front line. The trenches were ankle-deep with water and the Tutsi rebels honored our presence by firing mortars and heavy machine guns at army positions on the next hill, near the town of Byumba. Young fighters dashed across open spaces, and we followed as government guns returned fire.

Having gotten so close to the prize of Kigali, we angrily retraced our steps and pushed on, driving all night to Uganda's Entebbe airport. For the first time, we were blessed with a moment of serendipity.

We shared a lunch table with an official from the UN World Food Program (WFP). He took pity on us and arranged a flight on a cavernous Soviet Aleutian transport plane hired by the WFP to deliver relief food in central Africa. Flying in over Rwanda, we took turns in the cockpit and watched nervously as smoke rose from burning houses on the outskirts of Kigali. There was no secret anymore about what was happening down below. Upon touchdown, the plane was immediately quarantined and forced to turn around and fly back. But as our WFP savior argued with UN troops on the tarmac, we slipped out of the plane and made a dash for the airport terminal.

I was in.

There was the soap-sculpted Digit, SULFO flag still flying, who welcomed us like a ghost from a bygone era. Already his glass case was cracked by a single bullet that had sunk into his right foot. Digit's red eyes seemed to glow. We had arrived in Kigali just as hundreds of Belgian and French paratroopers deployed to extract 4,000 trapped foreigners. We bartered whiskey for food with the French, but soon they didn't need our supply: they broke into the duty-free shop, took what they pleased, and blamed the Belgians.

We woke on the cold floor of the airport terminal on 11 April 1994, and Mark Doyle reported that *one* of his shoelaces had been looted in the night—his second bit of bad luck. The Rwanda artillery crews (all Hutu) "protecting" the airport were having beer for breakfast, and their mood was already sour.

We ventured onto the streets for the first time with a French patrol collecting distressed expatriates—the policy seemed to be to rescue white people only—and I found that Kigali had become a city of choking, claustrophobic fear. Rwandans, of course, were left to their own devices—after all, French officers said, it was *their* country. And for many news editors the main story *was* the emergency evacuation, not the atrocities. But as the roadside ditches filled with bodies, there was no question which events took precedence in my mind.

Despite my hours of doubt and personal fear in Uganda, I was coming to grips with my anxiety. Once inside Rwanda, I was able to fend for myself and be safe in ways that were acceptable, or at least justifiable. The violence had only grown worse since the BBC's first breathtaking reports. But once on the ground, instead of being prey to wild speculation, I could calculate my own risks. That didn't mean that Rwanda was safe—for *anybody*—just manageable now, for me.

On one journey a crowd of killers lined a dirt road in silence as we passed, stopping momentarily from their bloody work like children caught stealing from a cookie jar. Armed with cudgels and machetes and long knives, their handiwork was nearby—three corpses bleeding into the wet sand. An hour later we returned with a group of Belgian evacuees, and the number killed by the silent crowd had risen to 11. Caught *in flagrante delicto* again, they paused. A Belgian woman peered over the edge of the truck and grimaced with fear: "Oh God!" she gasped. "Is it like that everywhere?"

The brutality among the lush green hills was inescapable. Violence seemed to lie in wait around every corner, along every muddy trail and behind thick undergrowth. My eyes scanned fields and buildings for any sign of life as we passed. Often there were half-hidden piles of corpses where the "work" was already complete, the stench kept down by heavy rains. But far more startling to me was the fact that any hint of life was suspect and dangerous: the terrible assumption was that anyone still alive must have been one of the killers. Evasive action at a checkpoint earned instant condemnation. I felt the threat everywhere. And I was only an observer.

Next to one stretch of road a young boy emerged, arms outstretched and pleading, crying for our convoy to take him to safety. No one stopped because to be found with that boy—a Tutsi—would have brought his death at the next barricade. But leaving him there, to be found anyway by a gang of Hutus or the army, virtually assured the same result. The risk was plain up the road, where another youth, a Hutu, brandished his homemade mace with confidence. All around him were bodies, including those of a pregnant woman and small child. The rest of his death squad was raiding a nearby house, while he stood guard, holding his weapon. The mace was a deliberate affair, spiny with 20 long nails hammered through the thick orb head. In the local Kinyarwanda language, the word for this flesh-ripping tool meant "No amount of money will save you."

This particular one dripped with blood, as the young killer glanced my way. His eyes were those of any 12-year-old. He knew very well what he was doing, but he didn't seem to care.

In a country where illiteracy was rife and radios were plentiful, the extremist mouthpiece Radio Télévision Libre des Mille Collines (1,000 Hills Free Radio, RTLM) was a constant reminder of the Hutu imperative to kill or be killed. In the first days of April 1994, the radio broadcast the names and addresses of Tutsi and moderate Hutu politicians on the primary death list. Its infamous message was simple: "The grave is only half-full; who will help us fill it?" Militiamen went to "work"—often observing normal office hours—with a machete in one hand and transistor radio in the other.

Outside the guest house where I had stayed in 1990 there was a militia checkpoint. Crumpled bodies appeared, then disappeared, and were replaced again and again. The city was so dangerous, the killers so volatile, that to bear witness with a camera was nearly impossible.

But from a distance, through a humid vapor to the next hill in Kigali, I saw some of the murder. Two men with machetes. One man with a machete hacked the neck of another man, who was on his knees and fell among several bodies—the magnified footage of the TV camera next to me showed gore sticking to the machete from that first strike, then it flinging off on the upswing. A woman with a sarong was next, on her knees and unmoving, as if waiting her turn. She fell over backward with the blow. The assailants kept striking, putting their weight into their strokes, making the bodies shudder with the blows. Then they eased off, moving back from the kill, shrugging to loosen their shoulders and overstrained latisimi dorsi muscles, holding their arms in the way that a professional tennis player ends exertion. It was clear that this killing was hard work and required commitment.

In Somalia and Sudan, the flow of modern weapons lubricated conflict and boosted the death toll. But in Rwanda that dynamic was reversed: the biggest producers of machetes in East Africa, the Chillington Company, sold more machetes to Rwanda in February 1994 than in all of 1993.[3]

Still, despite the Herculean physical effort and ubiquitous killing, there are few—if any—still photographs of even a single murder. Yet it happened one after another, close to 1 million times.

Prisoners in pink tunics drove garbage trucks, stopping at checkpoints to pick up the dead bare-handed. They might be on routine rubbish disposal—or even planting trees outside the national museum—for all they seemed to notice. This was not the first time Rwandan prisoners had been used to clean up a bloodletting, and this time they would collect 60,000 corpses. Belgian soldiers peered disbelieving into the back of the trucks, the dead so fresh that they smelled more of meat market than of mortuary. Bodies were dumped in city landfills like any other refuse, and bulldozed into the earth.

Riding in the open back of a Belgian military jeep during one evacuation run, we passed through a checkpoint where a group of *interahamwe* were drinking beer, again, for breakfast. Cold looks of contempt were cast our way, then one of the young killers lunged at me with a knife, screaming, "You shit!"

The Belgian army rescued a young European girl from a seminary in the center of town. She had been separated from her parents for days and was traumatized beyond her ability to articulate. She showed no emotion. During the long drive to the airport, past the atrocious scenes on the streets and murderous taunts of militiamen, she held a book in front of her face and pretended to read. She didn't once take her eyes from the words, and did not once turn the page. Transfixed too, at her reaction, I couldn't take my eyes off her.

Interahamwe raided one MSF hospital, killing 150 patients overnight. The team from the medical charity—usually one of the last relief organizations to leave a country at war—was distraught and pulled out: "We have decided it is no use to work here anymore," said an MSF doctor at the airport, waiting to depart. "It is useless to cure someone who is going to be killed. They were just lying in their tents, dead."

Hutu and Tutsi had not always been such enemies. This genocide couldn't be attributed to ancient prophecy, nor to some "age-old tribal hatred" cliché that made national suicide a foregone conclusion. Prior to the arrival of Europeans, in fact, there had never been systematic violence between the two groups. It is true that, broadly, there are some differing physical characteristics. There are also many exceptions. The majority Hutus are often shorter and stockier, with flat noses and very black skin. The minority Tutsis are often taller, with long thin noses and lighter skin. But the real divisions were formed in the late 19th century, by historical myths encouraged by Europeans who seized upon the system of Tutsi monarchy already in place as an easy means of control. It was the colonizers who first institutionalized tough minority rule.

Hutu and Tutsi speak the same language, have the same religion, and lived together on the same hills for centuries. Usually the Hutu farmed while the Tutsi raised livestock. But this caste system was largely apolitical: Tutsi came to mean "rich," someone with many long-horn cows; Hutu, or "servant," came to mean someone with fewer than ten cows. Hutus could become Tutsis in a special ceremony if they were wealthy enough, and Tutsis could fall into poverty. So the shape of one's nose in 1994 did not always determine whether you would die at a militia checkpoint during the genocide. Identity cards had to be checked before killers could be sure of their quarry.

For four centuries, Rwanda and and its southern cousin Burundi were ethnic nations in their own right, with a stability based largely on mutual dependence between tribes. "The political and social dominance of a Tutsi aristocracy forged by pastoral clienteles and princely marriages," noted one account, "gained a firmer foothold in both countries during the 18th century, but the label feudal does not fit: there were no Hutu serfs under Tutsi lords, only rich and poor in each group, both of which were the subjects of a sacrosanct [Tutsi] monarchy."[4]

Tutsis dominated the elite and—along with a handful of Hutus—were very hard masters who had the right of life and death. Their "citizens" were sometimes sold to Swahili slave traders. It was this period, and the transfer of its oppressive nature to colonial rulers, that blights the collective memory of Hutus today, so that they see themselves as perennial victims.

German colonialists and missionaries at the turn of the century capitalized on the Tutsi monarchy to reinforce an oral mythology that Tutsis were inherently superior and ordained to lead by God. Though there was no evidence for it, this "scientific" racial theory—which over time became official history—declared that Tutsis were a Nilo-Hamitic race from Egypt and Ethiopia that naturally ruled the Bantu Hutu.

One old traveler's book written in 1910 by Duke Adolphus Frederick of Mecklenberg during a tour of Imperial Germany's African colonies explained why Tutsis were so favored. The frontispiece portrait of *Into the Heart of Africa* showed this adventurer resplendent in spiked helmet and waxed moustache. "The Watutsi are a tall, well-made people with an almost ideal physique," he wrote, and speculated that they had migrated from Egypt or Arabia. By contrast he described the Hutus as "the primitive inhabitants. They are a medium-sized type of people, whose ungainly figures betoken hard toil, and who patiently bow themselves in abject bondage to the later arrived yet ruling race, the Watutsi."[5]

Another account describes how "missionaries in the grip of pseudo-Biblical myths . . . saw the Tutsis as 'Hamitic Semites,' or 'African Jews.'" The Hutus, on the other hand, have a "brachycephalous skull," a Belgian doctor wrote, and ". . . are childish in nature, both timid and lazy, and as often as not, extremely dirty. They form the serf class."[6]

To politicize the differences, in the 1930s the Belgian administration, which had taken over from the German occupation after World War I, conducted a census and found that 14% of the population was Tutsi and 85% Hutu. Anyone with less than ten cows was automatically classified a Hutu, and identity cards denoting ethnic group were issued for the first time.[7] Tutsis were systematically favored by the Belgians, and Hutus were largely denied education—except for those training for the Catholic priesthood.

The result would have far-reaching consequences, transforming past ethnic peace into modern violence. "The problem was the racialisation of consciousness affected everybody," Prunier writes, "and even the 'small Tutsi' . . . started to believe that they were indeed a superior race and that under the same rags as their Hutu neighbours wore, a finer heart was beating."[8]

By the late 1950s, however, the Belgians began to recognize that minority rule was no longer tenable. They bid to maintain influence by replacing Tutsi chiefs with Hutu chiefs. Unrest among the Hutu opposition was also encouraged. The result was the "Revolution of 1959" which—almost as if Belgian authorities had hit a switch—swept away the Tutsi monarchy. Hundreds of Tutsis were slaughtered and their houses were burned, sparking the first Tutsi exodus.

"The developments of these last 18 months have brought about the racial dictatorship of one party," a UN report warned in 1961. "An oppressive system has been replaced by another one. . . . It is quite possible that some day we will witness violent reactions on the part of the Tutsis."[9]

And sure enough, armed incursions of Tutsis from exile in the early 1960s set the precedent for the periodic bloodshed, mass migrations, and Tutsi incursions to follow. Tutsi guerrillas were called *inyenzi*, or "cockroaches." By 1964, some 10,000 Tutsis had died and between 270,000 and 370,000 had fled Rwanda. Anxious about erosion of their grip on power, Hutu governments ever since have sought to prevent Tutsis from returning. When Major General Habyarimana seized power in a military coup in 1973, he declared the return of Tutsi exiles impossible: Rwanda did not have enough land or food for the millions already squeezing it. The majority Hutus were brainwashed into believing that their very existence depended upon pure Hutu rule.

As Hutu extremists prepared for a "final solution" in Rwanda—the genocide—they inflamed passions by insisting that the Tutsi were preparing the same against the Hutu. The ideology of "Hutu Power" was born, and so with it the brand of extremist who saw the world in terms of "us" vs. "them." There was no question about it: the loser was to be annihilated.

In Kigali, the difficulties of working as a journalist in the early days of the slaughter were compounded because no one wanted witnesses. Travel through the city became more and more risky, then impossible, even though we commandeered vehicles left behind by fleeing foreigners. Many still had keys in the ignition. My Swiss embassy 4WD, chosen at the airport on 12 April 1994 from a fleet of abandoned cars—was pristine and white, with a sunroof, excellent stereo system, and—most important—more than a quarter tank of fuel. The transfer was hastily made, however, and I was separated from all my bags: portable satellite telex and computer, film, spare camera bodies, and lenses; all clothes, notes, and gear lost. I ended up at the Hotel des Mille Collines, with scores of Tutsis seeking refuge and a few UN troops. On the other side of Kigali, a civil war away, my equipment was first stuck at the airport, then vanished.

The Mille Collines was a hotel waiting for destruction. Like the Commodore in Beirut or the Holiday Inn of Sarajevo, it turned into a temporary haven for journalists who daily prayed that they would not be victim of the warriors who did battle all around them. The Tutsis hid in their rooms or waited in dark corridors, fearfully murmuring among themselves about whether or not the *interahamwe* would come today or tomorrow morning, to ransack the hotel and make the city's slaughter complete. It was a very real possibility: the Hutu soldiers who loitered in the lobby and waited outside with rifle grenades were not here for the Tutsis' *protection.* Remarkably, for a time the electricity and outside phone lines still functioned.

Passing the hotel office one day, I saw the same mechanical typewriter that I had borrowed five years earlier, when I had banged out my "Famine in the Green Hills" story while sitting happily beside the pool.

But the brooding sense of surrealism this time left no room for remembrance, and was defined by small, terrifying details. At night the waters of the pool glowed with underwater floodlighting, bathing the side of the hotel facing the war with an eerie opalescence. Over the prosaic lap of pool water, from my hotel window, I heard intense screams, true, true screams of danger, silenced by gunfire. There were two charged cries: of those being killed, and of those doing the killing *right now.* This maxim seemed to have gripped Rwanda: To survive the killers, you must be the worst killer; let die, so that you can live.

A Belgian hotel staff member casually mentioned that he *knew* Rwandans and would tell us when our safety was jeopardized. But later he ran out the front door in a panic, handing a piece of paper to a photographer.

"Here's a list of all the people in the hotel . . . Good Luck!" he said, without slowing down.

"How much food is left?"

"At least two days." And he was gone.

The first heavy fighting for Kigali erupted at 4:30 am on 13 April 1994, one week after the president's plane was shot down. The Rwanda Patriotic Front infiltrated the city to hook up with 600 RPF soldiers who had been deployed at the Parliament building as part of the 1993 peace deal, to protect Tutsi politicians. We had a front row seat as the civil war erupted around us. The explosions of heavy artillery rumbled across Kigali; the muzzles of 12.7mm guns flashed in heated exchange; bright tracer rounds arced through the sky, and our side of the hotel took a few stray bullets. The Tutsi fugitives were getting nervous—many had paid $300 for a "safe" Hutu escort to the hotel, but some felt now that that expense may have been in vain.

I shared a room with Mark Huband of *The Guardian*. We closed the curtain to stop spraying glass shards if we were hit, filled the bath while there was still water, and ate another *"Poulet et legumes,"* French combat meal #3. When the French food ran out, we had to eat cold greasy German rations. Euphemistically labeled "NATO approved," the lardy *hackfleisch* and spongy red *blutwurst* tasted bad out of an aluminum tin. Our fellow refugees, the Tutsis, had far less.

After eight hours of fighting, 2,400 rebels had joined up with the beleaguered battalion at Parliament. There was a pause, and the Red Cross made its first food distribution in a week. Outside the mammoth Ste. Famille cathedral, Hutus lined up, their machetes, lengths of pipe, and other makeshift killing tools—maybe just a dagger—hanging at their sides like a further appendage, just as Somalis carry their guns. Here were the demons, I thought, unable to feed themselves because of the destruction they had wrought.

These were the foot soldiers of the genocide, and they were hungry. They were waiting for a handout of beans, just a few yards from a ditch spoiled with mangled bodies. And an arm's length away on the other side was the church, where 5,000 Tutsis had sought sanctuary. Inside I found them camped under the Stations of the Cross, reading the Bible with children playing among the pews. Smoke from cooking fires burning on the bare floor mingled with the stench of overburdened toilets. Shafts of light from high windows—normally meant to inspire a sense of divine safety and goodness—cut mockingly through the smokiness. Wounded were being treated on the dais around the altar, and the arms of the cruciform cathedral had been converted into a makeshift emergency ward.

One Tutsi, unshaven and with a shaky voice, heard that other religious missions had been violated by Hutu soldiers and militias. "This is a house of God, but we are afraid of attack," he told me, pleading. "The army has positions above us and the rebels are below. We may die of hunger, but please not by knives and bullets!"

Back in the room, I slept badly. With so much killing so close by, it was not possible to feel safe. We were trying to rest in the midst of an engulfing crime, and my imagination was not yet prepared to accept its horrors. At dawn a thick fog coated the hills. The heavy fighting was finally blotted out by a downpour.

Once the last foreigners were evacuated, a general distribution of arms ensured that Rwanda's "final solution" of the Tutsi "problem" spread with methodical precision. Massacres had begun almost immediately in the north and northwest, the stronghold of the ruling class where the *interahamwe* were best organized. Within weeks of the 6 April kickoff, they had shifted to the south, the base of political opposition. In the intellectual capital of Butare, a Tutsi prefect kept order for nearly two weeks, but then was replaced by a hard-line Hutu. The same night, 20 April, Presidential Guard units were flown in from Kigali. Huge open pits were lined with burning tires and victims were thrown in alive. Even an orphanage was "cleansed": 21 Tutsi children were slain, along with the 13 Rwandan Red Cross workers who tried to protect them.

Three cease-fires announced by the UN dissolved in one week, and Canadian UN commander General Romeo Dallaire was despondent: "They haven't stopped fighting, so I haven't been effective," he said. Gangs of killers had been "conducting incredibly gruesome acts on human bodies" directly in front of the UN "peacekeepers," who said they were powerless to intervene. The killers, Dallaire said, were "like demons in human form."

I was ordered by the *Telegraph* to leave on one of the last evacuation flights. My satellite telex and computer were lost, I was out of film and, except for the two cameras around my neck, had lost all my camera gear. I hadn't changed clothes for a week. I was exhausted, but I had no problems—none at all—compared to the Rwandans I was leaving behind, if only temporarily. It was clear that the "Switzerland" of Africa was just beginning a very long free-fall, and that I would be returning.

The Belgian military plane was full of UN troops, and a handful of journalists. When the wheels left the ground, there was a cheer—*Bravo! Bravo!*—that made me cringe. I looked out the window, to the lush country below, until it was swallowed up by the rain clouds.

To a colleague, I expressed reservations about leaving—I was still undecided. He leaned across, straining the red nylon straps of his seat harness:

"Don't worry, this place is like 'Hotel California,'" he said, echoing the Eagles song. "You can check out, but you can never leave."

In the next weeks, the death toll began to merge into a statistical mass. In this village one Tutsi survived from a population of 400; in that town some 2,800 were slaughtered; dozens of parish churches were turned into abattoirs. To fully appreciate the nature of Rwanda's mass killing, however, requires extracting the terrific agony particular to each death. That is now an impossible task. But an extermination rate of 45,000 each day means little, unless you explore and taste the charnel house yourself.

Rwanda's plague in 1994 was genocide, and over the coming weeks, this is what it looked like.

Virtually every cluster of huts in Rwanda, this lush Garden of Eden, harbored a fresh outrage, evident in the overwhelming stench that hung where living people once were, their corpses now stuffed into back rooms and in muddy, shit-filled pits. Dogs roamed wild in the aftermath, or lay dead on the road, bloated after gorging on rotting human flesh. The evidence slowly disappeared, disintegrating under the ravages of sun and rain and excrement. Missions and parishes had traditionally been inviolable during Rwanda's previous bouts of killing. But this time identity cards of Tutsis—and of some Hutus—stuck to blood-caked church floors.

Though almost fantastic in its horror, the tale of the mission at Rukara was typical of the work of death squads at such sacrariums. For their "safety," they were told, Tutsis were herded into churches by Hutu officials. "The people sang hymns and cried and prayed" as they were massacred, said Father Oreste Incimatata, one of the few surviving witnesses. The windows were too high to give the murderers enough purchase with their assault rifles, so they tore off a section of roof to provide lethal access.

Oreste was spared, a militiaman told him, because "You'll have to say Mass for us one day."

Oreste recalled the onslaught matter-of-factly when I met him in the first days of June. Already just a few weeks after the act, his revulsion had been put away, buried deep within the folds of his brain, beneath layer upon layer of protective reasons and attempts to understand. His emotion was buried there, too. "After you see hundreds of people die in front of you," he explained, "you become like a tree."

The killing at Rukara went according to plan, and the evidence of the defense was still plain. The *interahamwe* threw stones through the church windows, forcing the 800 terrified people inside to stand the plank pews against the stained glass as barricades. Next day the killing began as grenades were dropped into the church. A small statue of Christ, palms open in supplication toward this battered flock—and oddly lit when I saw it, by a shaft of light from the "gun access" hole in the roof—stood witness as soldiers and militia swarmed inside. They finished off the wounded with bayonets and machetes as victims huddled on mattresses and beneath purple surplices. Hands clawed toward the dais; two wooden crucifixes had been washed away, carried by the river of blood that flowed down the sloped floor.

In a side room, packed with bodies and virtually blanketed from floor to ceiling with a layer of black maggot flies, one couple had died in each other's arms, on a chair under a picture of Pope John Paul II meeting a local parishioner. Even the 10-foot-high metal cross above the church entrance was thick with flies. In terrible counterbalance, a small cross on the ground outside was inexplicably formed by the bone of a baby, and the forearm of a small child, its withered hand pointing toward another cluster of sprawling bodies.

Such disturbing scenes of sacrilege—of sanctuaries violated for ethnic and political reasons—became too ordinary as Rwanda imploded. The atrocities piled one on top of another in relentless, damning succession. Like every witness, I couldn't believe what I was seeing, and I had to concentrate to control a physical reaction while I tried to do my "work."

Taking photographs at these places, I moved slowly with my cameras—looking to document crimes, while trying also to document the impact of their occasional intimate beauty, to realize art where one least expected it. I rarely spoke or heard speaking at these sites; it was like being silent at a funeral or church service, when you don't want to disturb the other spirits with your physical presence.

The Kabarondo Catholic Church of the Holy Sacrament was also violated by massacre. The desperate, feeble attempts to take final Communion by those about to die were scattered with the broken wafers: the wine vessel was smashed, the chalice tipped over, and the priest's robes were torn, stained with his blood. The testimony of unremitting carnage continued throughout the church, though the bodies of more than 1,200 had been dragged into a mass grave behind the building, where there was not enough earth to cover them.

As a rule, I never take sacred relics from war zones, because to me that is almost always profane. In Rwanda I never touched anything—except at Kabarondo. I had been so affected by these accumulating crimes that I felt I needed to have something *real* to hold on to, to remind me of Rwanda's atrocities, to ensure that my rage and my own deep trauma continued undiluted. That totem I still have—a simple dull brass cross that fits into the palm of my hand. It had been broken off the top of a stave and tossed into a corner, out of the way of the massacre. I almost put it back—instinctively checking myself from this grave robbery—but it was better that I kept it, for it has helped me to tell this story. This cross saw things that I hope I never will.

I later met a Dutch missionary priest, Father Jan de Bekker, who had lived more than 30 years in Rwanda and neighboring Zaire, before the genocide had swept like the plague through his parish. His hair was white with the effort, his face heavily wrinkled from grappling so long to reconcile God's grace with the evident frailty of the human body. "This is what happened everywhere," said de Bekker, at a rebel base near Rukara church. "All the Tutsis were allowed, even encouraged to go to the churches, because then it was easy for the Hutu to kill them, instead of trying to find them in the hills."

It was night, and the only light was from a candle between us that burned with a long smoking flame. As we sat there, de Bekker wandered to his darkest reaches, where doubt had begun to feed. He questioned his life's work spent trying to instill godliness among those who had become Rwanda's victims, and its killers. The genocide, he said, was moving inexorably toward completion. For decades Hutu and Tutsi had fought and made peace. Now both sides wanted to finish the argument. But could they ever forgive, after such an unholy orgy?

Without pause, he knew the answer.

"They can't."

In May 1994, one month into the genocide, only one relief agency had stayed in Rwanda. The ICRC hospital in Kigali was especially badly located, just on the Hutu side of the front line, and directly in the line of rebel Tutsi bombardments of the defense ministry. Shells fell short, into the ICRC compound, killing patients. Stacked sacks of relief food served as makeshift "sand bag" walls, but they were porous to shrapnel.

In a dark corner, I came across a young woman who moaned uncontrollably, her hands shaking with pain as she held them near her puffy, bruised face. After nine days here she was improving: she could open one eye slightly. Feeling had been slowly returning to her legs. Her arms and body were swollen as with infection; the wounds on either side of her head festered.

The woman had been buried alive for 36 hours, in a mass grave that included her entire family. Her body had been virtually destroyed, a nurse told me, by the sheer compression of all the dead packed so tightly around her; the weight of victims and earth together, crushing. Still, she had dug herself out and crawled away. Aside from injecting the woman with antibiotics, doctors were at a loss.

"There are no books written about dealing with someone who survives a mass grave," the nurse confided.

"No one should *ever* survive."

FIFTEEN

"DREADFUL NOTE OF PREPARATION"

I believe in Santa Claus.

> —A hopeful epithet turned epitaph,
> emblazoned on the sweatshirt
> of a murdered child

The wreckage of the president's plane lay mangled, shreds of wing and engine spread across a muddy cornfield that upon impact burst through the back wall of the garden and settled near a grimy, empty swimming pool. Burned beyond recognition, President Juvénal Habyarimana died here, on the grounds of his own mansion at about 8:30 pm on 6 April 1994. The tattered "Emergency Procedures Manual" came to rest under dirty cornstalks in the shadow of the crumpled tail of the *Mystère-Falcon*, a gift from the French leader to a regime that would turn genocidal. Two compact discs—the president preferred jazz and Tchaikovsky, it seemed—were melted and bent.

The large house reeked of death—and a curious mixture of spilled perfume—though the corpses were gone by the time I visited in late May. The Tutsi rebels had just taken control of Kigali airport, the nearby barracks, and this mansion. We were the first outsiders to see the wreckage and the residence—even UN investigators had been barred from the crash site while it was still held by the Rwandan army.

Laden with crucifixes and littered with family photos, the mansion provided clues to the sinister intentions of a man caught between Hutu extremists who insisted on a final, violent solution for the Tutsis, and those who begged for peace and reconciliation. Trapping himself in this dangerous game, Habyarimana pandered to both sides, and lost.

The three pillars that uphheld Rwanda's genocide were in evidence there, in the presidential mansion, and examining them is critical to grasping the roots of the carnage:

- Hutu fear of the minority Tutsi and detailed preparations to exterminate the Tutsi "problem";
- The acquiescence of the Catholic Church as those preparations became irreversible; and
- The French government's role in propping up the doomed regime—even *during* the genocide—with cash and weapons.

Theories abound. Was the president sacrificed by Hutu extremists before he could "capitulate" to power-sharing demands by Tutsi rebels? Considering the decades of anti-Tutsi propaganda and the increasing Hutu obsession with tribal purity and Hutu Power, did anyone else have better reason to assassinate a man seen by radical Hutus as a traitor?

Or did the RPF kill the president to take military advantage of what would surely result in chaos, advancing unopposed across much of the north and east of Rwanda within weeks? Few believe today that the RPF was involved. Even if it was, how could the Tutsi rebels have underestimated the feverish tension that so easily led to the deaths of 800,000 of their own people?

I wandered through the mansion, the personal effects of a failed leader strewn about every messy corner, along with a scattered collection of colorful first edition Rwandan stamps. RPF soldiers did not loot the silver or crystal, but the eyes of the late president had been scratched out of official painted portraits. A half glass of wine thick with bugs stood alone on the bar. Pictures of the president's eight children lined the fireplace wall. A mountain of gifts given to the head of state over the years was crowned with a kitsch copper clock inscribed with this obeisance: "The family that prays together, stays together."

Beside the president's bed were pictures of Christ, crucifixes, and a small altar. In his connecting den the weapons of a hunter were missing, but large-bore rifle rounds sprinkled the stained carpet. The most compromising documents were gone, but there was much to pick through among old confidential memos. A gold-plated shaving brush and razor, choked with hair, stood guard over a batch of Christian medals spilled onto the tiled bathroom floor. There was one from Pope John Paul II himself.

A Rwandan flag had been stuffed into the toilet.

"THE HUTU TEN COMMANDMENTS"

Passing through the dark lower level of the mansion, I saw an almost black fish tank raised up on stilts, shining darkly with importance like the Islamic Ka'aba at Mecca during the Haj. I moved toward it and found that the blackness was the water of the tank, turned into an oozing sludge-green scum soup after weeks of neglect. Some fish floated on the surface, belly up. Survivors swam with a deliberate slowness, conserving their energy in an effort to survive.

Electrical power was cut, so the aerator no longer worked. These fish were starved of oxygen, though the rebels flavored the brine copiously with food granules.

Nearby on the floor, I found the first clue to understanding the massacres. The glass picture frame was crushed, but the image was intact: a grainy black-and-white view of Tutsi huts on a hillside, in flames and coughing up columns of smoke. Like a historical artifact—revered obviously as an example for future generations—it had been carefully labeled "Apocalypse Révolution— Nov. 1959," to honor the overthrow of the Tutsi monarchy. Here was the symbol of Hutu supremacy, and of violence carried out in the name of majority rule—known in Rwanda as "democracy." The fact that this picture was so prominent in the Habyarimana household pointed also to the collective Hutu neurosis of ever losing power.

For decades Tutsis in exile had nurtured the "injustices" of the 1959 Hutu uprising and vowed to return. For them revenge was rooted in a never-forgotten series of ethnic transgressions. Like the perennial conflicts in the Middle East and the Balkans, they embraced the version of history that best matched their political aims. The Tutsi launched sporadic cross-border attacks, though these often resulted in massive rataliation by government forces and militias against the Tutsis still in Rwanda.

Shortly after I had left Rwanda's gorillas in October 1990, the Tutsi rebels, the RPF, invaded northern Rwanda from Uganda. They demanded that Tutsis in exile be allowed to return, and be given enough influence in the Hutu government to guarantee their safety. But their invasion sent shock waves throughout the country, on both sides of the ethnic divide. By then, Tutsis were a minority of just 9 percent,[1] but the incursion set in motion a series of defense mechanisms to preserve Hutu rule. The incursion was repulsed, though the threat immediately fed Hutu paranoia and gave ammunition to hard-liners.

For along with the reassuringly weak epithet "cockroaches" the RPF were also called—with measured reverence—*inkotanyi,* the name given to warriors of the former Tutsi monarchy: "relentless fighters."

Nearly every rebel was born outside Rwanda, and few had ever set foot on their native soil. Here were the angry children of the first Tutsi exiles, hardened by years away from Rwanda, trying to force their way back in, while clinging fiercely to the dream of milk and honey in their homeland, a dream that no longer existed in reality but had been passed down by their parents as a noble aim. Unlike previous incursions, in 1990 the rebels stated that Tutsi hegemony was not their goal. No matter. In official Hutu circles, there was no room for them.

"The Hutu Ten Commandments," published by the extremist Hutu newspaper *Kangura (Wake Up!)* in December 1990, laid down the new catechism of neutralizing this enemy of "the Bantu people." It was a new style of apartheid, and became the Hutu manifesto: any contact with Tutsis was an act of treason, and Hutus "should stop having mercy on the Tutsis." It was the duty of every Hutu, the tenth commandment demanded, to "spread widely" the supremacist "Hutu Ideology."[2]

President Habyarimana repeatedly warned that if Tutsis ever took control of Rwanda, they would find their families dead. Preparations to fulfil this prophetic undertaking were begun in earnest.

At the start of the civil war in 1990, the Rwandan army consisted of only 5,000 soldiers. Within one year 24,000 troops were in uniform to defend Hutu rule, making up an ill-disciplined force that institutionalized thuggery as much as did World War II Italian fascist Black Shirts or German Nazi Brown Shirts. During 1992 the army grew to more than 30,000 soldiers. Hand in hand with this increase came the formation of ultra-extremist Hutu political parties allied to the ruling Mouvement Révolutionnaire National pour le Développement (MRND) party. With President Habyarimana's help, the Coalition pour la Défense de la République (CDR) was created, with the sole mission of ensuring Hutu supremacy.

The MRND's militia, the *interahamwe,* and the CDR's *impuzamugambi* ("those with a single purpose") were designed to be the engine of the "cleansing" of Tutsis to follow. Finding Hutu followers was easy, in a country that ranked just 153 out of 173 nations on the UN's annual Human Development Index, which ranks countries' livability. "Young men, many of whom had no work and no prospect of work, were easily recruited with promises of land, jobs, and the material rewards to be reaped from their plunder," noted one analyst. "Rwanda's poverty, and political violence, again appeared to be intimately linked."[3]

The violence became so widespread that it caught outside attention. The

UN established an independent International Commission in January 1993, to look into growing violence and found the government's fingerprints everywhere. Hutu villagers who gathered for community service, for example, were regularly told to come to "work" with spears and machetes to "clear the brush," a euphemism for killing Tutsis. Some 2,000 had died already in that period of budding extremism.

Militiamen carried out attacks under organized leadership, dressed in camouflage uniforms. Telephone service would be temporarily cut during days of massacres—so killing could proceed in isolation—then restored a day or two later.[4] A grave with more than a dozen fresh corpses was excavated by the commission in the backyard of one government official, and the commission learned of many more such graves.[5] Even as the commission prepared to board the plane to depart, Capt. Pascal Simbikangwa—the presidential guard commander who had supervised killings in Kigali—publicly threatened to kill the Rwandan human rights activist who had organized the visit.

Not surprisingly, the commission concluded that a "climate of terror" reigned in Rwanda and that the government was doing nothing to stop it. "Authorities at the highest level, including the President of the Republic, consented to the abuses," the final report found.[6]

A second invasion of "cockroaches" in February 1993, in violation of a cease-fire, only strengthened extremist Hutu resolve. The RPF for the first time was responsible for several atrocities. Tutsis had been portrayed as devils, with horns and cloven hooves for feet. So to Hutus, news of killings simply confirmed that they were under siege by what they called the "Black Khmer."

Still, in August 1993, under strong pressure from abroad, President Habyarimana signed a peace agreement with the RPF in Arusha, Tanzania. It allowed for the rebel presence in a strip of land along Rwanda's northern border with Uganda. A power-sharing government was to be set up, and the Rwanda army and Tutsi rebel forces were to be cut back and merged. Some 2,500 UN peacekeeping troops—the UN Assistance Mission for Rwanda (Unamir)—were deployed along the cease-fire line. To Hutu Power extremists, however, this compromise was an act of treachery. So to keep control of hard-line elements within his government—and to nourish his own similar preferences—Habyarimana also continued to back radical factions intent on sabotaging the deal. He couldn't do both for long, and so may have made his own assassination inevitable.

The president's own hard-line inner circle—called *Akazu*, or "little house" after the old royal court—was unwilling to negotiate any end to the war that would accommodate the Tutsi. *Akazu* was first called *"le Clan de Madame,"* because it was run by First Lady Agathe Kanziga, higher born among political families than her husband, and so very influential. *Akazu* was the driving force behind the even more sinister "Zero Network," the cabal of elite military and civilian extremists who were instrumental in planning the genocide. Together, they turned the genocidal ideology into a national aim.

The crucial instrument for spreading the hatred of Tutsis was *Radio Télévision Libre des Milles Collines* (RTLM). Funded originally by the president's wife and wealthy businessman Félicien Kabuga—whose daughter married the president's son—this radio prepared the soil for a gruesome planting. To ensure a power supply in a crisis, the transmitter had been connected by underground cable directly to the presidential mansion.

So there was little sense of relief at the top in Kigali when the power-sharing peace agreement was reached in August 1993. Hard-liners determined to derail the deal pushed tension until the slightest spark would ignite an inferno. As militia attacks increased, lists of Tutsis and other "accomplices" of the rebels were created. Every social and church organization was forced to hand over lists of members to help identify "infiltrators." By early 1994 these death lists were so common that one could have his name removed for a fee.

Confidential intelligence and military documents found by Swiss journalist Jean-Philippe Ceppi of *Le Nouveau Quotidien* (Lausanne) and *Libération* (Paris) made clear that the inferno was inevitable. On 23 March 1994, two weeks before the president's plane crashed, the chief of civilian intelligence wrote urgently to the prime minister, warning: "The persistent tension is due to . . . the psychological fatigue of the population. . . . If the highest authorities of this country don't do anything to stop the gears of violence, this country risks falling into chaos."[7]

More evidence of explicit preparation was found in notes of a defense minister briefing from the Kigali prefect on 30 March 1994—just one week before the genocide began. Marked "TRÈS SECRET," it described the organization of "special operations cells" that could use traditional weapons such as machetes to "defend" their neighborhoods. Their mission was "to search and neutralize infiltrators in the different quarters of the city."[8]

If you did not have access to confidential files, you had only to glance at the local media to see that the constant rumors and predictions of widespread anti-Tutsi violence were coming together as never before. In January 1994, under the headline: "Who Will Survive the March War?" *Kangura* predicted that "it will be necessary then that the masses and their army protect themselves. At such time, blood will be poured. At such time, a lot of blood will be poured." Unamir, it warned "should also take into consideration these dangers."[9] Just days before the president was assassinated, RTLM predicted things would "get heated up" in the next few days, including "a little thing" on 6 April and after that "you will see something."[10]

Amidst this swirl of rumors, in early 1994 the government had attempted to bolster its weapons stocks, though Unamir caught on and stopped several deliveries. Habyarimana also delayed forming the new, joint Hutu-Tutsi government he had agreed to in Arusha. Daily incidents of criminality—kidnappings, targeted killings, and grenade attacks—finally became so severe that on 6 April, only a few hours before the president's plane was shot down, a decision was made by UN police to conduct a surprise cordon-and-search operation with the Rwanda army to rid a notorious section of Kigali of illegal weapons and grenades.[11] The search was never carried out, and within hours it became clear that the time to prevent an explosion had long since passed.

All was ready for the right signal. The plane crash was that spectacular signal. Within 30 minutes, the barricades were up, and presidential guard units were acting on the death lists. Hutu Power accused Tutsis of killing the president, a fiction used to encourage wavering Hutus to commit themselves to eliminating the "enemy within."

The radio of hatred came into its own, and put down the genocide marker: "Now," it announced, "it is time to bring in the harvest."

"HOLY MEN"

Climbing the narrow dark stairs of the president's mansion, from the fish tank in the basement to the attic, I found a hidden chapel. Beneath long wooden rafters and the low, sloping roof—up here, so close to God—appears to be a personal tribute to Catholicism, a private sanctuary in which to examine one's faith. A few carved pews faced a tall throne decked with opulent purple cushions. Vestments hung in a corner, beside the hurried remains of a special Eucharist. This chalice is gold, along with a gilt tray. I was surprised to find thin white wafers in the ornate ciborium. Like the frantic ritual before the Kabarondo massacre, was this also a Holy Communion cut short?

These icons are the second clue to understanding Rwanda's carnage. In few other countries have church and state blended so harmoniously, and been so mutually dependent on each other. The name of the president, Habyarimana, translates as "God is the creator of all things." I turned from these luxurious tools of the sacrament, and my eye fell upon a picture of the president meeting the pope. Here it held a particular significance, in a country where the archbishop was a political apparatchik. And where—despite all the Christian goodwill that should pervade the place—the Catholic Church did nothing to prevent genocide.

Disobeyed was the commandment: "Thou Shalt Not Kill." For all the apparent devoutness, and the gravity I could feel in the plush weight of the priest's robes, this private chapel represented failed religion and hollow faith.

Rwanda should be among the most pious nations in Africa. Its spirit has been formed by incessant preaching from a multitude of churches, the minds of its people forged in seminaries and convent schools. For a century the Catholic Church had molded Rwanda, converting the Christless to God. From the 1930s, to gain advantage in the Belgian administration, converts flooded in such that one elder wrote of "a massive enrollment in the Catholic army."[12] Church historians wrote of a "new Jerusalem" that "offers us the jewel of Africa." The conversion of a new king—and later his consecration of his kingdom to Christ in 1946—forged a closeknit church-state bond that would last for decades.

Still, Rwanda was "catholicized but not Christianized," the historian Prunier notes. "Christian values did not penetrate deeply, even if Christian prejudices and social attitudes were adopted as protective covering." Evidence would come during the genocide, when civil authorities would demonstrate a "moral override," causing people to kill inside churches.[13]

Like the colonial rulers, missionaries at first found the Tutsi monarchy a useful institution. But in the 1950s, thinking began to change. White clergy coming from Europe were no longer of such high social class, and increasingly identified with the disenfranchised Hutu. Those missionaries—led primarily by Flemish-speaking Belgians—played a significant role in the 1959 revolution by encouraging the majority Hutus to exercise their demographic dominance and overthrow the Tutsi monarchy.

Such political dabbling set a strong precedent. By the time of the 1994 genocide, elements of the Church had long been part and parcel of the Hutu regime. The archbishop of Kigali, the *Most Reverend* Vincent Nsengiyumva, had sat on the central committee of the ruling party for 14 years. The Vatican was not blind to the problem. The archbishop was forced by Rome to resign his political position in 1989. A further blow to cozy church-state ties came in 1991. Monsignor Thaddée Nsengiyumva, in a daring pastoral letter from Kabgayi, decried a political system in which "assassination is now commonplace," and where no one was serious about making peace between Hutu and Tutsi.[14]

Still, before and during the genocide, many clergymen decorated their robes with small images of the president. Some priests wore pistols beneath their habits. In their zeal to adhere to the Hutu Power line, in August 29 priests wrote a letter to the pope, denying any Hutu involvement in the genocide and blaming the RPF rebels for all atrocities.[15]

The toll on the Church in 1994 was high: 248 Catholic bishops, priests, and nuns died in Rwanda, fully one-third of the worldwide total of the past 30 years.[16] As early as 27 April, the pope had used the word "genocide" while condemning the killings.[17]

Abbé André Sibomana was a senior Hutu priest whose name nevertheless figured prominently on Hutu death lists because of his human rights activities. As editor of *Kinyamateka*, a critical Catholic newspaper and the most influential newspaper in Rwanda, André had exposed government corruption. Taken to court in 1990 for publishing the reports, he was acquitted after substantiating them with considerable evidence. Further distancing himself from the Habyarimana regime, he was known to have been the "chief inspiration" behind the 1991 pastoral letter that for the first time publicly separated the Rwandan Church from the state.[18]

I met André a year after the genocide, and he explained to me that guilt is best measured in a broad sense, rather than assigning blame to individual priests. It was an admission of a Church weak from spiritual depravity, with its morality rotten because of secular politics. Though the archbishop "was a friend of the president" and a ruling party stalwart, he "did nothing to stop the killings before they happened. It was the hierarchy of the Catholic Church: they can't say they didn't know. They knew. But there was not the pastoral attitude to stop it," André said.

He was not wearing a Roman collar. There had been no time for such details, because one year after the events, André was trying to rebuild. "If the Catholic hierarchy did everything at the exact right time, it was possible that genocide could have been averted. But to have that result we would have had to begin acting in 1989," he said, the sorrow evident in his voice.

Changing such a deeply rooted system would not have been easy, even if the will had been there. "Many people who prepared the genocide were baptized as Catholics, so the reputation of the Church has been damaged," André said. "Everyone knows that you don't only have holy people in the Church, but the point is that in Rwanda the Church is the opinion maker, the conscience of the country that must respect life. Here the Church was a friend of the government, and found it impossible to believe that the regime could do anything wrong."

Father Vjeko Curic, a Croatian priest who worked in Rwanda for 13 years, was one of the few Europeans to stay in government-controlled areas throughout the upheavals. As the slaughter got under way in 1994, his Hutu congregants told him that they were killing to "defend" Rwanda. Already he had seen it happen many times, this unchecked blotting out of life for the sake of misguided phobias. "I told the congregation that it was not true, that killing people was not the way to 'defend' the country," he said, a year after the genocide. "It is not possible that God can see this without consequences. It is a catastrophe; for the Church, too—a chance to see the account after 100 years' presence in Rwanda. It has come to nothing. The Church is destroyed."

Despite great personal risk—seeing hills so covered with bodies that they resembled "lawns of flesh" and witnessing "thousands of murders"[19]—he drove food convoys regularly for the UN from the border with Burundi, facing 30 militia checkpoints in 100 miles to carry food.

Vieko passed militiamen whose bayoneted rifles were so bloody that the barrels were plugged with the thickening paste. Old men used spiked clubs so heavy that they had to drag them behind when not killing with them. Vieko said his understanding was limited by his faith. "How can I explain what happened?" he told Sam Kiley of *The Times*. "It was possession, it must have been the Devil's work. Either that, or these people are just evil, evil—I am not allowed to think that."[20] Another priest described the breakdown: "Militiamen used to say, 'We have nothing to do with God.' They said the Virgin Mary was a Tutsi woman and she had to be killed."[21]

The spectacle at Kabgayi seminary—the largest in the country and known as the Vatican of Rwanda—was the result of this embattled morality. It showed the dilemma faced by the churchmen, and the thin line that separated an accomplice from those "forced" to do the "work." More than 30,000 Tutsis sought sanctuary at the complex in April 1994, but they found only partial peace.

Their existence was precarious. Hutu militiamen loitered near the gates, and daily extracted one or two dozen Tutsis to be murdered. They worked from lists, or, like Cambodia's Khmer Rouge, targeted anyone who wore eyeglasses—a sure sign of an "intellectual." Some victims were pointed out at random by unknowing children. One day 500 people were taken away. Those left were half-starved.

During the genocide, the Bishop of Kabgayi Thadée Nsengiyumva—the Rwanda primate who issued the Church's 1991 critical letter—was presented by the local prefect with a list of 306 names of "collaborators with the *inkotanyi*" who should be "sent to us for interrogation." It might as well have been a death warrant. Church officials say they do not know if their bishop complied, but such capitulation was standard elsewhere. One well-known case was in Kigali at the Ste. Famille cathedral, where I had seen smoky shafts of light mock hiding Tutsis. Father Wenceslas Munyeshyaka, the curate, while "protecting" the 5,000 Tutsis there, wore a flak jacket and pistol and never disguised his extremist views. Known as the "chaplain of the militiamen," he gave the killers free rein in the church to choose their targets for death. The "reverend" father was brought to France to continue his "ministry."[22] The French Catholic Church has also paid for defense lawyers to prevent his prosecution.[23]

At Kabgayi on the morning of 2 June 1994, Hutu militia and army units—sensing that their chance of slaughtering every Tutsi was slipping away with the fast-approaching rebel advance—mobbed the gates of the seminary complex. An ICRC delegate stalled the would-be killers for two hours, and a surprise RPF attack brought it under rebel control.

Days later, working behind RPF front lines, I was among the first handful of journalists to arrive at Kabgayi after it fell to the rebels. Here the genocide had failed, in the sense that only a portion were killed. But the human destruction was shocking, nonetheless.

Within the Kabgayi complex was a small school converted into a death camp, where 2,000 Tutsis were packed behind barbed wire and deprived of food. Foreign delegates of the ICRC had lived in a chapel across the road, but were afraid that publicizing the chilling conditions would jeopardize their own lives. In a barren classroom-turned-cell, one tangle of thin limbs—of people who died from lack of food—rested beneath a kitsch picture of Jesus praying that was nailed to a brick wall.

Down the dark hall, there was an auditorium turned into a makeshift chapel. Bodies lined the dark floor. In a corner opposite a tall wooden cross, a dead mother on a concrete slab cradled her dead baby girl. The flies had so far kept their distance. There appeared no chance that life could emerge, but a miracle occurred: a young rebel soldier touched the child, and her eyes reluctantly fluttered opened. Startled, we all jerked back, surprised. The soldier collected the baby in his arms and carried her outside. And there was light.

The scene outside was no less gruesome. The dead were knotted in all manner of contortion. Lying face down in a ditch, a woman grasped the root of a tree with fleshless arms, but she died in the effort and was now mortified this way. The last rays of the sun were poking through the trees, falling on this woman's being, immortalizing it for me. I couldn't tear myself away, as flies lingered on the brown skin of her arms, their shiny green-blue bottoms glinting brightly, defying anyone to save *this* cadaver. These images of Rwanda's misery evoked for me the all-too-familiar photographs of Germany's World War II death camps, in which liberating allied forces in 1945 found barely alive human skeletons and unutterable human ruin.

The sound of an artillery duel and small arms fire in the background served as reminder that to be rescued may not necessarily equal salvation. Abandoned people were dying there, at that moment, with no hope and little chance of rescue. No survivor could form tears.

The most powerful juxtaposition of the living coping with the dead was in Kabgayi's health center. Every room revealed a new horror, an almost unimaginable degradation of life. Innocent Rudasingwa was one of the few in charge of his senses enough to know that the original rebel evacuations had passed him by, and that he had finally been left alone. He was already resigned to dying there, without care. I promised to ask the ICRC to collect him, and they did the next day. When asked when he last ate, Innocent just laughed.

The bodies in the next room rotted ferociously. From his mattress he lamented to me: "We don't eat, we don't survive. You must help us . . . we are sleeping with corpses."

And he was right. The dead lay in their beds, some still pierced by now-cold intravenous needles, connected by tubes to plastic bottles in which their own blood had turned black. These chambers were crowded with swarming maggot flies. One man was sitting up—he was still alive—shrouded in his blanket and staring intently at a body decaying a few feet away. Weak with hunger, he swayed silently but couldn't turn away, because his broken leg was riven with metal stabilizing pins.

Like so many in Rwanda by that time, he must have been mad. Could the Church have prevented this suffering?

The collaboration between the "authorities" of the regime, their militias, and the Church made some holy men targets for revenge. Within days of the RPF takeover of Kabgayi, the archbishop of Kigali—Vincent Nsengiyumva, who had been a ruling party chief—two bishops (one of which was the liberal-minded Thaddée), and ten priests were murdered by rebel soldiers thirsty for revenge. The killing occurred apparently despite an offer from these churchmen to help mediate a truce. So the culprits were officially called "renegades." Few hands in Rwanda were free of blood, though these deaths seemed to some people to be a mix of divine retribution and yet more innocent lives lost.

The floor of the Kabgayi cathedral was uprooted to bury the three prelates. The funeral Mass began as the darkest moment of dusk turned to night, before a paltry congregation of a few nuns and some rebel soldiers who carried their weapons inside the cavernous church. It was one of the eeriest scenes I have ever witnessed. In the near darkness, the silence was broken only by the scrape of shovels across the hexagonal bricks of the transept floor. Rebel soldiers filled the graves beside the altar, dirt hitting coffins too deep to be lit by the feeble candlelight, with dust rising. A nun carried a simple 4-foot-tall wooden cross down the church aisle, and it was planted on the mound of earth and stone.

"Up to now we have been trying to control this emotion and reaction," said RPF Colonel Frank Mugumbage, who would later become RPF leader Paul Kagame's number two. He met us humbled, in a dingy, badly lit room near the cathedral, holding a crumpled list of the names of the slain men. Fifteen died in all. The deaths were tragic, he said, but not an unexpected consequence of ethnic war. The "renegades" who did this believed that these Hutu leaders—Roman collars or no—had organized the killing of many of their Tutsi brothers.

Surviving clergymen defended their Church, and pointed to the Kabgayi diocese as a good example in which the killing did not get out of control. Possibly 1,500 died out of 30,000—a small percentage, considering that most parishes were totally depleted. During the genocide, André himself returned to his home parish, hid some Tutsis, and made daily trips—bribing militiamen at checkpoints with beer and money—to Kabgayi to monitor the situation. Other churchmen also took risks to save Tutsis, or, like Vieko, did whatever they could to save lives.

A year after the events, André had become the apostolic administrator of the Kabgayi mission and sat reluctantly in his office, in the place of the dead senior clergy. His criticism of the old government had shifted to the new, and he was already in trouble with the new Tutsi-led regime.

"You must remember," he said, half-hidden behind the mountain of documents on his desk, "Kabgayi is the one place where there was not a mass massacre. It's true that there were many people taken from the camp, but proportionately few people were killed."

This request was for mercy, because not all priests were involved in the genocide or were silent, just as not every Hutu took up machete and screwdriver in the hunt for Tutsis. André was tired, and had many times mulled over the depth of Rwanda's moral failure. He also recognized the complexities of ascribing blame: "Please know," he said, "that if *all* Hutus were killers, then there would be *no* more Tutsis here."

"VIVE LA FRANCE!"

Stepping through a heavily wood-paneled secret door of the presidential mansion, I found myself in a narrow passageway that led to President Habyarimana's personal study. Inside, not far from the finery of the hidden chapel, stuffed hunting trophies and antlers lined the wall, interspersed with portraits of the leader standing triumphant beside bleeding game animals. There were formal meetings with important men. Photograph albums lay mangled on the floor, and files bulged with confidential documents. A small mortar had dropped through the ceiling, breaking glass and spreading debris throughout the hideaway.

Just 100 feet from the wreckage of the plane, the shelves of the study were heavy with books that might point to a man of refinement and learning. Habyarimana was unlikely to have been either. But as I glanced up, on the shelves I found the third clue to understanding how Rwanda's genocide so effortlessly engulfed a nation: the weighty, two-volume Dictionnaire de littérature de langue français. It was the bulkiest book on the top shelf and I pulled it down with difficulty. It was a personal gift in 1986 to Habyarimana from French

President François Mitterrand, just like the once-pristine Mystère-Falcon jet plane that lay mangled nearby. The relationship between the two presidents was close, and Mitterrand's son, in charge of Africa policy at the Quai d'Orsay for years, had a particular fondness for the Hutu leader.

Long before the mass killing began—and even well into it—France had infused Rwanda with weapons and intervened often to save a failing, French-speaking regime. Extremists rightly assumed that whatever the regime did— including genocide—Paris would turn a blind eye. This embossed dictionary represented that relationship, and French culpability in the genocide.

Colonial governments often look after their former colonies, but in Africa none more so than France. Though Rwanda had been under Belgian control and had received most of its post-independence military assistance from Belgium, allegiances began to shift. In 1975 a military and training agreement and French aid money helped bring Rwanda into the French "family" in Africa. And when the RPF invaded in 1990, Belgium cut off military aid, while France sent troops and filled gaps with fresh hardware. France has always clung irrationally to its supporters in Africa, and often served as the continent's gendarme. Commandos flying the *tricolore* have intervened a dozen times since the 1960s: in Chad to repel invasions from Libya, and regularly backing friendly dictatorships from Togo to Burkina Faso to Cameroon.

Under the ruse of protecting French nationals and for other so-called "humanitarian" reasons, these sacred French interests in Africa have often been protected with force. Rwanda's Hutu regime was happily sucked into this francophone orbit.

But the French interest went far beyond keeping up its reputation as African adventurers. To the French, the battle being waged was all-important and on a different plane: to preserve the gains of French culture and language against what were seen as threats from Anglo-Saxons. French conspiracy theorists saw the ghosts of a past world, believing that France was losing ground in Africa to English-speaking Rwandans, backed by Uganda and ultimately by Britain and America.

France proved to be the main bulwark of the Hutu regime. During the 1990 rebel invasion, some 4,000 Rwandan Tutsi soldiers and officers in the Ugandan army—all drawn from the ranks of exiled Tutsis—had mutinied overnight, taking their weapons and expertise to fight with the RPF across the border in Rwanda. The RPF had been planning this for years, and had infiltrated all levels of the Ugandan National Resistance Army. Despite official denials, these moves seemed to have the tacit blessing of Uganda's President Yoweri Museveni. His support for the Tutsi rebellion in Rwanda repaid Tutsis for their extensive help in the early 1980s when he was battling to win Uganda's own civil war.

That 1990 Tutsi invasion was stymied only with critical help from French combat soldiers. A leaked Rwanda government letter in fact showed that the French military had been given overall command of counterinsurgency operations.[24] When the rebels invaded a second time, in February 1993, the number of French combat soldiers and paratroopers more than doubled, to 680. Creative rotations kept the number above 1,100.[25]

Though officially only deployed to "protect" French nationals—not to intervene against the rebels—they manned artillery positions and checkpoints. Their true mission was hinted at by the French ambassador in Kigali, Jean-Philippe Marlaud, who said: "I don't expect the Rwandan army to suppress the RPF by itself." Though French advisers were observed taking part in combat operations and backing Rwanda army units with artillery, the ambassador hinted coyly to one human rights group: "When you are supposed to advise, you must advise however it is necessary."[26]

French commandos withdrew in December 1993, when UN troops were deployed to monitor the peace agreement signed the previous August. But French support never waned. Well-documented arms sales point to heavy French involvement with the Rwandan army and government, even as anti-Tutsi militias were being trained and other preparations for a mass killing were under way. France supplied heavy artillery and armored personnel carriers and kept operational six French-made Gazelle helicopters.[27]

When the president's plane was shot down, Madame Habyarimana, her family, and other *Akazu* and ruling party bigwigs were evacuated immediately to Paris by French troops. In the panic of the first days of the killing, senior Hutu officials gathered at the French Embassy and were evacuated, while all Tutsis—even Tutsi embassy staff—were left behind and killed. Upon arrival in Paris, Rwanda's First Lady received a gift of $40,000, which had been earmarked for "urgent assistance for Rwandan refugees," from the French Ministry of Cooperation.[28]

Despite the massive buildup, French training, and a field strength twice that of the rebel force, the Rwandan army fell apart as the RPF advanced. Rebel control spread across the north, the east, and by late May 1994 to the Kigali airport and Kanombe barracks on the edge of the city, bringing an end to the slaughter in those areas. Employing a strategy that will be studied at war colleges for decades, the rebels waited until the very end of their three-month advance to definitively capture Kigali, so that their precious few fighters were not tied up trying to hold the capital.

In violation of a UN Security Council arms embargo, the French came to the rescue of the francophone—and therefore brotherly—Hutu regime even during the genocide. The French secretly rushed to supply the failing army with munitions, delivering five cargo flights of weapons to Goma, Zaire, in May and June 1994, when the scale of killing was perfectly clear. The French consul in Goma said these were legitimate shipments that had been ordered and paid for long before. But subsequent shipments were facilitated by the French with Zairean soldiers assisting cross-border deliveries.[29] Still, the official line was that France was blameless: "We cannot be reproached for having armed the killers," said the French chief of staff, Admiral Lanxade. "In any case, all those massacres were committed with sticks and machetes."[30]

Mastermind of the RPF push was Maj. Gen. Paul Kagame, nemesis of the francophiles and a soft-spoken, spare man whose family fled Rwanda when he was just two years old. His ascendancy—and reputation for strict discipline and a formidable intellect—sparked the Hutu radio to demand the death of every Tutsi child, so that the "next" Paul Kagame would not survive. His long, fine features were set with a pair of eyeglasses more befitting of an academic than an unforgiving disciplinarian. With a disarmingly quiet demeanor, he was stern and rarely smiled.

Like many Tutsi exiles, Kagame fought alongside Museveni during Uganda's civil war. Kagame became Uganda's head of military intelligence, and his tenure saw a record number of treason cases. For this ruthless pursuit, he was nicknamed "Commander Pilate," after Pontius Pilate, who sentenced Jesus Christ to death.[31] Brought to bear during the RPF advance, such hardnosed discipline and ability to focus on the primary goal proved devastating to Hutu forces, which were distracted by their own involvement in mass killing.

The rebel leader had an even simpler explanation for the RPF sweep: the Tutsis had to end the slaughter of their fellow Tutsis. "Basically, every one of us was motivated. That was the main weapon of our success."[32]

French intervention to save the disintegrating Hutu army was a natural instinct for the "African Cell" in Paris and certain French commanders, especially by mid-June when defeat of the army and the extremist rump "government" was inevitable. Throughout the genocide, France had not uttered a word of condemnation. On the contrary, Paris acted sympathetically toward the genocidal interim "government" which was created by hardline *Akazu* militants whose known sole mission was annihilation of all Tutsis. Two senior extremist leaders—"foreign minister" Jérôme Bicamumpaka and CDR head Jean-Bosco Barayagwiza —were in fact welcomed to the Quai d'Orsay at the end of April and met officially with the French president.[33] Barayagwiza would later be indicted by the Arusha Tribunal for war crimes and at the time of writing was awaiting trial.

The long-standing Franco-Rwanda training deal meant that—"possibly without realizing it," Prunier notes—French troops had trained cadres of the *interahamwe* and *impuzamugambi* militias, which were the spearhead of the genocide. For this reason, in Rwanda President Mitterrand was nicknamed "Mitterahamwe." And on the back page of the 1990 issue of *Kangura* that published the Hutu Ten Commandments was a portrait of the French leader with the caption: "It is during hard times that one comes to know one's true friends."[34]

So when France's chosen allies were about to be routed—an embarrassing outcome, if nothing else, after such a deep French commitment to the regime—French forces stepped in. The genocide had been under way for two months; the bulk of the killing had already been done. But now, overnight, Rwanda's tragedy became all-important in Paris. Declarations of France's vital "humanitarian" interest took on a strident tone, in sharp contrast to the previous silence.

President Mitterrand took the offensive on 18 June: "Whatever happens, we will act. Every hour counts and it is now only a question of hours and days," he said. "Increasingly savage fighting [*sic*] is taking place and one can no longer wait . . . this is a matter of great urgency."[35]

But the belated call for "urgent" military intervention—which was backed by MSF and approved quickly by the UN Security Council—could not disguise its self-serving nature. France's history of manipulations in Rwanda and unabashed military support for so many other discredited African regimes made French troops the least welcome to all but the overjoyed Hutus. Days before the landing, RTLM was delighted, and in broadcasts told "you Hutu girls to wash yourselves and put on a good dress to welcome our French allies. The Tutsi girls are all dead so you have your chance."[36]

UN commanders in Kigali had begged for months for intervention, but they worried that the French offer to send 2,000 soldiers was ill-advised. Unamir needed neutrality even more than it needed troops. In private, Unamir commander Roméo Dallaire—a francophone Canadian himself, who was aware of the secret arms deals—was more forthright about the French mission: "If they land here to deliver their weapons to the government, I'll have their planes shot down,"[37] he said.

For the RPF, the French were forcing an end to the RPF advance, and the rebels reacted with fury. "We have never got a French body, but we hope to show you one very shortly," vowed one Tutsi officer.[38] But rebel rage did not matter to the French.

A clash sounded imminent, so I boarded a plane to the Burundi capital, Bujumbura—by chance with none other than Sam Kiley of *The Times*. We landed, filed stories, then teamed up and rented—with a guarantee to buy, if any damage was done—a very fine 4WD. In the dark we left and arrived very late in Bukavu, Zaire. The French were meant to deploy early the next morning, but it seemed we were in the wrong place. The French media had descended upon Goma to the north, but we were too exhausted to drive on. We slunk off to find rooms, then heard that there had been French soldiers, a "very small" advance team, at the local airport.

We arrived where the French had landed—the word "airport" seems too grandiose—let ourselves past the unmanned barrier, and drove toward a bright security light near a shack. The French unit was as surprised to see us as we were to see them. Their intention had been low profile, and instead here were journalists—English-speakers no less—here even before the French press had got wind of the change from the Goma plan. We arranged to deploy with them in a few hours.

The French crossed the border on 23 June 1994, and were met as liberators. They were heroes to the Hutus. The welcome party was outrageous, because it was clear that these European soldiers were saving the killers from all the demons that their violence and murder against the Tutsis had stored within their psyches. Freshly made *tricolores* waved from every hand; men chanted and danced with their machetes and bottles of beer. The crime had been committed, and now it was being absolved: they would be safe. Banners proclaimed *"Vive la France!"* and praised President Mitterrand for his mercy and care. Militia checkpoints evaporated when the convoy of troops passed. Confetti was thrown. I was jostled around by the crowd, as they tried to humor me and ply me with beer.

These Hutus had already forgotten the "lawns of flesh" they left behind, the communal evil, and skulls and machetes slick with blood. Remorseless, they could even ignore the bodies that, at that moment, were still piling up in their backyards as death squads kept up their work. For them, Rwanda was beautiful once again. But not for me.

Opération Turquoise in effect carved a Hutu "safe haven" out of southwest Rwanda. French commandos vowed to prevent the rebels from taking the area, thereby blocking complete RPF victory. The French commander declared that "no quarter" would be given if Tutsi rebels took him on, and troops did engage Tutsis on the borders of the self-declared security zone. These moves, of course, also saved the remnants of the disintegrating army and the collapsed hard-line rump "government" from total defeat. The interim "prime minister," John Kambanda, would later become the first man in history to be convicted of genocide. He pleaded guilty before the Arusha tribunal in May 1998.

Still, the French on 11 July 1994 offered any member of this quasi-government asylum in the zone. There the French kept the killers from facing justice, ensured that the vanquished forces could receive clandestine arms shipments, and that French influence with the Hutu majority would remain pervasive.

To demonstrate their "neutral" and humanitarian intentions, however, the French drove immediately to Nyarushishi Camp, one of the last havens for surviving Tutsis in the entire region. Some 8,000 people had been hiding here, their number cut down each night by militia raids. Colonel Didier Thibaut—the name the French commander gave to us—tried to calm the camp leaders, and declared "*Amahoro!* Peace!" The Tutsis responded, faces nervous and unwilling to accept that they would now be protected. Unknown to us or the Tutsi, the real name of "Thibaut" was Thauzin, a former French secret service officer and a former military adviser to President Habyarimana—an unlikely choice for a "humanitarian" mission. Thauzin was "itching to 'get at' the RPF," and so was later recalled, according to Prunier.[39]

But Thauzin knew his mission and put on a good display of appearing balanced. The Hutu prefect, Emmanuel Bagambiki—the man in charge of the camp and of the Hutu militiamen, who three days earlier had tried to organize the slaughter of every male refugee—lied to the colonel: "There are no militias here, and there never have been." Thauzin expected this lie, and I was surprised to see him pointing to his eye so that everyone could see his disbelief. One refugee explained: "Because [the prefect] knew that French soldiers would come, he wanted to kill us before. He read out the names of those to die from lists. He wanted to kill the able men at least, so that the French would take over a camp of old men and children."

Anglophobes were thick among French ranks that entered Rwanda from the Zairean town of Bukavu on 23 June. The French special forces did not sport blue berets, and in fact had stripped all insignia from their uniforms. The paratroopers were Somalia veterans of UN operations, too, who recognized my bald companion, Sam. He had helped them navigate a mined road in southern Somalia. We also had satellite telex machines with us and, apparently, by finding them in Bukavu in the middle of the night, good intelligence. So French officers came to believe that Sam was a British spy working for MI6. His name appeared on a "Wanted" list at checkpoints, and he was to be arrested if found. The situation became so tense—based solely on the imagined, yet common, fear among some senior military chiefs in Paris—that *The Times* complained to the French defense ministry.

Buoyed by the protective French presence, the *interahamwe* militia and army pressed on with their genocidal work. Far away from the main road, even farther away from the first French reconaissance teams, we came across a group walking up a hill on a mission of killing. Most of the 50 men and boys strung out along the road carried machetes, hardened clubs, and grenades. They had already decimated many Tutsi houses and carried away stacks of roof tiles and corrugated iron on their heads. Thinking we were French, they waved and smiled as we drove by, shamelessly oblivious of their daily destruction. Among them were government soldiers, "working" side by side with them to conclude the genocide.

At sunset, the warm air was thick with smoke, for nearly every one of the 200 houses in that Tutsi area was burning. Flames licked at the sky as though nothing had changed since the "Apocalypse of 1959."

Sam and I wanted to get ahead of the French deployment. But beyond the area of French *tricolores* and smiling Hutus, the land was still cursed. We traveled north toward Kibuye and the dirt road—this remote region had always been neglected by Kigali—was a treacherous gauntlet of hateful Hutu checkpoints. Some were just a couple of dusty men with machetes who had put a few stones across the track. Others were more deliberate, with gates and armed guards. It seemed that there was a new one around every corner. I counted 25 on the way to Kibuye alone. This was a final dragnet for any remaining Tutsis who might be naive enough to try to escape by road.

But even for us, passage was not easy. Luckily, a French journalist had joined us, Vincent Hugeux of *L'Express* (Paris), and at each stop Vincent would speak French and hand over our Anglo passports with his politically correct French one on top. The ruse worked, though after every checkpoint—practically in earshot of the Hutu guards—Sam would unnervingly shout: "You bestial killers! You *carnivores!*"

I didn't care much for playing Russian roulette behind the line of a genocidal government whose defeat was assured. Defeated armed men in Africa are always a bad bet for safety. And I was beginning to feel bad physically. Of course we were exhausted. The endless driving, little sleep, and then a night in the Nyarushishi camps conspired to knock us out. But the problem was something more. As we ticked off the Hutu checkpoints, I was slipping out of my senses. It was over 100 degrees, but I had the chills and wore a thick hat and all my clothes. Sam seemed to be driving fast and more and more erratically—that much wasn't a dream, until finally we whipped around a corner and sideswiped a battered army land cruiser coming the other way. We swallowed hard, for this could be disaster in such hostile territory.

I slumped over in my hat, ailing badly and fearing the worst. Vincent talked and Sam cursed. The officer was unimpressed. He wore a thin tank top and camouflage trousers, and he had scars on his chest and face attesting to a life of combat. He could easily mess us up. He wanted us to pay, and to go with him to his commanders—an absolutely no-win plan. We refused. But the result was terrifying anyway—a deal was reached, but as we drove on, the soldier reversed directions, passed us and proceeded through every check-point first, spreading bad news about us.

When we finally arrived in Kibuye, I immediately went to bed. My chills had given way to fever, so I lay naked and sweating on top of the bed. Suspecting malaria, I took a dose of something. But it was our physical situation that chilled my mind: there we were, stuck in Hutuland, with 25 hostile checkpoints on either side of us. I couldn't imagine a worse spot to be so incapacitated.

Next morning I pulled on my woolen hat in the heat, and we made a dash for Goma. I was on the verge of collapse, and when I finally got on a Red Cross flight for Nairobi, I did not have the strength to carry my cameras. At home in Nairobi I collapsed in tears, all the pressures of Rwanda that had stealthily built up rushing out in my state of weakness. I had been bitten by a malarial mosquito weeks before while camped at the sacred and abandoned Nyanza seminary in Rwanda. After many days in a Nairobi hospital, the fever of cerebral malaria passed.

Hutus flooded into their "safe haven" zone, and French soldiers winked with appreciation as shipments of fresh weapons for the beleaguered army arrived from Zaire.[40] Still, the final rout in Kigali on 1 July of the Rwanda gendarme and Presidential Guard troops reportedly sent "shock waves" throughout the French officer corps.[41] These elite Rwandan units were trained by French instructors at President Mitterrand's request in 1990. In Paris this was "defeat by the Anglo-Saxons," and one senior French officer warned: "The worst is yet to come. Those bastards will go all the way to Kinshasa now."[42] Nostradamus himself could not have foretold better.

French forces announced to the UN that they had disarmed the defeated army units in the zone. The weapons, they said, had been handed over to Zairean authorities. The extremist radio was told to stop its broadcasts from within the zone, and so moved across the border to Bukavu, from which it continued to incite Hutus to kill Tutsis.

Though French troops compiled their own lists of people accused of taking part in the killing, they were never given to the UN or the Criminal Tribunal set up to try war crimes. Though France considers itself the "home" of human rights, Paris has refused to allow its soldiers to testify before any court, and accuses the Rwanda tribunal of dispensing "spectacle justice." French troops withdrew in mid-August 1994, but left behind one weapons cache of 50 assault rifles and some machine guns for militiamen and soldiers "who remained." UN troops then took control, but the zone was a source of unrest for months.

Massacres of Tutsis barely slowed in areas where the French deployed. There were no trucks to rescue the handful of surviving Tutsis in the country-side—the French hardware was military only—and so the killing continued when it could find a target, by groups like that large death squad marching up the hill, machetes in hand. By the time French troops arrived, however, most signs of the carnage were gone, buried or washed from floors. But on closer inspection, I could see that sloppy cleaning had left dark trails of blood on walls or dripping down the sides of church rostrums.

And when the slaughter did finally ease, it wasn't because of the French: "It's not out of kindness," one Hutu had told me, "but because there are so few Tutsis left alive."

French officers seemed amazed to find one mass grave after another at churches, stadiums, and behind schools. Inspecting the remains of one orgy, I saw a genuinely shocked Frenchman turn away, exclaiming: "And these [Hutus] are supposed to be the *good* savages."

SIXTEEN

GENOCIDE DENIED

The flow of blood is an arresting spectacle. The color alone demands attention and calls to mind violent acts of piercing or cutting and the shocking sameness of all living creatures beneath the skin.

—Barbara Ehrenreich, *Blood Rites*

Rhetoric comes easily about ensuring that genocide never strikes again. Full-blown genocide doesn't happen very often, and what could be more noble—as a politician and as a human being—than to stand against the systematic decimation of entire strains of our species?

For more than half a century, as it should have been and still is, marking the evils of the World War II holocaust against the Jews has been sound politics. That attempted genocide still stirs deep emotion. As much as we might prefer to forget the haunting details of systematic slaughter—the images of long pit graves stacked with stick-starved Jewish corpses, of gas chambers and rooms stuffed with hundreds of thousands of shoes and shorn hair—how can we expunge them?

Inaugurating the Holocaust Museum in Washington, D.C., in April 1993, President Clinton spoke with full oratorical force about the need to "contemplate its meaning for us," and to "bind one of the darkest lessons in history to the hopeful soul of America." Then he laid down the standard. The evil was "incontestable," he declared. "But as we are its witness, so we must remain its adversary in the world in which we live." The president reserved special praise for "those known and those never to be known, who manned the thin line of righteousness, who risked their lives to save others, accruing no advantage to themselves."[1]

A year later, President Habyarimana's airplane was shot down over Kigali. Within days the United States—and that part of the Western world that had coddled a belief in its own goodwill and desire for justice—was faced with the start of the first indisputable genocide since World War II.

Despite more than 50 years of conditioning—and so much rhetoric from high-minded speech writers—the world unconscionably stood by as Rwandan Hutus began to kill Tutsis. There were many warning signs, and Western and UN leaders were aware of them. Genocide must be organized to be effective, and in Rwanda that took time and left many traces.

But Washington feared "another Somalia," and so the first instinct was denial that a genocide was even occurring—that would have legally required action to stop it. The second instinct was to disengage entirely, as the US sought to slash UN troop numbers. The third move—at least on the part of American policy-makers—was to bully any other nation from acting.

Ignored and uncensured, the killers carried their relentless work until the genocide had burned itself out or was snuffed out by the advance of Tutsi rebels.

UN commanders in Kigali were convinced that decisive action on their part with more troops would have stanched the killing, if not ended it—but none would ever come. General Roméo Dallaire, the Unamir commander in Kigali, was distraught: "The biggest crime of all," he said, "is that we weren't able to keep it from happening."

Evidence of a germinating, large-scale outburst of violence was accumulating in the months prior to 6 April 1994. Besides the hyperbole of the local newspapers and the government's lethargy in implementing the peace deal with the Tutsi RPF, there were signs that the "weapons free zone" of Kigali was becoming quite the opposite. Spurred on by *Akazu* militants, the regime attempted to bolster its weapons stocks. In the first months of 1994, Unamir learned of four secret planeloads of arms and intervened. It placed one shipment under joint supervision to prevent its distribution to the army and stopped delivery of three others.[2] In public, Unamir said nothing about the dangerous, organized buildup.

Officially, Dallaire felt his hands were tied by a limited, peace-monitoring mandate. This was supposed to be a straightforward mission, not unlike that of the ever-bored UN monitors in Cyprus and the Golan Heights. With a strength of 2,500, Unamir was small and with light arms to be used only in self-defense. In the early days of their arrival in November 1993, Unamir troops enjoyed barbeques with Rwandans at their stadium base and were well-respected. By some, they were even trusted.

But Kigali was was getting more violent, and political and ethnic killings of Tutsis were becoming *de rigueur*. As signs began to point toward something more serious, Dallaire's limited mandate began to infuriate him. "We had information on the location of weapons, training camps, information on the distribution of arms," said a senior UN official. Dallaire wanted to get the arms, but "he was dissuaded, he was instructed, he was cautioned: it was not in his mandate."[3]

Possibly the most critical example of how the UN let information of vital importance slip unnoticed—or at least unacted upon—through the system came on 11 January 1994. Tipped off by a high-level source in the regime about the plan to rid Rwanda of Tutsis, Dallaire sent an urgent fax to peacekeeping headquarters in New York.

Titled "Request for Protection of Informant," it made clear that his informant had been asked to "register all Tutsi in Kigali. He suspects it is for their extermination. Example he gave is that in twenty minutes his personnel could kill up to a thousand Tutsis." The source offered to show Unamir troops a weapons cache "tonight—if we gave him the following guarantee. He requests that he and his family (his wife and four children) be placed under our protection."

Though the weight of recent history in Rwanda—of periodic mass killings for nearly 40 years—alone should have convinced any UN bureaucrat in New York that a real "extermination" was possible, Dallaire added details of another operation.

This example left no doubt about Hutu extremist resolve. Dallaire's informant said he had been charged with organizing the killing of opposition leaders and Unamir troops at an official function. "They hoped to provoke the RPF . . . and provoke a civil war," Dallaire had written. "Deputies were to be assassinated upon entry or exit from parliament. Belgian troops were to be provoked and if Belgian soldiers resorted to force a number of them were to be killed and thus guarantee a Belgian withdrawal."[4]

The UN chief of peacekeeping was Kofi Annan—today the UN secretary general—who was still smarting from the disastrous events in Somalia in 1993. On Annan's letterhead, his deputy Iqbal Riza sent back a remarkable response: any action to be taken on this information, such as protecting the informant, was "beyond the mandate entrusted to Unamir." President Habyarimana—whose regime was intimately involved—was to be alerted to "these activities."[5] Dallaire later checked out the arms cache details and found them accurate.[6] "Serious mistakes were made in dealing with the cable," an independent UN inquiry found five years later: "It is incomprehensible . . . that not more was done to follow up."

When the genocide was triggered three months after the cable—as my colleagues and I were stuck in rebel territory, trying to reach Kigali—one act poisoned the Unamir experience that would serve as the catalyst for a UN retreat. That defining moment almost exactly mirrored the aborted plan divulged by Dallaire's source. The day after the president's plane crash, the moderate Hutu Prime Minister Agathe Uwilingiyamana sought protection from Rwanda's Presidential Guard, which had come to kill her. Ten Belgian UN troops were deployed to protect her, but they were confronted by Hutu soldiers who ordered them to lay down their arms. Three blue berets were injured immediately, but when the Belgian squad radioed back for instructions, they were told to comply and negotiate. Their Achilles tendons were cut so they couldn't run, and the Belgian soldiers—all of them privates—were castrated and died choking on their genitalia. The prime minister was killed.

The Belgian UN contingent—which served as the logistical and military backbone to Unamir—was enraged but powerless. The force wanted revenge, so was locked up for a time in an airport hangar to control their emotion. And beside their own crisis, there was a constant flow of Tutsis and moderate Hutus moving to UN bases everywhere, looking for protection. Nothing could be done. "We can't do anything for the civilians. We must stay neutral," one Belgian officer told me just days after the murders of his soldiers. He was anguished by the mandate, too. "I've seen women and children massacred there, in front of our compound, but we cannot intervene."

Dallaire chafed at this mandate, and tried to expand it. His job was complicated by the resumption of the civil war just days after the president's assassination. The RPF perforated the UN demilitarized zone in the north and marched toward Kigali to stop the massacres and "restore order."

Dallaire wanted more troops. It was clear to commanders on the ground that the risks for blue helmets in Rwanda would be far less than in the former Yugoslavia, for example, where bold Serb soldiers had routinely violated UN-declared "safe havens" in Bosnia and humiliated European UN troops by disarming them and taking them hostage. And it would be less dangerous than Somalia, where the UN had chosen an enemy and waged a war against him.

On the contrary, in Rwanda Hutu extremists were often just young men with machetes or ill-disciplined soldiers. Troops would not need to intervene *per se*, UN officers argued in vain. They would only need to provide a protective foreign "presence" around churches and stadiums where Tutsis had already begun gathering. None of the pitfalls of peacekeeping in the Balkans were likely to occur in Rwanda, so the strategy there may well have worked. The equation was simple: the number of lives saved would be a function of the number of soldiers deployed. With genocide catching fire all around him, Dallaire asked for 8,500 more peacekeepers. He was told by New York to "be more modest in his requests."[7]

UN officers were trapped between their moral compulsion to act and their professional commitment as soldiers to follow orders. "There is nothing preventing us from going any place to save lives," said Brig. Gen. Henry Anyidoho of Ghana, the deputy Unamir commander. "There are people dying who could be saved. That's why we are crying for more force to do it."[8]

For anyone who had been to Somalia and Rwanda during times of conflict, the only similarity seemed to be that their violence occurred on the same continent. Otherwise, there were few parallels: in Somalia there was anarchy, while in Rwanda tight political control was inescapable; in Somalia, as we have seen, the UN created its own war and and lost, while in Rwanda, as we will see, saving lives could often have been achieved by simply being present.

But in Washington, as the genocide surged ahead, a dangerous and telling link between Somalia and Rwanda appeared all too obvious. Their equation was simple: UN peacekeepers to Somalia in crisis equaled failure. Therefore, UN peacekeepers to Rwanda in crisis would also equal failure. Then add another political dimension unique to Washington: never mind the "We hate genocide" platitudes, at stake also was losing no more face after Somalia, and even how action or not might play in upcoming midterm elections.

Rwanda's agony was compounded by an unfortunate coincidence: Americans had made, just days before Habyarimana's plane was shot down, their final retreat from Somalia. That souring experience left them disparaging about policing the New World Order. The result was that US policy-makers drew the wrong conclusions from the Somalia debacle—that corrective intervention in Africa was impossible. Rwanda, shamefully, paid the price.

Fearing entanglement again in Africa, or of even footing the bill for another UN operation, the Clinton administration ruled out sending US troops, took the lead in cutting back Unamir, and then in blocking the deployment of *any* other force that might stem the violence. Instead of pushing to grant UN troops authority to actively protect civilians, the US lobbied strenuously to withdraw them altogether. The bosses of some Security Council ambassadors received telephone calls from Washington, requesting that they "lay off" the Rwanda issue, and certainly shy away from using the word "genocide."

As a result, among those instructed to "lay off" was Karel Kovanda, the Czech envoy who sat on the Security Council at the time. He had lost family members in the Holocaust, and so the hands-off policy was troubling. "When you come from central Europe, one has a sense of what holocausts are about," he told *Frontline*. "You recognize one when you see one. Here it was happening again."[9]

To save face, Belgian officials wanted more international backing to stay in Rwanda—or that everyone should pull out. Washington made it quite clear that they would be "on their own" if they decided to stay. Two weeks after the killing began, the Security Council yielded to American wishes: remarkably, Unamir was slashed from 2,500 to a skeleton force of 270. A key part of this "failure of political will," noted one former UN human rights official, was the "US determination to impose its interpretation of the lessons in Somalia on the Security Council."[10] That decision, a UN-appointed inquiry found later, would "always be difficult to explain."

Rwanda was the first ever case in which the UN responded to a crisis by reducing its commitment. Flabbergasted, UN troops on the ground prepared to leave. For the Belgians, who had been sheltering 2,000 Tutsis on their base at the Don Bosco school in Kigali, the withdrawal demonstrated how important their very presence could be. Hutu militias had been menacing the Tutsis, and drove by, threatening the Tutsis. Belgian Captain Luc Lumiere described an odd request: "They were afraid to be murdered by machetes. . . . They said, 'Please, we ask to be shot down [instead] by your machine gun.'"[11] When the Belgians pulled out, those Tutsis were slaughtered.

There was little opposition to UN dithering from member states, partly because the Security Council received inaccurate reports from its unabashedly pro-government envoy, Jacques-Roger Booh-Booh of Cameroon. Despite increasingly accurate press coverage of the systematic nature of atrocities against Tutsis, and Unamir's well-informed intelligence officers, he repeatedly described the killing as a free-for-all such that Boutros-Ghali's staff issued "blurred, sanitized summaries . . . depicting mutual and chaotic killing."[12]

"I have no doubt that Boutros-Ghali had complete confidence in Booh-Booh, and that Booh-Booh had complete confidence in Habyarimana," recalled Kovanda. "He sided with the dictator. He wasn't objective, he didn't report well enough. And when [Boutros-Ghali] got conflicting reports from Booh-Booh and Dallaire, he took Booh-Booh's."[13]

The acting legal counsel, Ralph Zacklin, had made clear: "What is happening in Rwanda I think on any definition amounts to genocide."[14] The UN, however, followed the American cue: on 30 April the Security Council condemned the violence in Rwanda using all the same language of the Genocide Convention, but rejected the word "genocide" itself to avoid its own legal obligation to prevent it.

The UN even thinned its criticism to the point of calling the genocide a "humanitarian crisis." Such a trivialization enraged many, including MSF. One report clarified the depth of UN cynicism: "Why not rename Kristallnacht a 'window crisis' and the policy of rape which occurred in Bosnia a 'gynecological crisis?'"[15]

Extremist Hutus had planned on such international indifference, just as they had banked on Unamir leaving if they killed a few Belgian troops. Referring to Somalia, Boutros-Ghali called it the "American syndrome."[16] These actions sent the strong and unmistakable signal to Rwanda's killers that they could act with impunity.

State Department officials had begun to use the word "genocide" among themselves to describe events in Rwanda just four or five days after the killing began, "but they didn't tell anybody else," said a journalist who has investigated the US role.[17] On 23 April, a secret State Department intelligence report on Rwanda used the word "genocide."[18]

And at the end of April, the lack of misunderstanding in Washington was made clear, perhaps not deliberately, when President Clinton appealed vaguely to Rwandan "leaders"—not to the government soldiers, or to the Hutu militiamen who paraded at checkpoints with shirts dried cardboard-stiff with the blood of their victims—"to recognize their common bonds of humanity."[19] A 5 May editorial in *The Washington Post* noted the growing cost of doing nothing: "As terrified UN peacekeepers evacuated Rwanda, other nations consoled themselves with the hope that the butchers would grow weary of the killing. This once seemed to us a likely prospect too, but it does no more. The savagery continues unabated. Anguished international onlookers, including Americans, now comprehend more fully the awful consequences of standing on the sidelines."[20]

But the unsavory framework for Washington's dillydallying was Somalia, and its legal fallout Presidential Decision Directive 25, which imposed strict conditions upon any peacekeeping operation before it could be given US approval. Signed into law by President Clinton on 5 May, it was invoked immediately so that the administration could stymie a mid-May UN troop deployment plan with financial and political obstacles. Britain and France eventually prevailed over US objections to sending a new UN force of 5,500 blue helmets, but the Clinton administration ensured that the deployment would proceed at a snail's pace.[21] As a result, not one soldier or armored vehicle arrived before the genocide and civil war were over two months later.

"The crocodiles in the Kagera River and the vultures over Rwanda have seldom had it so good," Kovanda scolded the Security Council. "They are feeding on the bodies of thousands upon thousands . . . who have been hacked to death by what has turned out to be a most vicious regime."[22] Recalling those moments later, the Czech envoy said: "To my mind, the whole Security Council demonstrated its incompetence, irrelevance, and impotence."[23]

Then-US Ambassador to the UN Madeleine Albright was unmoved by criticism of the American tactics and her own role in opposing Boutros-Ghali's troop request, despite the urgent circumstances: "Sending a UN force into the maelstrom of Rwanda without a sound plan of operations would be folly," she said. Anything else would be "pie in the sky."[24]

"We thought it was important to send a strong signal that the international community cared [*sic*] and was determined to do something," she said on 19 May. "But we felt that a phased operation here was more important."[25]

Boutros-Ghali didn't see it that way. "It was one thing for the United States to place conditions for its own participation in UN peacekeeping," he wrote in his memoir. "It was something else entirely for the United States to attempt to impose its conditions on other countries. Yet that is what Madeleine Albright did. . . . The behavior of the Security Council was shocking; it meekly followed the United States' lead in denying the reality of the genocide."

To the UN's top diplomat, that contrast was sharp: The US had spent $1 billion a day on defense during the Cold War, he said, but "had now prevailed upon other governments to withhold the relatively trivial sums to stop genocide."[26]

Philip Gourevitch, in his book about Rwanda, *We Wish to Inform You That Tomorrow We Will Be Killed With Our Families*, notes Albright's role: "Her name is rarely associated with Rwanda, but ducking and pressuring others to duck, as the death toll leapt from thousands to tens of thousands to hundreds of thousands, was the absolute low point in her career as a stateswoman"[27]

To limit American responsibility and avoid the moral pressure to act, US officials played word games. They were instructed not to use the term "genocide" in reference to Rwanda, other than to admit that "acts of genocide may have occurred."[28] This wan admission was calculated to absolve the US of its obligations to act as spelled out in the Genocide Convention. "In order to liberate mankind from such an odious scourge, international cooperation is required," the convention states. Article 1 could not be clearer: all signatories "confirm that genocide, whether committed in time of peace or in time of war, is a crime under international law which they undertake to prevent and punish."[29]

Still, in Washington the obfuscation was obvious, and reminded me of the twisted logic we were expected to believe about "successful" operations in Somalia. State Department spokeswoman Christine Shelly was asked by reporters to clarify the American position, which hadn't changed publicly even by 10 June 1994.

"We have every reason to believe that acts of genocide have occurred," she said.

"How many 'acts of genocide' does it take to make genocide?" a reporter asked.

"That's just not a question that I'm in a position to answer," she replied.[30]

For those with their eyes open to the systematic nature of Rwanda's bloodshed, such a careful construction was pure politics. "That was strictly an American issue," Ambassador Kovanda noted. "I don't recall anybody else insisting on 'acts of genocide' instead of 'genocide.'"[31]

Noting that China also had reservations, Antonio Pedauye, the number two diplomat at the UN for Spain, who also held a seat on Council at the time, pointed out: "What's the difference between 'acts of genocide' and 'genocide'? It's splitting theological or legal hairs. It's exactly the same thing."[32]

Fed up by the mounting criticism, US Secretary of State Warren Christopher finally admitted the obvious: "If there is any particular magic in calling it genocide, I have no hesitancy in saying that."[33]

But by that time, on the ground—as I and others began to examine the extraordinary scenes of mass killing, the incontrovertible evidence filling our nostrils—Rwandan Tutsis had given up any hope of outside help. The Hutu killers had banked on that, too. The RPF had advanced south to seize power and end the killing of their Tutsi brothers. No one else would do the job. Still, when the UN force was finally approved to "protect" civilians and secure relief routes, the majority of the 800,000 who would die had died, and the UN and Americans had yet to once use the word "genocide" in any official context.

Not surprisingly, such a late deployment was interpreted by the RPF as a ruse to deprive the Tutsi rebels of a hard-fought victory. They found it a particularly galling 11th-hour measure—a fair enough assessment. At one meeting, Kagame told us of his disappointment: "When genocide has been carried out almost with impunity, and when it is near completion, *then* people talk about intervention," he said at a hilltop base in northern Rwanda. "This is out of context, and will only protect the people responsible for the genocide."

One American "plan" was to keep any new UN troops outside Rwanda, by creating safe havens along the border areas and to avoid any entangling involvement at all. No one but the rebels seemed interested in stopping the mass killing. Kagame said the UN had ample opportunity to intervene when the crisis began, but now the RPF "have done most of the work for the UN."

Philip Gourevitch, the author and *New Yorker* writer, noted that US policy seemed to have achieved its aims. "We talk about Rwanda as a failure of US policy—a failure to intervene, a failure to recognize what was going on, and a failure to take action to stop genocide," he told *Frontline*. "But if you look at the Clinton administration's approach to it throughout the entire period, what you really see is that it was actually a success of a policy not to intervene. It wasn't a failure to act. The decision was *not* to act. And at that we succeeded greatly."[34]

The effect of that decision was all too evident in May 1994, when the few journalists in Kigali were forced to stay at the Meridien Hotel, which was well-placed on the rebel front line. RPF trenches and ditches branched out left and right from the main parking lot. At night from our balconies we watched the flash from the rounds of Tutsi snipers in the next building. The fighting made movement risky. In our hot-wired "stolen" cars, fueled by gas siphoned from abandoned vehicles, we could cross to the government side of the city only with a UN convoy. But even mundane journeys along the front—such as turning out of the hotel parking lot—were dangerous.

With our vehicle clearly labeled "PRESSE," I had driven often through one roundabout that straddled the line. But this time—with Peter Smerdon, a canny former Beirut bureau chief for Reuters as my passenger—a truce inexplicably failed. Turning into the roundabout, there were two bursts of gunfire—maybe ten rounds—from government sniper positions hidden in thick trees. Beyond the circle another burst seemed to come from inside and fumes enveloped us. The spare gas tank had been pierced—thankfully not by hot-burning tracer rounds—and Peter jettisoned it as we raced away, hunkering down in our armored vests behind the dashboard. Another round had ricocheted off the tire rim, and still another had carved its way through the back door and lodged in the chassis, four inches from Peter's rear.

It was a breach of truce that no one would notice, in a war that few seemed willing to stop, that was broken as we traveled to *peace talks* to end a genocide that few would ever understand.

For those who argue that Rwanda had become a "maelstrom" that should be left to itself—from which extracting UN troops was a top priority and sending more was out of the question—consider the heroic story of Captain Mbaye Diagne of Senegal. I had seen the captain from time to time around the Unamir headquarters. He had a calm face and was tall and unassuming. I heard him laugh a couple times too, a likable laugh just out of the corner of my hearing.

But the first time I got to know of the captain's real history was during an emergency: his emergency, a government checkpoint on the edge of the front line in Kigali. I raced down to a checkpoint with some other UN officers. The captain had stopped at the checkpoint, but before he could move on, a mortar shell land landed precisely on the center of his roof—it was a fluke shot and could not have been more accurate.

The captain was killed instantly, his blood coagulating thickly on the front seat. Within three hours his body bag, draped in a UN flag, had been carried to a plane. Soldiers wept, and General Dallaire wiped his eyes. But the captain's legacy had been firmly set in the minds of his comrades. It turned out that this one peacekeeper had singlehandedly saved the lives of scores of Rwandans.

"He was probably the bravest man here," Gregory Alex, a UN official who had shared many missions with him, told me. "He risked his life every day. He saved at least 100 people himself." The captain had saved one family early in the massacres by carrying them through 24 Hutu barricades. He saved the lives of Rwandan UN staff members, when UN and foreign troops were ordered to save only white foreigners. And he reportedly saved the prime minister's children after she was assassinated, by hiding them in his room for five days. According to President Clinton's remarks at the opening of the Holocaust Museum, Diagne in Rwanda must qualify as one of "those never to be known, who manned the thin line of righteousness."

Even in death he saved the lives of several Hutu soldiers at the checkpoint, who were the original targets: his car shielded them from the blast. The captain was killed less than 24 hours after the RPF and rump government forces held their first face-to-face peace talks—the same talks that Peter and I had rushed to get to, when we were shot up.

The lesson from the 100 people saved by the captain, and of the thousands more Rwandans who were saved by the tiny UN presence on the ground, made a strong case for more UN troops. And it made a strong countercase against those who, by not sending more UN troops in the first days and weeks of the killing, may be deemed partly responsible for lives of an uncountable number of Rwandans who almost certainly would have been saved with the simplest troop presence. Choking back tears years later, while testifying before the International Criminal Tribunal for Rwanda in February 1998, Dallaire said that with a well-armed force of 5,000 men of the proper mandate "the UN could have stopped the slaughter of hundreds of thousands of Rwandans." Filled with emotion and with his voice breaking, he said: "It seems . . . inconceivable that one can watch . . . thousands of people being . . . massacred . . . every day in the media . . . and remain passive." On the ground, he said, "It was an unimaginable frustration."[35]

The accomplishments of the few hundred Unamir troops still on the ground were impressive enough: some 12,000 people were under their nominal "protection" in Kigali alone. Hundreds of Tutsis were spared at the Hotel des Mille Collines, thanks to ten but sometimes just one blue helmet there. Weeks into the genocide, Unamir negotiated tricky "refugee exchanges," in which Tutsis in militia areas were traded for Hutus stuck in rebel areas. These were never easy: in early May, the first was aborted because the convoy of Tutsis was stopped at roadblocks, and militiamen dragged some Tutsis off trucks. One boy had been shot in the leg, and seven others were slashed with pangas.

During the next convoy from the Mille Collines at the end of May, I watched Tutsis file out of the hotel after almost two months. These were ranking people in Rwandan society, and all on the Hutu Power's "Most Wanted List," so they were dangerous cargo. Their faces were far more gaunt than I remembered them—the hotel had been off-limits for weeks—and they were terrified. Hostile government soldiers were everywhere, watching but not acting while the UN was there. I dashed into the hotel, and saw that the swimming pool—once a pleasant respite for me years ago, and later the sur-real backdrop to the first days of killing—was only half-full. A woman was filling a jug for drinking water from it, despite the brine.

In case of an emergency, the UN planned to call in "reinforcements"—such as they could muster—with the radio call sign "football kick." The ICRC hospital halfway along the route was put on standby in case of casualties. The Tutsis clustered in the backs of canvas-covered trucks. They clapped when the convoy left the hotel gates, and then we roared past *interahamwe* check-points, swerving to get past chanting killers who jeered with knives, rifles, and grenades. Ten miles west of Kigali in RPF territory, they unloaded with smiles and cheers. Some 480 people were saved that day. UN commanders could only dream of doing more.

Outside Rwanda, the *cri de coeur* from the victims was officially ignored, though this heroic work was simple proof that the presence of more troops—or even the original 2,500 blue berets, if they hadn't been pulled out—could have saved many more. Some 30,000 Tutsis were in Kigali alone, hiding like Alex Bizimungu, singly or in groups, cowering, waiting for protection or for rebel victory, or at least an easier end than one at the cutting edge of a machete.

The conversion came in mid-July, for those who had shied away from action during the actual genocide. One million Hutus—killers and innocents alike—had been ordered out of Rwanda by their local leaders, when their defeat was imminent. Overnight, the crisis changed from genocide to refugees.

The intensity of suffering was unmistakable in graphic television images, and Rwanda's crisis finally pricked the conscience of the West into action. During the slaughter not even a handful of relief agencies had worked in Rwanda. The ICRC and later MSF were the only notable exceptions. But in eastern Zaire, the sudden refugee problem was seen as simply that. Within weeks some 70 UN and relief agencies were battling for space in one of the most remote, lawless places on the continent. Around the world in banks, post offices, and newspapers, relief agencies appealed for funds to aid the suf-fering Rwanda "victims" piling up in Zaire. Like the columns of refugees, donations flooded in.

Spurred by the heart-rending footage—remember that there was virtually no "live action" footage of the genocide itself—Americans also finally demanded action. The US spearheaded the international aid effort with a $500 million commitment to bring water, airdrop food, and deliver 20 million rehydration sachets and other relief supplies. Many thought that they were helping victims of the genocide, and the Clinton administration may have believed this, too. Certainly, after doing nothing during the killing—or even less than nothing—"Operation Sustain Hope" salved many consciences.

The massacres were rarely mentioned, and Washington mounted the biggest emergency airlift ever. The chairman of the Joint Chiefs of Staff, Gen. John Shalikashvili, proclaimed that the mobilization was "a race against time," with every minute tolling another death in the camps.[36] Clinton said that the refugees had "now created what could be the world's worst humanitarian crisis in a generation," and then added this interesting line: "From the beginning of this tragedy, the United States has been in the forefront of the international community's response." US officials also claimed to have provided 40% of "all the relief aid in Rwanda," though only Rwandans *outside* the country—the killers—received any of that help.

The sudden change of heart resembled almost word-for-word France's too strident justification for Opération Turquoise one month before, when President Mitterrand declared that "every hour counts." Analysis of that French response could in many ways apply to the American one: the French had been "trying to glorify the Turquoise intervention in the hope of washing off any genocidal bloodspots in the baptismal waters of 'humanitarian' action," noted the French historian Gérard Prunier.[37]

And there was another remarkable turnaround. After so much American bullying of the UN Security Council to avoid any military entanglement during the massacres, President Clinton called on the UN to "move as quickly as possible to deploy an international peacekeeping force to stabilize Rwanda and persuade refugees to return home."[38]

Rhetoric meant to apologize for inaction during genocide seems to come as easily as rhetoric about preventing it. "Never Again!" was once the easy-to-mouth chorus, but Rwanda's genocide was the test case, and all that principled talk proved to be hot air.

When Kofi Annan—who had let the first warning cable slip across his desk in January 1994—visited Rwanda as secretary general of the UN in May 1998, he admitted that "the world failed Rwanda at that time of evil" and "must deeply repent this failure." He made no mention of the warning cable, nor that—claiming UN diplomatic immunity—he had refused to allow Gen. Dallaire to testify before a Belgian Senate commission that probed the Belgian soldiers' deaths in 1997. Instead, he said: "In the face of genocide, there can be no standing aside, no looking away, no neutrality."[39] When Annan visited a memorial site, where a table was laid with skulls, a survivor berated him for piling "evil upon evil."[40]

For those on hand during the genocide of 1994, that view is widespread. A UN official at the time recognized the shameful precedent set by letting the crime slip away. "The fact that the world can watch 800,000 people die is a failure for us," Charles Petrie said. "What credibility will we have? In Rwanda we are in danger of losing our souls."

But has that lesson been learned? A comparison to the impact of the holocaust film *Schindler's List* is instructive, says Alain Destexhe, the former head of MSF, who asked: "How many of those who wept during Spielberg's film shed tears for the victims of the recent massacres in Bosnia or Rwanda?"[41]

Another pilgrimage of apology was made by President William Jefferson Clinton, who arrived in March 1998 for a three and one-half hour visit. The engines of Air Force One were never turned off, and the president didn't leave the airport. Clinton used the 'G'-word with abandon. Genocide: it was the elusive word that didn't publicly exist in the lexicon of the Clinton administration until virtually all of Rwanda's 800,000 victims had died. But in his speech he used the word 12 times, and said he was contrite.

"We did not act quickly enough after the killing began," he said. "We did not immediately call these crimes by their rightful name: genocide."[42]

The president spoke not far from where Unamir had paid its last respects to Captain Mbaye Diagne, the day that brave African soldier was killed and bundled back home in a body bag, wrapped in a blue UN flag. The captain had lost his life, manning the "thin line of righteousness," and his actions saved the lives of 100 others.

But regarding Rwanda's genocide, neither William Jefferson Clinton nor Madeleine Albright can make a similar boast.

"It may seem strange to you here, especially the many of you who lost members of your family," Clinton said, a look of practiced atonement on his face. And then he broke from his script and delivered a most severe indictment[43]: "But all over the world there were people like me, sitting in offices, day after day after day, who did not fully appreciate the depth and the speed at which you were being engulfed . . . "

SEVENTEEN

IN PERPETUUM

Gorillas are much more peace-loving than men.

—Jean-Bosco Bizumurenyi,
Rwandan gorilla-tracker

The thunder erupted out of the dark camp, shaking the earth at night with the sound of 250,000 refugees running, screaming, their minds shot through with fear. Trouble was expected at the new refugee camp in Tanzania in May 1994. This ocean of Hutus had fled Rwanda only two days before, and were afraid in the black of night that Tutsi gangs might attack, seeking revenge for the genocide taking place on the other side of the border. Our small compound—protected by only two strings of barbed wire and a length of twine—was at risk. Aid workers had warned us before they left for the night that, with 20 tons of undistributed relief food stacked in piles beside our tents, we were also a target.

Even in daylight, tempers were explosive. With some 300,000 people, Benaco was one of the largest refugee camps in the world. The Hutus fought over chunks of raw meat and fistfuls of gruel and rioted with sticks, stones, and corn cobs. They had fled before the advance of Tutsi rebels, and at the border they dropped their implements of death. Thousands of machetes, hoes, knives, cudgels, screwdrivers and assault rifles—the tools of a genocide, some still bloodied from the hectic pace of killing—were left behind in piles.

Crossing the border bridge and looking down, the refugees could see the result. Swollen corpses swept over the Rusumo Falls by the dozen, their ragged clothes falling off as they caught in rock eddies, black skin sometimes bleached a pasty white. I, too, could not forget this cascade. Tutsis had tried to flee south into Burundi, but were kept back by Hutu soldiers. When captured, their legs were chopped off below the knee—literally making them less tall, to be more like the Hutu—and dumped into the river, which flowed northwards.

One senior official had declared as early as 1992 that Tutsis "belong in Ethiopia and we are going to find them a shortcut to get there" by throwing them in the river. "Know that the person whose throat you do not cut now will be the one who will cut yours," declared the vice president of the ruling party. "We must act. Wipe them all out!"[1] Relative to the scale of the crime, this jetsam was an insignificant number of dead. But Lake Victoria caught the noxious effluvium from this earthly River Styx, with more than 40,000 corpses poisoning the fish and washing up on sandy shores.

Not all the floating flesh had been cast away in anger, however. "On the banks of rivers, some parents threw their children into the water to spare them death with a machete," noted African Rights. "It was, in the words of one survivor, 'a last gesture of love.'"[2]

But the violence followed the refugees across the border. Some did a brisk business sharpening machetes on stones along the main camp road. They were used by "butchers" at makeshift abattoirs where fly-covered meat and pink-white hides were on display, blood trickling into fetid pools below. There was the thud of well-practiced hands cleaving meat and shearing bone. I was reminded with revulsion that these same Hutu hands—with machetes busy against Tutsi flesh instead of soup meat—were responsible for the slaughter.

In the first days, the refugees in the Benaco camp in Tanzania exhibited a particular, almost frightened gentleness. They had left Rwanda in droves, quickly, and then arrived slowly and silently, like a lava flow reaching the limit of its molten life.

But soon tension rose, and murders occurred. One woman accused of being a witch died due—the post-mortem said—to "cranial encephalic trauma," ironically the same cause of death at many Rwanda massacre sites. On the forehead of one slain Tutsi sympathizer, the words *Vive Kigali* were carved with a knife, in fond "remembrance" of the decimation of Tutsis there.

So I slept fitfully on that moonless night when I was there—protected only by two strips of barbed wire and a length of twine. And when a murderous shrieking engulfed the camp—there were no police, no authority at all, and no lights in this wilderness—it sounded to me like demons exorcising themselves. Was this the sound of the killing of Rwandans, the noise now of all the lives taken in the massacres, the accumulated roaring release of so many souls?

The camp roused immediately, as the noise of the thundering "stampede" spread down the two-mile length of the camp with an increasing cacophony. I rushed out of the tent to see that smoldering cooking fires amidst the invisible human sea of refugees were being stoked to create sinister bonfires, as menacing as an encircling enemy army.

I thought I had known fear, and I had let my imagination get the better of me in Uganda, listening to the first BBC reports of Rwanda's killing. That was a mental game. I could have just gone home. But in this camp, the sensation was immediately overwhelming, a deep, mind-altering fear. And now in this nowhere camp, engulfed in screaming and pounding and darkness, I felt it. I had seen too much blood spilled in Rwanda *not* to feel vulnerable.

I could see nothing except flashes of fire, but heard everything. The Tanzanian Red Cross workers—all others had left for the night—panicked, too. In the pandemonium we were all helpless: one-quarter of a million people seemed to be moving around us, many of them with an intimate knowledge of how to dispatch death, some of whom enjoyed doing so. I envisioned being rushed at in the darkness, the blade of a machete cutting deeply into my flesh, then deeper; or a single smashing blow to the head and my vision breaking apart and fading as my blood poured into the ground. Similar thoughts must have pierced Rwandans who found themselves the victims of their neighbors. Targeted, resigned, they had learned to tolerate their own deaths, to submit to the agony of a knife, often suffering in silence to deny their killers the satisfaction of seeing their pain.

Even the threat of such an end terrorized me. Magnified that night by impenetrable darkness and the awesome weight of human screams, I trembled. Rwanda's phantoms fed on it; the innocent couldn't escape. For a moment, I understood how fear could transform the usual, rational checks and balances into a single-minded impulse to survive—even if that meant killing to stay alive. This must have been the depth of fear drummed up in Rwandans that broke down every built-in human restraint, enabling them to kill and kill.

The clamor continued for 15 minutes, stretching on and on, sweeping up and down the camp in magnified waves that defied explanation. But no gangs stormed our compound. When the noise finally began to die down, Tanzanian Red Cross officials bravely mounted a journey with a megaphone, driving the length of the camp in a truck. "You are safe! You are safe! You are in Tanzania!" they shouted at the now-blazing fires. They established the cause of the great drama: someone thought he saw a lion, and when the alarm went up the refugees pounded their fists on the sides of plastic jerry cans and screamed. No raid by Hutu killers. No Tutsi "hunting" party—though these would emerge days later. No refugee throats slit under the cover of night: that night, no furthering of Rwanda's bloodshed here.

But in their terror, the refugees showed how easily and blindly they were drawn into a protective response, as effortlessly as their community back home had been drawn to systematically, almost perfectly, kill all Tutsis, when the time came to choose between "us" and "them."

Inside Rwanda there was another source of evil from which those refugees fled, besides the Tutsi rebels. It was on view at the Nyarubuye parish, where the Dark Side was fully revealed. A 6-foot-tall statue of a benevolent Christ stood above the cathedral entrance, arms open to those who sought refuge. But when I arrived in late May 1994, it was soon clear why one might rather begin life anew as a refugee than to remain close to that desecrated ground.

Deep in the countryside, 20 miles down a one-lane dirt track, the statuary welcome was deceptive. The prelude to this massacre ground was in the main sanctuary, on the floor next to the altar. A vase fashioned from a vegetable oil tin, labeled "Canada" by its well-intentioned donor, was tipped over beneath the first Station of the Cross. Spilled onto the floor along with the flowers— the whole mess once an "arrangement"—lay two greasy femurs and a shin bone. The violated *Baptizorum* ledger close by was smeared with bloody fingerprints by the last person who inspected it: a Hutu engaged in the goring. The spine of the book was crusty with dried blood.

Deeper inside the parish, among the cornstalks and well-tended garden flowers, beneath monastery columns and in classrooms, there was evidence and testimony. Hundreds of bodies dissolved slowly into hardening pools of human fat. Few were killed with bullets or grenades, except those victims in the back rooms, which were so choked with the dead that no other method of killing could have been so effective.

Children were lined against a wall, their softer skulls cut cleanly with the edge of a machete. Other skulls showed broad holes with jagged star edges, where the blow of a club forced bone and calcium fragments into the brain. Outside, few escaped such blows.

One of the child cadavers wore a shirt labeled "Pete."

A baby's body was crushed formless by a large stone.

Another was mortified with mouth locked wide open in a scream, a single tooth gleaming.

Maybe 1,000 Rwandans died violently here. Their souls were gone, though the organic leftovers shared an ignominious disintegration sprinkled with shards of glass and broken plastic buckets.

But there was a legacy for the living, too, whose senses were assaulted everywhere in Rwanda by similar massacre sites, at which cakes of fat turned rancid. I couldn't believe what I was seeing, because the horrific detail lay so far beyond my imagination, pushing even the limits of fiction. I left the corpses at Nyarubuye, infested with the fat brown fleas of the dead.

The drive to the border with Tanzania had been one of reflection. Sitting in the back of a truck after three weeks in Rwanda, in the warm afternoon sun and with the wind in my face, it was easy to let my mind wander. At this speed, detail blurred and the emerald green fields of springtime in Rwanda looked almost inviting, the hills part of a fairytale land. The genocide was still under way and I had seen many abominations. But the resplendent earth transported me to another reality: I thought on the beauty of children—clinching in my thinking for the first time, here of all places, the desire of now having a child with my wife—and on being home soon. This was going to be a satisfying departure, I felt, and those didn't come often enough in Africa anymore.

But the sun lowered to twilight, and my thinking darkened with the sky. Then one of the tires blew out, and my reverie with it. There was no spare, so I would have to walk, eerily following the exact footsteps taken by 300,000 refugees just weeks before: now it would be my turn. As the crow flies, we were less than 10 miles from the Nyarubuye sacrilege. And to the south, the border was six miles away, though at the end of the road would be the mountain of machetes, and a river of bodies. Suppressing that thought, I hoisted my backpack and camera bag, and with two RPF guards started to walk south.

All around it was silent. The road was paved well, and I was striding out, but my predecessors the refugees had obviously had a tough time. They dumped everything they couldn't carry, from pots to pans to furniture to clothes. There were broken cars, worn boots, and children's toys. But now, nothing else to mark their passing except the silence—and the trail of fibrous sugarcane chewed for its sweetness like gum and spat out.

As darkness fell, the only sound was my breathing, that of my two comrades, and the deliberate pad of rubber-soled boots on tarmac. The moon rose, but its glow did not dispel any demons—it just enhanced them with unfamiliar two-dimensional shadows. Here along the road were the leftovers of the refugees, tossed aside in time to reach the finish line, maybe cursed for having dragged down their owners long enough already.

These were the people who fled the ghosts of Nyarubuye, of Rukara and Kabarondo, of the betrayals in Ste. Famille and all those verdant villages struck down by atrocity, places where the Dark Side was dominant, where the word "Hutu" was scratched on the outside of houses, to protect Hutus from Hutu predators.

During this trek, we were on edge. One guard had one gun, but in a country as crowded as Rwanda, any prolonged silence was reason for suspicion. The hill down to the Akagera River, through a forest, finally came to an end, with a shuffle past the pile of machetes. From the bridge I stared down, but could see nothing in the blackness of the corpses that I knew to be heaving over the falls.

I turned to walk on, leaving behind Rwanda and its ghouls. But even on the high bridge, the sound of water rushing all around felt to me—as I'm sure it did to the relieved, fleeing Hutu refugees—like a baptism.

The refugees in Tanzania had rewritten the record books: their exit had been the biggest and the fastest ever recorded. So when an even faster and more massive exodus took place in mid-July, journalists found that we had used up our superlatives.

The swift advance of the RPF north of the French "safe haven" zone and the fall of Kigali set a new standard: more than 1 million people streamed into Goma, Zaire, in a flood of humanity of Biblical sweep. The rush was no accident. When defeat was inevitable, the *genocidaires* ordered the retreat. Radio des Mille Collines told Hutus to flee *en masse* for their "protection." The Tutsi "cockroaches," it declared, were killing and burning everything in their path, and aimed to eliminate every Hutu in Rwanda. Obedient as ever to the authorities of the old regime—which was still intact—the Hutus walked away from their country.

The exodus brought together the guilty and the innocent as refugees. For the army and militia, this ploy worked perfectly: civilians served as human shields for these perpetrators. They took food and aid from relief agencies and plotted their return. True refugees were intimidated, and told not to return to Rwanda until ordered. Just like in Tanzania, this subdued mob left behind machetes and assault rifles that piled up like a gruesome game of pick-up-sticks. It settled in Goma and a string of camps along the border to the north. Then cholera swept through the camps, multiplying the grisly toll. But there were no wounded, no victims of contact with the advancing "cockroaches," no witnesses of the crimes the Tutsi rebels were alleged to have committed against the Hutu.

As always, it was the weak and infirm, the children and women and the aged, who paid the highest price. The young strong men and "leaders" who had the sheer strength to carry out the bulk of Rwanda's killing would ensure that they would be the last to die. Some people starved and died from chronic dehydration, waiting for the international relief effort to kick in. Others tore open emergency medical bottles of undrinkable saline solution in an attempt to quench their thirst. Soldiers fished in the lake with grenades, the blasts shocking the catch into belly-up meals. They also lubricated their artillery pieces and mortars, ever confident that the counterattack would begin soon.

At the edge of the largest camp the Nyiragongo volcano turned active again, and it was taken as a sign of imminent destruction. When it last erupted in 1976, hot lava flowed 10 miles into Lake Kivu faster than most men can run, killing 500 people. The refugees were camped mercilessly on the sharp hardened spines of that flow. No holes could be bored in which to shit, or to bury the mounting dead. The words "divine retribution" were on many lips. Some argued that it had already come, as the death toll in the camps topped 50,000, growing as high as 1,800 in a day. But others knew that in Rwanda these "refugees" had killed 50,000 in a single 36-hour span, and had kept on going.

At night the brooding volcano bathed the refugees in an sinister red glow, the seething molten lava in the crater reflecting off the turbulent column of steam that rose heavenward.

Corpses were wrapped in grass mats and laid along the road for collection by Boy Scouts wearing gauze masks and plastic gloves who had a death-wagon service for pay. Standing in the back of the truck, during a visit in the first days of September 1994, I joined the scouts on one of these journeys. The earth-stained feet of our living mingled with the soiled feet of the dead. One time our driver braked quickly, and the body of a baby boy wrapped loosely in a gray garbage bag slumped over onto my leg, its small bones and still-supple flesh dropping onto my boot like a lifeless collection of waterlogged sticks. I was not as disgusted as I should have been, only because the horrible canon of Rwanda was large now, and my emotions bound together to mask my heart, protecting it. There was dirt under the fingernails of the tiny hand; in Africa, it was another small life so easily extinguished.

A sign said that we were collecting bodies on the edge of the Virunga National Park, famous for its tranquil mountain gorillas. But the peace of those hills had been long spoiled. Far away from the hardened lava flow and the refugee camp, we arrived at the mass grave. It opened like an irritated gash in the earth. The infant boy in plastic was tossed like a rag doll from the truck, arms outstretched and flailing. A still-bloody fetus followed him uncovered. In the pit, butterflies floated from body to body—a sharp contrast of beauty and the Dark Side. A dusting of lime, a makeshift wooden cross for the entire grave: one man's arms were crimped in frozen anguish, his head thrown back and face caked with lime, a medallion of St. Christopher strung on a necklace tight across his thrusting bare throat.

This dying may have been divine retribution, but the Hutu refugees did not see it that way. They didn't believe they were guilty, and so revised their history, recasting themselves as the innocent victims of a Tutsi genocide hatched by the "cockroaches" against them. They easily swallowed their own propaganda—those were the orders—and showed no hint of remorse. Extremists were placed in positions of importance by relief agencies in the camps, because they were often educated and had held responsible jobs back home.

In this universe, Hutus were absolved. It seemed that the only nightmares some Hutus had were about the Tutsis they did *not* kill.

A tract titled *"Le peuple rwandais accuse . . . "* was a typical example.[3] This was distributed by the self-declared "Minister of Justice" of the exiles in the camps at the end of September 1994, when the threat of hunger and thirst had been controlled by relief agencies, and hard-liners were beginning to turn their minds more fully to ethnic "injustice." The 19-page pamphlet blamed Rwanda's "catastrophic situation" on the "diabolical work" of the RPF with the assistance of the US, Belgium, Uganda, and the UN. It reversed reality, claiming that the RPF was guilty and the Hutus were its victims. There was no mention of dead Tutsis, but the RPF was accused of having "shown no respect for places of worship."

Outsiders—whose history of Rwanda often began with the refugee exodus, and not the genocide—were manipulated, too. I toured the camps with a spokeswoman for the British Red Cross who was so struck by the situation that she had adopted a Hutu orphan. Noble as this act was, her understanding of the past was rather selective. "You should hear the tales they tell. So many saw their entire families killed before their eyes. They have been traumatized!" And they were just that: tales. These Hutu certainly were witness to killing, but rarely that of *their* families.

Extremist leaders proudly flaunted their ethnic hatred. The former prefect of Kigali, François Karera, was also the head of the "Social Commission" that purported to represent all the refugees in the Zaire camps. Relief workers and the UN dealt with him every day. In one interview he said that the killing was justified because Tutsis were "originally bad" and "murderers." The Hutus were determined never to be ruled by Tutsis again. "If the reasons are just, the massacres are justified," Karera said. "In war you don't consider the consequences, you consider the causes. . . . We cannot use that word genocide because there are numerous survivors."[4]

Col. Theoneste Bagasora, an *Akazu* devotee, minister of defense, and chief engineer of the genocide, was even more brazen. Months into exile, he vowed to "wage a war that will be long and full of dead people until the minority Tutsis are finished and completely out of the country."[5] As of this writing, he, too, was awaiting trial at the Arusha tribunal.

When they fled, Hutus were told to expect to be in exile for 30 years, as the Tutsis had been. Preparations for that war began at the bottom. Despite its Catholicism, Rwanda once had a sophisticated family planning system. To limit the number of children, women were encouraged to have "Norplant" birth-prevention implants surgically inserted under the skin of their upper arms. But in the camps, extremists knew the power of the Malthusian imperative: women were told to give birth to as many Hutu babies as possible, so that the next generation of Hutus would definitively destroy every Tutsi in Rwanda. In ready compliance, women took knives to their own flesh and cut the "Norplant" inserts from their arms.

But the real *coup de grace* was that, even as the refugees fled the scene of their crime, they sparked the world's largest charity mission. Hutu extremists were ready to take advantage of the goodwill, to revitalize themselves and their genocidal mission. Relief agencies and the UN distributed food—the UN alone spending more than $1 million each day—using the same network of prefects and communes that had held sway in Rwanda and had been so instrumental in organizing the genocide. So the old authorities, with militiamen and soldiers, re-exerted their power. Population estimates were inflated, so the camps were swamped with food. Groups of thugs—modeled after Haiti's *Tonton Macoutes*—were created to enforce payment of "taxes" exacted in food, money, and relief goods to finance the "next invasion." Prostitution, bars, and other businesses, such as those selling the shoes of the dead, flourished.

On the military side, the Rwandan army-in-exile reorganized to include many militia, and its ranks grew to 50,000.[6] Hutu refugees from Burundi also joined up. Regular training took place in a series of semi-hidden military camps in Zaire, where military discipline was observed, soldiers carried their guns, and food was provided by the "relief" agency Caritas. In some camps soldiers kept groups of children on military bases to ensure continued supplies of relief goods. When the camps were finally broken up in November 1996 by Rwanda Tutsi forces, documents found crammed into three abandoned buses showed how the refugees had used the UN protection of the camps to launch an insurgency, train and rearm to recapture their homeland, and plot assassination of the new Tutsi leaders.[7]

The defeated army had little difficulty acquiring new weapons. The war chest was full of cash. President Habyarimana's widow and her brother, an *Akazu* financier, who purchased arms to resuscitate the exile army, had access to those assets in foreign banks. In October 1994, they placed a $5 million order in China for assault rifles, grenades, and RPGs.[8] The scale of that buildup was obvious: the total figure of *all* arms imported by Rwanda from 1981 to 1988 had also been $5 million.[9]

The most significant weapons supplies to the refugee camps came directly from Zaire, and indirectly from Bulgaria and Albania, Israel, France, and South Africa. Zaire supplied end-user certificates for some of the arms shipments which were then handed over to the Rwandan army. To make the shipments, pilots in Kinshasa filed false flight plans, paying a hefty $1,000 bribe to do so.[10] Like Somalia's gun market, arms in the Zaire camps became so readily available in market stalls that grenades sold for less than the cost of two bottles of beer.

The increasing stockpiles boosted the morale of the once-broken army. Heavy weapons originally confiscated by French forces in the "safe zone" and handed over to Zaire were slowly sold back to the Rwandans by Zairean officers. A command and control headquarters—complete with a sophisticated communications center—had been at work since October 1994, in a camp near Goma called Lac Vert. Trained guerrilla units made increasingly bold cross-border raids, killing as they could inside Rwanda with the express purpose of destabilizing the new Tutsi-led government.

The militarization caused nagging doubts among relief workers. The next war would begin here, and they had coddled the antagonists, nourishing them back to health. The pressure became too much for Médecins Sans Frontières, which withdrew in November 1994. They were fed up with death threats and the fact that the refugees were hostage to "leaders" who would kill them before letting them return home. "The situation has deteriorated to such an extent that it is now ethically impossible for MSF to continue aiding and abetting the perpetrators of genocide. Members of the former Rwandan authorities, military and militia exert total control over tens of thousands of civilians in the camps of Bukavu," MSF said.[11]

The dilemma was the same in Somalia and Sudan, though for the vast number of agencies who ignored abuses in the "humanitarian" interest, the act shouldn't be too carefully examined. "On the humanitarian level, you can't get too philosophical, just because Rwanda's recent history doesn't bode too well for the future," Ray Wilkinson of the UN High Commissioner for Refugees told me in Goma. "If the little baby in your arms is going to die in a few years because of more violence, you can't wonder why you go through the motions, or you would be paralyzed, you couldn't do anything."

The impulse was correct, to save lives with the political blindness required of the Hippocratic oath, but the conundrum remained. "Given that there was genocide, and that we are feeding killers in these camps, what is the alternative?" Wilkinson asked. "Could we make a case not to feed anybody? Can we make a choice? We can't put ourselves in a such a Machiavellian position: the world community has made a decision to feed and save people, and that bringing the killers to justice *has* to wait, unless you are going to plunge back into the Dark Ages. Because the only alternative is to say, 'Let them all die.'"

But much of the reason that the succor provided to the camps seemed so distasteful was because, during the Rwanda genocide, the "caring" outside world *did* regress to those Dark Ages and *did* say, "Let them all die."

In the coming decades, how many more people will perish because no one intervened to stem this mass killing, and instead nourished the guilty to a vengeful war footing? Tens of thousands were saved by emergency work in the camps. But how many of them would die during the next bloody encounter? Or does none of this matter, because these tragedies afflict a continent known more for its production of spectacles than for its contribution to the good of humankind?

Would justice have been better served by following a survival-of-the-fittest ethic and leaving 2 million Hutu refugees in Zaire and elsewhere—among them the perpetrators of the genocide—to die unassisted by the tens of thousands? Is it possible to stop singular and mass acts of revenge by Tutsi against Hutu?

Perhaps there is no way to correctly know the answers until it is too late to appropriately intervene. But I don't think so. Because there is always too much information—even about the elusive human nature—to ever say, "We didn't know." The result then hinges upon how that information is used. Referring to the knee-jerk reaction of sending "aid" to victims of ethnic cleansing in Bosnia and of genocide in Rwanda, outside the context of the crime, MSF notes:

> How can we think of passing food through the window while doing nothing to drive the murderer from the house, feeding hostages without attempting to confront their kidnapper, or, worse still, feeding the murderer after the crime? These are not humanitarian acts. Nevertheless, a purely humanitarian approach acts as a blindfold which allows us to bask permanently in the warmth of our own generosity.[12]

One method of ending this cycle seems obvious, if difficult: by making the killers accountable for their crimes. Justice may be the one solution—though complex and large, with so many guilty in Rwanda. The Nuremburg trials after World War II—aimed at what François de Menthon, the French prosecutor, called "the crime which is directed at the very nature of what it is to be human"—resulted in the execution of the leaders responsible.[13] When they died, they died for all the guilty.

But even at meting justice the UN and international community efforts were dogged by delay and incompetence. The result was the beginning of a bureaucratic turf war between UN agencies that led to a chronically underfunded, understaffed office in Kigali. One field officer, Irish human rights lawyer Karen Kenny, led a four-person team from July 1994 to investigate the murders of half a million people. Though overwhelmed with information about the massacres by Hutus and increasing reports of systematic revenge by Tutsi forces, the team had no car, no office space, and no computers. They were not even provided the few dollars necessary to buy cassette tapes to copy recorded broadcasts from Radio des Mille Collines, and—without an administrator for two months—wasted time drafting budgets and hiring cars. Karen Kenny resigned in September 1994 because the opportunity was being lost.

"The lack of resources got to be a joke," said one team member. "Never before has there been a genocide where the victims have been victorious. We have access to everything. The killing was so obviously organized, so simple, so easy, so open. No one has ever seen the quantity and quality of information here. If the in-depth investigation and monitoring began now, we could really change the history of Rwanda and break the cycle of impunity. It would be the beginning of the end of the culture of easy mass killing."

But it would be months before investigation teams began their work, and in many cases coordination by all the active parties—including the Criminal Tribunal—remains a dream.

How many killers are there? Soon after the rebel victory, the new RPF government compiled a list of 30,000 former officials who they said planned and executed the massacres. But even if they were the only guilty ones, they would have had to kill more than 27 people each. Did 100,000 Hutus take part instead, killing eight people each? Or did even more turn their machetes and hoes on their neighbors, slaughtering just a few apiece? Are the guilty so numerous that their acts of murder must be absolved, due to the sheer weight of mass complicity?

To understand the number of dead, look at it this way: imagine that every single word in this book is the name of a victim. This entire volume would then list only 150,000 of the dead, or not even one-fifth of the likely death toll. More than *five* volumes of this book would be required to list just the *first* names of every victim. Look at every word, and think of someone you know. Such a scale seems incomprehensible, as are the *blasé* reactions of those who took part. Exactly one year after the killing began, the new government brought the first cases to trial. One Hutu defendant was resigned, but said he felt no guilt: "It is true, I killed 900 people and I expect to be executed."

The human rights team finally began to take shape, but examinations of massacre sites were largely piecemeal and dependent on having teams of forensics experts seconded to the UN mission by foreign governments. A preliminary map of the largest killing grounds was drawn up by a group of Unamir troops who were lawyers, doctors, and intelligence officers. An American team conducted a thorough forensics examination of the killing in the chapel of Ntarama, 15 miles south of Kigali, establishing the brutality carried out countrywide. More than 300 smashed and sliced skulls were lined up for careful scrutiny—a handful of them stare at you from the cover of this book; bloodied clubs, machetes, and other implements lay among the human wreckage and were tagged as evidence.

But the work was slow and confused, the line blurring between UN and other separate efforts to bring justice. The Human Rights field operation in Rwanda at first deployed 130 monitors throughout the country, but many were young and inexperienced at human rights work, and unfamiliar with the depth of the tribal animosity. Their priorities were also unclear. Were they to keep an eye on revenge killings? Or to find evidence and witnesses that would assist prosecutors of the genocide? Monitors who resigned accused the mission of neglecting the greater crime and of exaggerating claims of revenge killing against the Tutsi-led RPF government.[14]

Still, invaluable information was revealed for the International Tribunal for Rwanda which was finally established—as an extension to the tribunal for the former Yugoslavia—in November 1994. For many Rwandans, however, this court was not satisfactory. Prosecutors said they would only go after the organizers, and in any event couldn't impose death sentences. The Tutsi-led government vowed to try every murderer in Rwandan courts, which could deliver the death penalty, but admitted that the task was too great. On top of that, it was torn into two factions: hard-liners who demanded revenge and forcing Hutus out of Rwanda forever, and those who wanted some kind of truce.

Rwanda's justice system no longer existed. Lawyers and judges were dead, in exile, or accused. The government had no money to cope with the guilty, and foreign governments were reluctant to fund a legal system that would surely execute those convicted. Still, in Kigali there were calls for immediate revenge, and a popular adage among new officials was "Justice delayed is justice denied."

Six months after the genocide, the ghosts of killing past still haunted the streets—streets that I will always find difficult to walk along calmly. My memories are of where the bodies once lay in piles, or where militiamen terrorized in their hunt for more human prey. For Rwandans, of course, the demons are much worse. I found the quiet in Kigali to be disarming. But surviving Tutsis were sometimes confronted secretly by the murderers of their families. One Tutsi was warned that he would be killed in "the next round." Another was asked, "How did we miss you?"

Just as there have been pockets of suffering, however, there have been moments of great joy as orphans were occasionally reunited with their families. More than 60,000 surviving children were lost, separated from their parents, or abandoned.

Hidden at the leafy edge of one Kigali suburb in November 1994, I was lucky enough to observe one homecoming. Just months before, this neighborhood had been transformed overnight. I saw bodies being dragged into the dirt street one after another by militiamen, from these same houses. In the confusion, little Eric Katabogama was lost. The day he finally returned, his face was the epitome of triumph. He could not stop smiling. He ran into the waiting arms of his mother, unbelieving. Tears ran down his mother's care-worn cheeks, for joy this time, not in sorrow.

"I didn't think that he would be alive!" she cried.

Other returns were less happy. There were people silently consoling each other, arms draped over shoulders. At one orphanage I looked into the eyes of injured children but found that there was little soul left to see. Most had been left for dead. My fingers tenderly probed scar tissue healing over deep, four-inch-long machete gashes that defiled arms, shoulders, and heads. Can they ever heal?

In a remote area of central Rwanda called Rukumbeli, I was alongside Anthony Mushoza in May 1994 when he went home. Machete in hand, he strode hard up a scant trail to his house, to see his family for the first time in weeks. In the glade, far off even dirt roads, deep in the heart of Rwanda's lush killing fields, they were not expecting him: they were dead.

Mushoza was bathed in sweat. The bloodstains on his shoulders were wet with an expectant sweat that I associated with preparing for close-in battle. Uncomfortably sticky, he saw his house through the coffee plants, and pointed to the first bodies embedded in a nearby patch of sorghum. His family were there, massacred with grenades and clubs. The huts were burned.

"They found the women and children gathered in the house," Mushoza said, without emotion, no longer impressed by the violence of his world. "We had put them all in one place for protection. But the militia came through the bush, and the real army came up from the road. I lost 24 people—my family and friends."

The dead smell. A baby had been dragged across a doorway, naked. A rotting hand reached through the door for help that never came. A group of nine children was collected outside in front of the house and beaten to death.

The wasted arms of one child poked through a small purple sweatshirt decorated with an image of St. Nick and a sprig of yuletide holly that read: "I believe in Santa Claus."

Without satisfactory justice, the memory of such phantoms will not disappear. Maybe it never will. So victims often took the law into their own hands, taking personal revenge when they could, their patience run out. Old scores were—and still are, to a large, even systematic degree—settled as Hutus were fingered by Tutsi survivors and arrested. Suspects disappeared, or were killed under the cover of darkness as undisciplined units of the former rebels—after their victory, they graduated to become the Rwanda Patriotic Army (RPA)—rounded up whomever they liked. "For each one of us killed, we liquidated 100," confided a Tutsi officer.[15]

Tutsi officials were convinced—and they may not be far from the truth—

that foreign focus on their acts of revenge was part of a larger conspiracy to "equate" the victims of genocide with their killers.

The tension finally exploded in the spring of 1995, publicly blowing apart much of the "moral authority" that the Tutsis had gained as victims. Tens of thousands of Hutus in the French-created "safe zone" in southwest Rwanda had lived precariously in a series of squalid camps for months. Using the anonymity there as a shield, remnants of the *interahamwe* conducted raids against RPA garrisons and Tutsi civilians. The RPA forced the closure of most of the camps, saying that for the innocent it was safe to return to their home villages. Soldiers then burned the stinking huts. Occasional "accidents" left more than a handful of Hutus dead. At least 400 Tutsi soldiers were arrested by the government for using their uniforms to exact their own revenge.

The last and largest camp, at Kibeho, was slated for closure at the end of April 1995. It was notorious for the militiamen hiding there. Hutus were gathered on the top of a single hill without food or drinking water, exposed to the rain and made to suffer. Camp leaders provoked the Tutsi soldiers with gunfire and broke through the cordon; so the Tutsis let fire. UN troops watched dumbfounded, as the Tutsis opened fire on the crowd—even with rocket-propelled grenades—sparking a five-hour spree. Slaughter continued into the night, with Australian UN soldiers reportedly making a body count that exceeded 4,000 before nervous Tutsi soldiers forced them to stop. No official tears were shed; certainly no remorse was shown by a single Tutsi soldier who took part.

Though the Hutus committed genocide against Tutsis and moderate Hutus—an act that Tutsis could never avenge—after Kibeho it was clear that no tribe is made up of angels.

Father André, the Kabgayi priest who kept watch on the balance of transgressions between Hutu and Tutsi, described a common capacity for wickedness: "We say that the previous government chose violent combustion, but this [Tutsi] one chooses quiet combustion: the result is the same"—though the scale was magnitudes different. "Genocide is a judicial expression, but the reality is that a human being is being killed. Even now many, many people are being killed, silently but seriously."

Under normal circumstances, incarceration would likely have been a blessing for Hutu suspects, who might otherwise have disappeared without trace from their villages as Tutsis sought revenge. But the rush to arrest choked Rwanda's prison system, making detention itself a high risk. By July 1995 more than 50,000 Hutus were locked up. The Ministry of Justice admitted that one-third may have been arrested on spurious grounds—one group of Tutsis in the town of Butare were known to work as "accusers for hire." Dozens died from the overcrowding each week, literally suffocating, or beaten to death by other inmates. By 1999, the number had ballooned to 135,000.

Festering in the Gitarama prison in mid-1995 were conditions described by representatives of the ICRC, the only neutral agency with the specific mandate to visit every prisoner in every nation, as the worst they'd ever seen. The RPA no longer kept wardens inside the prison, because it was too dangerous, and because there was no space for them. When a guard saw my pocket knife, he insisted that I leave it outside: "They will kill you with that!" he shrieked. The prison door was swung open just enough for me to slip through, into the steaming, sticky crowd of accused killers. The concrete ground inside was slick with feces and dark sludge, and other wetness left over from the rains. ICRC delegates visited daily to deliver food, and tried to provide help with latrines that were almost inaccessible in the crush.

Stewing in the hot moisture, 7,000 inmates stood, hunched, and tried to hide in an area built to withstand 400. They organized themselves, so the usual political and militia hierarchy existed: the weak were outside in the rain and the sun, their legs thick and packed with fluid, or sat on grimy steps between each other's knees, leaning on each other, their feet rotting and bleeding from the gangrene that would eat its way up to their senses and eventually kill them. The weak ingested little or nothing, and were the target of gangs among the prisoners who beat them mercilessly, concentrating their blows on their ears until they swelled with pus like cauliflower knobs. No one could escape the acrid smoke from the "kitchen" corner, which stung the eyes like Mace.

Appalled by the depravity, the ICRC and the UN took the unprecedented step of financing and building prison extensions and even entirely new prisons to relieve the pressure. Critics argued that such a contribution only encouraged more arrests—another "humanitarian" Catch-22.

In the prison hierarchy, the next rung up the ladder from the floor were the prisoners crammed into the three-level concrete cellblock. It was dark and so crowded inside that claustrophobia made me nauseated, as I was led by the dripping hand of Ferdinand, the chief cook. He took me through this crucible of sweating, shitting flesh. Every soul here wore shorts only, but heat rash was so common that I felt it would rub off on me if I scraped too hard past one more naked chest. In the darkness we were all entrapped, the cells packed with an efficiency that must have rivaled 18th- and 19th-century slave ships, vessels in which only the strong survived but everyone grew weak. Rough planks had been laid across the top fixtures of latrines and unused shower stalls, so the enterprising lay across them, their faces pressed against the metal grills to gasp outside air.

I went downstairs into the prison bowels, but could barely fend off the images of slaughter committed by these men, for—to my thinking—there was nothing preventing an outburst of violence *now*. Ferdinand's hand became like a hot, oily jellyfish, and was as difficult to keep hold of. As we continued into the sepulchral darkness, my nerve gave way. I had tried to sound kindly enough to these people—*Ça va? Ça va?*—though it was not my intention, just my instinct among strangers. I told Ferdinand that there was no need for me to *feel* my way around the farthest cells; the steady moaning chant was enough.

Every prisoner told a tale of injustice at the hands of Tutsis, of how they were innocent, of how they were beaten in detention centers by Tutsi soldiers before they were transferred to the jungle-law prison. The weak died, and even the not-so-weak. Ferdinand was probably among the killers, and his slick hand probably had blood on it.

"How can you survive this, Ferdinand?" I asked.

"Only God can know it," he said, then emitted the only laugh I heard in that place.

At the top of the food chain were the indisputable leaders: men of education and sometimes even refinement, who had taken for themselves the largest airy room. They controlled the gangs, got the food they wanted, and had a trusted foot soldier or two to wash their dishes in warm water and soap. They wore clothes, defended themselves eloquently, and bathed as often as they liked. In the midst of the squalor outside, their preening appalled. When I asked questions they came back at me with questions—and a particular look of defiance that seemed calculated to inspire a giddy fear. They knew that I knew all about what happened outside the prison gates, in the thickets and the chapels. In the ditches. They knew.

At the communal table in the center of their room during my visit, one short fat man stood alone, a clean white towel wrapped around his girth and spotless plastic sandals worn on broad feet. There was a mountain of solid corn porridge on a plate before him, which he spooned relentlessly into his mouth. This was hardly incarceration for him.

The prison was the effluence of an unfathomable evil, the Dark Side at work. I had seen it in many places in Africa, everywhere there was war, or hunger, or some psychological manipulation that twisted minds with reasons and excuses that made killing a necessity. British Army trauma psychiatrist Dr. Ian Palmer specialized in the Dark Side. He worked in Rwanda with British medics and found it difficult to pin down the extraordinary combination of fear and evident human capacity for violence that could lead to such widespread bloodlust. But he certainly knew that the possibility of a similar marriage was not peculiar to Rwanda. The genocide exposed the Dark Side that we are all afraid to see, he said.

So, I asked him, was Rwanda within every one of us?

"Absolutely."

While the guilty got by in prison, outside its walls others tried to make order out of what had gone before. Australian Major Bruce Oswald was shocked by the secrets hidden in the small Ntarama chapel in the woods in September 1994. The bodies were packed between the bench pews, two feet deep, 300 or so; another defilement that merited a red dot on the UN's massacre map. He and his team had arrived without masks. They wished they hadn't. Sometimes they crunched bones underfoot as they took photographs and diagrammed the site. They couldn't help it.

"I will never forget this scene for as long as I live," Oswald said, squatting down to photograph a cluster of children's bodies. "I have a feeling like this is unreal, like Disneyland. I'm looking at the skin on that guy's face, and I've seen it before in an Indiana Jones movie."

Children stood at the door, inspecting the bodies too, and played outside, numbed by months of watching the decay. Every day they played here. The stinking air stuck in their mouths, and they spit often. Inside, a useless rosary hung from a desiccated wrist. There was no one to bury the bodies—every family member had been killed.

Before leaving, Oswald gathered his team to pray for the spirits of the dead, which were all around them. White skulls nearby reflected the bright sun, as the men took off their blue berets and bowed their heads.

> "Lord," he prayed, "we stand here outside your church, where we have seen things that most people never will.

> "These people obviously sought sanctuary in your house, but it was not provided to them. May the spirit of their souls rest in your Heavenly abode forever; and for those who took part, may you find it in your heart to forgive them.

> "Also, we ask that you provide us with understanding, so that when we go away we will know how this can be your will. . ."

The slaughter at Nyarubuye, one of the worst scenes of genocide I had seen, was to be preserved. The site was to be set aside forever as a memorial to the crime, so that history would have some physical memory. But when I returned one year after the killing, when Nyarubuye was a must-see site for "body tourists," I was disappointed. The impact had diminished with the passage of time. The black *Baptizorum* book crusty with blood had been torn apart and tossed aside; the greasy femurs that made up the "flower" arrangement were thick with dust. Many of the skeletons had been overgrown by weeds, so that new paths crisscrossed over some bodies. Cobwebs hung between skulls.

The evidence of sacrilege was disappearing, something I found difficult to accept. The rains are hard, season after season in equatorial Africa, and so is the destructive power of the sun. Unliving organic matter simply can't withstand the extremes, and decays quickly. In Somalia, the dead turned to dust in the air; in Rwanda the dead fed the crops as they dissolved. The rich soil there takes in as quickly as it forces vegetal growth. So for the living, only memory and photographs can now be trusted to reveal this history.

To not be affected by all that had passed before me would not have been human. In May 1994, I was staying with several others in the abandoned hilltop seminary at Nyanza, in southern Rwanda, on the edge of a genocide and a war. The calm was deceptive while we waited for days to visit the front line, or at least to see what human wreckage had been left behind by it. This seminary had become our sanctuary, our place to hide, to confirm that daybreak in Rwanda was still worth appreciating.

We all slept on the floor. But one night I had a vision, a phantasm. I woke to see the apparition of a skeleton resting belly down on its ribcage, its chin resting on folded arms, empty eye sockets staring. As I stared back, my throat locked up, and the trembling fear overcame me.

I knew then that this parish—this country—could never again be graced by the Sublime.

EPILOGUE

More than 15 centuries have passed since St. Augustine first wrote about waging "just war." And as a new millennium begins, not many conflicts in Africa qualify for such a lofty distinction—except possibly the Tutsi advance to end Rwanda's genocide.

Still, Africa's warriors will tell you differently. They swear that they are fighting for "peace," or to right a wrong that was done to their clan, their family, or to their brother. For some, the degeneration has boiled down to what Somalis consider to be the last possibility: Me Against My Brother.

After years of kicking around the battlefields in Africa, I have seen how hard it can be for fighters to lay down their weapons. It is not easy to recognize that moment when the benefits of peace outweigh those of war. That is especially true in Africa, where war is so often practiced like a religion, as a faith in its own right.

"Just as it makes no sense to ask 'why people eat' or 'what they sleep for,' so fighting in many ways is not a means to an end," writes Martin Van Creveld, in *The Transformation of War.* "Throughout history, for every person who has expressed his horror of war there is another who found in it the most marvelous of all the experiences that are vouchsafed to man."[1]

Outside Africa there are "bigger" questions that matter: did the failure in Somalia shake the underpinnings of the New World Order, to the point that the subsequent failure in Rwanda was an omen? Or has that failure spurred action elsewhere? Did the US-led NATO bombing campaign of Yugoslavia in early 1999, to end ethnic cleansing by Serb forces in Kosovo, for example, aim to somewhat rebalance the scales of justice to good? Was the rush to intervene militarily in East Timor in September 1999—and the early insistent calls for human rights accountability there and a new war crimes tribunal—the fruit of a latent guilt felt by the global community over its shameful misreading of Rwanda?

In the battlefields, there are powerful instincts at play that are not always fully recognized by those whom President Clinton called "people like me, sitting in offices day after day."

There are the primary reasons that people go to war, "honor, fear and interest," as Thucydides made clear.[2] But there are instincts of revenge that we all share, too, which point to pursuit of the Old Testament wisdom of Moses' an eye for an eye, instead of Jesus' command to turn the other cheek.

In Africa these experiences have been all too frequent, partly because of sheer scale of the problems, of which war is just one. As much as I was humbled by my work in Africa—the human import so awesome to examine—I was exhausted by it, too, and so retreated to the Balkans. The Africa experience was so harsh, and the reasons to grieve were many and so often seemed incorrigible. One of my frustrations about this book is that it cannot portray the whole experience. I've had to be selective, lopping off entire battlefronts and nations at war, and with them, some of the human lessons worth learning.

You will never meet Nsabemana—"Patient 092," a Hutu who had been deliberately carved with six slashes that, from his ear, spread out across his face like sun's rays. The slashes were afflicted by a fellow Hutu because he had "too much money." Although Nsabemana was not made famous in words, his portrait—shot by Jim Nachtwey, while we were there together—became an icon for the genocide when it won the World Press "Photo of the Year" award.

Certainly I don't believe that if you've seen one mass grave, you've seen them all. But how many synonyms can be found for the word "killing," how many degrees of fear and anger can be conveyed when even the thesaurus lets you down? And considering that the technical term "genocide" has been overused and misused, and further cheapened by its non-use by politicians who should be *saving* us from it—how does the writer muster in the reader the requisite emotion? How can I get you to feel the heat of my tears, as I have sought to feel those of Africans? Is it through flowery rhetoric, which tires by the second paragraph? Or some turgid dissertation that, though serious, repels you in its density? Or is it sheer unaccustomed understatement that will make you take notice, that will take a toll on your heart?

So where are these African conflicts now, as the 20th century turns to the 21st? On return visits to the continent, I found many good things—despite the desperate events that I had the privilege to witness—and this was that the propensity to survive was in the ascendant. It reminded me of the conclusion of the old master, William Faulkner, on man: "He is immortal, not because he alone among creatures has an inexhaustible voice, but because he has a soul, a spirit capable of compassion and sacrifice and endurance."[3]

In Somalia, General Aidid was dead. He was shot by a sniper in August 1996, while on the front line in Mogadishu, commanding an attack against forces loyal to Osman Ato, the warlord's old financier. For some Somalis—and the families of Americans killed in battle in Mogadishu on the Day of the Rangers—death by bullet for Aidid was poetic justice. Others saw it as the death of Somalia's last patriot.

The most credible story about his passing was that his fighters had whisked him away and hid him in a house. The wound would not ordinarily have been fatal, but—without letting a doctor visit even once, so as to keep the secret—within five days it was. I could imagine the scene, and it reminded me of a decades-old dialogue from Gerald Hanley:

> [The Somali] had been speared through the chest days ago, and I knew, had it been I who had received the spear-wound, I would have been dead in a few hours, never mind the terrible journey tied to that camel across the bush waste full of his enemies.
> "Tell me who stabbed you," I said. "Tell me what you know and I will avenge you."
> "I will kill him myself when I am well," the warrior said to me in a whisper. . . . "I will get well, and I will kill him myself."[4]

When I returned to Somalia in the spring of 1999, it was relatively quiet. People were tired of fighting. Faction leaders were reduced to paying their own gunmen—battling for one's clan alone was no longer reason enough to die. Three separate phone companies were setting up lines across the city, when their cables weren't cut down by bandits. And the UN had finally worked out a system of getting food to the hungry, by making Somali contractors responsible for every sack. I met Aidid's son, Mohamed Farah. Educated in the US and with an American passport, he had inherited his father's mantle at the age of 34.

But General Aidid's legacy will be remembered most in Somali lore, and he may play a cameo role in future history books, under the chapter heading "The Failure of the New World Order," about how the end of the Great Cold War didn't yield the end of war itself.

I found Aidid's grave on the outskirts of town, where he had owned a plot of sand. Shaped like a square coffin with a roof, it had been carefully covered in white bathroom tiles. A light blue Somali flag was planted at one end. There was a small corrugated metal housing—the kind the American pilots used to blow away in their rotor wash—and that was all. On the drive back into town I noticed how large the mountains of trash had built up alongside the road during a decade of neglect. When rubbish blows free in desert towns in Africa, the result is always a waving sea of small plastic sacks, caught up on plants and any scrap of vegetation. They whipped in the wind, and on that day most of them were light blue, like so many Somali flags.

Every time I had visited Sudan, things were worse. I had been on the black list and unable to get a visa for years. But when President Clinton ordered Tomahawk cruise missiles to destroy a pharmaceutical factory in Khartoum in August 1998—based on exceptionally flimsy "evidence" that the plant was used to make chemical weapon components and was linked to the East Africa US Embassy bombings—the Sudanese government knew they had a good story to tell. We were allowed to wander at will across the wreckage.

But for me the real news was how things had changed—apparently for the better—in Sudan. The notorious Ghost Houses were mostly gone. Opposition leaders spoke openly, admitting that the Islamic regime had grown "older and wiser," while still criticizing the cruel dictatorship. Church officials were still nervous about creeping Islamization and gave many examples. But the brutal thrust of the early days was gone.

There were also promising divisions in the government, with a new moderate faction working to get Sudan off the American list of terrorist states. Carlos the Jackal had been handed over to the French in 1995, and Osama bin Laden—the prime suspect in the embassy bombings—had been kicked out in 1996. Riek Machar, the former rebel leader and Nuer Messiah, had sold out completely to the north. In his Khartoum office, the same Bible sat on his desk that had decorated his bush hut. He handed me a gilt-edged Government of Sudan business card with the title "President of the South." And there was a peace plan; north-south talks were starting yet again.

In the south itself, there were signs of hope. Though 417 villages had been destroyed during fighting between Dinka and Nuer, tribal chiefs sat down together in a remote village. "This meeting alone is a sign that you have decided to save your life," said one.[5] A peace deal was agreed in March 1999, and the applause that followed it turned spontaneously into a jubilant chorus of Dinka-Nuer song. "This," said a priest, "is the peace we have been calling for these many years."

Tired of waiting for justice in Rwanda, the Tutsi government held public executions of 22 *génocidaires* in April 1998—the first blood of justice to be officially spilled for the genocide, four years after the president's plane was shot down. Journalists were not allowed to take pictures or videotape, but it was deemed to be an "educational" experience by the Tutsi government. It was a big moment, for the former rebels had mounting problems. Fed up with an insurgency in northwest Rwanda emanating from the vast Hutu refugee camps across the border in Zaire, Rwandan soldiers had launched an offensive in late

1996 to break up the camps and to separate the armed men—who by that time had fully rejuvenated the former Hutu army—from the innocents.

More than 700,000 Hutus returned to Rwanda, in the face of a flurry of revenge killings. Those Tutsis who sought revenge for the killing of their families—and who quietly carried it out, day after day—can take heart that Article IV of the 1948 Genocide Convention goes beyond the attempt of the Arusha Tribunal to find only the ringleaders of the genocide. The convention is personal, and states that the guilty shall be punished, even if they are "private individuals."[6] Most Tutsi victims will argue stongly, like many Somalis, that only *vengeance* can satisfy honor.

Those Hutus from the camps who didn't return to Rwanda drove deeper into Zaire, chased by an insurgency led by Rwandan Tutsi officers. As a French officer so long before predicted, "those bastards" went all the way to Kinshasa, overthrew Mobutu Sese Seko, renamed Zaire the Congo, and installed Laurent Kabila as president.

But when Rwanda's Tutsi leadership had second thoughts about Kabila and ceated a *new* armed rebellion to oust him, Kabila reverted to a time-honored tactic. Echoing Rwanda's old Radio des Mille Collines, Congo's state-run radio in August 1998 primed the ethnic hatred: "Regarding the march on Saturday, it should be stressed that people must bring a machete, a spear, an arrow, a hoe, spades, rakes, nails, truncheons, electric irons, barbed wire, stones, and the like, in order, dear listeners, to kill the Rwandan Tutsis.

"We are clearly saying No! to the invaders," the radio declared. "Everything is ready to start the fighting. Open your eyes wide. Those of you who live along the road, jump on the people with long noses, who are tall and slim and want to dominate us. Wake up, be aware of our destiny, defeat the enemy."[7]

Such has been the fruit of genocide, its seeds planted in 1994, that were allowed to grow and propagate throughout central Africa.

As should be clear, my experience was small compared to the personal agony suffered by Africans in these war zones. After all, I still have my emotion.

I spoke to many who were traumatized beyond my comprehension, to the point where their in-built protective masks had been shorn away, breaking their will by exposing them, like a flash exposure from the radioactive core of a nuclear reactor, to the undisguised Dark Side, so that they were trapped in the same cell in which that ogre hunted. Their humanity had been replaced as if by rock. They couldn't cry. They sometimes couldn't muster even a single quiver of voice when describing moments of absolute horror.

After such a reckoning, you might think that there was no more room left for good. But that is not at the case.

Yes, there was the Nyarubuye convent in Rwanda, where among the bodies I found a mother and her daughter, curled together in fetal position. The mother had worn a simple plaid dress on her last day. Her daughter wore a sweater that had been pulled up toward her shoulders, and she lay on her mother's right arm.

Yes, this was failure, a stumble of momentous human proportions. But its inheritance is not inescapable. I found proof of that as the genocide was winding down, not far from Nyarubuye, a few dozen miles away. There a group of Tutsi survivors, after emerging from weeks of hiding in nearby swamps, had taken up residence in a school.

Early one morning on the broad, hard-packed red soil play area, I chanced upon another mother and her daughter, both very much alive. The little sprite of a girl, no more than five years old, had put her stool in the middle of that earthen field. Her mother was wearing a wound dressing on her forehead from some previous attack, and she was shaving the head of her child—with the gentle *tchk, tchk, tchk* of a straight razor on sturdy close-in hair. The daughter, too, wore a forehead bandage.

There were bashful smiles, from both mother and daughter, as I came nearer to watch. There was no reason to speak. The mother's splayed left-hand fingers sunk, tips gripping, into the freshly shaved skin of her child's bald scalp—tilting it from side to side, and tipping it forward—while her right hand fingers worked the razor. *Tchk, tchk, tchk.*

It was a ritual exercise, as common as any other mother might pull out the knots of her young daughter's hair with a comb—even like my own daughter's tangles today—jerking slightly with every stroke. But in these hands, as this girl stifled giggles, here was a spiritual moment of such great and common tenderness in Africa, a wellspring of love.

It was also an image of hope, because it was a moment of peace—and no one remarked upon how odd that was.

NOTES

INTRODUCTION

Lead quote: Barbara Ehrenreich, *Blood Rites: Origins and History of the Passions of War* (New York: Metropolitan Books, Henry Holt and Company, 1997), p. 20.

1. Ernest Hemingway, *The Old Man and the Sea* (London: Granada, 1981 [First published London: Jonathan Cape, 1952]), p. 89.

2. President Ntibantunganya, quoted in Alec Russell, "Drums Answer Burundi President's Plea for Peace; Burundi Is Terrified It Will Be Infected by Rwanda's Slaughter," *The Daily Telegraph* (London), 15 August 1994, p. 1.

3. William Faulkner, "Nobel Prize Acceptance Speech," Stockholm, Sweden, 10 December 1950.

4. Alain Destexhe, "De Solférino à Sarajevo," *Projet*, spring 1994, as quoted in François Jean, ed., *Populations in Danger 1995: A Médecins Sans Frontières Report* (London: Médecins Sans Frontières-UK, 1995), p. 87.

5. Jean, ed., *Populations in Danger 1995*, p. 87.

6. Matthew Connelly and Paul Kennedy, "Must It Be the Rest Against the West?" *The Atlantic Monthly*, December 1994, p. 84.

7. Leon Uris, *Mila 18* (Garden City, NY: Doubleday, 1961), p. 141.

8. Gerald Hanley, *Warriors: Life and Death Among the Somalis* (London: Eland, 1993 [First published as *Warriors and Strangers*, London: Hamish Hamilton, 1971]), p. 73.

9. William Wordsworth, "We are Seven" (1798), *Selected Poems* (London: Penguin, 1996), p. 5.

CHAPTER 1: LAWS OF WAR

Lead quote: Hanley, *Warriors*, p. 19.

1. For a good discussion of the historical roots of Somalia's warrior clans by the most renowned expert in the field, see any of the several books by Professor Ioan M. Lewis of the London School of Economics. These two quotes are from Lewis, *A Pastoral Democracy: A Study of Pastoralism and Politics Among the Northern Somali of the Horn of Africa* (published for the International African Institute, London: Oxford University Press, 1961), pp. 15–16.

2. Lewis, *A Pastoral Democracy*, p. 128, and other writings.

3. Ioan M. Lewis, "In the Land of the Mad Mullah," *The Sunday Times* (London), 30 August 1992, pp. 8–9.

4. John Drysdale, *Whatever Happened to Somalia?* (London: Haan Associates, 1994), p. 70.

5. Ioan M. Lewis, preface to Somalia Delegation, *Spared from the Spear: Traditional Somali Behaviour in Warfare* (Nairobi: International Committee of the Red Cross, 1997), p. 1.

6. This verse (p. 11) and several poems, proverbs, and commentary on traditional Somali rules of war are drawn from *Spared From the Spear* (esp. pp. 7–13), a remarkable joint ICRC/Somali Red Crescent Society project that pools the accounts of several Somali oral historians and elders to record this aspect of their country's culture.

7. Lewis, *A Pastoral Democracy*, p. 1.

8. Details of the Mad Mullah's campaign drawn from Ioan M. Lewis, *A Modern History of Somalia: Nation and State in the Horn of Africa* (Boulder, CO: Westview Press, 1988 [First published London: Weidenfeld and Nicolson, 1965]), pp. 68–79.

9. As quoted in David Lamb, *The Africans* (New York: Vintage, 1987 [originally Random House, 1983]), p. 197.

10. Quoting from Sir Geoffrey Archer's Historical Notes, in "British Somaliland and Its Tribes," document issued by the military government of British Somaliland, January 1945, p. 1.

11. Quoted in Lewis, *A Modern History of Somalia*, p. 222.

12. Ibid., pp. 209–210.

13. Quote and accounts of reactions to Americans from Lamb, *The Africans*, p. 204.

14. Ruth Sinai, "Somalia—Arms," Associated Press, 2 November 1993.

15. Ogaden adventure details drawn from Lewis, *A Modern History of Somalia*, p. 236 and elsewhere.

16. Figures quoted in Refugee Policy Group (RPG), *Hope Restored? Humanitarian Aid in Somalia 1990–1994*, a comprehensive after-action aid report prepared for the Office of US Foreign Disaster Assistance by the Center for Policy Analysis and Research on Refugee Issues, Washington D.C., November 1994, p. 7, and Sinai, "Somalia—Arms."

17. Organization for Economic Cooperation and Development figures quoted in African Rights and Mines Advisory Group, "Violent Deeds Live On: Landmines in Somalia and Somaliland" (London: African Rights, December 1993), p. 15.

18. Lewis, *A Modern History*, p. 256.

19. First estimate from Robert Gersony, in a report for US State Department, "Why Somalis Flee," August 1989, as quoted in Africa Watch, *Somalia: A Government at War with Its Own People: Testimonies About the Killing and the Conflict in the North* (New York: Human Rights Watch, January 1990), pp. 217–218. Second estimate by Africa Watch, p. 218.

20. African Rights and Mines Advisory Group, "Violent Deeds Live On," p. 21.

21. Recounted in Hussein Ali Dualeh, *From Barre to Aideed: Somalia; The Agony of a Nation* (Nairobi: Stellagraphics, 1994), p. 118.

22. Quoted in Africa Watch, *Somalia: A Government at War with Its Own People*, p. vi.

23. Africa Watch, "Somalia: Beyond the Warlords: The Need for a Verdict on Human Rights Abuses," 7 March 1993, p. 4.

24. Quoted in Mohamoud M. Afrah, *Target: Villa Somalia, An Eyewitness Account of Mogadishu's Fall to U.S.C. Guerrillas* (Karachi: Naseem, 1991), pp. 65 and 25. Printed in Somalia by the National Agency (Mogadishu, 1991).

25. Dualeh, *From Barre to Aideed*, pp. 36–37.

26. Quoted in Afrah, *Target: Villa Somalia,* p. 25.

27. Jonathan Stevenson, *Losing Mogadishu: Testing U.S. Policy in Somalia* (Annapolis, MD: Naval Institute Press, 1995), p. 34.

28. Lewis, "In the Land of the Mad Mullah."

29. As cited in Michael Johns, "Preserving American Security Ties to Somalia" (Washington, D.C.: Heritage Foundation, 26 December 1989), p. 2.

30. Quoted in Africa Rights and Mines Advisory Goup, "Somalia: Violent Deeds Live On," p. 21.

31. Recounted by Mohamoud M. Afrah, *The Somali Tragedy* (Mombasa, Kenya: Mohamed Printers, 1994), p. 17.

CHAPTER 2: "CITY OF THE INSANE"

Lead quote: Mohamoud M. Afrah, *Mogadishu: A Hell on Earth: A Journalist's Diary about the War in Mogadishu* (Nairobi: Copos Ltd., 1993), p. 2.

1. Mariam Arif Gassem, *Hostages: The People Who Kidnapped Themselves* (Nairobi: Central Graphics Services, 1994), p. 137.

2. Alex Shoumatoff, "The U.S., the U.N. and Aidid: The 'Warlord' Speaks," *The Nation,* 4 April 1994, p. 446.

3. Quoted in Afrah, *Mogadishu: A Hell on Earth,* p. 46.

4. Lewis, *A Pastoral Democracy,* p. 242.

5. Recounted in Gassem, *Hostages,* pp. 65–69.

6. ICRC, *Spared from the Spear,* p. 7.

7. As coined by the London-based human rights group African Rights.

8. Recounted in Gassem, *Hostages,* pp. 132–135.

9. Physicians for Human Rights, *Somalia: No Mercy in Mogadishu; The Human Cost of the Conflict and the Struggle for Relief* (New York: Africa Watch, July 1992), p. 15.

10. Africa Watch, "Somalia: Beyond the Warlords," p. 12.

11. Both quoted in Jane Perlez, "Somalia Fighting Keeps Aid from a Suffering City," *The New York Times,* 11 December 1991.

12. Quoted in Jane Perlez, "U.S. Increases Aid to Somalia After U.N. Balks," *The New York Times,* 15 December 1991, p. 6.

13. Quoted in Afrah, *The Somali Tragedy,* p. 90.

14. Recounted in James Schofield, *Silent Over Africa: Stories of War and Genocide* (Sydney: HarperCollins, 1996), p. 22.

CHAPTER 3: A LAND FORGOTTEN BY GOD

1. These quotes and proverbs drawn from ICRC, *Spared from the Spear,* pp. 12–13.

2. Secretary of State Lawrence Eagleburger nominated, and Andrew Natsios, the director of the Office of US Foreign Disaster Assistance, recommended the ICRC for the prize, as noted in RPG, *Hope Restored?,* p. 84.

3. "Barre," *The Nation,* Nairobi, Kenya, 15 May 1992.

4. Boutros Boutros-Ghali at 22 July 1992 UN Security Council meeting, as quoted in RPG, *Hope Restored?*, p. 22.

5. Quoted in Jane Perlez, "U.N. Let the Somali Famine Get Out of Hand, Aide Says," *The New York Times,* 16 August 1992, p. 12.

6. Mohamed Sahnoun, as quoted in Keith B. Richburg, "U.N. Envoy for Somalia Resigns Post, Blames Bureaucracy," *The Washington Post,* 30 October 1992, p. 31.

7. Mohamed Sahnoun, *Somalia: The Missed Opportunities* (Washington, D.C.: United States Institute of Peace Press, 1994), p. 35.

8. Mohamed Farah Jumaale, interview in Mogadishu, 8 March 1999.

9. Lewis, *A Pastoral Democracy,* p. 29.

CHAPTER 4: "CLUB SKINNY—DANCERS WANTED"

Lead quote: "Beautiful Somalia" (Mogadishu: Ministry of Information and National Guidance, 1978), pp. 4, 51.

1. RPG, *Hope Restored?*, pp. 2, 5.

2. "Letter dated 29 November 1992 from the Secretary-General to the President of the Security Council presenting five options for the Security Council's consideration," S24868, 30 November 1992, in *The United Nations and Somalia: 1992–1996* (New York: UN Department of Public Information, 1996), The United Nations Blue Book Series, Vol. VIII, pp. 209–210.

3. Quoted in Smith Hempstone, *Rogue Ambassador: An African Memoir* (Sewanee, TN: University of the South Press, 1997), pp. 229–230, from *U.S. News & World Report,* 14 December 1992.

4. Stevenson, *Losing Mogadishu,* p. 59.

5. Lewis, *A Pastoral Democracy,* p. 256.

6. Stevenson, *Losing Mogadishu,* p. 73.

7. Official US Marines figures quoted by John L. Hirsch and Robert B. Oakley, *Somalia and Operation Restore Hope: Reflections on Peacemaking and Peacekeeping* (Washington, D.C.: United States Institute of Peace Press, 1995), p. 63.

8. As quoted in RPG, *Hope Restored?*, p. 33.

9. Ken Menkhaus, "Getting Out vs. Getting Through in Somalia," *Middle East Policy* 3:1 (1994), p. 155, as quoted in RPG, *Hope Restored?*, p. 37.

10. Quoted in RPG, *Hope Restored?*, p. 34.

11. Ibid., p. 75.

12. Ibid., p. 34.

13. François Jean, ed., *Life, Death and Aid: The Médecins Sans Frontières Report on World Crisis Intervention* (New York: Routledge, 1993), p. 102.

14. Quoted in Jane Perlez, "Must US Strip a Land of Guns?" in *The New York Times,* 15 December 1992.

15. Recollection of Andrew Natsios, director of the Office of US Foreign Disaster Assistance, as quoted in RPG, *Hope Restored?*, p. 31.

16. Speaker identified only as a "disgusted colleague of Shinn's [David Shinn, director of the State Department's Somalia Coordination Staff] who had been a key

player and whom I shall call Frank," as quoted in Shoumatoff, "The U.S., the U.N. and Aidid," p. 444.

17. As quoted in RPG, *Hope Restored?*, p. 31.

18. As quoted in African Rights, "Somalia: Operation Restore Hope: A Preliminary Assessment," May 1993, p. 21. Spelling of Starlin Arush's name as in "Somalia's First War Lady," *The Economist* (London), 28 August 1999, p. 32.

19. Ibid., p. 20.

20. Wayne Long, interview in Nairobi, 12 March 1999.

21. Hirsh and Oakley, *Somalia and Operation Restore Hope,* pp. 104–105.

22. RPG, *Hope Restored?,* p. 74.

23. Ibid., p. 38.

24. Quoted in John R. Bolton, "Wrong Turn in Somalia," *Foreign Affairs* 73, January–February 1994, p. 104.

25. Mark Bradbury, *The Somali Conflict: Prospects for Peace; Oxfam Research Paper no. 9* (Oxford: Oxfam, October 1993), p. 46.

26. RPG, *Hope Restored?*, p 36.

27. Message Re: "30-day Attitude Adjustment," from Major General Charles C. Wilhelm, USMC, 12 January 1993, as quoted in Stevenson, *Losing Mogadishu,* pp. 65–66.

28. As quoted in *Africa Confidential* (London), 16 April 1993, p. 8.

CHAPTER 5: "CAMP OF THE MURDERERS"

Lead quote: Hanley, *Warriors,* p. 20.

1. Quoted in Tom Cohen, "U.S. 'Plucking the Bird' of Violence to Reduce Warlords' Power," Associated Press, 19 February 1993.

2. Drawn from "Report of the Commission of Inquiry Established Pursuant to Security Council Resolution 885 (1993) to Investigate Armed Attacks on Unosom II Personnel Which Led to Casualties Among Them" (New York: United Nations [S/1994/653], 24 February 1994) pars. 54 to 80, esp. 76 (pp. 16–19, esp. 19).

3. Recounted in Drysdale, *Whatever Happened to Somalia?,* p. 181.

4. Ibid., p. 178.

5. "Report of the Commission of Inquiry," pars. 102–103 (p. 23) and pars. 215–218 (p. 41).

6. Ibid., par. 92 (p. 21) and par. 212 (p. 40).

7. Ibid., par. 94 (p. 22).

8. Recounted in Drysdale, *Whatever Happened to Somalia?,* p. 6.

9. Quoted in RPG, *Hope Restored?,* p. 139.

10. Recounted in Drysdale, *Whatever Happened to Somalia?,* p. 6.

11. "Report of the Commission of Inquiry," par. 124 (p. 25).

12. As described by Ambassador Antonio Pedauye, *chargé d'affaires* from Spain, whose country had the rotating presidency of the Security Council at the time and had convened the emergency session of the council. Personal correspondence winter 1995, in Sarajevo, and July 1999.

13. "UN Security Council Resolution 837, S/RES/837 (1993)," 6 June 1993, in *The United Nations and Somalia*, pp. 267–268.

14. "Report of the Commission of Inquiry," par. 232 (p. 43).

15. Lewis, *A Pastoral Democracy*, p. 27.

16. Gassem, *Hostages*, pp. 129, 4.

17. Hossein Mohamed Farah "Aidid," then the 34-year-old leader of the SNA, interview in Mogadishu, 8 March 1999.

18. Quoted in Shoumatoff, "The U.S., the U.N. and Aidid," p. 446.

19. Lewis, *A Pastoral Democracy*, p. 252.

20. "Executive summary of the report prepared by Professor Tom Farer of the American University, Washington D.C., on the 5 June 1993 attack on United Nations forces in Somalia" (S/26351, 24 August 1993), as published in *The United Nations and Somalia*, pp. 296–300.

21. Drysdale, *Whatever Happened to Somalia?*, p. 185.

22. "Report of the Commission of Inquiry," pars. 186–188 (pp. 35–36) and par. 264 (p. 48).

23. Africa Watch, "Somalia: Beyond the Warlords," p. 18.

24. "Report of the Commission of Inquiry," p. 73, detail of 13 June citation.

25. Quoted in Donatella Lorch, "20 Somalis Die When Peacekeepers Fire at Crowd," *The New York Times*, 14 June 1993, p. A1.

26. Eric Schmitt, "Somali War Casualties May Be 10,000," *The New York Times*, 8 December 1993, A14.

27. Recounted by Patrick J. Sloyan, "Somalia Mission Control; Clinton called the shots in the failed policy targeting Aidid," *Newsday*, 5 December 1993.

28. "The Retreat," *The Economist* (London), 16 October 1993, p. 45.

29. "Report of the Commission of Inquiry," par. 231 (p. 43) and par. 225 (p. 42).

CHAPTER 6: THE FUGITIVE

Lead quote: Quoted in "Perspectives," *Newsweek* (international), 18 October 1993, p. 5.

1. Donatella Lorch, "Mogadishu Journal; To Find a Happy Ending, Somalis Take In a Movie," *The New York Times*, 8 March 1994, p. A4.

2. Lewis, *A Modern History of Somalia*, p. 91.

3. Ibid., p. 82.

4. Drysdale, *Whatever Happened to Somalia?*, p. 192.

5. Gen. Mohamed Farah Aidid, interview in Mogadishu, 21 December 1994.

6. Abdi Hassan Awale "Qaybdiid," interview in Mogadishu, 8 March 1999.

7. Hussein Mohamed Adbi "Sanjeeh," interviews in Mogadishu, 8–9 March 1999.

8. Lt. Gen. Thomas Montgomery (Ret.), telephone interview, 10 October 1999.

9. Testimony of Maj. Gen. Thomas Montgomery to the US Senate Armed Services Committee, 12 May 1994.

10. Figures drawn from "Report of the Commission of Inquiry," section on "Military Actions; 5 June–22 October 1993," pp. 60–67.

11. Rick Atkinson, "The Raid That Went Awry: How an Elite U.S. Force Failed in Somalia," Part One of series "Firefight in Mogadishu: The Last Mission of Task Force Ranger," *The Washington Post,* 30 January 1994, pp. A1, A26–A27.

12. First reported in "The Pitfalls of Peacekeeping," *Newsweek,* 26 July 1993, pp. 10–11, and confirmed by eyewitness accounts.

13. As quoted in "Prison beats Mogadishu on U.S. Independence Day," *Agence France Presse,* 4 July 1993.

14. An unclassified paper as quoted in *Defense Week,* "a Washington Newsletter," as quoted in Michael R. Gordon with John H. Cushman Jr., "Mission in Somalia; After Supporting Hunt for Aidid, U.S. Is Blaming U.N. for Losses," *The New York Times,* 18 October 1993, p. A1.

15. Quoted in Gordon with Cushman, "Mission in Somalia."

16. Recounted in Michael Elliott, "The Making of a Fiasco," *Newsweek* (international), 18 October 1993, p. 9.

17. Quoted in Donatella Lorch, "Envoy, With Glass Half Full, Toasts Operation in Somalia Despite Critics," *The New York Times,* 9 October 1993.

18. Recounted in Richard Ellis, "U.S. military were warned by SAS," *The Sunday Times* (London), 12 September 1993.

19. Recounted during 12 December 1994 interview in Nairobi with Keith B. Richburg of *The Washington Post,* who visited Gosende with Reid Miller of the Associated Press.

20. Mohamed Hassan Awale, interview in Mogadishu, 7 March 1999.

21. Richburg interview in Nairobi, 12 December 1994.

22. Specialist Jason Moore, interviewed for "Ambush in Mogadishu," PBS-WGBH/*Frontline* documentary, #1704, air date 28 September 1998, as quoted at http://www.pbs.org/wgbh/pages/frontline/shows/ambush/ interviews/moore.html.

23. CIA special agent Gene Cullen, interview for "Ambush in Mogadishu," PBS-WGBH/*Frontline* documentary.

24. Quoted in Gordon with Cushman, "Mission in Somalia."

25. Mark Bowden, *Black Hawk Down: A Story of Modern War* (New York: Atlantic Monthly Press, 1999), p. 91.

26. Patrick J. Sloyan, "How the Warlord Outwitted Clinton's Spooks," *The Washington Post,* 3 April 1994.

27. Patrick J. Sloyan, "Hunting Down Aidid; Why Clinton changed mind," *Newsday,* 6 December 1993.

28. Atkinson, "The Raid That Went Awry."

29. As quoted in Sloyan, "How the Warlord Outwitted Clinton's Spooks."

30. Kathleen DeLaski, as quoted in Sloyan, "Hunting Down Aidid."

31. Kent DeLong and Steven Tuckey, *Mogadishu! Heroism and Tragedy* (Westport, CT: Praeger Publishers, 1994), p. 8.

32. Atkinson, "The Raid That Went Awry."

33. Maj. Gen. William F. Garrison, "After Action Report for TASK FORCE RANGER Operations in Support of Unosom II; 22 August–15 October 1993," dated 5 January 1994, pp. 3, 5, released to author through Freedom of Information Act.

34. As recounted in Drysdale, *Whatever Happened to Somalia?*, p. 208.

35. Bowden, *Black Hawk Down*, p. 25.

36. Christopher Ogden, "Wrong Place, Wrong Time," *Time* (international), 13 September 1993, p. 43.

37. As quoted in Bowden, *Black Hawk Down*, pp. 26–27.

38. Reuters, "Quizzed on Somalia, UN Chief asks, 'What Cock-Up?'" 31 August 1993.

39. As quoted in Atkinson, "The Raid That Went Awry."

40. RPG, *Hope Restored?*, p. 41.

41. Garrison, "After Action Report," pp. 3-B-1, 3-B-2.

42. Ibid., pp. 3-C-1, 3-C-2.

43. Stevenson, *Losing Mogadishu*, p. 93.

44. As quoted in Bowden, *Black Hawk Down*, p. 27.

45. Quoted in Ellis, "U.S. military were warned by SAS."

46. Recounted in Bowden, *Black Hawk Down*, p. 23.

47. Recounted in Atkinson, "The Raid That Went Awry," with expletive from Bowden, *Black Hawk Down*, p. 23.

48. Long, interview in Nairobi, 12 March 1999.

49. Moore interview, "Ambush in Mogadishu." *Frontline.*

50. Atkinson, "The Raid That Went Awry."

51. Quoted in Keith B. Richburg, "Stuck in Somalia? American Mission is Unclear, Open-Ended," *The Washington Post,* 21 September 1993.

52. As quoted in Stevenson, *Losing Mogadishu*, p. 92.

53. As quoted in Gordon with Cushman, "Mission in Somalia."

54. Julia Preston, "U.N. Removes Italian General Impeding Somalia Operation," *The Washington Post,* 15 July 1993, p. A20.

55. Carter details recounted in Sloyan, "Hunting Down Aidid," and other sources.

56. Keith B. Richburg, "U.S. Somalia Envoy Urged Policy Shift Before 18 GIs Died," *The Washington Post,* 11 November 1993.

57. Keith B. Richburg, *Out of America: A Black Man Confronts Africa* (New York: Basic Books, 1997), p. 77.

58. Keith B. Richburg, "Under U.N.'s Nose, Somali Defiant," *The Washington Post,* 5 September 1993.

59. Quoted in Keith B. Richburg, "Reality in Mogadishu: A Conflict in Views; U.N. Officials, Journalists Differ Over Whether Safety Has Improved in Somali Capital," *The Washington Post,* 14 July 1993, p. A13. Richburg was so incensed at Albright's "gall" at telling journalists to "get around like her" that he sent a formal letter demanding an apology.

60. Keith B. Richburg, "Pen Mighty in Somalia: Gun Helps," *The Washington Post,* 9 September 1993.

CHAPTER 7: BLOODY MONDAY

Lead quote: Quoted in Michael Elliott, with John Barry and Karen Breslau, "The Neurotic Lion," *Newsweek,* 26 September 1994, p. 36.

1. Sanjeeh interviews, Mogadishu.

2. Qaybdiid interview, Mogadishu.

3. Sanjeeh interviews, Mogadishu.

4. Jean, ed., *Life, Death and Aid*, p. 107.

5. "Protocol Additional to the Geneva Conventions of 12 August 1949, and Relating to the Protection of Victims of International Armed Conflicts (Protocol I), of 8 June 1977" (Geneva: International Committee of the Red Cross, 1977), Articles 51, 52. Also Roy Gutman and Daoud Kuttab, "Indiscriminate Attack," in Roy Gutman and David Rieff, eds., *Crimes of War: What the Public Should Know* (New York: W. W. Norton, 1999), pp. 195–198.

6. Kenneth Anderson, "Afterword," in Gutman and Rieff, eds., *Crimes of War*, pp. 385.

7. "Report of the Commission of Inquiry," par. 152 (p. 30).

8. Quoted in Schofield, *Silent Over Africa*, p. 101, and Africa Watch, "Annual World Report 1994" (New York: Africa Watch, 1995), p. 49.

9. Jean, ed., *Life, Death and Aid*, p. 121.

10. US Department of the Air Force, Air Force Pamphlet No. 110–31, *International Law—The Conduct of Armed Conflict and Air Operations*, 19 November 1976, chapter 5, p. 9.

11. Montgomery interview.

12. Barton Gellman and R. Jeffrey Smith, "Course of Conflict Depends on the Success of U.S. Air Power," *The Washington Post*, 17 January 1991, p. A23.

13. Frank Smyth, "Gulf War," in Gutman and Rieff, eds., *Crimes of War*, p. 162.

14. H. Wayne Elliott, "Dead and Wounded," in Gutman and Rieff, eds., *Crimes of War*, p. 118.

15. Quoted in Donatella Lorch, "U.N. Counts on U.S. Rangers to Find Warlord," *The New York Times*, 26 August 1993, p. A8.

16. Notes of Montgomery interview in Mogadishu, 24 March 1994, provided to the author by Rick Atkinson of *The Washington Post*.

17. Julia Preston and Daniel Williams, "Report on Somali Clash Faults U.S., U.N., Aideed," *The Washington Post*, 31 March 1994, p. A28. Details of restrictions from Julia Preston, in personal correspondence, 11 July 1999.

18. "Report of the Commission of Inquiry," par. 238 (p. 44).

CHAPTER 8: MISSION IMPOSSIBLE

Lead quote: Angus Hamilton, *Somaliland* (Westport, CT: Greenwood, 1972) as quoted by Richard Dowden and Karl Maier in "The Darkness Gathers Again," *The Independent*, 21 February 1993, p. 14.

1. Atkinson, "The Raid That Went Awry," and Bowden, *Black Hawk Down*, pp. 28–29.

2. As reported in "Informed Sources" column, *Time* (international), 8 November 1993, p. 13.

3. Quoted in Atkinson, "The Raid That Went Awry."

4. Wayne Long, interview in Nairobi.

5. This account and quote drawn from Bowden, *Black Hawk Down*, pp. 110–111.

6. Quoted in Atkinson, "The Raid That Went Awry."

7. Ibid.

8. Rick Atkinson, "Night of a Thousand Casualties: Battle Triggered U.S. Decision to Withdraw from Somalia," Part 2 of Series "Firefight in Mogadishu: The Last Mission of Task Force Ranger," *The Washington Post*, 31 January 1994, pp. A1, A10–A11.

9. Video and lost convoy drawn from Bowden, *Black Hawk Down*, pp. 101–131.

10. As quoted in Elizabeth Drew, *On the Edge: The Clinton Presidency* (New York: Simon & Schuster, 1994), p. 322.

11. Lewis, *A Pastoral Democracy*, p. 198.

12. Quoted in Michael Gordon, "US Officers Were Divided on Somali Raid," *The New York Times*, 13 May 1994, p. A8.

13. Elaine Sciolino, "Pentagon Changes Its Somalia Goals As Effort Falters," *The New York Times*, 28 September 1993, p. A1.

14. As quoted in Barry Schweid, "Boutros-Ghali Warns U.S. Against Withdrawing From Somalia," Associated Press, 30 September 1993, and Elaine Sciolino, "U.N. Chief Warning U.S. Against Pullout of Force in Somalia," *The New York Times*, 1 October 1993, p. A1.

15. As quoted in Drew, *On the Edge*, p. 325.

16. Captive pilot Michael Durant interview with Mark Huband and Stephen Smith, as quoted in Huband, "'The People Killed Them. Chopped Them Up. I Consider Myself Lucky,'" *The Guardian* (London), 9 October 1993, p. 1.

17. Interview with Copley newspapers, as quoted in Tom Raum, "Clinton Says U.S. Must 'Conclude Our Role' in Somalia," The Associated Press, 6 October 1993.

18. Quoted in Elliott, "The Making of a Fiasco."

19. Oakley interview, "Ambush in Mogadishu," *Frontline*.

20. Bowden, *Black Hawk Down*, p. 345.

21. Quoted in "Letting Bygones Be Bygones," *Time* (international), 1 November 1993, p. 9.

22. Figures from RPG, *Hope Restored?*, pp. 2, 5, note 1.

23. Quoted in Donatella Lorch, "Americans Count Hours to End of Somali Mission," *The New York Times*, 28 February 1994.

CHAPTER 9: BACK TO ZERO

Lead quote: Lewis, *A Pastoral Democracy*, p. 246.

1. Gassem, *Hostages*, pp. 112, 113, 136.

2. Lewis, *A Pastoral Democracy*, p. 252.

3. Adm. Jonathan Howe, interview in Mogadishu, 12 September 1993.

4. Copy of Carter Letter to Clinton, faxed to Boutros-Ghali, as quoted in Boutros Boutros-Ghali, *Unvanquished: A U.S.-U.N. Saga* (New York: Random House, 1999), p. 104.

5. Lewis, *A Pastoral Democracy*, p. 244.

6. Montgomery testimony to the US Senate Armed Services Committee.

NOTES 339

7. Richburg interview, in Nairobi.

8. Letter as quoted in Mark Bowden, "How a relief mission ended in a firefight," *The Philadelphia Inquirer,* 14 December 1997, and first in Patrick J. Sloyan, "Full of Tears and Grief; For elite commandos, operation ended in disaster," *Newsday,* 7 December 1993.

9. Garrison testimony to the US Senate Armed Services Committee.

10. This "Washington lore" as described in Michael Hirsh, "At War With Ourselves; In Kosovo, America confronts its own ideals," *Harper's Magazine,* July 1999, pp. 60–69.

11. "Report of the Commission of Inquiry," par. 125 (p. 26).

12. Quoted in Ron Martz, "Slain GIs' Dads Won't Let Clinton Forget; Hearings on Mistakes in Somalia Demanded," *The Atlanta Journal and Constitution,* 29 March 1994, p. A15.

13. Larry Joyce, "Mr. Clinton, why did my son have to die?" KRT News Wire from *The Philadelphia Inquirer,* as published in *The Dallas Morning News,* 18 December 1993, p. 25A.

14. Quoted in Sloyan, "How the Warlord Outwitted Clinton's Spooks."

15. Clinton at a press conference after his first, subdued speech to UN General Assembly, 27 September 1993. Quoted in Thomas L. Friedman, "Clinton, at U.N., Lists Stiff Terms For Sending U.S. Force to Bosnia," *The New York Times,* 28 September 1993, p. A1.

16. "Report of the Commission of Inquiry," par. 244 (p. 45) and par. 233 (p. 43).

17. "The Retreat," *The Economist.*

18. Drawn from John A. Ausink, Pew Case Study 374: "Watershed in Rwanda: The Evolution of President Clinton's Humanitarian Intervention Policy" (Washington, D.C.: Institute for the Study of Diplomacy Publications, Georgetown University, 1997); and from Thomas H. Henriksen, "Clinton's Foreign Policy in Somalia, Bosnia, Haiti and North Korea," Essays in Public Policy (Stanford University, Hoover Institution on War, Revolution and Peace, 1996).

19. Ivo H. Daalder, Pew Case Study 462: "The Clinton Administration and Multilateral Peace Operations" (Washington, D.C.: Institute for the Study of Diplomacy, 1994), p. 7, as cited by Ausink, "Watershed in Rwanda," p. 4.

20. As quoted in Boutros-Ghali, *Unvanquished,* p. 116.

21. Daniel Williams, "Joining the Pantheon of American Missteps," *The Washington Post,* 26 March 1994.

22. Richard Holbrooke, *To End a War* (New York: Random House, 1998), pp. 216–217.

23. Alain Destexhe, *Rwanda and Genocide in the Twentieth Century* (New York: New York University Press, 1995), p. 49.

24. Quoted in RPG, *Hope Restored?,* p. 43.

25. As quoted in Schweid, "Boutros-Ghali Warns U.S.," and Sciolino, "U.N. Chief Warning U.S. Against Pullout."

26. Quote and comment in Michael Elliott *et al.,* "The Neurotic Lion."

27. Cost details drawn from Rick Atkinson, "U.N. Keeps Spending on Its Somalia

Base; Only 4% of $1.6 Billion Budgeted for Peacekeeping Reaches Streets of Mogadishu," *The Washington Post,* 24 March 1994.

28. Rick Atkinson, "In Divided Mogadishu, GIs Recall Losses; U.N. Keeps Sharks and Somalis at Bay," *The Washington Post,* 26 November 1993.

29. Quoted in Atkinson, "U.N. Keeps Spending on Its Somali Base."

CHAPTER 10: DIVIDED BY GOD

Lead quote: "Sudan Defends Its Record on Human Rights," Agence France Press, 23 February 1995.

1. Cyril Glassé, *The Concise Encyclopedia of Islam* (San Francisco: Harper & Row, 1989), pp. 375–377.

2. Herodotus, *The Histories,* translated by Aubrey de Sélincourt (London: Penguin, 1972 [this translation first published 1954]), pp. 137–141.

3. *Sudan: A Country Study,* Foreign Area Studies, American University, ed. Harold D. Nelson (U.S. Government Printing Office, 1982), p. 4, as quoted in Judith Miller, *God Has Ninety-Nine Names: Reporting from a Militant Middle East* (New York: Simon & Schuster, 1996), p. 130.

4. Milton Viorst, *In the Shadow of the Prophet: The Struggle for the Soul of Islam* (New York: Anchor Books, 1998), p. 114.

5. Francis M. Deng, *War of Visions: Conflict of Identities in the Sudan* (Washington, D.C.: Brookings Institution, 1995), p. 10.

6. Major G. W. Titherington, "The Riak Dinka of Bahr al Ghazal Province," *Sudan Notes and Records, no. 10* (1927), pp. 159–169, as quoted by Blaine Harden, *Africa: Dispatches from a Fragile Continent* (London: HarperCollins, 1992 [New York: W.W. Norton, 1990]), p. 139.

7. UN Commission on Human Rights, "Situation of Human Rights in the Sudan: Report of the Special Rapporteur, Mr. Gáspár Bíró, submitted in accordance with Commission on Human Rights resolution 1993/60," Economic and Social Council document E/CN.4/1994/48, 1 February 1994, p. 20. [Hereafter referred to as UN Human Rights Report.]

8. As quoted by Mohamed Omer Beshir, *The Southern Sudan: Background to Conflict* (London: C. Hurst and Co., 1968), p. 27.

9. Ibid., p. 51.

10. Ibid., p. 81.

11. Ibid.

12. Graham F. Thomas, *Sudan: Death of a Dream* (London: Darf Publishers, 1990), p. 198.

13. Miller, *God Has Ninety-Nine Names,* p. 136, note 16.

14. Isaiah 18: 1, 2, The Jerusalem Bible (London: Darton, Longman & Todd, 1966).

15. Ezekiel 38, 39, The Jerusalem Bible.

16. Revelation 20: 8, The Jerusalem Bible.

17. Alex de Waal, ed., *Food and Power in Sudan: A Critique of Humanitarianism* (London: African Rights, May 1997), p. 55.

18. Miller, *God Has Ninety-Nine Names*, p. 146.

19. Details drawn from Jean Gueyras, "Doubts over Sudan's new masters," *Le Monde* (Paris), 23–24 July 1989, as published in *The Guardian Weekly* (London), 30 July 1989, p. 17.

20. Figures quoted by Julie Flint, "Even If They Have to Beat Schoolboys Senseless the Rulers of Sudan Will Have Their New Society," *The Independent on Sunday* (London), 2 May 1993, p. 11.

21. "Rumour and red tape," *The Economist* (London), 11 August 1990, p. 51.

22. UN Human Rights Report, pp. 11–12.

23. Quoted in "Sudanese Leader Rejects U.N. Human Rights Report," The Associated Press in Khartoum, 13 February 1994.

24. As quoted in UN Human Rights Report, p. 15.

25. Jonathan Petre, "Adultery charge bishop flogged," *The Daily Telegraph* (London), 6 September 1993, p. 1; Richard Pendlebury, "Moslems flog bishop; Anglican is given 80 lashes in public after adultery charge by fanatics," *The Daily Mail* (London), 6 September 1993, p. 12; and "Archbishop condemns flogging of bishop in Sudan," Reuters, 6 September 1993.

26. As quoted in Africa Watch, "Denying the Honor of Living: Sudan: A Human Rights Disaster," March 1990.

27. As quoted in UN Human Rights Report, p. 23.

28. Hassan al-Turabi, interview in Khartoum, March 1992.

29. Deng, *War of Visions*, p. 5.

30. Hassan al-Turabi, interview in Khartoum, 27 August 1998.

31. *The Saudi Gazette*, 6 June 1995, as quoted in Miller, *God Has Ninety-Nine Names*, p. 498, note 22.

32. "Martyrs to the cause," *New African*, June 1994, p. 29.

33. Alfred Taban, "Sudanese civilians seek battlefield martyrdom," Reuters, 1 September 1993; and "Martyrs to the cause," Ibid.

34. Jinn details in "Sudan: Heavenly Powers," *Africa Confidential* (London) 33:18, 11 September 1992, p. 8.

35. As quoted in Mark Huband, *Warriors of the Prophet: The Struggle for Islam* (Boulder, CO: Westview, 1998), pp. 148–149.

36. Francis M. Deng and Larry Minear, *The Challenges of Famine Relief: Emergency Operations in the Sudan* (Washington D.C.: Brookings Institution, 1992), p. 113.

37. Detailed by Amnesty International, "Sudan: The Ravages of War; Political killing and humanitarian disaster," 29 September 1993, pp. 16–17, 19.

38. Quoted in "Sudan: Aspirations," *Africa Confidential* (London), 35:20, 7 October 1994, p. 8.

CHAPTER 11: WAR OF THE CROSS

Lead quote: The Jerusalem Bible.

1. Sharon E. Hutchinson, *Nuer Dilemmas: Coping with Money, War, and the State* (Los Angeles: University of California Press, 1996), pp. 103–104.

2. Hutchinson, *Nuer Dilemmas*, pp. 106, 108.

3. Quoted in Peter Smerdon, "Pyjama warriors by night in southern Sudan," *Reuters News Service,* 12 February 1995.

4. Ayatollah Sadeq Khalkhali, "Islamic judge," as quoted in Amir Taheri, *Holy Terror: Inside the World of Islamic Terrorism* (Bethesda, MD: Adler & Adler, 1987 [First published in Great Britain by Century Hutchinson]), p. 44.

5. Robert D. Kaplan, "Why Sudan Starves While Western Aid Pours In," *The Wall Street Journal,* 10 November 1986.

6. As quoted in de Waal, ed., *Food and Power in Sudan,* p. 61.

7. Ibid., p. 72.

8. As quoted in Hutchinson, *Nuer Dilemmas,* p. 355.

9. De Waal, ed., *Food and Power in Sudan,* p. 82.

10. Rakiya Omaar and Alex de Waal, "Components of a Lasting Peace in Sudan: First Thoughts," Discussion Paper No. 2, African Rights, December 1993, pp. 4, 15.

11. De Waal, ed., *Food and Power in Sudan,* p. 90.

12. Quote and Pol Pot detail in "Sudan: A time for decision in the South," *Africa Confidential* (London), 35:1, 7 January 1994, pp. 1–3.

13. Quoted in Roger Rosenblatt, "The Last Place on Earth," *Vanity Fair,* July 1993, p. 106.

14. Quoted in de Waal, ed., *Food and Power in Sudan,* p. 307.

15. Drawn from Jemera Rone, John Prendergast, and Karen Sorenson, *Sudan: Civilian Devastation; Abuses by All Parties in the War in Southern Sudan* (New York: Human Rights Watch/Africa, June 1994), pp. 126–127.

16. Quoted in Huband, *Warriors of the Prophet,* p. 163.

17. "Uganda/Sudan: Atlantic Traffic," *Africa Confidential* (London), 33:18, 11 September 1992, p. 8; and "Uganda: Missiles Incorporated," *Africa Confidential* (London), 33:17, 28 August 1992, p. 8.

18. Donatella Lorch, "Life in the War Zone: Boredom and Terror, Bullets and Hepatitis," *The New York Times,* 21 January 1996, Section 13, p. 10.

CHAPTER 12: THE FALSE MESSIAH

Lead quote: Quoted in Jeffrey Bartholet, "Hidden Horrors in South Sudan, *Newsweek* (international), 5 October 1992, p. 25.

1. Tale drawn from "SPLA Split Widens into Nuer-Dinka Conflict as Any Nya Two Destroys Bor," *Sudan Democratic Gazette* (London), January 1992, pp. 2, 4.

2. E. E. Evans-Pritchard, *The Nuer: A Description of the Modes of Livelihood and Political Institutions of a Nilotic People* (Oxford: Oxford University Press, 1968 [1st edition 1940]), pp. 185–188.

3. Ibid., p. 125.

4. Details from Amnesty International, "Sudan: The Ravages of War; Political killings and humanitarian disaster," 29 September 1993, p. 22, and body-count eyewitness Dan Eiffe of Norwegian People's Aid.

5. Evans-Pritchard, *The Nuer,* p. 126.

6. Ibid., p. 125.

7. *Sudan Intelligence Report,* no. 152, 1907, as quoted in ibid., p. 126.

8. Hutchinson, *Nuer Dilemmas,* pp. 338–339.

9. Rone *et al., Civilian Devastation,* pp. 102–103.

10. Evans-Pritchard, *The Nuer,* pp. 128–129.

11. "SPLA Split Widens," in *Sudan Democratic Gazette.*

12. Amnesty International, "Sudan: The Ravages of War," p. 23.

13. UN Human Rights Report, p. 37.

14. Hutchinson, *Nuer Dilemmas,* p. 297.

15. Drawn from Francis Mading Deng, *The Dinka of the Southern Sudan* (New York: Holt, Rinehart and Winston, 1972), p. 3, as quoted by Harden, *Africa: Dispatches from a Fragile Continent,* p. 136.

16. Francis Mading Deng, *Africans of Two Worlds: The Dinka in Afro-Arab Sudan* (New Haven, CT: Yale University Press, 1978), p. 70.

17. Quoted in Harden, *Africa: Dispatches from a Fragile Continent,* p. 145.

18. Evans-Pritchard, *The Nuer,* pp. 16, 49.

19. Hutchinson, *Nuer Dilemmas,* pp. 31–32.

20. Evans-Pritchard, *The Nuer,* p. 130

21. Beshir, *The Southern Sudan,* p. 19.

22. Rory Nugent, "Sudan: Rebels of the Apocalypse," *Men's Journal* (New York), September 1993, p. 109.

23. Ibid., p. 113.

24. Ibid., p. 112.

25. Ibid., p. 113.

26. Published as "The Church and Peace," *New Sudan Council of Churches News* (Nairobi), 2:1, March 1992, p. 3.

27. Quoted in Julie Flint, "Rebel divisions wreak lethal havoc in southern Sudan," *The Guardian* (London), 30 August 1993, p. 8.

28. Andrew Purvis in Ayod, "When the Flyers From Heaven Stop, We Will Die," *Time* (international), 12 April 1993, pp. 40–41.

29. Joshua Hammer in Kongor and Ayod, "Paying the Cost of 'Sharia,'" *Newsweek* (international), 19 July 1993, p. 12.

30. Radio message to Khartoum relief agency, 28 September 1988, as quoted in Rosenblatt, "The Last Place on Earth."

31. Amnesty International, "Sudan: The Ravages of War," pp. 23–25, and Nugent, "Sudan: Rebels of the Apocalypse," pp. 110–112.

32. Bishop Paride Taban, "Struggle of Sudanese People for Freedom and Peace and What I Have Learnt as a Christian and as a Human Being in the Sudan Situation?" address given at the Seminar on Solidarity, Madrid, 28–30 October 1994, p. 10.

CHAPTER 13: DARWIN DECEIVED

Lead quote: Author's interview with Philip O'Brien.

1. Quoted and drawn from Rone *et al., Civilian Devastation,* pp. 186–189.

2. "Sudan Situation Report No. 6," OFDA, 10 September 1993, as quoted in Rone *et al., Civilian Devastation,* p. 189, note 229.

3. Joint Task Force Report, p. 16, as quoted in *Famine in Sudan 1998: The*

Human Rights Causes (New York: Human Rights Watch, 1999), p. 121.

4. Hugh Nevill, "Aid agencies feeding two armies in Sudan," *Agence France Presse,* 27 July 1998.

5. "Corpse Explodes at Airport; Sabotage Feared," Associated Press, 29 December 1989.

6. Quoted in Andrew Hill, "U.N. document accuses SPLA of 'callous' killings," Reuters, 4 October 1992.

7. Save the Children-UK, as quoted by Ataul Karim (team leader), Mark Duffield, Susanne Jaspars, Aldo Benini, Joanna Macrae, Mark Bradbury, Douglas Johnson, George Larbi, and Barbara Hendrie (editor), *OLS: Operation Lifeline Sudan: A Review,* July 1996, p. 161.

8. Jean, ed., *Life, Death and Aid,* p. 17.

9. Ibid., p. 20.

10. Human Rights Watch, *Famine in Sudan 1998,* p. 42.

11. Ibid., p. 2.

12. Karim, Duffield *et al., OLS Review,* p. 153.

13. De Waal *et al., Food and Power in Sudan,* p. 352, 358.

14. Quoted in Peter Smerdon, "Five Foreign Aid Workers Freed in South Sudan," Reuters, 11 February 1995.

15. "Southern Sector, Operation Lifeline Sudan 1994 Assessment," October 1994, Nairobi, p. 3.

16. Human Rights Watch, *Famine in Sudan* 1998, p. 176.

17. Omaar and de Waal, "Components of a Lasting Peace in Sudan," p. 17.

18. Quoted in Robert M. Press, "Sudan Drought Threatens Millions," *The Christian Science Monitor,* 28 September 1990, p. 3.

19. "Rumour and red tape," *The Economist* (London), 11 August 1990, p. 51.

20. "Unicef and WFP Request Urgent Funding for War-Torn Southern Sudan," UN Operation Lifeline Sudan, press release, 14 February 1994.

21. "Nutrition and Mortality Assessment," US Agency for International Development Center for Disease Control report, as quoted in Rone *et al., Civilian Devastation,* p. 162.

22. Details of Ethiopian camps and early days of the "Lost Boys" drawn from Rone *et al., Civilian Devastation,* pp. 207–208.

23. Johannes Zutt, *Children of War: Wandering alone in southern Sudan* (New York: Unicef, March 1994), pp. 2, 30.

24. Quoted in Robert M. Press, "Sudanese Rebel Army Accused of Training Children for Combat," *The Christian Science Monitor* (world edition), 1–7 November 1991.

25. UN Human Rights Report, p. 33.

26. Estimates from two control groups of children at Nasir and Kakuma, presented in "OLS (Southern Sector) September 1994 Overview."

27. Quoted in Jennifer Parmelee in Kakuma, "We Think God Has Been Punishing Us; War in Sudan Sets Boys on Trail of Terror," *The Washington Post,* 1 February 1994.

28. Ibid.

CHAPTER 14: A HOLOCAUST

Lead quote: "Hutu and Tutsi: a false ethnic divide," in Jean, ed., *Populations in Danger* 1995, p. 31.

1. Alex Shoumatoff, "The Woman Who Loved Gorillas," in *African Madness* (New York: Alfred A. Knopf, 1988), p. 14.
2. Gérard Prunier, *The Rwanda Crisis: History of a Genocide* (New York: Columbia University Press, 1995), p. 261. Written by a French historian, this book is by far the best source written in English that details the history and roots of the genocide, especially the French role.
3. *La Lettre du Continent,* 16 June 1994, as quoted by Prunier, *The Rwanda Crisis,* p. 243, note 53.
4. "Hutu and Tutsi: a false ethnic divide," p. 30.
5. Aidan Hartley, "Prejudice-laced Book Gives Clue to Rwanda Horror," Reuters, 20 June 1994.
6. Quoted in "Hutu and Tutsi: a false ethnic divide," p. 31.
7. Guy Vassall-Adams, "Rwanda, An Agenda for International Action," Oxfam Publications, 13 October 1994, pp. 8–9.
8. Prunier, *The Rwanda Crisis,* pp. 38–39.
9. UN Trusteeship Commission Report (March 1961), as quoted by Prunier, *The Rwanda Crisis,* p. 52.

CHAPTER 15: "DREADFUL NOTE OF PREPARATION"

1. This figure is in dispute. Though most journalists referred during the genocide to a Tutsi population of 14% and the Hutu 85%, these figures were taken from a tribal census carried out by Belgian authorities in the 1930s. Since then the Hutu population has grown much faster and many Tutsis had been driven out. US Embassy figures in 1990 divided the population into 9% Tutsi and 90% Hutu.
2. "The Hutu Ten Commandments," *Kangura,* No. 6, 10 December 1990, as printed in Rakiya Omaar, *Rwanda: Death, Despair, and Defiance* (London: African Rights, August 1995 [revised edition]), pp. 42–43. This huge tome, and Alison Des Forges' also bulky *Leave None to Tell the Story: Genocide in Rwanda* (New York and Paris: Human Rights Watch and Fédération Internationale des Ligues des Droits de L'Homme, March 1999), are by far the two most comprehensive efforts to document the genocide.
3. Guy Vassall-Adams, "An Agenda for International Action," pp. 12, 24.
4. International Commission details drawn from "Beyond the Rhetoric: Continuing Human Rights Abuses in Rwanda," Africa Watch, 5:7, June 1993, pp. 19–20.
5. "Oubreak of Violence Follows Human Rights Investigation in Rwanda," Africa Watch, 27 January 1993.
6. As quoted in Vassall-Adams, "An Agenda for International Action," p. 25; "Arming Rwanda: The Arms Trade and Human Rights Abuses in the Rwanda War," Human Rights Arms Project, New York, 6:1, January 1994, p. 11; and Omaar, *Rwanda: Death, Despair and Defiance,* p. 33.

7. Confidential message addressed *to "Son Excellence Madame le Premier Ministre,"* 23 March 1994, from Dr. Augustin Iyamuremye, head of the intelligence service.

8. Letter to minister of defense from Chief of Staff Maj. Gen. Déogratias Nsabimana.

9. *Kangura,* as quoted in Omaar, *Rwanda: Death, Despair and Destruction,* pp. 71–73

10. As quoted in Prunier, *The Rwanda Crisis,* pp. 222–223.

11. Order for "Operation FRA," Unamir Civilian Police document, signed by Commander "Sangare, CPMT," Kigali, 6 April 1994.

12. Louis de Lacger, *Ruanda,* Kabgayi, 1959, as quoted in Prunier, *The Rwanda Crisis,* p. 31. Church history drawn primarily from Prunier.

13. Prunier, *The Rwanda Crisis,* p. 132, note 10, and p. 34.

14. Msgr. Thaddée Nsengiyumva (primate of Rwanda), *Convertissons-nous pour vivre ensemble dans la paix,* Kabgayi, 40 pp. (mimeo), as quoted in Prunier, *The Rwanda Crisis,* p. 132.

15. Prunier, *The Rwanda Crisis,* p. 252.

16. "Pope appeals for Burundi, recalls Rwanda dead," Reuters, 26 March 1995.

17. "Vatican Calls for Rwandan Peace Conference," Reuters, 27 April 1994.

18. Des Forges, *Leave None to Tell the Story,* p. 47

19. Quoted in Sam Kiley, "I saw hills covered with bodies resembling lawns of flesh," *The Times* (London), 14 May 1994, p. 12.

20. Quoted in Sam Kiley in an unpublished story commissioned by "The Magazine" of *The Sunday Times* (London) and written 10 June 1994. Editor Nick Wapshott found the 3,700-word story "too depressing" to publish, according to Kiley, and one editor said that his wife, after reading the rough draft, "was having nightmares."

21. The Rev. Octave Ugiras, as quoted in Edith M. Lederer, "Catholic Priest Examining Why Church Failed to Stop Massacres," The Associated Press, 16 January 1995.

22. Testimonies of survivors in *"Sous la soutane, la manchette . . ."* [Under the cassock, the machete. . .], part of an investigation *"Rwanda: La Machette e le Goupillon; De la responsabilité de l'Église catholiqudans le génocide du Rwanda,"* *Golias Magazine* (Villeurbanne, France), No. 43, July–August 1995, and elsewhere.

23. African Rights, "Father Wenceslas Munyeshyaka: In the Eyes of the Survivors of Sainte Famille," Witness No. 9, April 1999.

24. *La Libre Belgique,* 21 February 1992, as quoted by Prunier, *The Rwanda Crisis,* p. 149.

25. Prunier, *The Rwanda Crisis,* p. 164, note 9.

26. Both French ambassador quotes in "Arming Rwanda," pp. 23–24.

27. Drawn from "Arming Rwanda," pp. 4, 14–18, 28.

28. Alain Frilet and Sylvie Coma, *"Paris, terre d'asile de luxe pour dignitaires hutus,"* as quoted in Des Forges, *Leave None to Tell the Story,* p. 659.

29. Details of French weapons shipments and quote in "Rearming with Impunity: International Support for the Perpetrators of the Rwandan Genocide," Human Rights Watch Arms Project, New York, 7:4, May 1995, pp. 6–7. For a direct source, see Prunier, *The Rwanda Crisis,* p. 278, note 136.

30. Radio Monte Carlo, reported in *L'Humanité*, 29 June 1994, as quoted in Prunier, *The Rwanda Crisis*, p. 278.

31. Details from Crespo Sebunya (news editor of Uganda's *Business World*), "Paul Kagame: The Stern Commander," *New African*, September 1994, p. 35.

32. Quoted in "Kagame: From soldier to civilian," Reuters, as published in *The Nation* (Nairobi), 26 August 1994.

33. "Rwanda: A Double Agenda," *Africa Confidential* (London), 35:10, 20 May 1994, p. 8; Prunier, *The Rwanda Crisis*, p. 277; Des Forges, *Leave None to Tell the Story*, pp. 285–286, 658.

34. Nickname and *Kangura* caption as quoted in Prunier, *The Rwanda Crisis*, p. 165, notes 10, 12.

35. "Mitterrand Says Few Ready to Join Paris in Rwanda," Reuters, 18 June 1994.

36. RTLM as quoted in Prunier, *The Rwanda Crisis*, p. 292, note 21.

37. UN civil servant, as quoted in Prunier, *The Rwanda Crisis*, p. 287, note 14.

38. Quoted in Aidan Hartley, "Anti-French Rwanda Rebels a Force to Reckon With," Reuters, 20 June 1994.

39. Prunier, *The Rwanda Crisis*, p. 294, note 27. The historian had been asked to advise French officials on the Turquoise operation—to provide political cover as a critical academic, he says—and so had an insider's view of these events.

40. Details of clandestine weapons shipments from Zaire and elsewhere to the French-protected "security zone" of French weapons caches and French lists of genocide suspects in "Rearming with Impunity," pp. 7–8.

41. "Rwanda: Implausible Deniability," *Africa Confidential* (London), 35:14, 15 July 1994, p. 8.

42. Overheard and quoted in Prunier, *The Rwanda Crisis*, p. 337, note 49.

CHAPTER 16: GENOCIDE DENIED

Lead quote: Barbara Ehrenreich, *Blood Rites*, p. 25.

1. Official Transcript, "Remarks by the President at Dedication of the United States Holocaust Memorial Museum," The White House, Office of the Press Secretary, Washington, D.C., 22 April 1993.

2. "Genocide in Rwanda, April–May 1994," p. 9.

3. Quoted in John-Thor Dahlburg in Kigali, "Why the World Let Rwanda Bleed; Chastened by Somalia, a Gun-Shy U.S. Urged Caution On An Already Weary United Nations, Braking Efforts to Stem the Brutality," *The Los Angeles Times*, 10 September 1994, p. A1.

4. Outgoing Code Cable from Dallaire/Unamir/Kigali to Baril/DPKO/UNations New York, 11 January 1994.

5. Fax "From Annan, UNations, New York, 'Subject: Contacts with Informant,' to Booh-Booh/Dallaire, Unamir *Only No Distribution*," 11 January 1994; at www.pbs.org/wgbh/pages/frontline/shows/evil/warning/unresponse.html; and first reported in Philip Gourevitch, "The Genocide Fax," *The New Yorker*, 11 May 1998, pp. 43–46.

6. Lindsey Hilsum, "Massacre details were revealed months in advance," *The Observer* (London), 26 November 1995, p. 23.

7. Dahlburg, "Why the World Let Rwanda Bleed."

8. Quoted by Jeffrey Ulbrich in Kigali, "Rwanda-Massacres," Associated Press, 13 June 1994.

9. Ambassador Karel Kovanda, Czech envoy to UN in 1994, interviewed for *The Triumph of Evil*, PBS-WGBH/*Frontline* documentary, which aired 26 January 1999. Transcript at http://www.pbs.org/wgbh/pages/frontline/shows/evil/etc/script.html.

10. Ian Martin, former secretary general of Amnesty International and former chief of the UN Human Rights Field Operations in Rwanda, "After Genocide: The United Nations Human Rights Field Operation in Rwanda," Papers in Theory and Practice of Human Rights, No. 20 (Colchester, UK: Human Rights Center, University of Essex, 1998), p. 2.

11. Captain Luc Lumiere, Belgian army, interviewed for *The Triumph of Evil*, PBS-WGBH/*Frontline* documentary.

12. Julia Preston, "Rwandans Confound U.N. Security Council; Humanitarian Impulse as Mission Impossible," *The Washington Post*, 8 May 1994, p. A25.

13. Ambassador Karel Kovanda, Czech envoy to NATO in Brussels, telephone interview, 9 July 1999.

14. Preston, "Rwandans Confound U.N. Security Council."

15. Rony Brauman, "Genocide in Rwanda: We Can't Say We Didn't Know," in *Populations in Danger* 1995, p. 89.

16. Boutros-Ghali, *Unvanquished*, p. 132.

17. Private use among officials of the term "genocide" within days, as told to Craig Nelson, correspondent for The Associated Press, by State Department sources.

18. As reported in "The Triumph of Evil," *Frontline*.

19. As quoted in Keith B. Richburg, "Rwandan Rebels Close Border; Untold Thousands of Would-Be Refugees Prevented from Fleeing," *The Washington Post*, 1 May 1994, p. A34.

20. "Stopping Rwanda's Bloodbath," *The Washington Post*, 5 May 1994.

21. Stanley Meisler, "Albright Defends Rwanda Troop Delay; United Nations: Sending Extra 5,000 Peacekeepers Now Would Be 'Folly,' Ambassador Says," *The Los Angeles Times*, 18 May 1994, p. A4; Douglas Jehl, "U.S. Is Showing a New Caution On U.N. Peacekeeping Missions, *The New York Times*, 18 May 1994, p. A1; Larry Elliott, "Fury Greets US Block on Peace Force," *The Guardian* (London), 18 May 1994.

22. Quoted in Meisler, "Albright Defends Rwanda Troop Delay."

23. Kovanda, telephone interview.

24. Quoted in Meisler, "Albright Defends Rwanda Troop Delay;" Jehl, "U.S. is Showing a New Caution;" Dahlburg, "Why the World Let Rwanda Bleed;" and Pew Case 374, p. 7

25. Albright interview for *McNeil/Lehrer NewsHour*, according to transcript, 19 May 1994.

26. Boutros-Ghali, *Unvanquished*, pp. 135, 141.

27. Philip Gourevitch, *We Wish to Inform You That Tomorrow We Will Be Killed*

With Our Families: Stories from Rwanda (New York: Farrar, Straus and Giroux, 1998), p. 151.

28. Douglas Jehl, "Officials Told to Avoid Calling Rwanda Killings 'Genocide,'" *The New York Times*, 10 June 1994, p. A8; Thomas Lippman, "Administration Side-steps Genocide Label in Rwanda, *The Washington Post*, 11 June 1994, p. A1.

29. "Convention on the Prevention and Punishment of the Crime of Genocide," approved by the UN General Assembly in Resolution 260A (III) on 9 December 1948, and put into effect 12 January 1951.

30. Quoted by Lippman, "Administration Sidesteps Genocide Label in Rwanda."

31. Kovanda, telephone interview.

32. Ambassador Pedauye, interview and correspondence.

33. As quoted in Michael R. Gordon, "U.S. to Supply 60 Vehicles for U.N. Troops in Rwanda," *The New York Times*, 16 June 1994, p. A12.

34. Philip Gourevitch, author and writer for *The New Yorker*, interviewed for *The Triumph of Evil*, PBS-WGBH/*Frontline* documentary.

35. Lara Santoro in Arusha, Tanzania, "Rwanda Massacres Were Avoidable, General Says," *The Christian Science Monitor*, 27 February 1998.

36. John H. Cushman, Jr., "President Orders Pentagon Action to Aid Rwandans," *The New York Times*, 23 July 1994, p. A1.

37. Prunier, *The Rwanda Crisis*, p. 296.

38. President Clinton as paraphrased in Cushman, "President Orders Pentagon Action to Aid Rwandans."

39. Official transcript, "Secretary-General pledges support of UN for Rwanda's search for peace and progress," Press Release, SG/SM/6552/AFR/56, 6 May 1998.

40. Tom Masland, "Hardly a Hero's Welcome," *Newsweek* (international), 18 May 1998, p. 50G.

41. Destexhe, *Rwanda and Genocide*, p. 1.

42. Official transcript, "Remarks by the President to Genocide Survivors, Assistance Workers, and U.S. and Rwanda Government Officials, The White House, Office of the Press Secretary (Kampala, Uganda), at Kigali Airport, 25 March 1998.

43. Press Briefing by Mike McCurry, The White House, Office of the Press Secretary (Cape Town, South Africa) at the Civic Center, South Africa, 26 March 1998.

CHAPTER 17: IN PERPETUUM

Lead quote: Quoted in "Perspectives," *Newsweek* (international), 5 September 1994, p. 7.

1. Léon Mugesera, MRND vice president and official of the Ministry for the Family and the Promotion of Feminine Affairs, 22 November 1992, as quoted in Prunier, *The Rwanda Crisis*, p. 172, and in Des Forges, *Leave None to Tell the Story*, pp. 84–86.

2. Omaar, *Rwanda: Death, Despair and Defiance*, p. 798.

3. As quoted in "Rwanda; A New Catastrophe?" Human Rights Watch/Africa, December 1994, 6:12, pp. 3–4.

4. Quoted in Jane Perlez, "Under the Bougainvillea, A Litany of Past Wrongs," *The New York Times*, 15 August 1994.

5. Quoted in "Rearming with Impunity," p. 2.

6. Details of the former Rwandan army rebuilding drawn from "Rearming with Impunity," and "Rwanda: Arming the Perpetrators of the Genocide," Amnesty International, London, 13 June 1994.

7. Christian Jennings, "Documents Show Zaire Camps Used to Plan Rwanda War," Reuters, 19 November 1996.

8. "Zaire/Rwanda: Bears Guard Honey," *Africa Confidential* (London), 36:4, 17 February 1995.

9. U.S. Arms Control and Disarmament Agency, *World Military Expenditures and Arms Transfers 1990* (Washington, D.C.: Government Printing Office, 1991), p. 121, as cited in "Arming Rwanda," p. 18, note 17.

10. "Rearming with Impunity," p. 10.

11. "MSF Pulls out of Bukavu in Protest," MSF press release, 14 November 1994.

12. Jean, ed., *Populations in Danger* 1995, p. 14–15.

13. As quoted in Destexhe, *Rwanda and Genocide*, p. 2.

14. For an account of the initial failures of the UN Human Rights mission, see "'A Waste of Hope': The United Nations Human Rights Field Operation," African Rights (London), March 1995.

15. As quoted in Vincent Hugeux, *"Rwanda: La guerre sans fin,"* *L'Express* (Paris), 5 February 1998, p. 68.

EPILOGUE

1. Martin Van Creveld, *The Transformation of War* (New York: The Free Press, 1991), p. 161.

2. Thucydides, *The Peloponnesian War*, I.76.2, as drawn out in Donald Kagan, *On The Origins of War and the Preservation of Peace*, (New York: Doubleday, 1995), p. 8.

3. William Faulkner, "Nobel Prize Acceptance Speech."

4. Hanley, *Warriors*, p. 81.

5. As quoted in Karl Vick, "A New Peace in Sudan; Tribes Use Old Ways to End Modern War," *The Washington Post*, 7 July 1999, p. A1.

6. Convention on the Prevention and Punishment of the Crime of Genocide (1948), Article IV.

7. Broadcast translated from the French by BBC Worldwide Monitoring, as quoted in "Prelude to Genocide?" *Harper's Magazine*, November 1998, p. 24.

INDEX